Tales from the Western Generation

1967 Zen Okinawa Karate Kobudo Rengokai

Tales from the Western Generation

Untold Stories and Firsthand History from Karate's Golden Age

Matthew Apsokardu

Apsos Publishing
Pennsylvania, U.S.A.

Apsos Publishing
Apsos LLC
Pennsylvania, U.S.A.
http://apsospublishing.com

ISBN: 9780692436547

WARNING: Martial arts training is a serious and potentially dangerous endeavor. All training should be done under the careful guidance of a competent instructor.

The information contained in this book is for research purposes only. The reader assumes all risk of training and absolves the author, publisher, and interview guests of liability.

The opinions and recounting of facts in the following interviews are those of the interview guests. The author, Matthew Apsokardu, is not held liable for factual inaccuracies or statements interpreted as libelous.

Cover Photo: The main image features Jim Logue and Oyata Seiyu, reproduced with permission from the Logue family. The background image commemorates the landing of Commodore Matthew Perry on Okinawa.

Other images in the book have been supplied with the approval of interview guests, with proper attribution to their owners, or via public domain. No images can be reproduced without the express permission of their respective owners.

Editorial assistance by Christina Steffy and Lauren Apsokardu.

Dedication

For my family: Patricia Apsokardu, George Apsokardu Jr., George Apsokardu III, Samantha Apsokardu, and Crystal Apsokardu.

A special thanks to Lauren Apsokardu for her patience and support throughout the creation of this project.

1964 Okinawa Karate Championship Tournament

Table of Contents

Acknowledgements

A number of individuals were critical in assisting me in the development of this book. Without the Okinawan spirit of sharing passed down to senior practitioners in the United States, this project would not have been possible.

First and foremost, I want to thank my instructors C. Bruce Heilman and Ann-Marie Heilman. Their persistence in creating the International Karate Kobudo Federation was key in my meeting a number of other senior instructors in the United States. Furthermore, their reputation across the country opened doors for me and functioned as an effective letter of introduction, without which I could not have accessed so many top tier karateka.

I am also grateful to Rick Zondlo who has helped me tremendously on my personal martial arts journey. He has always shared his experience openly and has challenged me to live up to the higher standards of budo.

Bill Hayes has also been critical to this book's development, patiently guiding me in both my training and writing.

Finally, I want to thank everyone who helped me initiate meetings with the senior practitioners featured in this project.

Keys to Understanding This Book

The following is a primer in understanding how this book came about, the kinds of people included as interview subjects, and how information is organized so as to avoid bias and confusion.

The Purpose of *Tales from the Western Generation*

When doing research for karate, I often find myself wishing for just a little more recorded material from the old masters. I doubt I'm the only one. How valuable would a treatise be from Matsumura Sokon Sensei detailing his life and ideas?

In fact, we needn't go back as far as Matsumura Sensei. Even just a generation or two ago, with instructors like Gokenki, Shimabukuro Tatsuo, Nakamura Shigeru . . . we are left wondering about who they studied with, what difficulties they overcame, and how they viewed karate.

On Okinawa the tradition of oral transmission of information is well established. This practice has left holes in our understanding and has allowed room for apocryphal exaggeration. The devastation from the Battle of Okinawa only exacerbated an already growing problem.

We, as a modern culture, needn't make the same mistakes. If we stop for a moment, we'll realize that there are masters still with us, just now reaching the prime of their wisdom. It is our duty not only to look back at karate's history, but also to look around us as history is made before our eyes.

The purpose of this book is to record the stories of individuals who have been critical in retrieving karate from Japan and Okinawa, causing it to spread into the United States and ultimately the world. We do this so that future generations can benefit from understanding their circumstances and ideas.

How Selections Were Made For Inclusion

For a book of this scope, you may be wondering how I decided which individuals to include and which to exclude. It's an important question which I would like to address so that you can enjoy the book without worrying about the politics of martial arts.

My selection process utilized a system of checks and balances inherent in the world of old style karate. The more classical practitioners I spoke to, the more I was able to learn about events in years past from multiple angles. By cross-checking this information, I was able to learn about individuals who did a lot to contribute to the growth of karate in the United States. That is how I arrived at most of the guests included in this book.

That being said, I realized very quickly that there was no feasible way I could discuss all the men and women who were important to the development of karate; such a task would expand massively outward. Instead, I had to put the following restrictions in place:

- Interview subjects had to have grown up in the United States (although not necessarily born here). Although a number of immigrants were critical to the growth of karate early on (Demura Fumio[1], Okazaki Teruyuki, etc.) they were not considered for this particular project.
- Ideal interview subjects trained with either first wave Americans, original Okinawan / Japanese Sensei, or both. The subjects should also have made a lasting impact on the growth of their style.
- In an attempt to cover as many original styles as possible, I avoided including too many interview subjects of any one style.

Some individuals I had hoped to include were not reachable or were in ill health. Others were contacted, but opted not to participate. Still others had complex and confusing histories that were not verifiable. Others I simply missed due to the scope of the project.

I, the author, take full responsibility for any individuals who were missed but belong in a project such as this. It's my hope that the reader understands this is not designed to be a

---

[1] Japanese, Okinawan, and Chinese names are listed in the traditional fashion of surname first, followed by given name.

comprehensive encyclopedia of karateka, but more a collection of stories from a number of important practitioners who were critical to the growth of karate.

How Interviews Are Organized

In an effort to stave off any potential bias or political maneuverings, intentional or unintentional, I began my organizational process by placing the interviews in alphabetical order. First the styles had been listed alphabetically with the appropriate practitioners contained within. Then, inside that style, the practitioners were ordered alphabetically. Once I finished writing and editing the book, I realized that the flow of information could be improved upon. As a result, I made some strategic moves to enhance the reader's experience and create smooth continuity wherever possible.

I hope this method of organization keeps the information coherent and understandable while giving the interview guests their just due.

History, Interviews, Conclusion

While the primary purpose of this book is to share the stories of the interview guests, I decided it was critical to create a sense of context around the time period of their birth, maturation, and training. It is important for the reader to know why so many men were sent overseas during the '50s, '60s, and '70s, and why the Western Generation interview guests often cited Judo as their primary martial arts influence early in life. There were a number of other questions that I thought would best be answered in order to enrich the reader's understanding and appreciation for the world surrounding the interview subjects.

This book begins by taking a historical journey into America's past, observing some of the earliest contact between the United States and Eastern countries like Japan, China, and Okinawa. We observe the ways in which closed Eastern cultures came colliding with an expanding Western world. We then take note of the earliest immigrants coming into America, and how they chose to share their martial arts or keep them secret. Questions are answered, such as — why didn't America become a new fertile ground for kung fu during the Gold Rush Era? Why was Judo so captivating to Western minds? How did karate first make an appearance on U.S. soil?

The book then launches into the interviews, providing a brief synopsis of each style and the complete interview for each individual within that style. The book is concluded with a number of philosophical thoughts and practical observations by the author, which the reader is invited to consider while formulating his / her own conclusions.

Please enjoy, and best wishes in your martial arts journey.

General Disclaimer: *The author has attempted to verify as much information as possible in this project's historical content and interview subject matter. However, this book features personal stories and opinions from a variety of resources. As such, discrepencies may exist, especially when compared to the reader's personal experience and research. Such is the nature of karate research and must be understood when exploring personal accounts. Consider this book a tool, providing multiple viewpoints to a larger picture. The author can be reached (see "About the Author") if you'd like to share additional stories, questions, or comments; however, angry or impolite corrections / communications will be deleted without consideration.*

Chapter 1 –

Opening Doors to the East

Masts creaked as the *Empress of China* eased away from New York Harbor. It was February 22, 1784. The Revolutionary War had ostensibly ended the year prior, but its cost was still heavy on the minds of the citizenry and soldiers. A newly liberated American government decided to press outward and expand its influence around the globe. One of their primary targets lay half a world away, filled with untold possibilities — China. The *Empress* was to be the first true attempt at establishing long-term economic relations.

The Far East was notorious for its "closed door" attitude. Japan was so isolated that unapproved ships would be fired upon if they attempted to dock.[2] China, then operating under the rule of the Qing Dynasty, wasn't much more lenient. Foreigners looking to trade with China could only do so with certain, pre-approved merchants in the Guangzhou area. Countries such as England, France, and Denmark had established such trading arrangements, and America looked to catch up.[3]

The *Empress* made its long journey across the sea as a vassal of economic hope, landing successfully on Chinese shores. Unfortunately for the crew and America as a whole, full trade agreements proved elusive. Looking for a business angle that would pique China's interest, American traders soon realized the potency of opium as a bargaining tool. Britain had set a successful precedent of smuggling opium into China, acquiring large shipments

---

[2] "Perry In Japan - Brown University Library." 2011. 13 Jan. 2015 <http://library.brown.edu/cds/perry/people_Williams.html>.

[3] Embassy, U.S. "The Empress of China | Embassy of the United States." 2010. <http://guangzhou.usembassy-china.org.cn/the-empress-of-china.html>.

of tea in return. Capitalizing on this, America began to barter using its own opium resources.

The Qing Dynasty tolerated trade with Western powers while silver was the primary form of payment; however, when opium became the trade good of choice, they grew concerned. Qing lawmakers attempted to lock down the drug, ultimately seizing the goods directly from British merchants and destroying it. This perceived slight and economic "attack" prompted Britain to declare war.[4]

As with all clever political moves, the Opium War was only partially about the goods destroyed by the Qing government. In truth, it was a perfect excuse for Britain to flex its military might and establish a foothold in the East that it could control and dictate. The conflicts during the Opium War tended to be one-sided in favor of the British forces. At that time in history, European powers had greatly outpaced Eastern countries in terms of technology and modern military practices. The proud martial heritage of China had lagged behind the global pace, making them vulnerable to invasion.

When the Opium War began, the Qing Dynasty was bloated with political corruption, nepotism, and xenophobia. The Chinese armies were not well-led and relied on archaic methods such as horseback archery. The sophisticated cannons, volleys of gunfire, and well-trained tactics of the British left the Qing battered and defeated. For better or worse, trade was opened with China like a broken dam; Western influence flooded in while Chinese emmigrants flooded out.

Cracking the Political Armor of Japan

It wasn't long after the initial voyage of the *Empress of China* in 1784 that America also set its sights on Japan. In 1791, merchant vessels under the command of John Kendrick and James Douglas landed at Kushimoto, whereupon the captains attempted a ruse. Knowing the strict penalties in Japan for trespassing ships, they claimed to be shipwrecked and asked for refuge. Providing quarter for marooned sailors was common maritime practice; however, with the Japanese, it was still a gamble.

---

[4] Lorge, Peter Allan. *Chinese Martial Arts: From Antiquity to the Twenty-first Century*. New York, NY: Cambridge UP, 2012. 188. Print.

Kendrick and his crew were not killed, but neither did they succeed in their ultimate goal of establishing trade relations. They were sent away 11 days later with little to show for their efforts.[5] It would take more than 50 years before an American made significant contact with the Japanese again, and even then the goal of establishing trade proved difficult.

In 1846, Commander James Biddle anchored in Tokyo Bay with two warships, attempting to show military muscle in addition to economic interest. Despite the display, Biddle was rebuked. It is reported that Biddle was so thoroughly unimpressive to the Japanese that he was shoved callously by a Japanese soldier, who didn't perceive him as an authority.[6]

Unsatisfied with Biddle's results, Captain James Glynn was sent two years later under different auspices. Glynn was tasked with retrieving multiple American sailors that had been shipwrecked off the coast of Japan and who were believed to be alive.[7] Glynn's recovery mission was successful, but he made little economic progress otherwise. Before returning to the United States, Glynn stopped at a small island off the coast of Japan known as Loo-Choo (Lew-Chew, or Ryukyu), where he met an unusual people with kind faces and a remarkable lack of military implements. Unbeknownst to Glynn, the Ryukyu island chain and its main port of Okinawa would play a pivotal role in the eventual opening of Japan and the long term martial relations between East and West.

Despite the underwhelming results of its missions to Japan, the United States was beginning to develop real momentum in terms of military power and economic influence. There had been 18 expeditions, including four from America, that failed in their goal to secure full trade with the Japanese — the Dutch being the only nation to make small inroads. Nevertheless, being the first to force a permanent wedge into that iron cast closure was the key to significant strategic advantages on a global scale. U.S. authorities planned a bold mission to demonstrate the power of the United States Navy and persuade the Japanese to bargain once and for all.

---

[5] Johnson, Donald D., and Gary Dean Best. *The United States in the Pacific: Private Interests and Public Policies*, 1784-1899. Westport, Conn.: Praeger, 1995. 23. Print.

[6] Kerr, George H. *Okinawa, the History of an Island People*. Rutland, Vt.: C.E. Tuttle, 1958. 299. Print.

[7] Schodt, Frederik L. *Native American in the Land of the Shogun: Ranald MacDonald and the Opening of Japan*. Berkeley, Calif.: Stone Bridge, 2003. Print.

Captain James Glynn commanded the U.S.S. Preble to the coast of Japan and the Ryukyu Islands.[8]

In 1852, the American government arranged for Commodore Matthew Perry to sail to Edo using a team of two steam frigates (the *Susquehanna* and the *Mississippi*) and two sloops of war (the *Plymouth* and the *Saratoga*).[9] By all accounts, Perry was a man of excellent capabilities, matched only by his own sense of self-worth. He was a stern commander, expecting top performance and obedience from those around him. When he set out to accomplish a mission, anything that hindered his progress was met with extreme dissatisfaction.[10]

Perry's plans were ambitious. He intended to begin his economic conquest at the port island of Okinawa, which was known as a useful trading hub and refueling station. He then planned to touch down in Japan itself in order to lay out his aggressive proposals. He would then travel to China, which was the most well-established eastern base of operations for America, before returning to Japan for final negotiations.

---

[8] "U.S.S. Preble" by Per Honor et Gloria - Drawing of U.S.S. Preble (1839). Licensed under Public Domain via Wikimedia Commons.

[9] "A Brief Summary of the Perry Expedition to Japan, 1853". 2004. 13 Jan. 2015 <http://www.history.navy.mil/library/online/perry_exp.htm>.

[10] Kerr, George H. *Okinawa, the History of an Island People*. Rutland, Vt.: C.E. Tuttle, 1958. 297-301. Print.

Staking Claim in the Port of Okinawa

Okinawa is the largest island in the Loo-Choo (Ryukyu) island chain. Okinawa's people have always maintained a unique culture filled with special religious practices, clothing, and social hierarchy. From early in their history, the Ryukyuans interacted with various neighbors surrounding them, including China, Japan, Korea, Java, and more.

The convenient location of Okinawa made it a desirable port for countries looking to trade with one another. Even nations at war could still use Okinawa as a subtle means of exchanging goods. Of all the countries Okinawa interacted with, it was China and the Ming Dynasty that it admired most.

In the late 14th century Okinawa's Chuzan Provence, led by King Sho Hashi, achieved tributary status with China, which helped it overwhelm the opposing Hokuzan (Sanhoku) and Nanzan (Sannan) factions.[11] This ended the Sanzan period of Okinawan history and ushered in an era of relative peace.[12]

In the mid-15th century, King Sho Shin devised a series of crafty plans to maintain his power and keep Chuzan as the central dominance on the island. He mandated that families of high standing send one of their members to live in the central city of Shuri. Sho Shin also gathered the island's military arms and stored them at Shuri under the careful watch of his personal military force. This strategy effectively disarmed the outer regions of the island and made an uprising extremely difficult.[13]

Throughout the "Great Days of Chuzan," Okinawa prospered as a port and a people. They continued to integrate Chinese culture into their own, including art, pottery, architecture, martial arts, and more. The days of peace ended abruptly, however. In 1609 the Shimazu Clan of Satsuma, Japan, decided to flex its dominance over the Southern Islands.

---

[11] This is the prevailing theory of the Sanzan period based mostly on Chinese historical resources. Other theories are available, however, and research is ongoing.

[12] Kerr, George H. *Okinawa, the History of an Island People*. Rutland, Vt.: C.E. Tuttle, 1958. 83. Print.

[13] Turnbull, Stephen R. *The Samurai Capture a King: Okinawa, 1609*. Oxford: Osprey, 2009. 58. Print.

Despite Okinawa's cultural development of martial arts, its Shuri-centric military was unprepared for the might and swiftness of the Satsuma attack. In short order, Okinawa was conquered and a new era of Japanese oversight set in.

Japan's distaste for outside influence on its dominances transferred to Okinawa. While disarming the native populace, the Satsuma laid out a series of rules for how Okinawa was to conduct its business. Okinawans were permitted to continue trading, but were monitored and guided based on the needs of the Satsuma. This allowed for extended trading experiences for some foreign visitors while others were brushed along quickly.[14]

Significant American interest in China and Japan picked up in the 1700s, but it wasn't until the mid 1800s that serious interaction between the Americans and Okinawans began. Missionaries were among the first Westerners to manage any sort of staying power on the island, tolerated by the natives and their Satsuma overseers. The most telling account on record of the early interactions between Western visitors and the native Okinawans came from an eccentric British missionary by the name of Bernard Jean Bettelheim.

Bettelheim arrived via the British ship *Starling* with his wife, two infants, and two assistants.[15] The Bettelheims spent most of their time trying to convert the natives to Christianity, a task the local residents tolerated . . . but just barely. Despite his idiosyncrasies, Bettelheim proved a consistent source of information for visiting Western seafarers like James Glynn and Matthew Perry. In fact, Bettelheim's inside information aided Perry significantly as the Commodore planned his heavy handed strategies for dealing with Eastern nations.

Upon Perry's arrival in May, 1853, the Okinawans attempted to hinder his access to the island. They did so by traveling out to meet Perry's ships and proactively engaging in trade talks. The Okinawans hoped their efforts would be enough to send the Americans on their way in short order. Instead, Perry dismissed them without so much as an audience and informed them that he would only meet with those of the highest regal importance.

The Okinawans requested that Perry conduct his diplomacy through their senior regent, explaining that the queen and her young son were unavailable (the queen being quite sick

---

[14] For a more comprehensive exploration of Okinawa's trading habits, consult *Karate 1.0* by Andreas Quast.

[15] Kerr, George H. *Okinawa, the History of an Island People*. Rutland, Vt.: C.E. Tuttle, 1958. 279. Print.

at the time and the king having passed away). Despite these requests, Perry insisted on a meeting at Shuri Castle with the royal family. He organized a grand procession, complete with band, Marines, artillery, and a caravan upon which Perry himself rode, carried by eight Chinese servants.[16]

Perry successfully entered the palace despite strong objections. Inside he found unprepared halls and a vacant seat of power. Ultimately, Perry had to acquiesce and conduct his affairs with the regent. The two arranged multiple meetings with elaborate dinners and political posturing. In the end, Perry established a more permanent base on the island and gave a promise to return after his dealings with Japan.

The Commodore Seeks His Prize in Japan

In 1853, Perry arrived near Edo and proceeded to sail toward Kurihama. While sailing off the coast of Japan, Perry shelled a handful of buildings to demonstrate the power of his artillery. The predominantly wooden cannon of the Japanese could not come close to matching the range, accuracy, or destructive power of the American ships. The Japanese, surprised by the gaping difference in technological and combative capability, allowed Perry to land at Kurihama. Perry delivered to Japanese delegates a letter from President Millard Fillmore, along with a white flag. He informed the delegates that if they did not deliver the letter to the Emperor, that they could use the white flag to surrender when Perry began his military incursion.

With his threat clearly laid out, Perry promised to return in 1854 to finalize the details of Japan's full opening. He then set out to China to continue strengthening relations there as well.

Perry returned to Japan, as promised, in 1854 with even more firepower than when he left. Although the Japanese attempted various political maneuverings to get Perry to budge from his goals, Perry remained ironclad. After all alternatives had been exhausted, the emissaries for the emperor declared that they would meet with Perry in person. The Commodore, in typical fashion, created a grand processional for himself complete with

---

[16] ""A Brief Summary of the Perry Expedition to Japan, 1853"." 2004. 14 Jan. 2015
<http://www.history.navy.mil/library/online/perry_exp.htm>.

Marine squads, bands, and gun salutes. At the meeting, the Japanese agreed to open a coaling port for the Americans within five years time, but Perry pushed further. Negotiating for nearly a whole month, Perry achieved a much more comprehensive treaty.

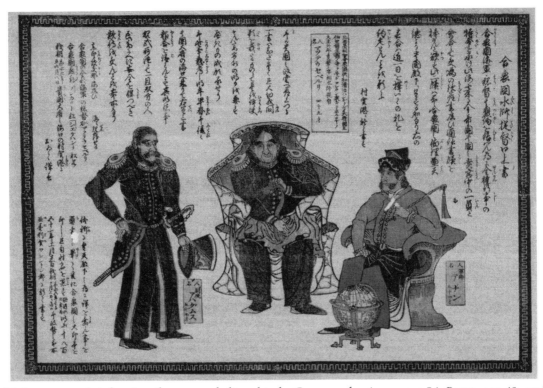

"A Japanese print showing three men, believed to be Commander Anan, age 54; Perry, age 49; and Captain Henry Adams, age 59, who opened up Japan to the West."[17]

Perry's work was unprecedented and represented the first full opening of Japan to an outside nation. Soon after, Japan experienced a harsh internal split between the citizens and administrators who wanted to re-close the country and endure American retribution, versus those who wanted to capitalize on the newly opened global economy. As the Meiji Restoration took hold in Japanese politics, more Western powers were permitted trade and Japanese culture spread across the globe.

---

[17] "Gasshukoku suishi teitoku kōjōgaki (Oral statement by the American Navy admiral) minimal restoration" by Unknown - Library of Congress. Licensed under Public Domain via Wikimedia Commons.

After his dealings in Japan, Perry returned to Okinawa as he said he would. It was then that he formally established the "Loo-Choo Compact," an agreement that allowed island access for trade purposes, guaranteed the safety of shipwrecked American sailors, and provided other conditions for favorable treatment.[18]

While international relations grew thanks to the efforts of men like the Commodore, back in the U.S. a few adventurous and industrious miners were picking their way up and down California. Some found little golden nuggets peeking out of the soil. Once word go out that California was the land of golden mountains, a place where fortunes were made, the fate of the United States and the Far East changed forever, becoming intertwined in wholly unexpected ways.

---

[18] Kerr, George H. *Okinawa, the History of an Island People*. Rutland, Vt.: C.E. Tuttle, 1958. 335. Print.

Chapter 2 –
Chinese Immigrants Venture to Gold Mountain

Around 1848, rumors of riches began quietly spreading from California. A few letters from Chinese immigrants back to mainland China spoke of golden nuggets found in the mountains, and opportunity for any individual with enough courage and enterprise to make his way into the mines. Whispers soon turned to talks, and eventually entire desperate towns were abuzz with the prospect of wealth from across the sea. Of course, fear and trepidation quelled many serious conversations of America. Most Chinese peasants knew nothing of the outside world and feared the worst from Americans. However, the possibility of a better life and a fresh start inspired more and more brave men to book passage for the West Coast.

Travel to America was precarious, to say the least. Ships were crowded, expensive, and often operated by abusive or dishonest emigration outfits. If a Chinese citizen did not acquire travel arrangements through reputable means, he could wind up with dangerously poor accommodations, unfair work agreements, or delivery to a different country entirely.

Once arriving in California, almost exclusively in the rough port town of San Francisco, Chinese immigrants did not find an easy life. The town had little in the way of accommodations and was both violent and lawless. The West was experiencing a massive land grab and was occupied by ambitious and / or ruthless men. With no organized law besides that of firearms and force, the town averaged about five murders every six days.[19]

Despite the hardships, Chinese immigrants realized that if they could persevere for a few years, find gold or consistent work, they could return to their families in China with relative wealth and change the course of their family's fate. So they set out for the mountains and worked the hardest jobs Westerners saw fit to give them, which was usually placer mining (a.k.a. "panning for gold").

At first, American pioneers and governing bodies seemed to tolerate Chinese immigrants gladly. Before 1850 there were only about 50 Chinese immigrants in the whole country, so their presence was both a novelty and a non-issue. However, as a steady stream of Chinese came to work, the numbers began to concern the empowered white populace.[20]

Although possessing a reputation for hard work, cleanly appearance, and respectful manner, diligent Chinese laborers were often forced away from the mines or taxed for their findings so harshly that it made the work unsustainable. The more the white frontiersmen complained about the influx of Chinese labor, the more legislative bodies did to repress opportunity for the immigrants. The frontiersmen grew more and more violent toward the Chinese, who they perceived as a threat. Reports and rumors flowed regarding bands of Chinese workers being beaten, chased, and killed, given no more rights or concern than average livestock.[21]

The Chinese realized their plight in America, and their growing Western population became very insulated. They knew that they would not receive fair judgment from the government, nor would they receive kind treatment from frontiersmen. As a result, they cultivated their own food, education, and martial arts strictly within themselves.

Understanding that mining was severely restricted as a work option, the Chinese decided to branch out in their enterprises. Few amenities were available in San Francisco and other frontier towns, so Chinese men began opening small rudimentary businesses such as laundry services, food services, and medicinal herb shops. At first these businesses served

---

[19] Chang, Iris. *The Chinese in America: A Narrative History.* New York: Viking, 2003. 36. Print.

[20] Chang, Iris. *The Chinese in America: A Narrative History.* New York: Viking, 2003. 51. Print.

[21] Ambrose, Stephen E. *Nothing like It in the World: The Men Who Built the Transcontinental Railroad, 1863-1869.* New York: Simon & Schuster, 2000. 150. Print.

only Chinese communities, but once word got out regarding their quality, even the disgruntled frontiersmen were inclined to partake of them.

A Forced Opportunity on the Transcontinental Railroad

In the mid 1800s, America had an audacious idea. Realizing the grand expanse of the country, and the value of connecting the new gold rush towns with the established East Coast, a plan was concocted (primarily by Theodore Judah[22]) to build a railroad that spanned the continent. This transcontinental railroad would traverse mountains, deserts, great plains, and more. Nothing so ambitious had ever been attempted before via mass transportation, and the sheer scope of it led many to comment that it was patently impossible.

Despite the challenge, two groups of investors took the chance. They realized that if they achieved success, the profit and impact would ensure a rich legacy. In the East, the Union Pacific started building out of Iowa. On the West Coast, the Central Pacific spearheaded its work from California. It was the Central Pacific investors that changed the lives of thousands of Chinese immigrants looking to make a better life in America.

[23]

In 1862, plans were finalized and approved for the Central Pacific to begin work. In 1863, they started laying track. The method of track laying was complex and arduous, involving many different teams of both skilled and unskilled labor. Contractor Charles Crocker was

---

[22] Ambrose, Stephen E. *Nothing like It in the World: The Men Who Built the Transcontinental Railroad, 1863-1869.* New York: Simon & Schuster, 2000. 19. Print.
[23] "Central Pacific Railroad Company (CPRR) Logotype 1869". Licensed under PD-U.S. via Wikipedia - http://en.wikipedia.org/wiki/File:Central_Pacific_Railroad_Company_(CPRR)_Logotype_1869.jpg#/media/File:Central _Pacific_Railroad_Company_(CPRR)_Logotype_1869.jpg

charged with oversight of the project, relying heavily on his chief foreman James Strobridge. Strobridge, along with Crocker and the other financiers, were all generally concerned about the massive influx of Chinese immigrants in the country. They resolved to use white workers exclusively, primarily of the Irish persuasion. When first arriving in America in significant numbers, the Irish had been considered an inferior breed, and tended to occupy many of the "blue collar" positions. By limiting his labor pool, Crocker could only fill about 800 labor positions out of roughly 4,000 openings.[24]

Work was slow and inefficient at first for the Central Pacific. Most of the white workers quickly abandoned the job for mine work. They realized that a few weeks or months on the railroad could help finance their mining prospects, which tended to be easier, safer, and more lucrative. In short order, the Central Pacific was in desperate need for laborers, and the only solution that presented itself was hiring non-whites.

New Chinese railway workers, about 50 to start, proved diligent, intelligent, and quick to adapt.[25] Despite management's early reservations, and the general anti-Chinese sentiment of the country, the Central Pacific continued to employ more and more "coolies" (Chinese laborers) after that. In fact, the railroad worked closely with American and Chinese brokers responsible for the importation of immigrants. The brokers used the promise of gold mountain mining to entice peasants, who found themselves hustled to the front lines of railroad work upon arrival.[26]

Other non-Chinese workers saw the coolies as pests, undercutting their rates and invading their homeland. As a result, the Chinese were inclined to stay insulated amongst themselves in camp. Outside observers commented on the organized fashion in which the Chinese operated, citing gambling as their only noticeable vice.

At its peak operation, the Central Pacific Employed over 10,000 Chinese laborers, roughly 90% of its workforce. The coolies were considered expendable, and many laborers died

[24] "Workers of the Central Pacific Railroad ... - PBS." 2011. 16 Jan. 2015 <http://www.pbs.org/wgbh/americanexperience/features/general-article/tcrr-cprr/>.
[25] Ambrose, Stephen E. *Nothing like It in the World: The Men Who Built the Transcontinental Railroad, 1863-1869.* New York: Simon & Schuster, 2000. 152. Print.
[26] Ambrose, Stephen E. *Nothing like It in the World: The Men Who Built the Transcontinental Railroad, 1863-1869.* New York: Simon & Schuster, 2000. 161. Print.

from over-exertion, illness, and blasting accidents. When work crested the Sierra Nevada Mountains, many workers froze in avalanches and massive snow falls.

While the Central Pacific was pushing its way eastward, Chinese mercantilism was booming in San Francisco and other early Western towns. Entire city sections developed where Chinese laborers banded together for safety and comfort, becoming known as "Chinatown" blocks. Organizing, importing, and protecting new Chinese immigrants became such big business that large-scale organizations came to power, made up of the more industrious and powerful Chinese businessmen. These organizations became known as the Six Huiguans, or Six Companies, and held sway in the social, economic, and cultural aspects of most Chinese communities in early western America.[27]

The Six Companies, also referred to as the "Chinese Consolidated Benevolent Association," provided a lot of valuable services during their reign of power. They arranged for labor housing, organized worship, and security from abuse. Of course, as their power grew, so did their corruption.

Ambitious and aggressive outcasts from the Six Companies organized into new groups referred to as "Tongs," or secret brotherhoods. The Tongs used the powerful Triads of China as their template, engaging in acts of clandestine smuggling, gambling, drug selling, and prostitution.[28] They attracted members from a large population of Chinese immigrants who felt abused, underpaid, lonely, and angry. In short order, their influence grew . . . so much so that the Tong groups frequently feuded with each other in bloody engagements.

"The Tong Wars" raged on for more than 30 years, sometimes quietly, sometimes openly. The Tongs imported an extensive number of women to work in their prostitution rings, and also employed teams of "hatchetmen" who conducted violent acts to gain territory, seek revenge, and enforce Tong rule. The hatchetmen, while infamous, were also some of the earliest examples of Chinese martial arts in the United States.

The Six Companies and Tongs alike operated with the knowledge that "outsiders," those native to America, actively resented the Chinese. The secrecy and privacy that came as a

[27] "The Six Companies - FoundSF." 2009. 16 Jan. 2015 <http://foundsf.org/index.php?title=The_Six_Companies>.
[28] Chang, Iris. *The Chinese in America: A Narrative History.* New York: Viking, 2003. 83. Print.

result only served to incite non-Chinese further, especially as the Tongs became more dangerous. In 1871, a white policeman and white bystander were both killed during a Tong battle. A riot erupted as a result, now known as "The Chinese Massacre," in which enraged mobs shot any Chinese they saw, dragged them from their homes, looted their possessions, and lynched victims at will.[29]

Matters worsened in 1873 as the country headed toward its first great industrial depression. Despite the Chinese population's hard labor and willingness to endure even the most difficult and unwanted jobs while being heavily taxed, they were singled out as a primary cause for the country's economic woes. This anti-Chinese sentiment grew in ferocity, resulting in a steady decline of rights and an increased risk of physical violence for Chinese immigrants.

In 1882, the United States Government signed into law The Chinese Exclusion Act, which stopped immigration of both "skilled and unskilled laborers," constituting virtually all Chinese individuals looking to get into the country. It also made non-citizen Chinese incapable of receiving citizenship. This initial bill, designed to last for 10 years, ushered in a cruel era known as "The Driving Out," during which Chinese residents across the country were pressured by white mobs to leave under the threat and execution of violence.[30]

Despite its initially prescribed run of 10 years, the Chinese Exclusion Act was renewed, revised, and otherwise enforced for over 60 years, not being repealed until 1943. Cut off from their homeland, hated by those around them, constantly under threat of violence — it is no mystery why the Chinese community remained insulated. It is also evident why the Tongs and other Chinese martial artists chose not to share their martial secrets with Westerners.

---

[29] Chang, Iris. *The Chinese in America: A Narrative History*. New York: Viking, 2003. 121. Print.
[30] Chang, Iris. *The Chinese in America: A Narrative History*. New York: Viking, 2003. 132. Print.

Opening Doors, Breaking with Tradition

America did not become a "second home" of kung fu[31] throughout the late 1800s and early 1900s, a fact which we now understand. The true surprise is that traditional Chinese arts were shared with non-Chinese at all. While it's impossible to know each and every Chinese instructor who decided to teach Western students, we do have reports of some of the earliest programs to open their doors. It should be noted that most pioneers of the Chinese arts were met with strong cultural resistance, some of which could be ignored, some of which had to be fought through figuratively and literally.

In 1922, one of the first organized kung fu clubs began under the the supervision of the Chinese Physical Culture Association in Hawaii; however, it was a closed door club. It wasn't until 1957 that Tinn Chan Lee began teaching Taijiquan (Tai Chi Chuan) openly, allowing access to non-Chinese Hawaii residents.[32] In mainland United States, Ark-Yueh began teaching Shao-lin openly in 1964 in Los Angeles. The Bruce Lee craze developed throughout the 1960s and '70s in California, bringing Chinese arts to the forefront for the first time. It's surprising to think that within our modern history, kung fu was still a closed experience. This attitude is reflected even today in some parts of the Chinese community.

The earliest karate schools in the United States arrived in the late 1940s and early 1950s, before any "open door" kung fu schools became well known. It makes sense that the earliest karate pioneers in the U.S.A., and the men and women who grew up in the '50s, found so little influence via kung fu. In fact, a large number of the interview guests in this book cite Judo as the only Eastern martial art available in their early lives.

---

[31] The word "kung fu" is the most frequently used term to refer to Chinese martial arts. However, kung fu by definition more closely relates to "achievements/merits of a man," rather than "martial arts." In fact, martial pursuits in China cannot be encapsulated with a single word.

[32] Corcoran, John. "The Untold Story of American Karate's History." *Black Belt Magazine*. 1 May 1977: n. pag. *Google Books*. Web. Date of Access. <http://books.google.com/books?id=l9UDAAAAMBAJ>.

Chapter 3 –
Judo Takes Main Stage

With the gross mistreatment of Chinese immigrants in America, it might be easy to assume that Japanese immigrants suffered the same fate. Indeed, they were repressed and treated poorly, their history in America its own unique tapestry of trials and challenges. Despite that, Americans have always had a fascination with Japanese culture and the subtleties of its people. As a result, America was more open to working with, and learning from, the Japanese than most other Eastern nations. Judo, the sportive throwing art of Japan, became the first truly widespread Eastern martial art in the U.S.A.

Any conversation regarding Judo must begin with Kano Jigoro, founder and architect of Judo. Born into a financially stable family in the saké business, Kano had access to certain societal perks from a young age. One perk that he put to great use was education. A student of classic literature, philosophy, and pedagogy, Kano quickly became one of the bright minds of his day. In addition to his regular studies, he dedicated much of his life to the pursuit of jujutsu, Japan's classical Samurai throwing and combative art.

Kano Sensei, who was born in 1860, came into adulthood right as the Meiji Restoration was picking up steam. One of the key elements of the Meiji Restoration was an "opening of doors" to Western powers, providing access and legal trade to outside nations. While many Japanese citizens and lawmakers resisted the idea of mingling with foreigners, rebuking the forceful interactions of men like Commodore Matthew Perry, Kano saw it as an opportunity to grow. Not only did Kano do significant work to get Judo and kendo (sport fencing) involved in the Japanese school systems, he was also constantly looking for opportunities to enhance and empower Japanese culture as it related to the outside world.

During the Meiji Restoration, the extreme privilege offered to the old Samurai class was reduced, and the interest in lethal hand-to-hand fighting was replaced by Western firearms and tactics. Kano was aware of this change, but also aware of how valuable rigorous sports with ethical and philosophical underpinnings could be. As a result, he started making pedagogical and technical changes to his jujutsu background, creating Kodokan Judo.[33]

In 1879, President Ulysses S. Grant embarked upon a worldwide goodwill tour and visited the Emperor of Japan. While there, Grant witnessed a jujutsu demonstration, of which Kano played a part. This demo sparked an interest in jujutsu and Judo which quickly worked its way back to the United States. Despite negative attitudes prevailing in the U.S.A. regarding Chinese immigrants, professors and men of influence in the U.S. began traveling to Japan in order to train, some even inviting Judo instructors to America in order to share their art.

The following two decades (1880s and 1890s) were critical in the early integration of Judo into Western culture. In 1882, William Sturgis Bigelow traveled to Japan and began studying under Okakura Kazuko Sensei. In 1889, Professor Ladd from Yale University began studying at the Kodokan (the home of Judo) itself. By the early 1900s, regular Judo practice was observed in Hawaii and programs began cropping up in the continental United States. Kano Iitaro[34] opened a program in Seattle and Samuel Hill arranged for Yamashita Yoshitsugu Sensei to teach his children. Kano Jigoro, the founder, continued to support and spread the art as well.

William Sturgis Bigelow and a police officer named J. J. O'Brien introduced President Theodore Roosevelt to the idea of training in Judo, and, as a result, may have changed the course of the art's popularity. Yamashita Yoshitsugu Sensei visited the White House at the behest of President Roosevelt, and although Roosevelt did not become a lifelong student, he did speak very highly of the art and increased its reputation and exposure. Starting in

[33] Brousse, Michel, and David Ricky Matsumoto. *Judo in the U.S.: A Century of Dedication*. Berkeley, Calif.: North Atlantic ;, 2005. 15. Print.
[34] No familial relation to Kano Jigoro, founder of Judo.

1905, Judo began its long-term integration into the American military system, where it would stay and grow throughout the 1900s.[35]

The military wasn't the only portion of the American population growing more enthusiastic about Kano's art. Men such as Tomita Tsunejiro, Maeda Mitsuyo, and more began teaching and putting on demonstrations across the country. Some Judo players took on all comers in challenge matches and appeared in popular professional wrestling troupes. Judo became a spectacle, whereupon seemingly undersized and outmatched individuals could trump larger opponents. Women were getting in on the action as well. In 1907, Daisy Peterkin displayed "jujutsu dances" on stage, integrating locks and throws to the delight of audiences.

Of course, Judo's integration into American culture was not entirely smooth sailing. With the Chinese Exclusion Act well underway as Judo gained momentum, not all Japanese immigrants found life in the U.S. easy and hospitable. A number of Judo clubs closed down shortly after their creation, and other instructors were unhappy with their lot as sideshow spectacles.[36] As unappealing as American treatment could be, land taxes were increasing at an alarming rate in Japan and conscription into the military was rising. Many Japanese opted to engage in "dekasegi," a principle in which Japanese workers traveled overseas for a time in the hopes of gaining enough money to return home and improve the lives of their families. This was quite similar to the plight of the Chinese at the time.

Shifting economics and national politics inspired a generation of Japanese citizens to consider the opportunities America had to offer. Quite a few of them landed in Hawaii on their way to California, adding to Hawaii's growing value as a martial gateway to the West. These first generation Japanese immigrants were known as "Issei," and they often did their best to preserve the culture of their ancestors even after moving overseas.

The children of the Issei, known as "Nisei," tended to be born with more rights in the West than their parents and thus had a more open and inclusive attitude toward Americans. As the Nisei came of age throughout the 1920s and 1930s, they took Judo with them into universities, helping create numerous clubs. America found itself in possession of some of

---

[35] Brousse, Michel, and David Ricky Matsumoto. *Judo in the U.S.: A Century of Dedication*. Berkeley, Calif.: North Atlantic, 2005. 27. Print.

[36] "The Father of Judo - Google Books." 2012. 1 Jan. 2015. 97.
<http://books.google.com/books/about/The_Father_of_Judo.html?id=cTmEiO5UrMYC>.

the best Judo practitioners from the Issei generation and a blossoming generation of Nisei willing to share their art. Judo was on the rise.

On December 7, 1941, the Imperial Japanese Navy launched a surprise attack on Pearl Harbor. This was a pivotal turning point in World War II, leading to the direct military involvement of the United States against Japan, Germany, and the Axis powers. At home in the U.S., President Theodore Roosevelt was experiencing extreme pressure from the state legislature about the potential espionage risk of Japanese citizens residing in the country. On February 19, 1942, President Roosevelt issued Executive Order 9066 which resulted in the mandatory relocation and internment of Japanese citizens in pre-designated, military controlled areas.[37]

The general perception of Japanese people in the U.S. throughout the 1940s was bleak; however, not all was lost in terms of growth for the martial arts. Judo players, many of whom resided on the West Coast, found themselves incarcerated together as a result of Executive Order 9066. In addition, highly skilled Judoka were sometimes used in the internment camps as peacekeepers. This was a time of condensed learning and sharing, and when the war was over and Japanese citizens released, the art spread back out with a renewed vigor.

As history shows, America was able to defeat Japan and help bring about an end to World War II. This victory did not come without a heavy price. The Battle of Okinawa took place in April of 1945, lasting 82 days and incurring thousands upon thousands of deaths for the Americans, Japanese, and native Okinawans. The battle destroyed the Okinawan countryside, leveling towns and killing entire bloodlines. The Japanese used the Okinawans as distractions and tools, convincing the natives that it would be better to kill themselves than surrender to the "barbarian" invaders. In August of 1945, after securing Okinawa, America utilized atomic bombs to decimate Hiroshima and Nagasaki. The Emperor of Japan submitted his surrender that same month.

America maintained an occupying force in Japan after the Emperor's surrender, ensuring the country's continued pacification and military disarmament. Over the course of the war it became apparent that Japan was using its long history of martial culture to bolster

---

[37] Hatamiya, Leslie T. *Righting a Wrong: Japanese Americans and the Passage of the Civil Liberties Act of 1988.* Stanford, Calif.: Stanford UP, 1993. <http://books.google.com/books/about/Righting_a_Wrong_Japanese_Americans_and.html ?id=SGVHxKe-nC4C>.

nationalism and loyalty in its soldiers. As a result, the American forces created Directive 548, requiring "the removal and exclusion from public life of militaristic and ultra nationalistic persons."[38] This included the closure of the Dai Nippon Butokukai (a central hub for Japanese martial arts), and placed every art under close scrutiny.

Thanks to the foresight of Kano Jigoro and his senior inheriting students, Judo was not crippled by Directive 548. With established rules, tournaments, and controlled techniques, Judo was seen as a sport instead of a classical military art. Judo also enjoyed an established history within the U.S., making it a known commodity. In fact, as opposed to shutting Judo down, a number of U.S. military personnel engaged in training while stationed in Japan. This would serve as a source of Judo resurgence as the 1940s closed and the 1950s began.

---

[38] "JCS: Documentation Regarding the Budo Ban - EJMAS.com." 2003. 2 Jan. 2015
<http://ejmas.com/jcs/jcsart_svinth_1202.htm>.

Chapter 4 –

The First Karate Wave - Immigrants and Men of War

To understand the journey of karate, we must first revisit the critical pipeline that is Hawaii. America was certainly aware of Okinawa and its people throughout the 1800s, thanks in large part to the early expeditions of Matthew Perry. However, it was in the year 1900 that the S.S. *City of China* arrived in Hawaii with a group of Okinawan immigrants, some of whom brought karate with them.[39] While it is unknown if there were small pockets of karate outside of Okinawa before this, the arrival of the S.S. *City of China* was undoubtedly one of the earliest and most notable exports of the art.

There is research indicating karate's use as early as 1902 in North America, but it was Yabu Kentsu in 1927 that first brought broader attention to the art, giving two demonstrations in Hawaii. Yabu Sensei's second demonstration was widely attended, the audience including military personnel and reporters.[40] The 1930s saw Motobu Choki, Mutsu Mizuho, Higaonna Kamessuke, Miyagi Chojun, and more landing on Hawaii's shores. Men like Thomas Shigeru Miyashiro took advantage of this influx of karate and began teaching on the island, which was noteworthy because the classes were open to Asian and non-Asian students alike.

---

[39] "The Roots of Okinawan Karate in Hawaii." 2002. 2 Jan. 2015 <http://seinenkai.com/art-roots.html>.
[40] "JCS: Karate Pioneer Kentsu Yabu, 1866-1937:Svinth." 2003. 3 Jan. 2015
<http://ejmas.com/jcs/jcsart_svinth_0603.htm>.

Much like Okinawa itself, Hawaii was a small island with a lot of cultural influences melding together. In the 1940s, James Mitose mixed his experiences in striking and throwing to create an effective self defense methodology, which would eventually be integrated by William K.S. Chow and referred to as Kempo. Hawaii also saw the birth of Kajukenbo, a mixture of karate, jujutsu, kempo, and boxing. It was a time of both experimentation and preservation.

Karate's Survival Throughout World War II

One of the primary reasons karate was imported from Okinawa into Japan was to benefit the education system. The Japanese intended to use the physical fitness aspects and discipline of karate to instill strong fighting spirit and loyalty in their future soldiers. Funakoshi Gichin, Itosu Anko, and other karate pioneers recognized these requests from the Japanese Ministry of Education and made changes to the art, emphasizing clean linear techniques that resembled the mindset of kendo and integrated a spirit of "perseverance through suffering" in every club. The revised karate could be learned on an abbreviated timeline, which was perfect for university students or soldiers.

Influenced by Kano himself, Funakoshi integrated the belt ranking system into his clubs, initially containing just white belts and black belts but eventually expanding into a diverse range of colors. By the time the Americans arrived, Shotokan and other Japanese styles of karate were engaging in sporting competition with regulations for legal techniques. Although a departure from its Okinawan roots, the changes made by the early Japanese karate pioneers helped save the art during American occupation.

Karate survived in Japan and Okinawa, but only a handful of Western individuals studied the art at first. One of the earliest to return to the American mainland and teach karate was Robert Trias, who began instructing in 1945 and opened his own small program in Arizona in 1946. After that, karate slowly trickled in through Hawaii and via soldiers returning from military tours in the East.

Although the re-spread of Judo took precedence after the conclusion of World War II, Oyama Masutatsu's visit to America in 1952 went a long way in popularizing karate. Around the same time, Emilio Bruno, supervisor for the U.S. Strategic Air Command in Japan, began investigating karate and how it might integrate into American military training. Judo had proven a successful venture in military combatives, and karate seemed like a logical, hard hitting counterpart. General Curtis Lemay, empowered by Bruno and the S.A.C., initiated an eight week training program for Air Force members via the Japan Karate Association, working closely with Nishiyama Hidetaka, Kamata Toshio, and Obata Isao. This event truly kickstarted the study of karate by Westerners in Japan and the migration of karate instructors into America itself.[41]

The Burgeoning Karate Scene in the U.S.A.

1954 and 1955 were critical years for the influx of martial arts talent in the U.S. Ed Parker moved back to Provo, Utah, and begun the spread of his brand of kempo. William Dometrich came back to Kentucky, bringing Chito Ryu with him. Dewey Deavers opened his school in the Pittsburgh area, teaching a combination of jujutsu and karate. Oshima Tsutoma began organizing classes at the Konko Shinto Church, soon paving the way for future Japan Karate Association (J.K.A.) greats like Nishiyama Hidetaka. The mid 1950s was also the beginning of formalized karate events. Robert Trias Sensei put together the first Arizona Karate Championships held at the Butler Boys Club, which proved to be one of many increasingly impressive competitions.

Korean arts were also coming into prominence in the U.S. Some of the Korean styles, like Tang Soo Do, had direct roots in Shotokan Karate and quickly became part of the "karate scene." Atlee Chittim, for example, returned to Texas from Korea as a brown belt in taekwondo. He taught at San Antonio College and became a prominent resource for martial arts in Texas. Chittim was instrumental in bringing Jhoon Rhee into the United States, who would go on to become one of the most influential taekwondo instructors on the whole East Coast.

In the late 1950s and early 1960s, karate was beginning to make a noticeable impact on the martial arts landscape. Pioneers like Dan Ivan, Cecil Patterson, Don Nagle, Phillip Koeppel, Peter Urban, Maynard Miner, George Mattson, Robert Fusaro, Louis Kowlowski, Roger Warren, Charles Gruzanski, Ed Kaloudis, Aaron Banks, Harry Smith, Wallace Reumann, Ron Duncan, Chris DeBais, Anthony Mirakian, Steve Armstrong, Virgil

---

[41] Corcoran, John, and Emil Farkas. *The Original Martial Arts Encyclopedia: Tradition, History, Pioneers.* Los Angeles, CA: Pro-Action Pub., 1993. 230. Print.

Adams, Ralph Lindquist, James Wax, Gary Alexander, and other "notables" were cropping up. Although there are too many to list at this time, each pioneer made an impact and deserves recognition in his / her own right.

The Tournament Scene and the Vietnam Influence

One of the great divides in karate's practice and dissemination has always been sport competition. In Japan and Okinawa, there was a growing split between sport karate and old-style karate even as the first Westerners began to train. Thanks to Judo's influence, many Americans were drawn to the competitive aspects of martial arts. However, a number of U.S. military members learned karate with the express intent of using it for combative purposes, wishing to keep as much of the violent efficacy intact as possible. The result was a birthing of some schools in America that were business minded and sport regulated, others that mimicked military boot camp, and others still that mirrored the Asian cultures from which they came.

The tournament scene in America began in the late 1950s but truly came to prominence throughout the '60s, leading to a boom in popularity in the '70s. A large influx of Korean schools in the 1960s, combined with the existing sport karate presence, created a significant momentum shift toward the sporting side of the art.[42] Nishiyama Hidetaka created the All American Karate Championships in Los Angeles, held in 1961, which focused predominantly on Shotokan participants. The North American Karate Championships were held in 1962 at Madison Square Garden, sparking widespread interest as Oyama Masutatsu wowed audiences. In 1963, Robert Trias, with the cooperation of John Keehan, created the first World Karate Tournament, one of the earliest and biggest multi-style events, at the University of Chicago Fieldhouse.

Of particular note in 1963 was the work of Allen Steen, Pat Burleson, and a few other Texas pioneers. Steen created the Dallas Southwest Karate Championships, which proved to be a gathering place for some of the toughest and grittiest fighters in the country.[43] Competitions increased in frequency throughout Texas, each event having its own loose

---

[42] Corcoran, John, and Emil Farkas. *The Original Martial Arts Encyclopedia: Tradition, History, Pioneers.* Los Angeles, CA: Pro-Action Pub., 1993. 244. Print.

[43] "Black Belt - Google Books." 2011. 11 Jan. 2015. 16. <http://books.google.com/books/about/Black_Belt.html?id=iM4DAAAAMBAJ>.

set of rules. The sparring in these Texas tournaments often ended in broken bones, black eyes, and busted lips. This period is often referred to as the "Blood 'n Guts Era," a name justified by the powerful, unrefined methods of fighting often exhibited during matches.[44]

Some of the biggest martial arts personalities in American history found the spotlight during this era as well. Chuck Norris made a name for himself as a champion-level Korean stylist. Victor Moore began breaking boundaries for African Americans as he continuously beat the most renowned karate and taekwondo practitioners of the day. Bill "Superfoot" Wallace melded karate technique with incredible high kicking skill, adding personality and flair to fights. Joe Lewis seared through the competition as one of the toughest and brashest competitors in the world. The popularity and success of tournaments had far reaching effect as karate became a commodity across the United States.

Vietnam Draws Military Forces Overseas

While the tournament scene grew after World War II, global conflicts continued to send American servicemen overseas. The U.S.A. relied heavily on its bases in Japan and Okinawa as the Korean War sparked in the early 1950s, and the Cold War kept armed forces all over the world on edge. American martial and military science developed rapidly as a result of these conflicts. However, the most significant pipeline for karate's transmission was developed as a result of the Vietnam War.

Okinawa was a key staging area for American troops going into and out of Vietnam. The close geographic location, pre-existing military bases, and tropical climate made Okinawa an ideal environment to acclimate soldiers. The high ranking military officials on the island realized that highly fit and able soldiers were arriving on Okinawa with just enough time to benefit from learning the deadly fighting art native to the island. Military coordinators began working closely with Okinawan karate instructors, hiring them to teach on bases and accept soldiers into their dojo(s).[45]

---

[44] "Martial Arts Biography - Pat Burleson - U.S.A.dojo.com." 2006. 11 Jan. 2015
<http://www.usadojo.com/biographies/pat-burleson.htm>.
[45] Dojo, a term for karate schools, is also pluralized as dojo. The same applies to the word sensei, or teacher.

Although some Okinawans wanted nothing to do with American occupying forces, many karate sensei realized that working with military organizers was a path out of poverty. Okinawa had long been a poor country, repressed and controlled by Japanese rule. The destruction of the island during The Battle of Okinawa only exacerbated the problem. Teaching karate allowed a number of Okinawans to improve their desperate situations, and even save their families.

Shimabukuro Tatsuo was one of the first major instructors on Okinawa to establish a contractual relationship with the Americans. Uechi Kanei, Shimabukuro Eizo, and Shimabukuro Zenryo did the same. A number of instructors also allowed Westerners into their schools, including Nakamura Shigeru, Kise Fusei, Toma Shian, Odo Seikichi, Nakazato Shuguro, Higa Seiko, Oyata Seiyu, and more. During the Vietnam Era, military personnel struggled to secure long periods of time on the island (often cycling between Okinawa, Vietnam, and the U.S.A.), but, while there, had incredible direct access to various high level instructors.

It is in this timeframe, after World War II and throughout the Vietnam Era, that the interview guests in "Tales from the Western Generation" matured. The karateka[46] featured in this book either studied directly in Japan and Okinawa or with the earliest pioneers in America. Their areas of interest span the spectrum of karate, some achieving fame as champion competitors, others quietly spreading the culture and art of their teachers. Altogether, they represent the foundation upon which present-day karate stands, and the potential upon which future karate will be built.

---

[46] Karateka is a term that refers to someone who practices karate.

Interviews with the Western Generation

Chapter 5 –
Goju Ryu

One of the most widespread Okinawan styles, Goju Ryu is respected worldwide and has experienced multiple permutations throughout the 20th and 21st centuries. The lynchpin figure in the history of Goju Ryu is Miyagi Chojun, a powerful karateka and influential figure.

It's believed that Miyagi Sensei was introduced to karate by Aragaki Seisho at a young age, but he began his primary study with a gentleman named Higashionna Kanryo at the age of 14.[47] Higashionna's flavor of karate became well known throughout the city of Naha. Miyagi Sensei expanded upon his experience with "Naha Te" (the hand of Naha) by traveling to China with Gokenki, a tea merchant who lived on Okinawa and had developed a reputation for his skills in White Crane Kung Fu (Baihequan).[48]

In addition to being a powerful practitioner, Miyagi Sensei was also a prolific teacher. Throughout the 1920s and 1930s, Miyagi was involved in a number of important demonstrations, including those for the Crown Prince Hirohito of Japan. Miyagi Sensei was integral in the early development of karate for school programs on Okinawa and traveled to both Japan and Hawaii to put on demonstrations and teach some of the art.

As a result of Miyagi's efforts, multiple branches of Goju Ryu spawned and disseminated. In Okinawa, a number of senior students carried on his tradition, including (but not

---

[47] Alexander, George W. *Okinawa, Island of Karate*. City of pub: Yamazato Publications, 1991. 53. Print.
[48] Bishop, Mark. *Okinawan Karate: Teachers, Styles and Secret Techniques*. City of pub: Tuttle Publishing, 1999. 27. Print.

limited to) Higa Seiko, Miyazato Eiichi, Yagi Meitoku, and Toguchi Seikichi. Miyagi's most famous Japanese student was Yamaguchi Gogen, nicknamed "The Cat". It was this inheriting generation that first introduced the art of Goju Ryu to Western military men.

Glenn Keeney

Born in 1942, Glenn Keeney grew up in an unassuming Indiana town with a large family in a small, modest home. As he came of age, the very first wave of American martial art pioneers were beginning to emerge in the United States. Little did Keeney know that a budding interest in karate as a youth would eventually turn him into one of the winningest tournament competitors of all time.

Keeney Sensei established his karate foundation in Goju Ryu, but became something of an early collector, always on the hunt for top tier fighters and kata men to learn from. In time he not only built his reputation on the fighting circuit, but also became respected as an organizer. Keeney Sensei had a direct hand in some of the biggest organized karate events in the country and has become a household name for those interested in the world of early karate competition.

Q: Keeney Sensei, what was the general state of martial arts in the U.S.A. throughout the 1950s?

In the central Indiana area there wasn't much to speak of. I know Judo was the prominent art / sport in the United States around that time. For me there might have been two YMCA-style Judo clubs and one Korean club in a 60-mile radius.

I first heard about martial arts from a guy named Bruce Tegner. He wrote small paperback self-defense books (I still have one or two actually). It was interesting to me at the time, trying to pick up a few tricks from these books.

Q: Did anything in your childhood lead you to martial arts early on?

I really didn't go looking for trouble as a kid, but I was feisty . . . and quite poor. There were seven of us growing up in a two room house, which led to some rough housing. I enjoyed my siblings and parents though. Other kids would sometimes make fun of us because we were so poor, and I wouldn't stand for it. I got a few ass whoopings that way which led me to the martial arts. I wanted to try to find something that would give me an edge.

Q: Those early scraps led you to joining a martial arts school around 1957. Could you describe how you went about finding a dojo, given their rarity?

It started with a conversation I had when I was 14. I was talking to a guy I knew, a truck driver who drove freight between Anderson, Indiana (where I lived) and Cincinnati, Ohio. He told me about this karate school on Redding Road. He stopped in, noticed that no one was speaking English, and decided to skip it . . . but gave me the address anyway.

After I got out of school on Friday a few weeks later, I hitchhiked down to Cincinnati about 115 miles away. I found Redding Road and went a block or two back where the road turned into gravel and dirt. There was a shack down toward the end with a little efficiency apartment hooked up to it. I found out that the person in charge was named L. Kim who spoke almost enough English to understand you (but not quite). I let him know that I wanted to take karate and he asked, "Money?" I had four dollars and gave him three of it. I guess that was enough!

He took me over to the corner and demonstrated a few basic techniques. He had three or four people come in, all adult Korean men. We did some exercises and techniques and then they finished with kata. After class I told him that I had brought a sleeping bag and was hoping to sleep in the dojo. He had me sleep outside, but it was springtime and warm so I made do.

The next day I went back to class again. He had the same people come in and they worked out and let me join in again. This same training routine went on until Sunday when I hitchhiked back to Anderson. I got to doing that almost every weekend for about two to three months. Unfortunately I went back one Friday and the school was closed. I went back a few weeks later and it was closed again. At that point I realized he probably went out of business.

Q: Did you ever find out his full name?

No - it was always just "L. Kim.". I asked if he meant maybe "El," or "Ele," but no. He just said "L."

Q: Did your parents have any reaction to you traveling to take these classes?

My parents were pretty old school and poor. They thought it was a waste of time but figured I was getting old enough to make my own decisions. My mother didn't like the idea of me hitchhiking, but my dad didn't mind as much.

Q: So this first experience introduced you to the habit of training, but it wasn't particularly long-lived. What was the next step in your martial arts journey?

I was disappointed that the first school had shut down and I spent most of my time afterward trying to learn out of books. In 1961 I discovered a club in Indianapolis. I was about 18-19 years old when this happened. I first heard about the group from a gentleman in town who studied Judo there. I was able to bum a ride down with him to check it out a few times and decided to sign up for the karate course they were offering. It was a Shorin Ryu Six Month Program and cost $405.

The course was being taught by a gentleman named James Wax. Mr. Wax was an early Western student of Matsubayashi Ryu. The two assistants were Robert Yarnall and Greg Helm.

Q: Could you describe the content of that particular karate course?

The classes were set up in one and a half hour increments. The first 30 minutes were exercises, then 30 minutes of basics, and the last 30 minutes were one step sparring drills with a partner (preset combo movements).

After about two to three months, they taught me two kata. There was a third gentleman who taught some of the classes but it was Mr. Yarnall and Mr. Helm who I enjoyed and learned the most from. They helped me establish a karate foundation.

Glenn Keeney sparring with Robert Yarnall. Chuck Norris acts as referee.

Even though the program was said to be run by James Wax, we were never taught by him. I saw him about four times throughout the course. He would come into the dojo and talk to the instructors. One time he was talking to Mr. Yarnall, and they kicked off their shoes and went onto the floor. Mr. Wax went into some flying kick routines with Mr. Yarnall being uke. The one time I saw Mr. Wax teaching a class it was for more advanced people and I wasn't allowed to stick around.

After the course I didn't see Mr. Wax again until around 1975-1976. By then he had been affected by drug use and his mind wasn't what it used to be. He had gotten married and his spouse was helping him day-to-day. I got to talk to him quite a bit at that point and his story was sad to hear.

Q: Are there any particularly memorable lessons or evenings from your time in the Shorin Ryu Six Month Program?

One night I was out on the floor before class, running the first kata they had taught me. I was really running hard at it. The Tuesday before this particular night, I was running the kata and Mr. Helm had corrected me on a few things. So I was training and Mr. Yarnall came by and "recorrected" the techniques another way. When I told him Mr. Helm had recently corrected me a different way, he took a moment and then said, "Well here's what you do. Practice 100 times the way he told you to do it. Then practice 100 times the way I told you to do it. That way you can do it either way depending on who is teaching."

I started to laugh at the thought and Mr. Yarnall said, "What are you laughing at? You've got 200 kata to do!"

Q: Having a karate program with a set amount of time (six months) is a little unusual. How did that work exactly?

The instructors worked for a company led by James Cahn. Unfortunately Mr. Cahn eventually got caught up in tax evasion . . . but he had a club set up in St. Louis. He would run it for six months or so, and if it was successful he would sell the franchise to his best student for next to nothing. The best student would have to honor a preset agreement and help set up the organization. Then Mr. Cahn would move on to the next city through Missouri, Iowa, Illinois, Indiana, and Ohio. He probably started thirty-some schools by the time he was done.

Mr. Cahn would come into a city with his crew and set up shop somewhere. They would operate out of a trailer if they didn't have a building yet, but they usually managed to find buildings quickly. They would put together a dojo and sell contracts as best they could for five to eight months. Once a person emerged as a top student, they began the process of giving control of that dojo over to him. The individual taking over the dojo would be bound by the financial agreements of the organization but would be entitled to any profits beyond that. Unfortunately these franchises tended not to last.

The school I personally attended within this organization ended up closing shortly before my contract time was up. They must not have found a proper guy to sell it to in order to continue it. I was disappointed, but there was a brown belt by the name of Ed Erler who opened a school a few weeks later. I remember he had joined the Cahn club as a green belt and got to brown before it shut down. He opened his own club but then decided to join the Navy and had to shut down a few months later.

Q: Your early experiences were diverse to say the least, but your next big break in terms of training came in 1964. Could you tell us about your introduction to Goju Ryu at that time?

In 1964 I met a gentleman named Larry Pickel. He lived in Chesterfield, which was three miles from where I lived in Anderson. He had spent time in Okinawa studying under Miyazato Eiichi, one of the senior students of Miyagi Chojun. My buddy and I went over to his house in Chesterfield to ask if he would teach us. Without much fuss he said, "Sure." So we all started up in my one buddy's garage. It went on that way from 1964-1966.

Q: How did you find out about Pickel Sensei?

Everyone seemed to know him. He played linebacker at a local high school, which is notable in a Midwest American town. When he got back from the military I must have heard half a dozen people talk about his return. There were whispers about Larry Pickel "learning all that karate in the East.". He had been back for maybe three to four weeks at the most before we got a hold of him ourselves.

Q: When you started Goju Ryu did you have any trouble adapting your previous experiences in karate, namely Shorin Ryu?

I didn't have trouble adapting because I didn't really know anything. I found a lot of the basics to be quite similar, with just a few adjustments (things like where we chambered the punch). Some kicks were a little higher or lower, that sort of thing. I had already been augmenting my previous training with books from Nishiyama Hidetaka of Shotokan so I was starting to see some of the consistent basics across the styles and was willing to adapt to what my teacher needed me to do.

Willie Perry, Jerry Brown, Glenn Keeney, Larry Pickle
Dick Brinkley, Larry Davenport, Clarence Burk

Larry Pickel (standing) with winning competitors, including Glenn Keeney (third from left).

Q: What was Pickel Sensei like as an instructor? Did he bring his military background into the dojo?

Yes, he was very militaristic. Our typical class was 30 minutes of hard exercise, 30 minutes of hard basics, and 30 minutes of whatever content he felt you needed. He used the word "kumite" to describe the seven, one-step sparring drills he used (pre-arranged block / punch combos). Then he used the term "jiyu kumite" for his two-step drills even though we know now that term tends to refer to freestyle fighting. He had never sparred at the Miyazato dojo on Okinawa. I, of course, liked to spar but he never got into it. There were times when he wasn't around, and I got some folks to spar with me.

Q: Considering the hard, militaristic style of the training, did you ever consider quitting?

Absolutely not. He couldn't run me off with a gun. I didn't miss classes often either. We were very disciplined about such things. I remember that we would clean the training space after every evening of classes. Equipment maintenance was the same way.

As some of Pickel Sensei's earliest students, we helped build the training space. None of us knew what we were doing when we laid the floor, so we often had to wear tennis shoes or slippers because the cement had little edges sticking up. Before class we would often get hammers and knock down as many little sharp areas as possible. After a few months we got it to the point where we could go barefoot.

Q: What was it that attracted you so much to the discipline of training?

I think it had something to do with the way I was brought up. I lived out in the country and my dad was a very strict person. I couldn't be out of shape based on the chores, work, and running around I had to do on a daily basis. I liked the physical part of training and I liked the people I was working out with. I felt like I was becoming tough and that maybe I could whip somebody if it came down to it. I got proven wrong a few times . . . but I still felt like I was improving.

One thing that always appealed to me, in training and regular life, was travel. From 1963 and beyond, any time a club would open up within 70-80 miles I'd be right there talking to them and working out with them. I didn't care if they were Judo, jujutsu, karate, Aikido[49], grappling . . . it didn't make a difference. I always wanted to see what they knew and see what I knew.

A lot of people know about Bill "Superfoot" Wallace, one of the greatest karate and kickboxing competitors in U.S. history. Well he and I met in 1968, and every year during the summer we took off for two to three weeks with our blue jeans, sweatshirts, and gis in order to travel around to different karate clubs. We would call ahead to these clubs, visit for two to three days, and sleep on the mat. We would work out, take instruction, and then go on to the next dojo. This went on for about six years in the late '60s and early '70s.

---

[49] Specific styles of martial art like Aikido (founded exclusively by Ueshiba Morihei OSensei) tend to be capitalized, while broader terms like karate or jujutsu remain lower case. A capitalized example of karate would be Shotokan Karate.

Q: Did you find most of the instructors you were visiting to be receptive to you, or was there a little bit of closed door secrecy?

They tended to be receptive because I laid out the agenda before we left. I had met most of these people at tournaments so there was already an introduction and relationship there. Indiana was one of the first and best karate states, believe it or not. A lot of it was thanks to the business efforts of Jimmy Cahn. He had set up dojo(s) in Fort Wayne, Marrietta, Muncie, Indianapolis, and so forth throughout the mid-to-late '60s. Mel Wise, Parker Shelton, Robert Bowles, Bill Wallace, and others all helped make the scene in Indiana really lively.

I'd call up these individuals, tell them where we'd be traveling, and find out if it was ok to pop into the area. They were all for it. I turned out to be a pretty good kumite player so they liked to have me around. Also, if I went to events, I worked my ass off to help with the set up and operation of the event. All day long I'd work, then I'd do kumite, and then go home or go back to the dojo. I would also help spread the word about their events so I would end up bringing them attention and entry fees.

Q: When did you actually start your tournament career, and what were some of those early events like?

I saw my first tournament in 1966 in Aurora, Illinois. From then on I was hooked. The first tournament I competed in was in 1967 in Convington, Kentucky. It was put on by William Dometrich, and I got beat my first match. I was thoroughly convinced that I was going to walk in and whip everybody in that gym. It didn't work out that way, which turned out to be an important lesson. After that I had one more tournament as a green belt, which I won, and then as a brown belt I never failed to place. By 1970 I had competed in around 60 tournaments, so I kept an active schedule.

For kumite there were no pads of any kind. Rules changed a little bit from place to place, but in general if you wore pads you were scoffed at by the other competitors. However if you could remove the pad and show that you had a significant injury, it was generally considered acceptable.

Sportsmanship was at a peak at that time, in my opinion. You didn't talk back to anybody, you followed the rules, and that was that. Contact was acceptable — if the opponent was still conscious, you were considered to be in the bounds of the rules. The mindset of competitive fighting was a little different then compared to modern events. The general theory was that if you started forward on your opponent he could make you pay for it, even if it meant knocking you into next week. It was understood that he was defending against your attack.

I will say that the viciousness of those early fights tends to be exaggerated sometimes. If it was as bad as you hear, none of us would have survived it. One important thing about making contact — it had to be done with technique. If you went out and started brawling or using Western boxing skills, you wouldn't get points and you'd be reprimanded or disqualified.

Q: You mentioned that you did quite a lot of travel with Bill Wallace, who would become a very famous full contact fighter. Did you and Mr. Wallace train and spar a lot with each other as well as with other dojo instructors?

We sparred on average about five hours a week. He had enrolled at Ball State Teacher's College and that was only 18 miles from my house. He had studied under Mickie Generic in California and then studied overseas with Shimabukuro Eizo. He was in Okinawa for eight to nine months and was given a black belt, which the Asian teachers were known to do for a lot of the Westerners.

Bill had a handful of kata and basic drills but he really loved to spar. The first few times my students and I fought with him, we did really good. He hadn't had a lot of experience in freestyle sparring yet, and I had been around karate for awhile. That unevenness didn't last long though.

Here's the thing: Bill is brilliant. I don't specifically know his I.Q. but I do know it's high. He is a speed reader and has something akin to a photographic memory. For example, one time we stopped in Chicago while traveling to ask for directions to a local Y.M.C.A. The person rattled off nine or ten steps to get there and I had to say, "Whoa stop, let me get a pencil." Bill just said, "No it's fine, I got it." He learned karate the same way.

When I learned karate, it was a long process. If I saw someone at a tournament doing something I liked, I'd take them off to the corner and try to learn from them. I would practice it then for two to three weeks, then I'd say, "Hey Bill, come on out here. Let me show you something." We'd go through it and I'd show him my best version of the technique. Then I'd go into the office or something and come back out five minutes later and he'd be doing it better than I could. The first time Bill ever did full contact, he won the world championship. A lot of people think of him as a boxer or kickboxer but it was his karate foundation that allowed him to win championships. I think he had nine or ten under his belt before he had his first actual boxing lesson.

Glenn Keeney and Bill Wallace enjoying a moment of conversation after one of their many competitions.

Q: In the early 1970s, you started getting involved in organizing and running tournaments. Why did you decide to undertake this, and what challenges did you encounter?

I kinda got stuck with it. I wanted to be in karate bad. I was addicted to it and I wanted to learn. I owed a lot to Mr. Pickel as my teacher for a number of years . . . but things got in the way when it came to training with him. He had a bad marriage, and a man who had never drank a beer in his life became almost a drug addict. He quit the martial arts. We had just bought a dojo in 1966 (four of us, including him) and I was a brown belt. Once Pickel Sensei quit, I realized I had two choices — either take over the dojo or close the doors.

I realized there was nowhere else to go nearby and I refused to close the doors, so we decided to buy it. Jerry Brown, Larry Davenport, and myself scrounged up enough money and bought out Mr. Pickel's share of the school. Two and a half years later, I bought out Mr. Davenport and Mr. Brown and became the sole owner. Both of my partners had family responsibilities, and the karate school was simply taking too much of their time.

Owning that school led very naturally to an increased role in tournament play. If I found out about a tournament anywhere in the country, we would find a way to get there. My students and I would all crunch together in a few people's cars and all slept in the same hotel room. Sometimes we would just drive down to the event and drive straight back. Despite all the competing, I worked very hard to keep my club traditional. We made new students watch every week for nearly a month before allowing them to join us out on the floor.

Eventually I decided that instead of just spending money all the time going to tournaments, we might actually make some money by hosting one. We needed new equipment in the dojo, so that settled it for me. I drew up flyers and sent them out saying that anybody who came and supported my tournament would have my support in return. This occurred in February of 1968.

The basic idea was that if schools sent students to participate in my tournament I would send equal or more students to their tournament. If I couldn't arrange for that, I would send them the money as if we were attending. I ended up with about 325 competitors at my first event when the average tournament was around 100 attendees at that time.

Unfortunately, I had no idea what to do when over 300 people arrived at my event. Fifty people I could have handled no problem, but this was different. Luckily William Dometrich had decided to attend. He came up to me and said, "Do you want some help with this?" I said, "Please, yes!" He took over in short order, lined everyone up by rank, and started counting off in fours. He then split everyone up into divisions and got the show on the road.

While traveling to other people's tournaments, I got to know Master Robert Trias. One time I went to Kansas City to attend his Nationals event put on by Jim Harrison. While there, Trias Sensei asked me to hold a Grand Nationals with his backing. I took that very seriously. I spent the biggest part of five months promoting that tournament, set to be held in 1970. I had every sign in the city of Anderson with that tournament plastered on it and twenty pages in the newspaper talking about it. I ended up with 900 competitors and 6,000 spectators.

Q: Could you talk a bit more about Trias Sensei as a person and as a martial artist?

I always admired Trias Sensei for his work ethic and knowledge. People know the United States Karate Association (U.S.K.A.) as a big organization, but when Trias Sensei started in the U.S.A. he was teaching off of his back porch in Phoenix, Arizona. Later he moved to a modest dojo on McDowell Road in town.

His karate was absolutely awesome. I had limited knowledge myself, but I did get out an awful lot and saw other practitioners at work. I also brought a number of people to my dojo both to live and train for periods of time. Even with exposure to all those people, I knew that Mr. Trias was special. I remember every time I saw him I was just as impressed as the very first time I met him.

Trias Sensei had the ability to help you understand what you were doing. He could take a little movement of yours, tweak it, and boom — there it was. He had a mechanical and conceptual understanding that was very rare.

Glenn Keeney receiving correction from Robert Trias Sensei.

Q: Throughout that period of the early-to-mid-70s while you were competing and promoting, were you able to continue your own personal study in Goju Ryu? Were there any particular teachers you connected with, perhaps back on Okinawa?

No, I was not able to make any connection of that sort during that era. Mr. Pickel had continued to teach me up until black belt level, sharing the kata(s) Gekisai Dai Ichi and Ni, Saifa, Shisochin, Sochin, Sanseru, Seipai, and Sanchin. He also taught one bo kata and one sai kata as well as the one / two step sparring drills.

I had my foundation in Goju Ryu and then filled in gaps with exposure to other practitioners and traveling around the country. I was able to secure some books on Goju, but finding them in English was next to impossible. I also got serious about learning Shuri Ryu once my relationship with Master Trias developed (Shuri Ryu being the style he developed). At the time, Mr. Phillip Koeppel was also studying that and he was a great inspiration and teacher whom I learned a lot from.

For a long time there was actually a stylistic intermingling called Shorei-Goju under Trias Sensei, but eventually it just became known as Shuri Ryu. I was one of the individuals involved in the combined concepts of Goju Ryu and Shuri Ryu.

Q: Did you ever have any worries about being labelled eclectic as opposed to traditional? Perhaps being thought of as not pure enough in your training?

No, not really. I was a Goju practitioner and I both practiced and taught the system faithfully. I learned the Shuri Ryu system and practiced that faithfully, too. I never mixed the kata up. I took the time to learn the basics of both so that I could do the kata properly. It got confusing at times, but then I just slowed down and reminded myself of what I should be doing.

As far as cross-training, I tried to do it all. I took boxing lessons and even went to college on a wrestling scholarship (until I flunked out). I studied jujutsu, Aikido, and more. I mixed those lessons into my kumite and self-defense, but did not let them sneak into the preservation of my styles.

One trick I've developed over the years is relying on others to help keep me straight. When I'm training with my really good black belts, I assign them a kata. That person is not allowed to forget that kata and has to retain as much detail as possible. Even if he / she quits karate, they still have to remember that kata. We can all then go to that person just in case I forget something or need to brush up.

A natural fact of karate training is that eventually you will develop a favorite kata or two. You'll keep on practicing those favorites while letting the ones you don't like as much slip. Sometimes the movements of your favorite kata will start to sneak into the other forms, so you need to make sure you have a resource to double check yourself and see if any habits are sneaking in.

Q: Do you remember how many national championships you won before retiring? Also, how did you know when it was time to retire?

I honestly don't remember in terms of tournament wins. Keeping track of numbers like that wasn't important to me. Not to mention, titles have always been cheap in karate since the popularization of tournaments. I was more about finding the toughest competition and earning the wins that I thought had value.

Winners row in Chicago, 1974. From left to right: Fred Wren, Bill Wallace, Glenn Keeney, Owen Watson, Ron Van Clief, and John Davis.

I remember traveling specifically to New York one time to fight a guy named Joe Hayes who I heard was a really good fighter. Another time I went to a Trias event and ran across Victor Moore. I got to watch him fight in 1967 and was really impressed. I studied him as much as I could and ultimately drove to Kansas City specifically to fight him. That weekend I was helping Jim Harrison run the tournament and he came up to me and said, "Glenn thanks a lot for the help you've given me — you work like a slave! Is there anything I can do for you in return?" I said, "Yea, line me up with Victor Moore in the first match." He said, "Really? Well, I can do that."

That first match was me and Victor Moore . . . and Victor gave me an ass-whooping worse than my father ever gave me. I had gotten beaten in matches before, sure (if you fight enough you are bound to lose sometimes). He was the only guy to have ever given me a straight ass-whooping.

Q: Did you get to fight any of the other great competitors of the era, like Mike Stone?

I fought almost everyone at one point or another, but Mike only competed for a short amount of time. He was actually a brown belt when he won his first world tournament in 1963 in Chicago. He was from Texas and they said to him, "Well, why don't you just fight with the black belts?" He continued to fight into 1964, '65, and '66, but that was about it. He made a few semi-full-contact appearances around 1970, but those were one-off bouts.

Personally, I would put Mike Stone in my "top ten" for fighters. The only knock might be his longevity. He was as good and as tough as anybody else of his era. I sparred him about half a dozen times during seminars and the like. His instructor, Yamashita Tadashi of Kobayashi Ryu, had moved to Mishiwaka, Indiana, around 1967. Mike would come down to visit him on occasion (around 1969-1970), and we would work out then. At the time that I sparred him I could hold my own, but in 1963 and 1964, when he was in his absolute prime, I doubt I could have.

Q: How about Joe Lewis, student of Shimabukuro Eizo and famous full contact competitor?

You know, I never got a chance to fight Joe Lewis in a tournament. He was my hero, though. When I looked at Joe I thought, "Now that is a karate man." He had just gotten back from Okinawa in 1966, and he competed in Jhoon Rhee's big international tournament in Washington, D.C., and took first place in both kata and kumite. He was a very arrogant type of person, but he was the baddest man walking.

I went to every seminar of his that I possibly could. He was so far ahead of us in karate at the beginning . . . it took me ten years to understand what he was teaching me. Oddly, after 20 years he still seemed to be doing and teaching the same thing and ended up a little behind the rest of us. But at the beginning — wow.

I wanted to fight him in 1973 in Memphis, Tennessee. A guy named Bill Gardo was putting on Mr. Trias's tournament. I went down and fought in that tournament. Two days before the event started, I was down there and so was Joe. We were all hanging out around the gym and I called him and said, "Hey, would you show me some stuff?" At that time I had been working on refining a few really good techniques, and naturally when Joe and I were working out I didn't use those. So I was just setting him up and setting him up, letting him get the best of every exchange. I thought I was being really clever and said to myself, "When I get him in this tournament I'm really gonna have the advantage."

So the tournament started and I won the lightweight division, Joe Lewis won the heavyweight division, and Bill Wallace was National Champion coming in. We each had to fight Bill Wallace if we wanted the National Championship title. If we both lost, we would end up fighting each other. The winner of the consolation match would join on a European tour.

Joe got out there first to fight Bill, but Bill beat him. I got out there and Bill beat me, too. So I figured that Joe and I would fight next as the tournament dictated. They called my name and I reported to the ring, but Joe was nowhere to be found. I looked at the center judge and said, "Hang on a minute." I ran down to the dressing rooms and there was Joe getting undressed. I said, "Hey Joe, we're supposed to fight! Come on let's go!"

He said in reply, "Look, I came to win this tournament. I've been to Europe twice and I don't want to go again. I'm going home." So he left. On the plus side, I got to go to Europe for 30 days. I wanted that match so bad, but it wasn't meant to be. Shortly after that, Joe dabbled in full-contact as well as movies and seminars, so the opportunity never arose again.

Q: As you continued your own journey through tournament competition, you eventually established the Professional Karate Commission (P.K.C.). What was that, and when did you decide to create this governing body?

The P.K.C. started in 1986. Full-contact karate was becoming big and getting television attention. The Professional Karate Association (P.K.A.), which was a major body at the time, couldn't sanction its own fights. P.K.A. was at odds with the World Karate Association (W.K.A.), so P.K.A. needed a sanctioning body.

I had been working hard for years to conduct my karate affairs in a forthright fashion, so my reputation was steady both as a businessman and competitor. I was in touch with the P.K.A. due to the "Battle of Atlanta" event, and eventually they became interested in having me take a bigger role in helping kickstart the full contact side of things. So they helped fund the start of the P.K.C., which became my sanctioning organization.

Q: In the development and growth of the P.K.C., what are you particularly proud of in terms of its accomplishments? And is there anything you would change in hindsight?

I don't believe I would change much. I tried my best to get really good people to help me make the thing work. I didn't intend to be a big organization, so I wasn't unhappy about growth at any point. I will say that it seems to me that in some ways karate is a dying art, and I wish there was more I could have done for that . . . but there isn't.

Eventually, as time went on, I realized that I wasn't quite fitting in anymore, and that's when I started stepping away from the organizational aspects. "Change, migrate, or perish," is what I say. It was time for me to step back and unload what I had before I changed too much.

Q: You mention you didn't feel like you were fitting in anymore. What do you mean exactly?

Martial arts organizations are big business nowadays. Unfortunately, you see a lot of people in charge who are not capable of being the psychologists, ministers, caregivers, and role models they advertise themselves to be. These groups are being run by amateur people and are, at best, babysitting clubs and, at worst, a danger to students. I didn't run my schools like that, and I don't like seeing it happen.

A big problem in today's martial arts culture is young people being put in the care of individuals who claim credentials but are not ready for the responsibility. Worse yet, in the dojo these teachers behave as kings and eventually start to believe themselves kings. One thing I've noticed is that a lot of new instructors will study only for a short time with their teacher, maybe until green belt, then leave. Afterward, a student of theirs studies until green belt and they leave. Eventually you have clubs opened by people so far removed from knowing what they are doing there is no lineage or quality to speak of. Then they are left to make up things or mix and match techniques from half a dozen arts they know very little about.

Q: In your mind, how can karate correct its course and once again become valuable to young adults and individuals in need of a life-improving pursuit?

I believe there will always be a few good karate clubs out there, but the larger landscape of karate cannot correct its course. The way of money and business has too far influenced how karate is both seen and practiced. People getting into it now won't realize how far it's gone, and won't even realize it needs correcting.

Q: For those individuals who are trying to make karate a lifelong pursuit, could you give some thoughts on how you've made your training work for you in a healthy manner as you've gotten older?

Well, I had good teachers who helped me understand how I should train. I also listened to some good medical advice, which helped prevent me from making some "young and dumb" decisions. I avoided a lot of the stuff like banging my fists against walls and kicking my shins against pipes.

In the '60s and early '70s, there was a lot of legitimately insane activity going on. Looking back I realize people mainly teach how they were taught, and that's how a lot of bad habits and bad mindsets got perpetuated in today's karate.

I had one eye-opening experience in particular. I remember there was a long time before I let women and children into my club. Once I did, though, I remember taking a 12-year-old boy to a tournament. He got beat pretty bad. While he was lying on the floor, hurt, I went over and started screaming at him to get up. I was kicking him to get up. In my mind I heard the military discipline my instructors used on me. Suddenly I realized I was behaving insanely. I realized that different students needed different treatment, and I needed to adjust the way I conducted myself.

Sometimes it's important to step back and look at yourself. If you can assess yourself honestly you might say, "I don't like that person." It happened to me, and it was an important step. The funny thing is, when I was "that person" I got a lot of respect (or what you might call some sort of fear-based respect), and I walked around like a big shot. But I didn't like who I was.

Another example occurred in 1976. I was still heavy into that tough guy stuff, and I was bragging to another guy that I had only promoted 18 people to black belt since I had been in karate. I went on and on, explaining how I told students when they started that they wouldn't make it to black. He responded simply by saying, "Yea, and when you told them that . . . they believed you. Of the 18 black belts you promoted, how many thousands of students have you run off?" I really had to stop and think about that. He was absolutely right. Those people that I ran off, if they had been given proper guidance they might have been some of the best in the world.

So that's how I've developed mentally, but physically I've had to tone down my training as I've gotten older. Now that I am in my 70s, I train in shorter spurts, two to three times a week. I run through kata and I like to work my heavy bag. I won't go longer than 40-45 minutes.

Q: A lot of studies suggest that the key to health and happiness in older age is a sense of purpose. Do you feel that karate provides you with this sense of purpose? Something to wake up for and pursue?

My wife, my three daughters, and karate — that is what gets me up in the morning. My wife is brilliant and helps me out in so many ways. But really the only thing I've had in my life since I was a young boy is karate.

Lee Gray

A Texas native and Marine Corps veteran, Lee Gray Sensei represents one of the earliest Westerners to have extensive contact with Goju Ryu in Okinawa. Stunned by the tropical climate and beauty of the island, Gray Sensei found himself welcomed by a kind and generous people even though he spoke no Japanese or Uchinaguchi (the native language of the Okinawans).

Gray Sensei's original interest was in Judo, which he had heard about during his youth in Texas. While pursuing Judo in Okinawa, he eventually stumbled across the native art of karate and was intrigued by it. He discovered the Toguchi Shoreikan Dojo in Koza City, where he began his lasting study under Shinjo Masanobu Sensei.

In addition to his military service and study in Okinawa, Gray Sensei became one of the leading traditionalists in Texas, bringing back authenticity and skill that made him a desired commodity at tournaments and seminars.

50

---

[50] Image courtesy of Brian Berka, owner of Torii Weapons.

Q: Gray Sensei, could you provide a little background on when you were born and what kind of neighborhood you grew up in?

I was born in Amarillo, Texas in May, 1941. My father was in the grain industry for many years. We didn't live on a farm but I was very farm and ranch oriented. I grew up understanding the problems of farmers and ranchers. I went all the way through high school in Amarillo, looked into going to college, but decided that I wanted to join the Marine Corps.

Q: Was there any pressure for you to join the farming community considering you were so closely connected to it?

Not really. I was very fortunate that my parents wanted me to do what I felt was best. They gave me freedom to explore and determine my own future. At that age I didn't know for sure what I wanted to do, so I decided that I could benefit from the structure and direction of the Marine Corps. Not to mention I would have an opportunity to see some of the world.

Q: In your youth did you hear anything about the martial arts in the United States and were there any demonstrations near Amarillo?

Not so much, but wrestling back in those days was very popular. It was a little different compared to the big spectacle of modern professional wrestling. We had a local group of wrestlers in our town that always drew a crowd. Amongst them was a Japanese gentleman who called himself "Mr. Tojo" and claimed to be a Judo expert. Occasionally they would have "jacket matches" where one of the other wrestlers would challenge Mr. Tojo and they would don Judo gi tops. They would tug around in Judo fashion for a while, but eventually Mr. Tojo usually won.

Going to these wrestling events with my grandfather introduced me to the idea of martial arts and I eventually learned about Judo's origins in Japan . . . but that was about the extent of my early martial arts exposure.

Q: Were you athletic as a kid or was most of your time dedicated to work and school?

I played basketball, football, and ran track through my school programs. Football is very big in Texas, especially at the high school level. I was aware of athletics, fitness, and keeping in shape.

Q: After high school when did you decide to join the Marine Corps?

I joined in 1960 and actually left Amarillo during a snowstorm, headed off to boot camp in San Diego.

Q: Could you describe your early experiences in the military? Was it a culture shock to you?

I would definitely say it was a culture shock for me (and for most people that join the Marine Corps). It was not what I had expected right off the bat; however, I did anticipate it was going to be tough. My dad broke his back when he was young so he wasn't able to join the military, so I didn't have a lot of access to preparation through my family except via an uncle. The only advice I got was pretty simple, "Do what they tell you to do."

Once you are in the service for a while you stop being scared to death of your drill instructors and so forth and you realize it's a job that you have to get done. You do what you're told and you learn how to do your job well and everything gets along ok. Once I fell into that mode, things were fine.

Q: Why did you choose the Marine Corps over other military branches?

The Marine Corps had the reputation of being the toughest and the hardest, which appealed to me as a young man. The thing that I liked about the Marine Corps was that they had a policy of not leaving soldiers behind in battle. If you were wounded, shot, or dead . . . they would go back for you. I thought, "One way or another I'll wind up back home with the Marine Corps."

Q: Did you get deployed directly from San Diego to Okinawa or were there some assignments in between?

I finished my recruit training and then went into a rifle company at Camp Pendleton. I stayed there for about a month before getting orders to go to Okinawa.

Q: Were you aware of karate before shipping off to Okinawa?

No, I had not heard of karate at all. To me, the martial arts just meant Judo and I only had a vague awareness of other things out there. I knew there were Samurai with swords and things like that, but as far as categorizing arts I was definitely not aware.

Q: What were your expectations when you got deployed to Okinawa, especially in regards to world conflicts of the time?

The Cold War was in full swing, so that was always on our minds. Vietnam was not on the radar yet and I didn't really know much about it. Going to Okinawa, I had known that the island was a battlefield in World War II and that it was a very intense struggle there. It was one of the last strongholds the U.S. needed to invade. We had learned about such things in our Marine Corps history program. They showed us pictures and lectured about the different islands and so on. I heard rumors from other Marines regarding what it was like to be stationed there - some spoke highly of it, others did not.

On my way over I didn't know what to expect. I was not shipped with a large deployment, and in fact went on individual orders. The usual mode of getting to Okinawa was by ship, but instead I flew in a little twin engine plane. I was the lowest rank individual on the plane, sitting with Colonels and Majors and individuals of that stature. We went from the U.S., to Hawaii, to Guam, and to Wake Island as refueling stops. I enjoyed being able to see all those places along the way.

We would have a few hours of layover and they would give us some leeway to go out and look around. On Wake Island you could stand on one end and see the other. By the time I got to Okinawa I wasn't sure what to expect.

Q: What were your duties when you arrived on Okinawa and where were you stationed?

I went to Camp Butler which was also known as the Tengan Camp. It was stationed right outside of Tengan Village. It was a small base that was service oriented. We had the mechanics, public works, builders, and so forth that did work for the other bases. It was a small base around with around 150 people.

Q: What were your earliest impressions of Okinawa and its people?

Okinawa was a beautiful island. I'm originally from the Texas panhandle, where the wind blows freely across the plains and the air is dry throughout the prairie. On Okinawa I was surrounded by the ocean in areas that were densely populated (from my perspective). I found myself particularly drawn to the ocean, and have been ever since first spending time near it on Okinawa. The water was very clear and blue, as you might imagine when picturing a tropical paradise. Of course, I knew right away that I wasn't there for vacation.

There was a language barrier with the Okinawan people, but enough of them spoke a small amount of English that I could get my point across and so could they. I found them very receptive and friendly. I didn't find many Okinawans that disliked Americans. Generally, they treated Americans on a case-by-case basis according to how they were acting. If an American was being a jerk they treated him as such, if the person was nice then everyone got along. I tried to be nice as much as I could.

I realized early on that their customs and courtesies were a little different from ours. I didn't try to make fun of those differences; I wanted to understand them and accept them in order to get along. When you first got to the island in those days the military bases would give you a big orientation. You couldn't get off the base for a couple of weeks until you finished this orientation. They told you about some of the customs, and differences, and so forth. Generally, they cautioned you about the bad things.

Around any military installation there will always be some trace of a bad element, including people looking to take advantage of you. Of course, at that point all of Okinawa was one interconnected military installation. As such, during the orientation they put some fear in you to watch out for traps and problems. The scare tactic worked on me for a while, as I would venture out during the day but be back on base by night.

The nearby Okinawan towns contained a lot of things to appeal to the G.I.'s. There were a lot of bars, nightlife, and things that go along with that. I tried to avoid those scenes and stayed pretty much to myself.

Q: After you settled into your military life on the island how did you first go about discovering karate?

My introduction to karate happened in a roundabout way. I actually started studying Judo when I first got on base. I knew about Judo from my youth so it was the first thing that captured my attention. Tamaki Sensei, a Judo instructor on the island, had a club on my base. I started there. I felt fortunate because I got to spend a lot more personal training time with Tamaki Sensei than most. He had been a professional Sumo wrestler in Japan . . . one of the few Okinawans who accomplished that.

Tamaki Sensei was pretty advanced in age at that point but still very mobile and technically sound. I can remember trying to throw him at times and I might as well have been trying to throw a house. It just did not work.

Q: A lot of Sumo players you see are heavy and large. Did Tamaki Sensei fit that description?

He was quite tall, especially for an Okinawan. If he wasn't 6' he was very close. He wasn't huge in weight and girth but was still strong. He had very large hands as well.

Q: Did Tamaki Sensei talk about where he got his training?

I know he had spent time in Japan training directly with Kano Jigoro Sensei in Judo. He also had the opportunity to learn Aikido from Ueshiba Morihei Sensei. According to other Okinawans I had spoken to, he was the most senior Judoka and Aikidoka on the island at that time. The impression that I got was that Tamaki Sensei's goal was to spread Judo and Aikido across Okinawa as best he could.

Q: Was there a language barrier during your lessons, especially during the classes when it was just you and Tamaki Sensei?

There was a barrier, although we could communicate via small bits of broken English. Most of the communication was done through technique though. If he wanted to emphasis something he had a way of getting his point across so that I felt what he meant.

Q: What was the content of the Judo class like?

It was very technique based. I would come in and he would show me some warm-up exercises. Generally if he showed me a warm-up he would expect me to do those on my own in future classes. Then I would start going through ukemi (rolls, falls, etc.) on my own. There were a few training devices we had on hand to help with technique. There was a big, heavy sandbag that was a little larger than a duffel bag. We had cut and attached inner tubes to it which you could hold on to while trying to sweep the bag. The bag probably weighed about 200lbs. In addition to sweeps you could work throws on the bag but it was really heavy so you had to mind technique.

After that Tamaki Sensei would come out onto the mat and have you try to throw him in one way or another. He would make corrections, fixing your posture and your approach. He was very adept at foot sweeping so he spent a lot of time moving and sweeping my feet. He would often sweep my feet out from under me but wouldn't let me fall, just jerking me back upright so that he could sweep me again. He encouraged me to try to replicate the technique, correcting me along the way.

Eventually he started introducing me to some other Judo programs around the island so that I could work out with and gain experience from other people. It was from these other schools that I learned about Tamaki Sensei's seniority and experience.

Q: How did that Judo training transition into karate training? Did Tamaki Sensei introduce you to a karate teacher?

No he did not. In fact, he discouraged me! I discovered karate through a woman who worked at my base named Ms. Nakamura. She spoke English very well and even lived in the United States for a time. She started a little cultural program on the base where on weekends she would take G.I.'s out into the local population, visiting restaurants, cultural locations, cultural events, and the like. She would explain things as we went.

At one of those events there was a karate demonstration. I was very impressed, although I don't recall who conducted the demo or what style it was. Ms. Nakamura said to me, "You train in Judo but this is karate."

Later I went to an Okinawan bullfight. During intermission between matches a gentleman named Taira Shinken conducted a bo demonstration with a 9' bo. I was stunned as this small gentleman came out, winging a nine foot stick around like it was a feather. When he swung it over his head I thought he had generated so much force it might just pull him off the ground like a helicopter. That really intrigued me and I asked Ms. Nakamura about it, to which she replied," Yes that is a very old Okinawan art." I asked how I could get involved in it and she said, "No, that is more cultural. I don't believe you can do that."

At that time I started looking around about getting involved in karate and asked Tamaki Sensei about it. He said, "No don't do. You concentrate on Judo." Nevertheless, I kept looking around. Shimabukuro Tatsuo Sensei of Isshin Ryu was teaching at Agena, so I went out to visit his dojo. He had a contract through Special Services. If you went to his class and had him sign a letter of attendance, Special Services would pay him for that lesson. As you might suspect, he was interested in getting as many Americans as he could. Money was very scarce on Okinawa in those days. They were still rebuilding after World War II, trying to get their economy up and running.

I went out and attending a couple of classes with his group, which consisted mostly of Americans. My concern was, if it was mostly Americans . . . would I be getting the real thing? A warranted concern or not, I wanted to find a place where the Okinawans trained. So I kept looking and visiting schools, finding similar situations to that of Shimabukuro Sensei.

By that time I had grown comfortable with the Okinawan people and didn't feel scared like I had when I first got on base and went through orientation. I realized the Okinawans weren't going to drag me down a back alley somewhere, and I could walk around and interact in relative safety. A friend of mine on base mentioned that he had passed a karate school and told me about its location . . . so I went in search of that.

When I found the dojo he had described I stood outside and watched the class going on inside. There were no Americans that I could see so I began to wonder if I could actually be accepted as a student. I then made it a habit to go to this dojo in the evenings in order to watch classes. After a week or two the Okinawans started to notice me standing just outside and watching. One of them came over and invited me to come in. I went in and sat down and watched.

The next day I went back and assumed it would be ok for me to go in, sit down, and watch again. Nobody seemed bothered by me or even paid any attention to me. Eventually one of the instructors came over and asked if I wanted to join in. I said yes, and that's how my training started there.

Q: Do you recall where that dojo was located? What was the dojo itself like?

The name of the school was Toguchi Shoreikan in Koza City. The dojo was a beat up old building with cracks in the walls and leaks in the ceiling. The floor was made out of wood. They put it together just for karate training, as opposed to being someone's house or anything like that. After class the doors were just left open. I never saw the dojo's doors closed except to keep rain out.

Sometimes when I arrived for training the place would be jam-packed full of students, other times there would only be four or five. Consistently though there was one individual who became what I consider my primary instructor, and that was Shinjo Masanobu Sensei. I studied with him at the Shoreikan Dojo for about a year until he decided to move and open his own school, calling it the Shobukan. At that time I moved with him.

Toguchi Seikichi Sensei was not at the Shoreikan dojo himself, so Shinjo Sensei was in charge. Toguchi Sensei had moved to Japan and I never had the chance to meet him in person.

Q: What was it about Shinjo Sensei that you really liked? What made you decide to follow him even as he created his own dojo?

He was very relaxed and open. He wasn't overly friendly, but he wasn't hostile either. When we were in the dojo he was all business, and didn't show any favoritism among students. He corrected us all the same way regardless of our race or background. I really appreciated that and never got the sensation that he was holding things back from me just because I was an American.

Shinjo Sensei's own performance and skill was incredible. He was a powerhouse with dynamic movements. When you saw him you knew that was something special going on. He had respect amongst many of the Okinawan karateka. My goal was to one day become like him.

Shinjo Masanobu Sensei during a student test in the 1960s.[51]

Q: What did Shinjo Sensei like to focus on in his teaching?

He was very strong on the fundamentals. Every class we practiced the basics. He would make sure that stances were correct, blocks were correct, body alignment was correct, etc.

---

[51] Image courtesy of Darrell Bailey.

When he got the sense that you were performing at a certain level he would push you to move to the next level.

While training technique, if we violated a basic principle he would stop and take us back to the fundamentals and explain why they had to be in place. He would then explain how that foundation allowed the technique to work and why it was needed in order to connect to other techniques. He would conduct this same attention to detail in his own training. As such, we could use him as a guide in how to hold oneself to strict standards and ensure improvement even in solitary training.

Q: Did Shinjo Sensei integrate sparring in his classes or was it mostly two person drills and kata?

There was a lot of two person drills and kata, but there was sparring as well. After class ended is when most of the sparring took place. It tended to be unsupervised, or if Shinjo Sensei hung around to watch he would make suggestions for us. I only sparred with Shinjo Sensei himself on a few occasions. Most of the sparring sessions with Kinjo Sensei came about when I couldn't get a particular technique to work, so he would show how it was supposed to be done.

Q: Did you use padded gear during your fights or was it all control based technique?

There was no padded equipment and only sometimes was there control.

Q: Did Vietnam take you away from training for a time?

Yes. My original time on Okinawa spanned from 1960 until the end of 1964. I started my karate training about six months after my arrival. I also continued my Judo training long enough to be granted a black belt from Tamaki Sensei.

In 1964 I was sent back to the United States in order to go through drill instructor school and become part of the hand-to-hand combat section. Later on, hand-to-hand would be combined with rifle skills and knife defense and was called close-quarters combat. Around 1968 I got orders to return to Okinawa and was dispatched to Vietnam shortly thereafter.

I did a one year tour in Vietnam before being sent back to the United States. Once in the U.S., I put in a request to be stationed again on Okinawa, which they allowed after about six months. I stayed for two years on Okinawa before I was sent into Vietnam for a second time. After my second tour I was once again sent back to the U.S., stationed at El Toro Airforce Base. After about 18 months I was once again allowed to return to Okinawa (around 1971).

Q: It sounds like you established something of a pattern, traveling between the U.S., Okinawa, and Vietnam. During those times, did you get into kobudo at all?

I got into kobudo more in the '70s than in the '60s. I had seen it and talked to Shinjo Sensei about it. Shinjo Sensei liked to use karate principles even with a weapon in hand. I didn't pursue kobudo actively until I returned to the island in the '70s.

Tonfa was one of the earliest weapons practiced by Lee Gray Sensei.

Shinjo Sensei's dojo had some weapons around like bo and tonfa. Occasionally some of the more senior students in the dojo would practice with the weapons, especially when there weren't many students in class. I would follow along with them as best I could, which provided me with an introduction to manipulations and a few kata with the weapons. Finally someone suggested that I travel down to Naha in order to meet Matayoshi Shinpo Sensei.

I visited Matayoshi Sensei and he was kind enough to accept me as a student. Even while training in kobudo, karate was always my true emphasis.

Q: Were there any other instructors on the island who made an impact on your training?

Interestingly, I ended up with something of a social friendship with Shimabukuro Tatsuo Sensei of Isshin Ryu. He remembered when I came and visited his school when I first got to Okinawa, and that led to conversations and friendly visits. He would often ask questions about Goju Ryu, how the style was organizing and progressing, etc. Shimabukuro Sensei told me that he had trained with Miyagi Chojun Sensei, although there is some debate about that. Nevertheless, he seemed knowledgeable about Goju Ryu.

One Saturday afternoon I went to visit Shimabukuro Sensei and when I arrived I noticed an older Okinawan gentleman sitting with him who looked vaguely familiar. I realized shortly after it was the man I had seen do a bo demonstration in the bull ring a few years ago - Taira Shinken. His dojo was south of Agena and he invited me to come visit. I went and met Akamine Eisuke Sensei while there. We talked about the differences between their concept of kobudo and what Matayoshi Sensei's concept was. I personally jumped back and forth between Matayoshi Sensei and Akamine Sensei, learning from both.

Q: Was there any issue about you visiting different instructors and training with them, or was the mindset of sharing fairly open?

I didn't encounter any problems in terms of visiting other instructors. Whenever I would tell Shinjo Sensei he would simply nod and tell me it was fine.

Q: Could you talk about some of the subtle differences in concept between Taira Sensei's methods and Matayoshi Sensei's methods?

One of the most noticeable differences was in the way they used the bo. Matayoshi Sensei noticed right away when habits from Taira Sensei began showing up in my technique.

Matayoshi Sensei knew that there was a conceptual difference between the two and asked me to pick one way or another to do my kobudo. I opted to stay with Matayoshi Sensei.

Matayoshi Sensei had a huge knowledge of technique and kata. I never saw someone do a kata that Matayoshi Sensei did not also know or at least was able to immediately trace the form's lineage.

Q: When did you end up settling back into the United States?

Around 1978 I was transferred back to Coronado Island in order to teach at the amphibious warfare school. That proved to be my last tour. I had made up my mind that I was going to get out of the Marine Corps, which I believe was the biggest mistake of my life.

Q: Oh, why such a big mistake?

I had passed my twenty year mark in the Marines, but I had some big ideas that I was going to retire, open a dojo, and make a bunch of money with a ton of students. I quickly learned about the difficulties involved in operating a dojo in America. I realized it was something of a contradiction hoping to run a school with the same intensity and focus that I had experienced on Okinawa while also expecting the business to be highly profitable.

Q: Could you talk more about those challenges in the early days?

When I first started teaching I did so in recreational centers, apartment complexes, and Y.M.C.A.'s. Eventually I found a more fixed location in Escondido, California. People would come in and I was very upfront with them, asking, "Do you want to train or do you not want to train?" They wanted to be sweet-talked like a customer but I wasn't going to do that.

Once I got a few people signed up I started teaching the same way I was taught on Okinawa. We would spend three hours going up and down the floor working on blocks, punches, kicks, etc. Lots of sweat and aching muscles. We did a lot of contact drills, including kote kitae, Sanchin, and conditioning exercises. The students kept dropping out and I couldn't figure out what was going on. It didn't make sense to me.

It took me a few years to realize that the people in the United States didn't really understand karate and were more interested in learning what they saw on television and in the movies. My Marine Corps Drill Instructor mentality was not suitable to get students in the door. I had virtually no kids in my classes . . . but then again parents weren't signing their children up for that sort of thing in those days.

Q: How did you eventually balance softening your teaching methods while not losing the quality of your content?

I found that it was effective to be a little kinder and gentler when students first came in, especially the younger students. Eventually though, the students that really wanted to learn would make themselves apparent. Those students you could effectively push and challenge without fear of them quitting. One of the keys was watching for students who were willing to push themselves to the next level. It was then I knew I could work more closely with them.

It took awhile to develop effective habits like that in the U.S. I remember one of the first sessions I taught on a military base back in the States had almost 200 military personnel show up to train. It was a two hour workout, and in the middle I stopped to give them a break. Only about 50 came back after the break. I wound up with about ten individuals who stuck with it after that initial class.

Q: Did you get involved with tournaments and demonstrations?

I liked doing tournaments and competing. Demonstrations never played an important part in my training or teaching. I find that they don't convert well into new students, especially if you aren't doing outrageous kicking and jumping and breaking.

In the early tournaments I competed with a lot of the guys who would go on to become big names, like Chuck Norris. I found I had to adapt my kumite in order to lessen the contact I generally made. I got disqualified frequently in the beginning. Sometimes I would just compete in kata knowing that I wouldn't be able to adapt to stringent sparring rules.

One of the best parts of tournaments was being able to meet a variety of people. I encourage my students now to compete for those same reasons, although I don't pressure anyone.

Q: Did you get to go back to Okinawa at any point in the 1980s?

Yes, I went back in 1986. The Okinawans celebrate the anniversaries of individual's deaths every so often. 1986 was set to be the last major celebration of Miyagi Chojun's passing so they had a "Miyagi Festival". Shinjo Sensei and Yagi Meitoku Sensei had formed the Okinawa Goju Kai and hosted the festival. I went over with a number of my students in order to partake in the festival, see the island, and train in the Hombu dojo.

It was during that trip that Shinjo Sensei told me, "I haven't been feeling good for a long time." It was shortly after that I learned he had been diagnosed with Leukemia. In 1993 he passed away. After his passing, I backed away from organizational efforts in the United States and even stopped training for a while.

Q: What are some of the most important ethics and principles you use to maintain good quality people in your school and organization?

Attitude is a big principle for me. Sometimes people ask me what I look for in a student and I tell them that attitude is first and foremost. I find that a lot of youngsters in the 12-16 age group have no understanding of loyalty and integrity and hard work. I try to instill those things into them. I always say, "Nobody is going to give you anything. Anything that you get out of life you are going to have to work for. If you don't work for it, you're not going to get it." I try to impart values that make them independent and self-reliant. I try to build their confidence through challenges and stay with them until they overcome their own perceived limitations.

I set goals for students at first, but eventually I expect them to start setting their own goals. I make them write down those goals and give them to me. I then check in from time to time, asking how they are progressing in achieving those goals. This isn't limited to just karate. I want them to use the principles of karate to improve their everyday life.

Q: Did you find your karate training helpful during your time as a correctional officer?

Yes, absolutely. I moved back to Amarillo, Texas to help my parents. My mother had been diagnosed with Alzheimer's Disease and my father needed assistance in her day-to-day care. I had to have a job, of course, to help support them and my own family. I didn't train much during that time as all of my energies and hours went to my job and family.

However, after my parents passed away, I decided it was right to get back into training and teaching.

I went to work for the Texas Department of Criminal Justice. When they found out about my military and martial arts background they had me instructing correctional officers and police officers. They had a horrible defensive tactics program and I helped them revise that into something that was practical and easy for the average individual to use and retain.

As a correctional officer I worked in the psychiatric ward where we housed aggressive, mentally-ill offenders. There were days when you would go in and it was one fight after another with those guys. You have to take them out of their cells to shower them, feed them, etc. When you have individuals who are combative in nature you find yourself in combative situations when you are required to interact with them.

I found a lot of the techniques I had trained were extremely effective, although they had to be toned down. Smashing heads and what-not was not an acceptable treatment of prisoners. You had to control them. I started learning and analyzing my karate and realizing the depth of control techniques that were available.

Q: Was there anyone in the United States that became a mentor or training partner to you?

A Chito Ryu stylist named Robert Hunt became a good friend and we have had many discussions regarding karate, bunkai, etc. However, I like to talk to anyone who trains about their karate, regardless of rank or style. I find that if you listen to others for long enough they will usually present an idea you may not have considered before. Often there is a little jewel that you can take away and use in your own training. If I disagree with what they are saying I may or may not voice it, but I always hear them out.

Q: Goju Ryu is well known for its powerful rooting, stancework, breathing, and technique. Have you had to ease your training at all as you have gotten older? Does Sanchin kata change as you get older?

Everything changes as you get older. You'll find that it's not the technique that changes, but the body that learns to adapt. I still do things the same way but they're different. In time the strength of the technique takes over for strength of the body.

Not too long ago I was performing Seisan kata in front of a group. Afterward one of the spectators came up and said, "Wow, you get a lot of power out of that kata!" I replied, "No, the kata is powerful."

Q: What kind of content do you like to focus on when you are teaching?

I stress fundamentals and kata. Other exercises like hojo undo (body development drills) and yakusoku kumite (pre-arranged sparring exchanges) are used to augment and emphasize fundamental aspects or pieces of kata. In addition to reinforcing kata, supplementary exercises also help with visualization. A hands-on experience through yakusoku drills gives students a physical sensation which they can attach to the kata instead of just going through the motions for aesthetic purposes.

Q: Is there anything else modern karateka can do to ensure they practice kata as it was originally intended?

You need to analyze what the purpose of kata is. It's not just a dance that will put trophies on your mantle. Kata is the heart of karate and without kata there is no real karate. You need to analyze every aspect of kata, thinking about each movement and asking, "Why is it there? Why is it done that way?" Be careful in kata not to change things simply because you don't like them or you think you have a better way. Find out why it was done a certain way and discover the real meaning of it, making sure to look at it in a realistic light.

It's easy to get caught up in elaborate explanations of kata. I had one individual explain a technique as a method for kicking someone off of a horse. Now, how many times in history have you ever heard of someone getting kicked off a horse? Was it really such an important concept that it would make its way into a kata? Once you eliminate the far-fetched or unlikely scenarios you can start looking into real explanations.

I liken kata to textbooks. When people started developing kata they either couldn't write or didn't want to write their concepts down. Instead, they preserved combinations of movements so they could be remembered and passed on. Starting in the late 1800s kata started losing its meaning as people wanted to keep the meaning secret from one another. As a result, it began getting passed on either incorrectly or incompletely. Luckily we have the ability to examine deeply what the kata could have been intended for, relying on our own research and the research of others to educate ourselves.

The only staunch requirement Shinjo Sensei ever put on me was, "Don't change the kata."

Q: What are some of the most important things for future generations to remember in terms of passing on Goju Ryu as Shinjo Sensei and Miyagi Sensei intended it?

I think karateka have to be honest with each other and honest with themselves. It's easy to kid yourself. They have to look at what they are doing and be certain to keep it real. Don't get carried away with the fantasy and hype of karate. Don't give up and say, "Old karate is dead. This is the new karate." Try to keep up the tradition of kata and keep it grounded in reality.

Chuck Merriman

Peter Urban and Chris DeBaise were two of the earliest Goju Ryu practitioners on the East Coast. Urban made a name for himself as a top tier fighter, learning directly from Yamaguchi Gogen as well as Masutatsu Oyama of Kyokushin fame and Richard Kim, the noted researcher and philosopher.[52] Urban established himself as a karate authority in the late 1950s and early 1960s, organizing some of the earliest competitions and events in the country.

Chuck Merriman was a direct student of both Urban and DeBaise, and was an accomplished Judo competitor. Throughout decades of training and competing, Merriman Sensei became renowned as a tournament champion, event coordinator, and national coach. He expanded his experience beyond Japanese Goju, later melding it with Okinawan influences. As a result, Merriman Sensei has become one of the most sought after resources for insights into Goju Ryu and modern competition.

Q: Merriman Sensei, was there anything in your youth that got you interested in the martial arts?

My interest started in 1960 when I was working at General Dynamics in Connecticut, building submarines. There was a guy there that was training in Judo. I had no concept of what Judo was, but it interested me because I was always more interested in one-on-one sports versus team sports. He invited me to watch a class and I thought it was great — something I could really put time and effort into.

Q: Did you try to join his Judo club right away?

---

[52] Noble, Graham. "An Interview With Goshi Yamaguchi." *Hawaii Karate Seinenkai,* 2009. Web. 12 Nov. 2014. <http://seinenkai.com/articles/noble/noble-gyamaguchi.html>.

Actually I watched for about a month, two to three classes a week. They eventually invited me to come on the floor and start training. Once I started, I just kept at it. There was a limited amount of people in the class because it was a small dojo, so they figured if a student couldn't put the time and effort in to watch, then they didn't deserve to train.

Classes were held in Norwich, Connecticut, and were conducted by a gentleman named Norbet Bellinger. Unfortunately, after about six months, Mr. Bellinger stopped showing up for classes, which kinda left us in a tough spot. I didn't want to stop my training, so I went to New York City in order to find a new dojo. Once I found a school, I explained to them that I wanted to train but couldn't afford the lessons while trying to support my family. They told me that I could sleep in the dojo, keep it clean, open and close it for classes, etc. in exchange for training. So that's what I did.

Q: You mentioned trying to support your family. Did your wife and child come with you to NYC, and how did you manage that travel?

To make ends meet, I sent my wife and child down to Pennsylvania to live with her mother. On the weekends, I would travel down to PA to visit them.

Q: Training must have been very important to you in order to make those kinds of life changes!

Oh yes. It's like when you find something that you didn't know you were looking for . . . when you find it you grab on to it and do your best not to lose it.

Q: Did you ever find out what happened to your first instructor, Mr. Bellinger?

No, none of us ever found out. It was unusual when it happened. There were no announcements or anything of that nature. We just showed up one day, he wasn't there, so we stood around looking at each other trying to figure out what to do. For a few weeks we tried to make do and work out on our own. Eventually one of our brown belts decided to contact the local Korean Judo College to ask for an instructor. They sent a gentleman named In Soo H'Wang. I got to train with him for awhile, but by that time I had already made arrangements in New York at my new school, so I continued my training in the city.

Q: Did you ever get to know In Soo H'wang in greater depth?

Yes, I did. A few years after I began my training in New York, I was able to move my family back up north into NY. On the weekends we would all go to Connecticut to visit my mother, and that's when I started my real training with In Soo H'Wang.

Q: Could you go into more detail regarding the New York dojo? Who were the instructors, what was training like, etc?

It was operated by a pair of brothers known as "the Judo twins", Bernie and Bob Lepkofker. The twins were identical . . . and I mean identical. I was in that dojo a good six months before I could figure out who was who. They were very big guys — 6'7" or 6'8", 260-265 lbs. I started my competition years in New York City with them at that time.

Merriman Sensei during his early days in New York.

I trained with them through the '60s and into the '70s. In 1970, I was able to move my family out of New York and into Connecticut, although I continued to live in New York. At that time I was working a lot of different jobs, including security detail for the United Nations. I was a commercial artist for Harper & Row Publishing Company and I was doing modeling at the same time. Just a lot of different things that kept me in the city. Whenever a job started impacting my training too much, I would move on to a different job.

Nakabayashi Sadaki was also teaching and training at the Judo twins' dojo a couple of times a week. He was a great guy, truly humble even though he was a three time All-Japan collegiate champion. He was very generous with his time and knowledge, and he became something of a father figure to most of us in the dojo.

Q: Was your New York training with the twins and Nakabayashi Sensei different than what you experienced in Connecticut with Bellinger and In Soo H'Wang?

It's important to understand that Judo is Judo. In karate you have many different styles, but Judo operates under set rules with specific techniques. That being said, Korean Judo was very strong and very physical. Originally, Judo was intended to be more of a finesse game, feeling out your opponent and sensing weaknesses. Korean Judo was more about attack. A foot sweep to them meant that if you didn't move your foot, they were going to break your ankle.

In Soo H'Wang's training ethic was really inspirational to me. He trained like a demon, and he pushed himself as hard as he pushed everyone else. He was a young guy just out of college and was very happy to be in the U.S.A. Taking over that dojo in Connecticut was a great chance for him to get started in the States.

Q: Having had exposure to both Korean and Japanese teachers, did you notice any difference in treatment between Asian students and Western students?

No — everybody got the same attention, criticisms, and time. In a broader, countrywide sense, racism was probably there, although I didn't see too much of it personally. There was (and still is) a little mental bias believing that if you are born Asian you have the martial arts in your blood . . . something non-Asians will never truly understand. It's not true, of course. In fact, the biggest sport in Japan is baseball. Sports and martial arts don't follow ethnic lines.

Q: Could you describe early Judo competitions in the '60s and '70s?

The competitions were a pretty good size in NYC. The city was something of a focal point, and people from other parts of the country would come to compete. The matches were strong at that time. It was rough. The techniques were less refined technically than what you might see in modern events.

Q: How did you fare in those matches early on? Were you successful right away, or did you experience some bumps and bruises along the way?

Oh there were always bumps and bruises. Judo is a rough sport, especially back then. Competition became even tougher because of what was at stake. Being in New York, we tended to get the best and most skilled competitors.

Q: While your Judo training was going on, you also began to explore karate in 1962. Could you discuss how this came about and who you studied with?

The opportunity really came about because I was living in the Judo twins' school. I was never much for going out and drinking and such, so I was often found in the dojo. I practiced Judo 6-8pm, and then a gentleman named Chris DeBaise taught karate from 8-10pm. At first I just hung around and watched the class. I was intrigued by how DeBaise Sensei was able to move, and the whole thing just caught my eye.

What impressed me the most about DeBaise Sensei was that he was stern and focused. He expected a lot from his students, but he gave a lot as well. He struck me as a good leader, someone you wanted to emulate. He was also kind and considerate. When I told him about my situation of living in the dojo, he was very understanding and took me into the class.

Q: Debaise Sensei was a Goju Ryu practitioner. As such, could you describe the day-to-day training and how he liked to operate class?

Thanks to all the Judo training, I was able to slip into karate more easily than might otherwise have been expected. DeBaise Sensei never concentrated on any one kind of drill, and there weren't any real competitions to organize around or prepare for. The first competition I remember hearing about for karate was in 1962 when Mas Oyama came to Madison Square Garden. Peter Urban Sensei, S. Henry Cho Sensei, and Oyama Sensei ran the event. I wasn't qualified to compete, but I was able to attend and watch.

Q: That 1962 gathering must have been impressive to see. Could you talk a little bit more about that?

It was a huge event, not strictly in terms of participation but more in a newsworthy way. Having Mas Oyama over from Japan was a huge story in itself. Peter Urban Sensei had trained with him over in Japan and had invited him to New York and proceeded to put on this showcase in Madison Square Garden. The event was smaller than you might think, especially by today's standards, consisting of about 200 people.

Q: At that time Mas Oyama was fairly famous for feats of strength (chopping off bull's horns and the like). Did his demo in New York involve anything like that?

No, nothing so extreme. I was very young in my karate training at the time of the demo, so I wasn't party to a lot of things outside the dojo and didn't get a chance to interact with

Oyama personally. I did get a chance to meet Urban Sensei, though, because DeBaise Sensei was good friends with him.

A few years after I started my karate training (around 1964-1965), DeBaise Sensei had some disagreements with the Judo twins and quit teaching. At that time, DeBaise Sensei took me to Peter Urban's dojo and wanted me to train there.

Q: Can you elaborate a little more on the transition to Urban Sensei's program?

When DeBaise Sensei told me he was shutting down his program, we went up to 17th Street in order to visit with Mr. Urban. Mr. DeBaise asked Urban Sensei to take me in, which Urban Sensei did as a favor to Mr. DeBaise. About a year or so later, DeBaise Sensei actually joined Urban Sensei's program himself. We all had the chance to train together, which was great.

During that time I continued to live with the Judo twins, up until about 1970.

Q: Peter Urban is one of the most well-known pioneers of American karate. What were his classes like, and what was he like as a person and teacher?

In regards to his classes, after establishing the 17th Street dojo Urban Sensei also developed his "Chinatown Dojo". The training there was very strict. We trained from 6pm-10pm every night, five nights a week. Saturday was an open dojo where anyone in the city could come and jump on the floor. We focused on kumite during those times.

When Sensei said to line up at 6pm, he didn't mean 6:01. If you weren't on the floor at 6pm you weren't getting on the floor, at least not without a problem. I tended to be there every night.

During the first hour of training we focused on warm-up exercises, stretching, and body conditioning. The second hour was basics. The third hour was kata. The fourth hour was kumite. At the time we were in the Goju Kai under Yamaguchi Gogen Sensei, and the main emphasis of the Goju Kai was sparring, so we put a lot of focus into that. It should also be noted that Urban Sensei did not integrate hojo undo tools (nigire game, chi ishi, etc).

Q: Did Urban Sensei ever tell stories about any of his instructors?

Yes, he used to talk about training with Yamaguchi Sensei. He would mention how much he revered him and what a great man he was. Later on he had problems with the Yamaguchi family, and that's when he severed his ties with the Goju Kai in Japan and started American Goju.

Yamaguchi Gogen (in black) during a visit with the Goju Kai in the United States. This image was taken in the late 1960s after Peter Urban's departure. Chuck Merriman is featured top left, Robert Taiani is third from left, and Chris DeBaise is fourth from left in the back row.[53]

I was actually in the room when he made the statement about making this change. The atmosphere of the dojo was very tense that evening. Urban Sensei was sitting in front of about five or six of us who were the highest ranking individuals in the dojo at that time (Nidans and Sandans, which were the highest he would promote to at that time). He got very emotional and reached under the table he was sitting at. He pulled out a meat cleaver

---

[53] Image courtesy of Joe Lopez.

and slammed it into the table and declared, "I sever my ties with Japan!" That kind of behavior was actually fairly typical for him. He was a very theatrical person. At the time Urban Sensei was a highly sought after referee, and he brought that drama with him to the ring as well. With Sensei everything was always a production.

Q: Did his personality lead to conflicts with other instructors and organizations?

Sure, eventually. In the beginning not so much — remember that there were only a few dojo in the area anyway. Criticisms came later after he left the Goju Kai and started his own American Goju. What he did was unheard of at the time, and the fact that he was an American and would break ties with Japan was horrendous to a lot of people.

I found that most of the people who criticized him were the ones who didn't train with him, which aggravated me. They would also pass along stories that they had heard from second-hand sources, gossiping and spreading rumors. I didn't appreciate that behavior.

Q: You mentioned the focus on kumite in the Goju Kai, and indeed two of the most prominent fighters of the early karate era were Don Nagle (Isshin Ryu) and Peter Urban (Goju Ryu). Were their reputations warranted?

Quite warranted, although those two gentlemen had totally different styles. Urban Sensei was a bull, stocky and really developed. He was fantastically strong, and Goju is a very rooted and fundamental style. Nagle Sensei was tall and lanky so he had more distance and speed concepts during fighting. Urban Sensei had the desire to grab you and punch you until someone said, "Stop." Nagle Sensei was more mobile and integrated a number of kicks. They were both great fighters in their own right.

In 1966, I had the privilege of attending an exhibition match between the two men. It wasn't a win-or-lose situation; they were just trying to demonstrate some of the differences in their methods. They complimented each other very well, and it was a tremendous story at the time. The fact that these two people of such renown would get up and do something like that was very notable.

Q: In regards to tournaments, is it true that Urban Sensei was an important piece in the development of modern tournaments and how refereeing works?

That is definitely true. He was the ideal that many people tried to follow in refereeing and judging. He had both precision and dramatics in the way he ran competitions. He was considered the premiere official at the time. Of course it's important to note that we are talking about a different era in tournaments. It wasn't as sophisticated back then as it is now. Having seen the growth of tournaments personally on an international level, I can say that what they did then and what we do now is quite different.

Q: Did Urban Sensei do a lot of traveling and teaching internationally?

No, that only came much later on. He didn't get out of New York much unless he was going to New Jersey.

Q: When did you make the leap to opening your own dojo, and what was that experience like?

I opened my first dojo in 1970 in Connecticut. I still had a few friends in the state whom I visited on the weekends to play Judo. A few of those guys wanted to start studying karate. They asked, "If we drum up some student interest, would you be willing to come and teach?" I said yes, so they got people together and built a really nice dojo with beautiful hardwood floors. Almost 50-60 people signed up early on. I started going twice a week to teach.

Q: Did you have to get specific permission from Peter Urban Sensei to teach?

It didn't really work like that at the time. You always try to pay courtesy, of course, but actually I was already co-teaching in a NYC dojo on 38th Street and 6th Avenue. We were called the Midtown Dojo under Urban Sensei, and there was another dojo in Harlem called Uptown Dojo. I just made sure my teaching was ok from a courtesy standpoint; there was no formal protocol.

I also started getting involved more heavily in judging and refereeing, which seemed natural given Urban Sensei's influence on me. Eventually I connected with the Amateur Athletic Union, a large non-profit body that oversaw the growth and development of amateur sports in the United States and the interaction of those sports abroad. I got invited to the first A.A.U. Nationals in the 1970s. By that time karate competition had begun to flourish, and my involvement snowballed. The organization started spreading nationally and, eventually, internationally.

Chuck Merriman with Bill Wallace and Ron Van Clief during their competition years.[54]

Q: When did your interest in Goju Ryu expand to its birthplace (Okinawa)?

Ever since I began karate, I was always very curious about origins. I had done a lot of research, studying, going to seminars, etc. I found out that Okinawa was the birthplace of karate, not Japan, and that Yamaguchi Sensei did not start Goju himself. I discovered that

---

[54] Image courtesy of Glenn Perry.

Goju Ryu was started by Miyagi Chojun and carried on by a man named Miyazato Eiichi. At that time I began planning my journey to Okinawa, hoping that one day I could learn from the source and start transitioning into Okinawan Goju.

Over the years I trained with different folks and slowly integrated Okinawan concepts and adjustments into my own methods. I had known Higaonna Morio for a number of years and always tried to train with him and talk to him whenever I could. I finally asked him one year at the Ozawa Cup if I could become his student, and he said yes.

At the time, I was under the impression that he was connected to the Jundokan which was where Miyazato Sensei was. I figured Higaonna Sensei would prove to be a direct pipeline to Miyazato Sensei and would maybe even allow me to train at the Jundokan itself. I trained for about a year with Higaonna Sensei, but then decided to leave for personal reasons.

Soon after, I had gotten an invitation to a seminar in Canada featuring Yasuda Tetsunosuke, a senior student of Miyazato Sensei. This occurred around 1994. We got along great, and he invited me to train in Okinawa. This was a great honor for me, and I jumped at the chance.

I made arrangements and spent three or four weeks on Okinawa, training two or three times a day. It was really a wish come true for me after all those years. It was surreal when I got a chance to be on the floor training with Miyazato Sensei, the successor of the style. I got into the dojo as much as I possibly could. Although it was evident that I was there for training and not anything else, I still had a chance to socialize. The social aspect is important in the Jundokan and on Okinawa, so we would all go out and have dinner after training.

Q: What were some of the changes you had to make in order to transition from Japanese Goju methods to Okinawan Goju?

Well, I don't like to use the term "changes." Change is scary for a lot of people, including my students. I used the word "adjustments" instead because it wasn't a matter of hard right and wrong, just different.

The emphasis in Okinawan Goju is kata and self-defense. The emphasis in Japanese Goju has always been kumite (sparring and sport fighting). That was an adjustment in that I needed to shift my focus from freestyle fighting to a deeper understanding of the techniques and kata and how it relates to self-defense.

I also had to adjust to the method of teaching. I was used to formal class situations where everyone did the same thing at the same time, but in the Jundokan everyone trained one-on-one. By that I mean you were expected to work on what you needed while the instructors and seniors would go around and adjust you individually. I got used to the Jundokan way really quickly because I am a one-on-one kind of person. The attitude of training with the Okinawans was different. I noticed a lot of Chinese habits and influence rather than Japanese. Even the habits of one-on-one and deep research reflected more of the Chinese way of doing things. In the Goju Kai, tournament and competition was heavily focused on, partly because Yamaguchi Gogen Sensei was an important part of developing the tournament scene in Japan. That all made sense historically.

I was fortunate in that Miyazato Sensei only had to make adjustments with my kata . . . nothing too reconstructive. I had already started studying the Okinawan methods years before I got to Okinawa, so I was on the path already. Creating that relationship with Miyazato Sensei was a milestone for me, and I was happy to keep it alive even beyond my initial visit.

Q: What were your impressions of Miyazato Sensei when you were with him in terms of personality and teaching methods?

Kata was extremely important to Miyazato Sensei, as was the refinement of technique. He was a very kind man as well as generous. On first impression, he gave off a sensation of being gruff. He spoke in a commanding voice and seemed quite stern. The purpose, of course, was that he was trying to determine your intentions. He wanted to know why you were there. Some people came to take a picture and say they trained in Okinawa, others were there to study, and others yet were willing to do whatever it took to get better. Miyazato Sensei would feel out which kind of student you were and teach you accordingly.

Once Sensei realized I intended to use as much of my time as possible for training, he opened up and helped me quite a bit. He told me I could take pictures or video as needed and would provide answers to questions whenever I asked. One time he said to me, "There are no secrets to karate." Then he pointed at me and said, "You're the secret, it's in there. Now you just have to figure out how to bring it out." Of course he wasn't referring just to me, but to every karate student.

Q: Koshin Iha Sensei inherited Miyazato Sensei's Goju Ryu upon his passing. Did you meet Koshin Sensei around that same time?

Yes, I had the opportunity to train with him around the same time. Iha Sensei was actually a contemporary of Miyazato Sensei. When Miyagi Chojun passed away, no one did anything organizationally for about a year. Waiting a year is an Okinawan custom in order to pay respect. After that year, Miyazato Sensei opened up the Jundokan. All the seniors and equipment went over to the Jundokan as well. Iha Sensei became his cohort in teaching at that time, running classes about three days a week. I got to train with him quite a bit.

There was a significant size difference between Iha Sensei and Miyazato Sensei. Iha Sensei was quite small while Miyazato had more of a bull-like physique. Miyazato was a Judo champion in addition to karateka and clearly had the build for it. Iha Sensei was different, and it showed in his

Merriman Sensei with Miyazato Eiichi (center) and Iha Koshin (left), two of the most senior Goju Ryu instructors on Okinawa.

tendencies. His specialty in terms of kata was Suparinpei and Tensho. I spent quite a bit of time on those two forms with him. Miyazato Sensei focused heavily on Sanchin kata. He said it was the basis for everything else that we did, which is interesting because Sanchin is a very strong breathing and muscle development form. Tensho is just the opposite, with circular and soft movements.

Q: While improving your Goju and expanding your exposure to different teachers, you maintained a presence on the tournament scene. What kept you interested and involved with competitions?

I've always been a strong believer that proper training in karate can be put to a lot of different uses; competition is one of them. I never stressed competition or trained my students specifically with those objectives . . . we just trained. We then took it out into the circuit in order to see how we were progressing. The concepts we used (timing, distance, targeting, body shifting, etc) in an unknown circumstance was valuable. You never knew where exactly you would be or who you would be facing, so you learned to adapt.

One thing that I've always been proud of is that I know when to move on and grow in my personal development. I was a competitor for a long time in kumite because that is mostly what early tournaments consisted of. Then kata began to grow as part of tournaments, and, coincidentally, I was getting older and was healing slower after kumite bouts. I realized it was smart for me to get more involved in kata. As I progressed I eventually realized that younger and faster guys were coming up behind me even in kata, so I moved on to refereeing, judging, teaching seminars, and things like that. Because of this ability to let go and move on, I'm still here!

Q: When did you get into coaching on a national level?

I personally started as head coach for the A.A.U. karate team in 1978 and stepped down in 1982. I coached the first U.S.A. team to win gold, which occurred in Spain. We also went to Tokyo and won gold. In 1980, I took the team to France and we fought twice in Bordeaux and Paris and won three out of the four matches. We had some great teams. Later on, in 1995, karate was selected to be in the Pan Am Games which took place a year before the Olympics. I was named coach for that, and we were able to win seven medals. I was fortunate to be a part of those milestones.

Q: What motivated you to take on large national-level challenges and continue to push the boundaries of what American karate was capable of?

Well, karate training is all about challenges, and I felt these were worthwhile challenges to take on. Trying to develop ideas for training and putting together teams was interesting. I knew I was getting a lot of different people from a lot of different areas and only for a short period of time. I certainly wasn't going to be their full-time karate teacher. Of course, they already had a pretty high level of skill; otherwise, they wouldn't have gotten to the national level. I knew in just a few weeks I wasn't going to be able to help them punch any harder or kick more accurately. However, elements like timing and targeting were certainly things that I could help with. I developed drills and methods that we worked on as a team.

Q: In regards to your own personal training, have you continued Sanchin training as you've gotten older? Are there any changes you've made to the performance of the kata in order to keep it safe?

Actually, you don't change Sanchin; your body changes it. You keep doing the same principles, and the body adapts to it. At this point, I'm so used to the inhalation and exhalation that it simply behaves as it will.

Q: What are some of the most important aspects of Goju technique, in your opinion?

Okinawan Goju Ryu is all about personal research. Miyagi Sensei taught kata to each student according to their particular body structure. He didn't teach all the kata to every student except Miyazato Sensei, who served as his assistant in teaching at the police academy (so he had to know all the forms). Miyagi Sensei figured that if you had three or so kata that fit your body, you didn't particularly need more.

I don't think people pay enough attention to the fact that karate training is based on physical principle — it's that simple. Physical principles are undeniable. When I do a move from one stance to another, I'm transferring weight from one stance to another. If my upper body is attached to my hips, common sense tells me that my hips should move first. If I move my hips, the upper body will naturally come with. How do I move my hips? Through my legs. Seemingly obvious principles power everything we do in karate, and we try to optimize them.

Early in the U.S.A. we were all engulfed in a sense of mystery when it came to the martial arts (and to some extent this still goes on today). We all heard stories about "The Far East" and the great feats of strength that went on there. Of course, those stories tended to be exaggerated. Sure, we can condition the body, but the body is the body and it follows natural laws. If someone weighs 350 lbs and hits you, you are going to get hurt. I know this from working directly with members of the National Football League. You could also look at Anton Geesink who was the first non-Japanese man to win the World Championships in Judo. He had a lot of technique but was also a huge guy. The idea that technique completely eliminates size and power is over-exaggerated. The truth is effectiveness comes from a combination of all of those things.

Keeping fundamental physical principles in mind is a very effective way to self-correct. If you have a problem with balance or power . . . just look in the mirror and figure out why. Watch the pieces of how you move and decide if it is in proper natural order. The Okinawans were pragmatic and used these same methods.

I think a lot of us from the early days of American karate went through stages. We had to figure out a lot of things the hard way. Heck, I thought that Yamaguchi Sensei was Goju's founder at one point. The key is to always be a student, and to be a student means to study. I research and get as many viewpoints as I can while distilling things down to commonalities. This has always informed the way I practice and the way I teach.

Q: In terms of teaching, do you tend to operate in an Okinawan way or do you mix in some of your earlier, more formal Japanese experiences? Also, do you individualize kata to each student or do you utilize a standardized curriculum?

I teach all kata sequences the way we do it in the Jundokan, but I stylize it to the needs and abilities of the student. Over a period of time, each person's body starts doing what is comfortable and adapts to certain kata more easily than others. In essence, kata tend to pick people versus people picking kata. You aren't going to do something that goes against your body tendencies and is uncomfortable. During some kata, you may think to yourself, "Yea I know it, but I'd rather not do it again." Then other kata you think, "Ohh yea, now *that* feels good." If you listen to your body, it can teach you a lot!

Q: How would you like to see Goju Ryu and competition in America continue to grow?

Competition has come a long way since I competed and coached. Sometimes people ask me if I ever get the itch to coach again, but I really don't. I would have to go back to "school" and learn the game all over again. The rules are different, the techniques score differently, etc. The rules constantly change and evolve. I try to keep up as best I can, but there's no purpose for me to stay up-to-the-minute. Competition will always be around as there will always be people with personalities to suit it. This is fine as long as competitors understand that tournaments are for a short period. Put that period to good use, but if you want longevity it can't be your main focus.

Goju itself has morphed into a lot of clones and offshoots in recent years. My way of thinking is that if I could get back as close to the original as possible (which was my effort with Miyazato Sensei), it would be a worthwhile effort. Don't get me wrong, this isn't to suggest things don't change. I often tell my students that when Miyagi Chojun died, the original Goju died with him. After that, it's everybody's ideas and interpretations.

Here's a good example — years ago, two of my students went over to the Jundokan and trained with Miyazato Sensei. After training, Miyazato Sensei gave a lecture. These two people sat side-by-side and told me two *different* versions of what was said in that lecture. I don't mean that to be good or bad; it simply points out the reality of interpretation. Words and context will lead you to a different conclusion than anyone else sitting in the room. If you multiply that over individuals and generations . . . things have a way of getting off-track. This is just people being people.

Sometimes I see people adding kata or changing kata. If you change a kata, to me it's like changing the alphabet. Urban Sensei talked about this, and I still use a lot of what he taught me. He said, "Karate is like the alphabet. Why is William Shakespeare William Shakespeare and I'm not? We use the same 26 letters."

All the great works in the English language are composed of those 26 letters. It was the skill of creating prose, satire, poetry, drama, sarcasm, irony, and on and on. It is different expressions that make those works significant. If you simply started adding letters or

taking them away, the whole thing would devolve into chaos.

If I have 12 kata, why would I need more if I can understand how to use the many infinite combinations of movements within those 12 kata? I would only need something else if I can't decipher the original content myself. A lot of that is happening these days.

Q: How does this relate to your pursuit of understanding kata through bunkai?

Every time I do a seminar, I ask, "Does anyone know what 'bunkai' means?" Immediately a number of hands go up, and the answer is "application". The word "bunkai" actually means "to analyze." First, a kata must be analyzed, and then you take that analysis and put it into practical use. Bunkai changes constantly depending on partners, timing, speed, knowledge base, and more. You have to make those adjustments while you are working with a partner and analyzing the kata. Add to that the fact that you change over the years (your body, your knowledge, your ability to analyze). Bunkai is never one thing; It is in a constant state of change just as you are.

Kihon bunkai is essentially the same as kihon karate. We're all in the same style, we all do basics the same way, and we all analyze the kata the same way initially, to give us a foundation. Oyo Bunkai allows us to take those "alphabet letters" and rearrange them in a way that makes sense in the context we are given. The details of Oyo have to change given the variables of the situation and opponent. Keeping that in mind, bunkai becomes a constant re-evaluation of scenario and opponents.

In our version of Goju, we also have something called Renzoku Bunkai which is essentially our version of kumite. It's a continuous application of kata from start to finish.

Kata and bunkai have a tendency to grow over a lifetime. Kata mean something different to me now than they did 10, 20 years ago. That growth of meaning is one of the true purposes of training.

Consider this — I used to train a handful of broadway dancers back in New York City. How long do you think it took them to learn kata? Not only were they physically gifted but retaining patterns is what they did for a living. They could learn a kata in an hour and do the movements very well. They could essentially learn all twelve of our kata in a day. They were learning a pattern, but it wasn't the true intent of kata as we know it. A pattern must eventually become kata; it doesn't start there.

Q: For someone just starting out in karate, what are some of the best pieces of advice you could provide to help them make it a lifelong endeavor and grow with it in a healthy way?

Healthy, to me, is balance. Miyazato Sensei taught balance; Miyagi Sensei taught balance. Life is all about balance, the good with the bad. The up times and the down times. We say in our dojo kun, "Train according to your physical abilities.". If you're injured, you don't train so that you are going to injure yourself more. You take care of that injury. You take care of family and work and these other important things so that you can maintain a balance in your life. Karate training is a part of that.

Merriman Sensei with Miyazato Eiichi Sensei on Okinawa.

Continuity and patience are the true keys to me. Continuity means that if I train twice a week, an hour each time, it's better than if I train five days in a row, six hours a day, and then don't train again for a month. With steady training on a regular basis, the mind will retain more and the body will react better. In our Western culture, we tend to lack patience. It's just not as focused on, especially as gratification comes quicker and quicker. One thing about Japanese culture is that they are taught from a young age to value patience and respect. This helps them during their martial arts pursuits. This cultural reality actually adds value and importance to the martial arts training we do in the West as it gives us an avenue to express these ideals.

I often tell people, "Be as hard as the world makes you be, but be as soft as the world lets you be." Through karate, you can choose soft and not be resigned to it. I also impart the idea that karate isn't what I do, it's what I am. I hope others find their way to that feeling as well.

Kimo Wall

As a marine stationed on Okinawa before and after the Vietnam conflict, Wall Sensei had the opportunity to learn Goju Ryu directly from Higa Seiko Sensei. He also became a student of Matayoshi Shinpo and a friend of Odo Seikichi, two of the great kobudo luminaries in Okinawan history.

Wall Sensei was one of the early influencers of western karate as he brought back Goju Ryu, Kingai Ryu, and even Thai massage. Wall Sensei eventually became one of the most traveled instructors in the world, sharing his art throughout the Americas and beyond.

Q: Wall Sensei, what was your earliest exposure to the martial arts?

My training began in Kamuela, (Waimea), Hawaii, in 1949, when I was six years old. This was before Hawaii was even a state, believe it or not!

As a kid, I had a breathing problem. My one playmate's mother was the wife of a karate instructor in our community, and she thought that she could help me with some breathing exercises that would make my lungs and heart stronger. I will never forget it. It was a simple warm up and stretching exercise, and after a few days we started something like Sanchin with lots of deep breathing and slow punching, but no turns. Just walking forward and backwards, doing the same thing — concentrating on posture, relaxing, and listening to my heart and lungs. Before long, I could hear my heartbeat and the air going deeper into my lungs. I did this for several weeks. It didn't take much time to get my breathing and heart in good shape.

The formal karate teachers in my village were Walter and Sam Higa (Higa is a common name in Okinawa), father and son. The father, Sam, had learned karate in Okinawa sometime before WWII. He had studied with Master Miyagi Chojun and Higa Seiko in the early days of Goju Ryu's development. I know he studied under Master Higa Seiko because he sometimes received letters from him and sent a letter of introduction with me when I went to Okinawa in the Marine Corps. Sam Higa Sensei immigrated to Hawaii with his wife, Haruko, and son, who was born in Okinawa. I believe they arrived in Hawaii around 1939. In 1949, Sam Sensei was about 60 years old and Walter was about 35. Walter learned from his father and Master Higa Seiko, from an early age. Sam Sensei taught kata — Gekisai Ichi and Ni, Sanchin, Tencho, Saifa, Seiunchin, Shisochin, Seisan, Naihanchin, (Naihanchin was a part of Master Miyagi's training in the early years), and Kururunfa. There were more kata in Master Miyagi's system, but, I think that was all Sam Sensei learned before he emigrated to Hawaii. I only studied up through Shisochin. Sam Sensei passed away in 1968, and Walter passed away in 1988.

Q: What led you to join the Marines in 1961, and were you stationed on Okinawa right away?

I joined the Marine Corps in 1961 after working in Vidalia, Georgia, for a few months while visiting my mom's relatives. I went to Boot Camp at Parris Island, South Carolina; attended Infantry Training at Camp Lejeune, North Carolina; Weapons Training at

U.S.M.C. Schools, Quantico, Virginia; and other schools during my first year. After that, I was sent to Okinawa.

Q: How did you first meet Higa Seiko Sensei on Okinawa? What made you decide that this was the individual you wanted to continue your karate training with?

I met the Higa family at their dojo in Yogi Machi, Naha, Okinawa. I came with a letter of introduction from my teacher in Hawaii. I was well received. The Higa dojo, Sho Do Kan, was a typical dojo of the times. It was old and in a residential area. Master Higa lived with his son and daughter-in-law, their two sons and, soon, a little girl. They had a nice home just in back of the dojo. I always considered it my home dojo, but I also studied at Sho Rei Kan, in Koza City. I'll explain that more a little later.

Kimo Wall with Higa Seikichi, son of Higa Seiko, 1986.

At the same time, I met Matayoshi Shinpo Sensei, who lived in an extra room in the dojo with his wife and daughter, and, soon, his son. He had recently returned from Kawasaki, Japan, where he had lived since WWII. Matayoshi Sensei lived in the Higa dojo until about 1972 and was a renowned kobudo practitioner on the island.

Q: What was day-to-day training like with Higa Sensei?

I think the training was like most Goju Ryu dojo(s), or other styles. From 7-9pm each night, we trained. Strong warm ups, a lot of hojo undo with many implements, basics, lots of kata and "imi-wa niwaka touben" (bunkai). For several years, there was training after the 7-9pm class at the honbu dojo, sometimes until midnight. Most senior students came to this session, where Higa Sensei and Takamine Sensei taught. After training, we had tea and cake or sushi and always went to the local public bath, Sinto, for 15 cents. In those days most homes in Okinawa didn't have baths. In the Marine Corps, while stationed in

Okinawa, I had mostly night duties, so I spent most of my days at the dojo. In that way, I received a lot of private lessons from the great masters.

At the dojo, I met many lifelong friends from Okinawa, such as Master Takamine, Gibo, Kanai, Kyuna, Ushiro, Yamagawa, Yamashiro, Gakiya, Tamano, Shinoda, and especially Odo Seikichi who was a great teacher of Okinawa Kenpo. He came to our dojo to study kobudo, Sanchin, and Tensho with Matayoshi Sensei. My peers in the dojo helped to inspire me to be as good as I could be. I spent many special, private hours in the dojo doing extra training.

Q: Could you share an interesting story about Higa Sensei that people might not know?

Once, Higa Sensei was visiting Masanobu Shinjo Sensei in Koza, Okinawa. He [Higa Sensei] was on the street when a young boy asked him to watch his shoeshine things for a moment. Koza is just outside of Kadena Air Base, which means there were plenty of G.I.'s (American soldiers) about. One G.I. was a little drunk and stopped to ask Higa Sensei to shine his shoes. Sensei did not speak much English at all. The G.I. got a little heated, "Papa-San, shine my shoes!" Master stepped back and said, "Waiting." Maybe the G.I. thought Sensei was " waiting" for some action. He rushed Higa Sensei but ended up on the ground. Angrily, the G.I. started to swear at Sensei. Sensei said, "WAIT!" He picked up the shoeshine box and punched it so hard that it went flying across the street even though Sensei hardly moved his body. The G.I. was so surprised, he looked where the box had gone, looked at Sensei, and apologized.

Q: You mentioned the term "imi-wa niwaka touben," essentially meaning "bunkai". Could you break down what that phrase literally means, and if it is different than the typical western idea of bunkai?

Good question. "Bunkai" means "to analyze," which means that a punch or kick that is thrown at you is blocked. In most bunkai that you see, everything is blocked, until the end of the kata, and someone wins. In a real situation, you must end the altercation as soon as possible. You would never have the chance, or opportunity, to do a whole string of movements. The term "imi-wa niwaka touben" was explained to me with those words, and in several other ways. There are meanings in the Okinawan languages that can't be explained in simple terms. Consider this — after a block or a movement from a sudden confrontation, what will you do? By training your kata properly for many years, you will respond with the right answer.

You can break any Okinawan kata down and find the meaning behind, "What would you do after the block, or movement, that you do?" The answer is, "Punch, kick, throw, KILL, as quick as possible."

Q: Toguchi Seikichi was another prominent Goju Ryu karateka on Okinawa at the time and was very close, personally, to Higa Sensei. Did you get to know Toguchi Sensei at all?

Toguchi Sensei lived in Tokyo while I was in the Marines but came to Okinawa once in a while. I met him in Okinawa around 1969 and then in New York City in 1972. He and Matayoshi Sensei came for a demonstration for Sho Rei Kan. Then, at the end of 1972, he came to my wedding in Okinawa.

Master Higa Seiko was always there in the dojo until he passed away in 1966. His son, Seikichi, lived at the dojo, so I was with him everyday. When Higa Sensei passed away, Seikichi was not the senior dojo member; Takamine Sensei was. In 1989, there was a celebration turning the dojo over to Seikichi Sensei. Many Sho Do Kan senior members were there, including Toguchi Sensei. I also attended the event with some of my students from the University of Massachusetts.

I learned that Toguchi Sensei had been a student of Master Higa Seiko for 30 years. In the 1950s Toguchi Sensei was working on his ideas at Higa Sensei's Sho Do Kan dojo, but, according to tradition, he [Toguchi Sensei] opened his own dojo to exercise his own way of teaching. Of course, he was a master in his own right with many followers, so this was seen as acceptable. He was even helped by Master Higa in setting up his dojo in Koza.

Q: How did you formally become a student of Matayoshi Shinpo Sensei?

I met Matayoshi Sensei on the first day that I went to Sho Do Kan. He was in the dojo with Odo Seikichi Sensei of Okinawa Kenpo. I introduced myself, and Matayoshi Sensei said that Higa Sensei was with Takamine Sensei in Naha and would be back soon. He [Matayoshi Sensei] invited me to wait, so I spent time getting to know both him and Odo Sensei.

I thought I knew what I was in for when I walked into the dojo, but . . . wow, it was quite a surprise when they started performing kata. Odo Sensei seemed like a very relaxed fellow, sitting and drinking tea, maybe around 5' tall. He stood up to do a kata called Chinto, moving slowly and easily at first. He faced the kami dana and bowed, then turned to the dojo. His eyes and his manner seemed to change almost instantly. He began his form and was fast and smooth and jumped extremely high. I had never seen much about other styles before arriving on Okinawa, and Odo Sensei really made an impression on me. His movement was like lightning and his kiai was so strong. When he finished, I'll never forget, he just melted back down to the floor like nothing had happened. Matayoshi Sensei did Kakuho kata next and was amazing as well. I was just a kid (19 years old) in the Marines, and here I was watching two of the best martial artists in the world.

Matayoshi Sensei was quite a unique master. He was very sharp and disciplined, but he had a most pleasant and comical personality. When I was in the Marine Corps, my duties usually required me to be on post at night, so I spent my days with him. Matayoshi Sensei taught me all the kobudo that I know, except Chizi-kun-bo and two training Bo katas that I developed. Plus, he shared his Kingai Ryu katas that he learned from Gokenki, a White Crane specialist who lived in Okinawa.

I spent many wonderful years with the Matayoshi family. For 10 years the family lived at Higa Sensei's dojo in Yogi Machi. Then Matayoshi bought land on Sobe Hill in Naha and built his beautiful dojo and home. When he moved, it was only a few miles from Yogi Machi, I went to both dojo(s) to continue my training in kobudo. Like in the Marine Corps, most work I got in Okinawa was night work. When I became a civilian, Sensei helped me get jobs when I was on the island, like teaching English, unloading ships, working at Naha's city market, etc.

After I had moved back to the United States, Matayoshi Sensei came and visited several times. Sensei and I took a round trip tour all across America in my Plymouth Voyager van, and even flew down to Puerto Rico together. In 1992, Sensei and I were invited to participate at the Butokukai in Kyoto, Japan, with demos from all of Japan's top martial artists.

Q: What was the Butokukai demonstration like in 1992?

The Butokukai event in Kyoto, Japan, happens once a year. The top martial arts masters of Japan and their students get a chance to demonstrate in the Great Hall of the Butokukai. That year I was given the honor of demonstrating with Matayoshi Sensei. He did White Crane katas from Gokenki and I did Pichurin and Kama.

Kimo Wall with Matayoshi Shinpo at the Butokukai demonstration in Kyoto, Japan.

At that same event, Master Wally Jay from Hawaii did his Small Circle Jjitsu and Patrick McCarthy Sensei did Tonfa and Sai. I think we were the only foreigners there. It was a great honor for me. I will never forget how amazing Matayoshi Sensei's Kingai Ryu kata was and how much he was respected by the whole group of demonstrators and the government officials.

Q: Where did Matayoshi Sensei collect his extensive kobudo and White Crane repertoire?

Matayoshi Sensei's extensive repertoire of Okinawan Martial Arts was taught to him by his father, Shinko. He learned Shorin Ryu Karate from his father. The Kingai Ryu was taught to him by Gokenki, the Chinese immigrant from Fuchou, Fukien, China. He learned Goju Ryu from Master Higa Seiko and Grandmaster Miyagi Chojun.

Q: Matayoshi Kingai Ryu has very well-preserved elements of White Crane. Was Matayoshi Shinko (father to Shinpo) the senior student of Gokenki? Also, did the Matayoshi White Crane System involve kyusho vital point striking as well as seizing and gripping techniques?

Yes, Matayoshi Kingai Ryu is a very powerful and complete system. Gokenki taught several people his system, especially, Matayoshi Shinko. I know Shinko Sensei was a top student of Gokenki, and Gokenki was often a guest at the Matayoshi home. Eventually, Gokenki stayed in Okinawa, married, and had a family. He has many family members there today.

The vital point striking, kyusho, was taught only after you reached a high level of proficiency. Not many people reached that point. But, it is very similar to what we are taught in Goju Ryu. Like Goju Ryu, it came from Fuchou and some things are the same.

Q: You mention that Odo Seikichi Sensei was at the Sho Do Kan with Matayoshi Sensei on your first day there, and you got to know Odo Sensei more over time. Did you train directly with Odo Sensei at any point, and if so what was that training like?

Right after my first meeting with Matayoshi and Odo Sensei (described earlier), I became a member of the dojo. Odo Sensei came once in a while to train the Sanchin and Tencho katas with the karate class. This was after 9 PM, when older men trained with Higa Sensei. On the weekends, Odo Sensei came to train kobudo with Matayoshi Sensei and that is when we became friends. His [Odo Sensei's] dojo was on the way to my Marine base, so I gave him a ride home many times.

Wall Sensei at the Matayoshi Dojo in Naha, 1972.

I was a beginner in kobudo at that time, and Master Odo was a very high level student. He had even trained before the war with Matayoshi Sensei's father, Shinko. I trained, usually in the daytime, with Matayoshi Sensei, but on the weekends Odo Sensei came and he and I both studied together. His kata was higher than mine as he was a very advanced student. Often, he would get information from Matayoshi Sensei and train by himself. I always had the chance to watch Odo Sensei's training. I was amazed at his skill and power. He could make the Bo quiver with power at the end of each technique. After a few years, I was studying the Kama and he was studying it with me. He knew another Kama kata but this one was a new for him, so we shared the time together. I could always remember, he was what I would aspire to be like.

Odo Sensei was a very confident martial artist. He had trained with Master Nakamura, who was a very respected leader in Okinawa Kenpo. Until Odo Sensei passed away, every time I went to Okinawa, Mr. Nakasone from the Shureido Company would call Odo Sensei and he would come to Naha to meet me. Sometimes we went to Nakasone's home or to a local soki soba restaurant.

Mr. Nakasone is another wonderful person who became very close to me, so I will tell a quick story. Mr. Nakasone trained in karate, and at that time he had a sports store (this was around 1967). His store sold general sports equipment, baseball stuff, mostly, but he had someone who could make gis. So I had one made through him. I suggested that he should concentrate on martial arts equipment instead of spreading his attention around other sports. There was a growing amount of karate students, mostly G.I.'s who needed better-fitting equipment. Eventually he saw the trend and decided to give up on other sports gear. A friend of mine, Toshio Tamano Sensei, made the first Shureido emblem, and I made the first ad — in English — for his store. If you have been to Naha, Okinawa, you must have gone to Shureido. You will see what a great businessman he is.

Q: As a Westerner, did you ever feel like you were being kept in an "outer circle," different from how the Okinawans trained amongst themselves? How long did it take for the Okinawans to trust you given the wartime history between America and Japan, culminating in the Battle of Okinawa?

I don't think I was ever kept in an outer circle from anyone in the dojo. The only thing that separated us was the language, but I had many friends who helped me. I learned to take notes in the Marines, so I took many notes and had a friend that could explain Okinawan words to me. Some martial concepts are complicated, even for Okinawans to understand, like the meaning of "what comes after bunkai." It is very deep, and you must love what you are doing and persist in doing it for a long time.

I found that the Okinawans would grant me trust readily. Understand, the Japanese caused a lot more damage than the Americans. They caused the Okinawans to commit suicide (the term "suicide cliff" is well known in Okinawa). My wife's father was shot by the Japanese army for stealing food from a garbage can to feed his family.

In our modern times, the relationship between America and Okinawa is a bit more tense due to the cultural involvement of communism as well as rape cases by a few wayward American G.I.'s; however, I think most Okinawans are very welcoming to Americans and have really benefited from the U.S. forces paid to be there. You talk to any American who has spent many years on Okinawa, and they can tell you the same. I love Okinawa, the people, and its culture.

Q: After your time on Okinawa was up, what were the early days like starting a program in the U.S.A.? Did people understand what you were trying to teach?

In the States, at first, I only taught in the Marine Corps. I began teaching in Puerto Rico in 1965 while stationed at the Marine Barracks in San Juan. A lot of Marines and sailors trained, but I had a few civilians in the dojo and some are still training today. When I got out of the Marine Corps in 1970, I returned to the University of Puerto Rico to teach again.

In 1965, I think true karate was very much unknown in Puerto Rico, but from my dojo we developed a large group of very strong and talented followers.

Q: After years of study and teaching, you ultimately named your branch of karate Kodokan Goju Ryu. What was your primary objective in establishing Kodokan?

It was to help promote Okinawan Goju Ryu Karate and Kobudo outside of Okinawa. Kodokan means "home of the ancient ways".

Q: What have been the biggest challenges in growing the Kodokan while maintaining a level of quality and integrity in your art?

Time was / is the biggest challenge. I lived in Okinawa for a long time thanks to my military career. It is more difficult now for students to find the time and finances to stay for as long as I did. After becoming an instructor myself, I traveled a lot and didn't spend enough time with most students to take them to higher levels. Despite my shortcomings, I am very proud of those who have been able to continue training the Kodokan way. I see them as much as I can in Puerto Rico, Guatemala, California, Massachusetts, Tennessee, New Mexico, Arizona, and the list goes on.

Q: What inspired you to investigate Thai style massage and physical therapy?

In the Sho Do Kan dojo, there was a teacher who taught acupuncture and herbology on Saturdays. I took advantage of this, and studied until he passed away. Many teachers in the old days practiced some type of healing. It was the dojo's responsibility to help anyone who might get injured in training; that inspired me to study more about ways to heal people in my dojo. I studied Thai massage in Chiang Mai, Thailand, and received a teaching diploma from The Traditional Medicine Hospital and The International Thai Massage Center. It is used in Thailand by Mauy Thai fighters at all boxing camps for healing and therapy. I worked at the Traditional Hospital and International Thai Massage Center in Chiang Mai, and that experience has proven an effective means of healing and conditioning.

Q: How has your training changed as you have gotten older? Are there any forms or training methods which you prefer or avoid? Is there anything you did as a youth which you would warn others against?

I am almost 70, so I don't put as much time and focus on rigorous training. Kata and meaning are important. My advice is to just grow old gracefully. Don't smoke, don't drink, have faith, and believe in God.

Train hard and train often. Always practice kata, making sure not to neglect Sanchin and Tensho. Replace fear and doubt with knowledge and understanding. Open your mind and be joyful in training. Really LOVE what you are doing.

All our kata(s) were developed by Grandmaster Miyagi Chojun. Unfortunately, WWII virtually destroyed Okinawa and set it back several years. Miyagi Sensei passed away before he finished his development of Goju Ryu. Now, we who love Goju Ryu must find our way through the kata. I don't think there are any "superior kata" because they all have their importance and meaning. Grandmaster Miyagi said, "The secrets of Goju Ryu are in the kata." So, we must always study kata . . . even the simple kata Gekisai Sho has a whole system within itself.

Chapter 6 –
Chito Ryu

Although karate originated in Okinawa, a number of skilled practitioners helped it spread to Japan in the early 20th century. While Funakoshi Gichin reigns as the most famous of these early traveling pioneers, Chitose Tsuyoshi was counted amongst the most skilled and important men to carry karate to mainland Japan.

Chitose Sensei was born in 1898 in the Kumochi area of Naha, Okinawa.[55] He began his karate studies at seven years old under Aragaki Seisho. As he grew and developed, Chitose Sensei was exposed to training under a number of other prominent karate experts, including Itosu Anko, Kyan Chotoku, Higashionna Kanryo, and more.

Upon moving to Japan in 1922, Chitose Sensei became a student at the Tokyo University Medical Center, graduating in 1924. While establishing his medical practice, Chitose Sensei would often visit with Funakoshi Gichin, Ohtsuka Hironori, and other individuals pivotal to the development of karate in Japan. He would also occasionally return to Okinawa to visit family and maintain contact with his own teachers.[56]

At the onset of World War II, Chitose Sensei served in the Army Medical Corps, bringing his years of medical experience to bear. It was only until a year after the end of the war, in

---

[55] "The United States Chito-ryu Karate Federation." United States Chito-ryu Karate Federation, 2003. Web. 10 Nov. 2014. <http://www.chito-ryu.com/index2.html>.

[56] Colling, Michael. "Chitose Tsuyoshi: A Bridge Through Time." *Dragon Times,* 2002. Web. 10 Nov. 2014. <http://www.dragon-tsunami.org/Dtimes/Pages/article33.htm>.

1946, that Chitose Sensei had an opportunity to fully re-establish a dojo and formalize his style, Chito Ryu, named after the ancient Chinese methods upon which it was based.[57]

William Dometrich

William Dometrich Sensei (1935-2012) was one of the most instrumental individuals in the global propagation of Chito Ryu. He studied under Tsuyoshi Chitose (1898-1984) and is best known for starting the United States Chito Ryu Karatedo Federation.

In June of 1950, the Korean War broke out and a remarkably young William Dometrich tried to participate. Thwarted by his youth, he was forced to wait a year until he could join the 187th Airborne Regimental Combat Team stationed in Korea.

Two years later, at the end of the war, Dometrich's unit was restationed to Beppu City on the Southern Island of Kyushu, Japan. It was there, at 18 years old, that Dometrich Sensei would begin his training with Ichiro Shirahama and ultimately Tsuyoshi Chitose, and would be the very first Westerner to do so.

Q: Dometrich Sensei, when asking Chitose Sensei if you could train under him, were you afraid of rejection or an angry response?

It never entered my mind. I was a young man and never gave it a thought. I just wanted to study karate. I was stationed in Beppu and first encountered the art via Shirahama Ichiro. I realized shortly after that the style didn't come directly from him, but from Chitose Sensei,

---

[57] Buret, Andre G. "History of Chito Ryu Katas." *Calgary Chito Ryu Karate Club*, 2009. Web. 11 Nov. 2014. <http://www.calgarychitoryu.com/history.html>.

who had a dojo in Kumamoto.

I had to wait for military leave and then go down to visit Chitose Sensei's school. It took a few visits before they let me train.

A young William Dometrich wearing the patch of his instructor, Tsuyoshi Chitose.[58]

Q: What was the training like once you were accepted as a student?

---

[58] Pictures courtesy of William Dometrich prior to his passing or Barbara Dometrich.

It was quite rigorous. I wasn't sure at first if they wanted me there due to how hard they pushed me; however, in hindsight, I believe everyone trained hard and I just wasn't quite ready for it at first.

Q: During your sankyu test, you had Chitose Sensei watching as well as Funakoshi Gichin Sensei. Did this make you nervous?

Who knew? I had no idea who anyone was except the small group I trained with. I just knew that Dr. Chitose was the man for Chito Ryu.

Q: It's often claimed that Chitose Sensei spent seven years learning one kata in his youth. Do you know if this story is true, and do you believe others should try to study in the same way?

William Dometrich with his instructor, Tsuyoshi Chitose.

The kata that Dr. Chitose practiced for seven years, I was told, was Seisan. I asked Chitose Sensei on several occasions what his first kata was, and he told me Seisan. There are those who disagree with this — they believe his first kata was Sanchin. Sanchin really sounds more like it to me . . . but on at least two different occasions Chitose Sensei told me Seisan, and he should know. He was an exceptional martial artist. I suspect sticking with one kata for seven years was a combination of ability, desire, training, and who knows what else. Others should study in the way best for them.

Q: What was it about Chitose Sensei's karate that made him so powerful and yet so graceful?

Chitose Sensei could generate a great amount of power for his size. He had total body control and had developed vibration ability (not to be confused with hip snap). It seemed he could move his internal organs to increase his power while his outside body moved hardly at all. He moved like a ballerina when he walked. People just never seemed to bump into him when he was on the street.

Q: Could you talk more about the vibration and hip movement utilized in Chito Ryu?

In Chito Ryu, we teach students to increase their power through the rotation of the hips, thrusting of the hips, snapping of the hips, lifting of the hips, and dropping of the hips. This we can teach. The vibration, I believe, must be learned by the students through individual practice.

Q: What are the origins of the Chito Ryu patch?

The patch we use currently was the design used for the All Japan Karatedo Federation. I had heard that Dr. Chitose was instrumental in its design with the assistance of Tsuruoka Masami. When the Federation failed or closed up, Dr. Chitose took the patch and changed the center kanji from renmei-federation to Chito-Kai. In 1993, I changed the "All Japan" to read "All United States" and added the color blue to the patch making it red, white, and blue.

Q: In 1955, you returned to the United States and attempted to open your own karate program at Fairmont State College, Fairmont, West Virginia. This program was short lived, and you weren't able to establish a more stable program until 1961 when you connected with Harvey Eubanks in Cincinatti, adding your program to the Vine Street Dojo. What did you learn from these early struggles to start a program?

When I started teaching karate, I found out how little I actually knew. I was, to put it mildly, dumber than a brick. I did not have a good understanding of karate and was not a good teacher.

Q: Could you discuss the different training mindsets you encountered in Japan and when you first got back to America?

When I first returned to America very few people knew anything about karate, especially in West Virginia where I grew up.

Q: After establishing yourself in the U.S., you turned your attentions to competition and organizing events. During your first large tournament, there was a black belt champion who was technically sound, but behaved disgracefully. What made him disgraceful?

The contestant had a bad attitude. He thought he was a superhero (he read too many comic books), and I told him off.

Q: You trained with a lot of very impressive martial artists all over the country in the 1960s. Was there a sense of community amongst Western martial artists, and do you find more stylistic barriers these days as opposed to mutual learning?

I found more barriers in the old days. There was bad blood between a few various karate styles and groups. Today is much better as a whole.

Dometrich Sensei (seated front and center) at an early tournament in Covington, Kentucky, circa 1967.

Q: Could you discuss the atmosphere at some of the early tournaments in the West? There seemed to have been a lot of injuries.

A few of the early tournaments ended up in blood baths. Injuries were caused because of the following:

- Poor tournament rules — they tend to be better established now.
- Poor referees and officials — today they are very good in most instances.
- Lack of technique — a great many of the early karate students were bar fighters and the tournaments suited them.

Q: In 1968, you agreed to host a black belt instructor from Japan named Kazunori Kawakita for a year. When Kazunori Sensei instructed at your school the attendance dropped to almost nothing, mostly due to the extreme intensity of his classes and his tendency to injure students. Do you regret hosting him because of that?

Kazunori Sensei (Kita-San) was a great individual, an outstanding karate man, and is still a very good friend today. He was not a student of Dr. Chitose directly, but studied with Yamamoto Mamoru (who was a student of Chitose Sensei). Kita-San was a rough guy, but that was the way they trained at Yamamoto's dojo in Japan.

While in America, Kita-San had a few run-ins at tournaments, fighting with full contact as he had done when in challenge matches in Japan. As a result, he was often disqualified. I can say for certain that he improved the kumite (fighting) abilities of those students who did manage to stick around.

Q: During one of your visits to Japan, Chitose Sensei wished to have your name legally changed to Chitose Tsuyoshi. Can you elaborate on the significance of that gesture?

After studying for many years with Chitose Sensei, I met his oldest son. He was my age and lived in Okinawa. His last name was Chinan. I was a police officer and he was a police officer. He was paralyzed from the neck down after being struck by a drunken taxi driver in 1961. Enough said.

Q: Why is the practice of Seisan Kata so important in Chito Ryu?

All kata have some good and bad in them. I feel that the movements in Seisan make it the best all-around kata.

Q: You endured extremely harsh martial arts training and tough treatment in the military, and yet you thrived in that environment. Is that level of severity necessary for success in the martial arts? Was there anything that you believe was too harsh in your training that you wouldn't recommend for future generations?

In the early years, we (Japanese and Americans) did some stupid things. Today's training is much better in terms of understanding the body and how it works. We have better instructors, better sports medicine, better clinics, better tournaments etc. No matter what, though, the desire to train and endure has to be there.

Q: You had some amazing experiences in Japan when meeting Chitose Sensei and throughout your martial arts career. For individuals who cannot afford to make the trip overseas, what can be done to properly follow the martial way? Is there something special / irreplaceable to be gained by going to Japan / Okinawa?

For those who do not have the opportunity to travel to Japan, there are some very qualified instructors here in the U.S. Do the research required to find one because there are also some instructors who claim to be something they are not. When you find an instructor, just be loyal to him / her and have a beginner's mind.

Chapter 7 –
Isshin Ryu

Isshin Ryu is one of the most prolific styles of karate in the United States. Creator of the style, Shimabuku Tatsuo Sensei[59], was a skilled karateka and innovator with a personal background in Goju Ryu, Shorin Ryu, Motobu Ryu (Motobu Choki's brand of karate), and more. He synthesized his experience and created Isshin Ryu, the "one heart way."[60]

How Isshin Ryu became so popular in America was a matter of coincidence, good timing, and business savvy by Shimabuku Sensei. As American bases became more established on Okinawa, they began to interact more closely with the Okinawan populace. Military leaders quickly realized that karate could be used to enhance the skills and fitness of their soldiers, and set about hiring reputable instructors from nearby towns. Shimabuku Sensei quickly became one of the most active instructors. As a result, some of the earliest military members to study karate in Okinawa and bring it back to the United States were Isshin Ryu students.

Don Nagle became one of the most prominent karate men in America, demonstrating extreme speed and skill in fighting and kata. However, Harold Long, Steve Armstrong, and Harold Mitchum were considered fellow pioneers. The first generation was not limited to these influential men, as Shimabuku Sensei continued to teach soldiers actively. While not a prolific traveler himself, Shimabuku Sensei saw fit to send Okinawan instructors to the

[59] Tatsuo Sensei's last name was originally Shimabuku. Later the honorific "ro" was added, making it Shimabukuro. Both versions are considered acceptable and are used at the interview guests' discretion.
[60] Advincula, Arcenio J. "Isshin-ryu Karate-Do History." *University of Mississippi,* 15 Jan. 2008. Web. 13 Nov. 2014. <http://www.olemiss.edu/orgs/karate/2008%20commerative.htm>.

United States to help spread his teachings, including his son-in-law, Uezu Angi, and his eldest son, Shimabuku Kichiro.[61]

Marilyn Fierro

A few decades ago, women were actively taught not to resist a violent male attacker in the hopes that he might have mercy. Marilyn Fierro, and other pioneering women, realized that this helpless mindset, dependent on the whims of external forces, was no way to live. That is why they pushed through barrier after barrier to become the first wave of female martial artists in the West.

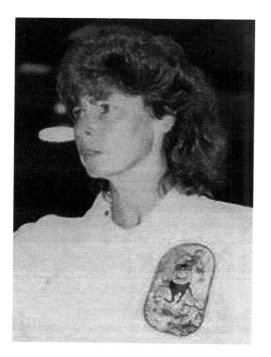

As we know, karate was primarily brought back to the United States through servicemen. These tough, able, and intrepid individuals grew up inside of a strict, male-dominated hierarchy. There was no perceived room for women and children in the deadly activities that made up their livelihood. These soldiers continued their male-centric mindset while developing their early martial arts programs. It was a challenge, in more ways than one, for Marilyn to walk into one of these tough schools in New York City in the hopes of taking lessons. Yet she did just that, and persisted in her training until she became one of the seniormost Isshin Ryu practitioners anywhere in the world, counting Nick Adler and Uezu Angi amongst her most significant influences.

Q: Fierro Sensei, could you give us some basics of when and where you were born? What kind of neighborhood did you grow up in?

[61] Long, Harold and Tim McGhee. *Isshin Ryu Karate: The Ultimate Fighting Art.* Mascot, TN: Isshin Ryu Productions, Inc., 1997. 25. Print.

I was born in 1942, and grew up in an apartment complex in the Bronx. Our neighborhood was a mixture of race and religion. For instance, I am Jewish and my best friend is Catholic.

Q: What are some of your earliest memories of martial arts in the United States? Were there any particular movies, books, actors, or local individuals that caught your attention?

I did not grow up looking at any martial arts films or having any desire to study it until I tried it at a health club in 1972.

Q: What were the circumstances around that first training experience?

I had joined a health club to lose weight after the birth of my second son. That was when I took a woman's self-defense program. I liked it much more than just exercising. The instructor was a taekwondo black belt named Dan. When the health club stopped offering the program, some of the girls and I began training in taekwondo in my living room.

Q: How did you transfer that experience into full-time training elsewhere?

I did not join an actual dojo until 1973. I was enjoying my training, but Dan had a job and was going to college and could no longer find the time to teach us. I began to look for a dojo at that point. While looking around, I was told that I could only take self-defense programs and NOT train in the actual arts with men.

Eventually I found an ad for a martial arts program at a Jewish Center. I called and received the same response (no women), but I wanted to train. At that time I had no knowledge of styles or systems, I just wanted to do martial arts. Eventually the instructor, Jimmy Papa, agreed to let me take karate and the self-defense class. That was my introduction to Isshin Ryu.

Q: Could you talk more about this early experience with Isshin Ryu?

Jimmy Papa introduced me to the style, and I loved the natural movements of it. The vertical fist seemed to be perfect for me and far easier and stronger than the rotated fists of taekwondo. My sister-in-law at that time was taking Judo which seemed a more feminine martial art but, again, not what had piqued my interest. One day, Master Nick Adler came to our class and showed a movie clip of the founder of Isshin Ryu, Shimabuku Tatsuo. It was the first time I had met Mr. Adler. At that time, he only addressed my instructor and not any of the students. After class I went up to thank him, but he basically just looked at me, or more like through me. When I left, I thought I would never attempt to train with him. Adler Sensei is not the easiest person to get to know, and for sure my first impression was not favorable.

Q: Given the rough start, how did you eventually establish a more lasting training relationship with Adler Sensei?

When Jimmy stopped teaching (he was also a college student and played guitar with a group), I began to look for a more established dojo. I had earned my yellow belt in Isshin Ryu by that time, and the cultural stigma against women in the dojo was beginning to ease up. I checked out several schools, but by then I had fallen in love with Isshin Ryu and wanted to continue. To be honest, I did not even check if there were other Isshin Ryu schools around; I knew Mr. Adler was Jimmy's teacher and that he had to be good. I decided to contact a friend, David, who had been training with me under Jimmy and convinced him to go with me to see Master Adler. We both signed up that day, but, unbeknownst to me, Jimmy had previously taken David to Sensei's dojo for a kyu test. Hence David retained his yellow belt and I, on the other hand, became a white belt once more.

Adler Sensei had some karate magazines in the dojo, and I think that was my first introduction to a broader understanding of what was going on with martial arts. At that time, Peter Urban (the father of American Goju Ryu) was writing a recurring column for "Black Belt Magazine". In one article he actually said, in so many words, women didn't belong in the dojo because men were damned if they hit a woman and looked bad if they didn't.

Q: What was the dojo and student body like when you joined Adler Sensei's dojo? Were you the first / only female, and did that amount to different treatment?

Almost all the students were male with the exception of one woman black belt. There were no children when I joined Sensei's dojo in Bayshore.

Marilyn Fierro with what would become her two greatest influences — Nick Adler and Uezu Angi.

There was no difference in the training for the women. We all did the same thing. His girls were really tough and excellent fighters, but I was definitely not. It was a painful growing process for me both emotionally and physically. When I was at Jimmy's class, the guys were easier on me and they took the time to help me. It was far harder in Sensei's classes. I ask myself even today how I managed to do it because I was also a little older than the average student. I muddled through the fighting aspects, and eventually Sensei told me that if I was not going to be doing a lot of kumite then I needed to be great at self-defense — so that became my true focus.

Q: Could you elaborate on the training content and how fighting was mixed in with other matters, such as basics and kata?

We always started with warm ups, then basics, 10-15 times on each side. That was followed by kicking drills, kata, and sparring. Classes were two hours long but basically lasted as long as Sensei chose to teach. It should be noted that the dojo was two stories up when I joined, and within the year he had moved the dojo to the third / top floor. You needed to be in good condition just to get to the dojo with all the stairs and your gi bag. In the summer it was an oven, and even with everything open it took a long time to cool down. We just had floor fans, and they were really noisy. In the winter, it was the total reverse with a huge noisy heater.

Q: What was Adler Sensei like as a person and practitioner?

It was not until later in my training that I began to understand Adler Sensei and his ways. He was / is not easy and is a demanding instructor, but I watched as he produced many good fighters. He, himself, was a ferocious fighter. He had no fear and fought as if it were for real in the street. I remember one time Don Nagle Sensei had a shiai (gathering for competition) and Adler Sensei went there with some of his fighters. I was not there. The next time I saw them at the dojo, I heard the story of how another instructor wanted to fight Adler Sensei, so Nagle let them go at it. Evidently, the other instructor came at him quite hard — I believe he tried to kick him in the groin, so Sensei punched him in the face (remember there were no lawsuits in those days). I was told that the other guy got quite a shiner. About a week or two later, S.Henry Cho held a tournament in Madison Square Garden, and I saw a man there with the biggest black eye I had ever seen. Someone told me it was the same man Sensei had hit.

Q: When did you begin competing in tournaments? What was your motivation for doing so?

I hate to admit it, but competition was never something that interested me. I kept seeing a more spiritual aspect to the martial arts and found it to be a more fitting path . . . so my training was a pursuit of more lofty goals initially. Eventually I realized that I could grow through competition, and each time I went out in front of judges and an audience I was conquering my own fears and building my confidence as well.

I do not remember if I competed before spring of 1976. If I did, I did not do well. I remember participating in some demonstrations for our dojo on a regular basis. However, in April of 1976 there was a tournament in honor of our founder, Shimabuku Tatsuo, who had passed the year before. It was a special event, and most of our school participated in it. I was the only girl from our dojo to compete. At that time, there was only one division for women — white belts through black belts. I was still a kyu and did poorly at the event.

Sensei was big on competition no matter where the event was hosted. After '76 I went to many tournaments, some of them in the toughest areas. It was frightening to me at first, but through karate I began to accept the fact that we all had a common bond. Sure people are serious in the arena when competing, but outside the ring we gain many friends.

Fierro Sensei performing Seiunchin during her early competition years.

Q: Could you describe what early tournaments were like for you and other women? Was there obvious prejudice or lack of accommodation?

Unfortunately, there were not that many women in the earlier days, so we usually got lumped into one or two divisions no matter the difference in skill or size. There was no division for women to do weapons, and the men did not want us to compete in their divisions.

I remember one tournament when Ann-Marie Heilman and I had to fight to get into the men's weapon division. At that same event, the organizers discussed making separate Shodan, Nidan, and Sandan divisions to ease the pressure on the guys. Someone asked about making higher rank divisions for women too, and the tournament director said, "Well women rarely make Nidan, and if they do they would not get Sandan." You can't believe how fast Annie and I jumped up, as I believe we were both Sandan at the time.

Since most of the tournaments were in school gyms, there were normally locker rooms for each gender and ours were mostly empty.

Q: In 1978, you co-opened Smithtown Karate and took full ownership in 1980. What were some of the challenges in those early days of teaching and dojo ownership?

When Adler Sensei and I opened the dojo together, it was easy. Sensei basically taught and I assisted. When I sold lessons to newcomers, I sold Adler Sensei as the focus because of the quality of his instruction and reputation.

When I took over on my own, I was Shodan and did not feel qualified to run a dojo. I did not have the confidence to use my own abilities as a selling point, so I relied on the reputation of Isshin Ryu itself. It was a very difficult time of growth. At first I tried to be like Adler Sensei, to teach like him, but that was not working. I finally had to find my own identity and teach what I knew . . . but in my own way. I continued my training and tried to constantly improve, but I was alone managing the dojo, and I felt the burden.

That first year was probably the most difficult time I had ever known. There were three ladies training that began to assist me with office work and some classes, which helped. Eventually our school grew, with men and women together. The biggest challenge came when someone came into the dojo looking for the Sensei and finding out it was me, which resulted in a negative reaction. I would tell them they didn't belong in my dojo if they could not learn from a woman, and asked them to leave.
There were other incidents of men who came into the dojo and started criticizing our

Isshin Ryu vertical punch. I had to tell them they were going to feel the striking end of that punch if they did not leave immediately. There were numerous such incidents, especially during that first year. As I handled each incident I found that they were not as threatening as I had first perceived, and my confidence grew. One time I had a male secretary who was a brown belt. Someone came into the dojo looking for the Sensei and went to him assuming he was in charge — I looked at him across the room and gave him the cut signal across the throat. It was not worth speaking to someone like that at all.

Q: When did you begin teaching programs specifically for women? What was your motivation and intention for this kind of program?

I love the word karateka. Not a man, woman, child, or adult. Just a person who studies the martial arts. I had trained with the men and did not separate myself from them. I was quite resistant to teaching just women. I figured they needed to train like I had, with a mixed group. But, in 1978, I participated in a joint program with the police department on safety. At that time, the police were telling women NOT to fight back. They recommended letting the attacker do as they wanted; the victim's goal was to stay calm and hope to stay alive. I felt that there was no way a woman should just give in — the results from doing so would last a lifetime. I told the police that there were ways women could defend themselves, and I finally began to offer self-defense workshops.

At that time most women were not like those of today, and it was difficult to get them to do anything. It took me a while to realize I had to make them steaming mad and understand the consequences of non-action before I could get action. My program started as a six-week workshop of technique and mindset, with the last week defending against a padded male attacker. While I was teaching these programs, I was also lecturing at various schools and organizations. I had an opportunity to present my karate class on a TV show in The Hamptons, Long Island, New York. That show was submitted to the Suffolk County Film Festival and we received a runner up award for it.

Q: When did you first begin training with Uezu Angi Sensei? How did you meet him, and what was that first meeting like?

It was probably at our Isshin Ryu Friendship Tournament in 1986 where he was our guest. Adler Sensei knew him before that time.

Anyone who meets Uezu Sensei likes him immediately. He is always so pleasant and treats everyone fairly. He is such a patient man who takes time to sign autographs whenever asked. I remember we would have a line of people looking to meet him and chat with him — we had to ask them to stop so he could rest. He did not just sign his name, but also the person's name and he wrote in English and Japanese as well. He always says that patience is of utmost importance.

Master Uezu has a great heart and likes people who show they are true. He believes in bushido, and one of his best compliments would be to tell you that you are a good bushido man or woman in my case. When we trained, we trained hard and he demonstrated everything before watching the class. His English was good, but some people could not understand him. After a while I found it easy to have conversations with him, and he would share many insights into his training with Shimabuku Tatsuo Soke.

Q: Could you describe Uezu Sensei as an instructor? What was his teaching style, and what kind of content did he like to focus on?

We always started each class with a bow in and short meditation. Basic warm ups and stretches followed, including the 15 upper body basics, then the 15 lower body basics and kicking techniques. Depending on the emphasis of the day, we would sometimes go into sport kicking drills or self-defense, and other times we would work on kata and bunkai.

Depending on the time allowed, we would also work weapons.

He loved teaching and enjoyed watching someone who had good kicks or technique. I once told him I was having a problem with a technique, and he said, "That's okay. Chinkuchi most important." By "chinkuchi" he meant that everything had to be executed perfectly with proper stance, speed, snap, etc.

He rarely tells someone they are not good, so one day when a practitioner at class asked Uezu Sensei how he looked, I was surprised to hear Sensei answer, "Kicky no understand, punchy no understand. More practice needed." Wow, that got me, so I bravely asked if what I did was okay and he said, "Joto (okay), back kick not too good."

Q: You met and trained with a number of pioneering American Isshin Ryu Sensei, as well as multiple Okinawan Sensei while they were in the States. Did you ever get to visit Okinawa itself?

I remember many of the male practitioners told me Okinawa was not a good place for a woman to go, so I was concerned. Master Uezu said it would be fine and that I should go, but I was quite hesitant. In 1991, I had the opportunity to participate in a Master's Demonstration in Okinawa. Adler Sensei and I were part of a group of Americans training and participating. It was quite an experience. Master Uezu also took us sightseeing. I found out later that he checked everywhere to be sure there were western toilets available for me. His concern was amazing.

As the years have passed, Master Uezu suffered some strokes and is no longer able to teach the same way . . . but his spirit is strong and he continues to make every effort to teach whenever he is well enough to return to the United States. He is a perfect example of Isshin Ryu's "one heart way," and a role model for anyone who ever faces a challenge.

Q: Were there any other instructors that were instrumental for your development as a martial artist? If so, how were they instrumental?

Fierro Sensei with Isshin Ryu pioneer Don Nagle.

Because Adler Sensei has always encouraged his students to study multiple arts, I have been most fortunate to have met and trained with more great masters than I can even begin to list. My higher ranks from 6th Dan and above all came jointly from Master Adler and Master Uezu who are my main Isshin Ryu teachers. I have had the opportunity to spend time with all four of the Isshin Ryu Pioneers, Don Nagle (who helped teach Adler Sensei), Harold Mitchum, Harold Long and Steve Armstrong, each of whom brought their own take on Isshin Ryu (which teaches us that differences are okay). I also hold the rank of 1st Dan with the International Karate Kobudo Federation (operated by Bruce and Ann-Marie Heilman) and Master Odo. It was an honor and privilege to have trained with Odo Sensei who was very much like Uezu Sensei with his quality instruction as well as kind and patient manner. I was already a 4th Dan in Isshin Ryu when I tested for 1st Dan with Odo Sensei and the Heilmans in Okinawa Kenpo, and had not tested in years. I found it extremely stressful and rewarding all at the same. It was a good reminder of what our students go through.

Other instructors I met through seminars, some I met more than once and others more often, but always with the purpose to gain knowledge and never rank. Each person that enters into our lives brings us a lesson. Maybe you meet someone once in a casual encounter and there is a lasting impression. It could be a word or a deed but something that changes us forever. I met Don Bohan, Isshin Ryu, probably sometime in the late '70s or early '80s. I did not like him initially as he was rather distant and not the kind of person I normally gravitate to. I did not train with him but would see him at tournaments and events. One day I was getting coffee and I asked Adler Sensei and Bohan Sensei if they wanted one too. When I brought back the coffees Bohan said to me, "You don't like me do you?" I said no, so, he asked, "Then why did you bring me coffee?" I told him that liking someone and respecting them can be two different things.

Later that evening, Bohan Sensei and I sat up in the lobby of the hotel talking until about

3:00 a.m. I learned more about him and his time in the military. I realized that although I had never considered myself judgmental, I was certainly acting the part. I formed an opinion of Bohan Sensei based on what I *expected* him to be like. That was quite a lesson. After that day we became close friends, and Bo was a great supporter of me. He understood that there were very few women in the martial arts and I was hanging in and working hard to grow with the art. Bohan Sensei passed away in 1998; a great loss to the Isshin Ryu community.

Soon after, I was at a tournament and his student, Wayne Wayland, told me that while Bo was in the hospital Wayne began asking him many questions. One of the questions was, "Who do you admire?" Bohan Sensei's answer was me. Wayne was shocked as am I still today. Wayne asked him why, and he said, "Because she was there at a time when there were few women. She stayed, worked hard, and did well." I guess we never know who will make a difference in our lives.

Q: You created the "Taking Charge" martial arts television program in the early '90s. How did that get started, and what was your ultimate goal with it?

In 1992, I had the opportunity to bring a group of students to The Hamptons to participate in a public access TV show with Lois Wright. We did an episode about karate and self-defense. As mentioned earlier, this show was submitted to the Suffolk County Film Festival and won a runner up award. I took our show to my local cable station to have it aired. This piqued my interest in TV and making shows.

That same year I did a five part series with Dave Porello on "In Your Interest" about self-defense. At the same time, I was developing my Woman's Attack Prevention program and needed a tape to use mainly for phys-ed teachers to incorporate into their curriculum. I contacted Chris Cook who was in charge of the film festival to see if he knew someone who could help me create my program on tape. After many calls I was finally put in touch with a B.O.C.E.S. (Board of Cooperative Education Services) program and given a grant to make the tape, which was completed in 1993. Through that program I learned a lot about editing footage.

In June of 1994 my program had gained some acclaim and I received a call from Councilwoman Pam Greene who had a TV show called "Women in the '90s." I appeared on her show and used a section of my new tape to reinforce what I was teaching. By

September I also did a news special on our local channel 12 who came in and filmed some of my women's program at the dojo.

My interest in TV had been piqued but still I was not doing anything about it. It was not until 1997 when I was being inducted into the Jewish Sports Hall of Fame (and was already a 7th Dan and considered the highest in my system) that a radio announcer, David Weiss from WALK FM, said, "So what's next?" I was blank. What could possibly top this year with my rank and now the recognition of being the first karate person to be inducted into the Jewish Sports Hall of Fame, not to mention the second woman ever? What could be next? His next question was, "What do you love?" That was easy — I loved TV work. His response was, "Then create a show!"

By April of 1997, that is exactly what I did. I debated long and hard as to what I could call the show. I kept saying that I wanted to help people learn how to take charge of their lives, and the title became obvious. The show turned out to be mostly martial arts based with many subjects and systems covered, but also spiritual in nature. It is, as the name says, about taking charge of yourself and learning to be the best "You" you can be. I have done shows with horses for physically challenged people, with puppies for the guide dog foundation, crystal healing, spiritual channeling, chiropractic methods, and other healing modalities. To date I have produced 121 half hour shows. While my goal has been to introduce people to a variety of arts and healing techniques, I also have had the opportunity to meet, film, and interview many great people in their fields.

Q: You are the first woman to be recognized as 7th Dan and then 8th Dan in Isshin Ryu. Could you describe how you felt when achieving this, and what it means to you upon reflection?

When I began this wonderful journey, I never expected it to take me to the point I am today. My initial goal, besides finding myself in karate training, was to achieve my brown belt. I figured by then I would be able to defend myself. I never even thought of becoming a black belt. But with training and perseverance, that goal and others were achieved. My next goal after I began teaching was to be 3rd Dan because that was considered true teaching level. Other ranks came with time and, as I got closer to higher levels, I had the desire to be the first red / white belt woman in Isshin Ryu. In the United States the red / white belt is sometimes awarded at 6th Dan, but in Okinawa it is not until 7th. So 7th Dan in 1996 became a major accomplishment for me.

Fierro Sensei receiving her promotion to 7th Dan in 1996.

Achieving a goal is an excellent feeling, but, for me, it is a matter of, "What's next?" I believe we need to keep growing, learning, and re-defining ourselves. It is true that I am recognized as the highest woman in Isshin Ryu by our Centurion Association (headed by Nick Adler Sensei), Master Uezu's Okinawa Isshinryu Karate Kobudo Association, and several other reputable Isshin Ryu associations . . . but it does not mean there are no other women in other associations. In 2007, I took my third trip to Okinawa and brought my student, Rita, with me. Master Uezu was so proud and would introduce us and say this is Marilyn-San — Hachidan. Everyone I was introduced to would begin to talk about it (the ladies especially would get so excited). I finally asked Uezu Sensei why he was introducing me in that way, and he told me that in all of Okinawa there was no woman Hachidan. He was so proud of me, and that made me extremely happy.

Q: How did your personal training change and mature as you grew older and more experienced?

I have found that as my body ages there are things that I can no longer do physically, but I still need to be an excellent teacher in order to help my students do certain moves. I now need to wear something on my feet when I teach in order to take the pressure off my back. It took a long time for me to get used to it, but without these changes I would not be able to continue to grow in the art I love so much. As we age and grow with the martial arts, I believe we get smarter. It's like watching things in slow motion, and I can anticipate what a student is doing before he or she does it. I have learned how to move better and smoother than when I first started training.

Q: What are some of the most important lessons you hope your students will carry on into the future?

I believe in values — honesty and integrity. They are as much a part of the martial way as learning how to fight or perform a good kata. It is knowing you have a skill but choosing not to use it. It is respect for others and having a kind heart. These values are very important to me.

Q: What do you think needs to happen for Isshin Ryu to grow in a healthy way worldwide?

Unfortunately Master Uezu's health is not the best and, to me, he has been our greatest connection worldwide. Through his tape series and organization led by Christopher Chase he continues to influence people all over the globe, but he is not able to travel as much as he had in the past. There are other organizations that have similar recognition, but the idea that we can have one unified Isshin Ryu seems to be more of a dream than a reality. We, the Centurion Association, support all associations and attend each of their World Championships or Grand Nationals annually. But, sadly, most stay within their own groups. In a perfect world we could be as our style of Isshin Ryu says, "one heart way."

Nick Adler

In the 1960s and 1970s, New York was one of the hottest spots for karate activity. Training in the city was intense and focused with an edge about it born from constant competition amongst schools. Nick Adler trained and fought his way through the heart of the New York scene, developing a reputation as a skilled fighter, talented kata performer, and savvy instructor.

Adler Sensei's Isshin Ryu experience came primarily from the earliest first generation instructors to come back from Okinawa after their tours of duty in the United States military. He augmented that by training with visiting Okinawan teachers, arranging for many of their stays and acting as a hub of interaction between many senior practitioners of different styles and backgrounds.

Q: Adler Sensei, You got your start in the martial arts in 1956. How old were you at that time, and what inspired you to get started?

I was 18 years old and got my start in the military. At that time, there wasn't much karate around. I was in S.A.C. (Strategic Air Command), and they had a Judo club.

Q: Who were your instructors in Judo, and when did you begin karate training?

My instructors were from the military in the Air Force Judo Club. It was after I left the Air Force that I began doing karate with Ed McGrath. Although I was enjoying karate and studying regularly, I began missing the close quarters combat which I had become used to with Judo. So, I joined jujutsu with Moses Powell.

Q: Did you travel frequently due to your enlistment in the Air Force? Were you ever sent to Okinawa or Japan?

During my time in the Air Force, I went to Japan for a short time and then was stationed in Korea.

Q: How were martial arts treated in the U.S.A. in the '50s and '60s? Were they understood, or were there a lot of misconceptions?

Karate in the '50s and '60s was definitely hardcore. It was being taught by ex-military personnel, no children and very few, if any, women. The average person had no interest in it. We were more of a novelty.

Q: Could you talk more about your experiences with Ed McGrath Sensei starting in 1962?

Ed McGrath was a senior student of Don Nagle and was a Lieutenant in the Marine Corps. While studying with McGrath Sensei, I always considered Mel Sutphen as my main instructor. He was one of McGrath's black belts and really took time with me on a day-to-day basis.

Q: What was your early training in Isshin Ryu like? What kind of mix was there between kata, kumite, basics, etc?

We did a lot of basics and a lot of kumite with very little kata. The majority of people in Isshin Ryu were Marines. They didn't spend a lot of time on Okinawa training and were young (teens and 20's) with a macho man mentality. Their emphasis was to bring back more of the fighting aspect of the art.

Q: How did you meet Don Nagle, and was training with him different than your previous experiences?

I met Nagle Sensei many times in New Jersey when I participated in interclub competitions and tournaments. Ed McGrath retired from teaching in 1966 and started his communication business, so I started going to New Jersey to train with Nagle Sensei in addition to teaching my own classes.

Nick Adler with Don Nagle and Harold Long in 1984 practicing Isshin Ryu punching technique.

Nagle Sensei was a police officer in New Jersey and did a lot of undercover work. I would go there on Saturdays to train, traveling one and a half hours each way. Nagle was the best fighter I have ever seen, even when compared to the big name fighters of then and now. After class he would continue to train himself and all who wanted to stay. Usually it was just me, and we would work for hours on just one technique to get it down until he felt it was perfect.

As a police officer, he was so feared in NJ that a contract was put out on him. Eventually it was rescinded because they were afraid of the consequences if they missed. Nagle Sensei was one of a kind.

Interesting to note: Nagle Sensei did all of his forms the way Shimabuku Sensei taught him . . . which was different from how others taught the forms. I was a brown belt when Shimabuku Tatsuo came to the United States and Nagle Sensei asked him if he wanted him to change. Shimabuku Sensei said, "Keep doing what I taught you." It should be understood that Shimabuku Tatsuo was still evolving his system and made changes quite often.

Q: There seems to be some confusion or controversy regarding rank in Isshin Ryu in the early days, especially as given to American servicemen. What do you make of that situation, and what were Shimabuku Sensei's intentions?

I believe Shimabuku's intentions in the early days was to elevate four of his senior people who came from different parts of the United States in order promote the growth of Isshin Ryu. When Nagle Sensei came back to the United States, he was a 5th Dan even though he spent a short time on Okinawa. Shimabuku Sensei did it knowing that Nagle Sensei would be that rank if he continued training, thinking it likely that he would not return to Okinawa. On Shimabuku's second visit to the United States, he promoted all of these four pioneers to the rank of 8th Dan.

Q: How did you eventually come to study with Angi Uezu Sensei? What made him stand out as someone you wanted to be affiliated with?

Uezu Sensei was the ambassador for Shimabuku Sensei and was sent to teach Isshin Ryu. I met Uezu Sensei in 1966 or 1967. He spent two years teaching in the U.S. with Harry Acklin. Uezu Sensei's forms were different from the way I had been taught, so I began to learn another set of forms. I trained with him every year he was in the United States and each time I visited Okinawa. Nagle Sensei knew I was doing this and gave me his permission. Uezu Sensei was so sincere in what he taught. He did not make anything up. If he did not know the answer he would say, "Shimabuku no say." He genuinely cares about his students — it does not matter what rank a person is, he takes the same amount of time to work with them. Uezu Sensei has a great smile and personality. To this day he is loved by all who know him here, in Okinawa, and worldwide.

Q: Could you discuss your early efforts in starting martial arts schools in the United States? What was the climate like in the States, and did you have trouble staying afloat during fads like the kung fu craze?

Bruce Lee was the heyday for any martial art. We used to turn people away there were so many interested. I never had contracts and didn't believe in them. If you didn't have the character I wanted in a student, I could ask you to leave and vice versa.

Q: In addition to your Isshin Ryu experience you are also known for your kobudo work. Who were your major influences when studying weapons?

Uezu Sensei, Odo Sensei, Oyata Sensei, Guru Dan Inosanto, and many different people through the years . . . but these were my main instructors.

Q: How did you first meet Odo Seikichi Sensei? Could you describe your study with him?

I met Odo Sensei through Bruce and Ann-Marie Heilman. I do not remember the actual year, but from that point on I trained with him each time he came to the States and even hosted him at my dojos in the early '80s.

Q: Could you share a funny or interesting story about one of your teachers that readers may have never heard before? Something that might give an inside peek at the individual's character and personality?

Nagle Sensei was very unique and quite perceptive. One day I was sitting near him and was quite angry at him for promoting someone I felt didn't deserve it. He simply said, "You're too close, my son, to be thinking that."

Q: Over the years you've successfully developed a network of schools and clubs, calling it the Centurion Program. When did you come up with the concept, and what is the driving philosophy behind it?

The Centurion was a Roman soldier. The original Roman soldiers were the greatest warriors of their day. They switched to lighter armor so that they could move swiftly in combat. They also switched to a short sword because they found that stabbing led to more consistent kills (you can slice somebody but they may continue to fight). I wanted the same mindset and results for my people. I believe speed, mobility and agility conquers all — a strategy suitable for male, female or whoever.

Q: After multiple decades of training and teaching, what keeps you motivated to go to the dojo every week and travel frequently to seminars?

For one thing, I like working with people of all ages. It's very rewarding to see their development. I've been fortunate in that the people who have made black belt with me have also accomplished many things in the outside world through the discipline they gained from martial arts training.

As for seminars . . . I enjoy both taking them and teaching them. It keeps you fresh in the way things are done, whether it be different types of drills, new conditioning exercises, or reinforcing techniques we already do. I enjoy being both a student and a teacher.

Q: Given the benefit of hindsight and experience, what is one thing you would tell less experienced martial artists to focus on during their training, or one mistake to definitely avoid?

Try to never miss a workout. That's the biggest secret! Never believe you know everything. One of the most important things: you can do martial arts for the rest of your life and you can ALWAYS improve.

Q: What message would you give to future generations to ensure that the true spirit of martial arts is preserved?

There will always be people who love the martial arts and will continue teaching. Unfortunately, in this country everybody wants everything now. There is nothing wrong with competition for the people who can handle it mentally and physically, but most people didn't get involved with the martial arts for competition; most got involved for self-defense, self-confidence, conditioning and coordination — that "Yes, I can!" attitude that you need for other sports and life.

I have been in the martial arts for almost 60 years, teaching two classes a day and enjoying what I am doing. It would be very hard for me to do that if I were a football player, soccer player, or any other kind of athlete. It is the job of the teacher to inspire the students to stay in the martial arts and even teach, helping other people the way it helped them. You can still be involved in other activities, but martial arts is the one thing you can do for the rest of your life.

Ed McGrath

In 1957, Don Nagle had returned to the United States, fresh off of a tour from Okinawa where he had been studying directly with Shimabuku Tatsuo of Isshin Ryu.[62] Nagle Sensei quickly established a karate program in Jacksonville, North Carolina, near Camp Lejeune. Thanks to a partnership with Ernie Cates, one of the preeminent Judo experts in the U.S., the program grew in reputation.

Signing up early in 1958 was a young Ed McGrath (1935-2014). McGrath Sensei had been studying Judo with Cates Sensei but found himself intrigued by the new Okinawan art. The relationship McGrath Sensei started with Nagle Sensei in North Carolina spanned decades, with McGrath Sensei becoming not just an important practitioner of Isshin Ryu, but also an ambassador of karate throughout the U.S. and even into pop culture.[63]

Q: McGrath Sensei, could you tell us when and where you were born? What kind of neighborhood did you grow up in?

I was born June 10, 1935, in Brooklyn, New York, in an Irish, German, and Italian neighborhood. We were all very sports-oriented. The Brooklyn Dodgers were our neighborhood idols. We also loved the New York Rangers. The streets were tough and as ball players we rode our bikes from park to park. Fighting was something that happened quite frequently while riding through some of the tough neighborhoods.

Q: During your youth what was the general vibe of martial arts in America? Were there any big trends in Judo, jujutsu, or karate?

---

[62] Corcoran, John, Emil Farkas, and Stuart Sobel. *The Original Martial Arts Encyclopedia: Tradition, History, Pioneers.* City of Pub: Pro-Action Pub., 1993. 235. Print.
[63] Images acquired with the assistance of Daniel Vena.

Martial arts were sparse, but Judo was known. Boxing was big in our neighborhood; we all paid attention to "Friday Nights at the Fights."

Q: When did you join the United States Marine Corps?

In 1956, Officer Candidate School.

Q: In 1958, you began your martial arts journey with Don Nagle Sensei. Was Nagle Sensei then teaching at Camp Lejeune, and how were you first introduced to him?

Yes, he was teaching at the original New Bridge Street Dojo in Jacksonville, North Carolina. Ernie Cates, my first Judo instructor, introduced me to Nagle Sensei.

Q: Could you describe some of your first experiences with karate training? Did you find it particularly difficult, rewarding, etc.?

Marines are supposed to train and get in great shape, so we were looking for a way to train outside of work in the Corps. Nagle Sensei came back from Okinawa with the gift of Isshin Ryu and said, "Fellas, look at this."

These were tough Marines in Nagle Sensei's dojo. If you wanted to survive, you had to learn how to fight like Sensei. I am proud of the fact that Rick Niemira, a tough fighter and senior student, never knocked me out, but I broke his nose twice and knocked him out three times. Rick was our first black belt under Nagle Sensei, and if I did well against Rick, Nagle Sensei knew I could fight.

Q: What was the Nagle dojo / training area like? Could you describe the kinds of students who were studying at that time?

I'd like to describe two of the training areas:

1. Jacksonville, North Carolina, consisted mostly of United States Marine Corps personnel. There were a few officers in that original dojo, and I was one of them. The students were as tough as nails. Don Nagle, Don Bohan, Rick Niemira, and Lou Lizotte, just to name a few. The workouts lasted about three to four hours and covered the entire Isshin Ryu

curriculum, including all the particular information Sensei learned while he was stationed on Okinawa.

2. In New Jersey and on Long Island, Nagle Sensei's dojo consisted of police officers, school teachers and working people. He trained some of the finest instructors in Isshin Ryu when he started teaching back home in New Jersey.

Q: What was Nagle Sensei like as a teacher?

I was an officer taking instruction from an enlisted man, so our relationship was flipped in the dojo. At work I was the authority; in the dojo, he was the authority. Nagle Sensei wanted us to learn what he had learned from Shimabuku Tatsuo Sensei — that's all that mattered. I hope you get the underlying message of this answer. Sensei knew how to instruct, and used his experience to convey his teachings clearly and concisely.

Ed McGrath with Don Nagle and Gary Alexander in front of an honorary photo of Shimabukuro Tatsuo Sensei.

Q: What material did Nagle Sensei like to focus on (kata, sparring, basics, weapons, etc)?

Fighting was the focus.

Q: In 1959, shortly after you started your training, Nagle Sensei was discharged and left the military base, headed for civilian life. Was it difficult losing your teacher, and what made you decide to teach in his place?

It was not a difficult loss because he told me that when I returned home we would pick up where we left off. When he departed and returned home in 1959, he left me in charge of the Jacksonville, North Carolina, dojo. It was Nagle Sensei who made that decision.

Q: Were you able to stay in touch with Nagle Sensei after he left? How did you continue your personal training at that point in your life?

I did manage to keep in touch, and he continued to support me until I returned home. Once I returned home, we got together and I opened my first dojo in Queens, New York.

Don Nagle testing Ed McGrath for his 1ˢᵗ degree black belt in 1959.

Q: Are there any moments in your training from the late '50s and early '60s that are particularly memorable for you? Could you describe them for us?

In the 1950s, Nagle Sensei and I worked on demos for the Marine Corps. In the 1960s, Aaron Banks, Gary Alexander, and Peter Urban were all working together to promote martial arts. I worked for all of them, mostly in the ring and announcer booth. It was the best time in martial arts — pure arts from direct students.

Q: Many of your students went on to become tournament champions. Did you compete as well in tournaments? If so, could you describe what those early competition days were like?

Yes, I competed often! They were tough fights back then; however, the center judge had an easy job — go until a knock out or someone couldn't continue.

Q: Was it important for your students to compete? Did you stress that kind of training in your dojo(s)?

No. No. We trained for real-life work. Most of my students used their martial arts skills on the job (police, soldiers, etc.).

Q: What kind of material did you like to focus on (kata, sparring, basics, etc.)?

I emphasized fighting applications, control techniques, and submission techniques. Again, our training reflected danger at all times when on duty. As for kata and kobudo, we also used that part of the curriculum to develop the drills that are required for the inherent "jitsu" practical methods.

Q: In 1969, you moved to Long Island, NY, and began teaching there. What prompted this move, and what lasting memories do you have from this Long Island dojo?

The move was prompted by our family growing and needing more room for the children and dogs.

My fondest memory of this time was meeting a young man named Barry Steinberg who began training alongside his brother. With me now for almost 50 years, this individual [Barry Steinberg] has proven time after time to be both loyal and humble. Steinberg Sensei turned out to be one of the most talented karateka I have ever met, and his knowledge is above reproach. His delivery of instruction is so easy to understand that Shimabuku Tatsuo Sensei would be proud that Barry picked Isshin Ryu Karatedo as his life's journey.

The students that followed me to Long Island and the one's that went off on their own have, of course, progressed in a way that I cannot put into words. These men have persevered in teaching the art of Isshin Ryu. Malaki Lee, Richie Bell, Mel Sutphen (my first black belt). Bobby Baker — one of my most deadly fighters ever. Jack Jameson, Frank Klos, John Pinghero, Kenny Laskowski, Stevie DiLorenzo, Dan Vena, John Dumbrowski, Joe Burgess, Nick Adler, Frank Black, Greg Melita . . . the inner fiber of my senior deshi. The Long Island experience produced my finest work because I lived there the longest. The students turned out by these Sensei are my finest work. They continue to display what we refer to as "Nagle-isms," so again these Sensei do my work every day when they teach Isshin Ryu.

Q: Did you ever have the opportunity to visit Okinawa and study directly with Shimabukuro Tatsuo and Shimabukuro Kichiro?

I never went to Okinawa, but Nagle Sensei brought the founder here, and I did get a chance to meet him. I did meet Kichiro Sensei when he was here in the States, but I never trained with him.

Q: In addition to being a renowned competitor and teacher, you also became known for your commentating skills, acquiring the nickname "The Voice of Karate." Could you describe this turn of events and what you gained from becoming an event announcer?

I worked for a brokerage firm in Manhattan, and they wanted me to do an advertising campaign for a new aftershave product, "Hai Karate", they had been planning to release. The World's Fair was going on at the time in Flushing, Queens, New York, so I had several students prepare demos of routines that worked well for the audience. We had several opportunities to display Isshin Ryu and we were all excited about that, and I guess it showed. I was asked by Aaron Banks and Gary Alexander if I would work future events and help promote what is now considered the early days of martial arts in North America. Gary Alexander Sensei has been running his event for roughly 50 years now, and I did his very first one. I gained friendships, promoted camaraderie, and worked with so many great martial artists who all worked to change how martial arts were perceived in the United States.

Q: You remained a loyal student to Nagle Sensei throughout his life until his passing. At that time, you were named the successor to Nagle Sensei's A.O.K.A. (American Okinawa Karate Association) Isshin Ryu lineage. Could you tell us about how Nagle Sensei handled that handing down of the art?

He named me inheritor on his death bed, and for that I remain humbled and forever in his debt. I truly loved my Sensei; he was my best friend and teacher.

Q: What do you think are some of the key elements to understanding Isshin Ryu, both in terms of philosophical intent and physical execution?

The simplicity of the curriculum is amazing and is the most modern of all the Okinawan curriculum. Isshin Ryu adapts to you, you don't have to adapt to Isshin Ryu. Its design and architecture is implemented in a way that is deadly and highly effective.

McGrath Sensei during his final years of teaching.

Q: What do you hope your lasting impact on Isshin Ryu will be?

I have always stressed uniformity, camaraderie, and creating the best instructors to train the best students.

Q: If you could give future generations advice for properly preserving the spirit of karate, what would you tell them?

Karatedo is not a sport; it is a way of life. Your dojo is where you are standing. Treat all people as if you were in front of your Sensei, with respect and honor. Train hard and train safe. Never give up. There is no "I" in team. Always respect your parents and your Sensei. You never stand so tall as when you stoop to help a child or the elderly.

Chapter 8 –
Matsumura Seito

Soken Hohan was a unique and highly regarded martial artist on Okinawa throughout the 20th century. He bore familial lines back to one of Okinawa's greatest warriors — Matsumura Sokon Bushi. Matsumura was famous for his integral part in the protection of Okinawan kings and in the development of karate and kobudo on the island. The branch of karate known as Shorin Ryu is attributed to Matsumura and his teachers.

Soken Hohan is said to have studied directly under Matsumura Nabe, grandson and student of Matsumura Sokon. As such, Soken Sensei's art is referred to as Matsumura Seito (The Orthodox Path of Matsumura Sokon).

In 1924, Soken Sensei immigrated to Argentina and did not return to his homeland for almost three decades. However, when he did return, he eventually agreed to teach his karate methods. While resistant to the idea of teaching non-family members at first, Soken Sensei eventually took on a number of students who became well known experts in their own right (men like Kuda Yuichi, Kise Fusei, and Yabiku Takaya, among others).[64]

---

[64] Estrada, Ernie. "Interview With Soken Hohan: The Last of the Great Old Time Karate Warriors - Part 1." *FightingArts.com,* 2004. Web. 15 Nov. 2014. <http://www.fightingarts.com/reading/article.php?id=426>.

James Coffman

James Coffman Sensei is a man of many firsts, and is a staunch guardian of the old ways of Okinawan karate. An Air Force veteran who was stationed on Okinawa in the early 1960s, Coffman Sensei turned a lucky meeting with Kise Fusei of Matsumura Seito into a lifetime of training.

Born in 1943, James Coffman grew up in a disciplined household. He took that discipline and transferred it into a successful military career. After becoming the first western student of Soken Hohan and a dedicated student of Matsumura Seito, Coffman came back to the U.S. and spearheaded a number of Matsumura Seito programs, including the earliest program at Fort Bragg.[65]

Since his time in Okinawa, Coffman Sensei has continued to train and study, drawing a hard line on traditional matters such as rank and lineage. He is considered a critical link to the ways of Soken Hohan and the legacy of Matsumura Sokon.

Q: Coffman Sensei, your earliest experience with karate was 1959, here in the United States. Who did you train with, and what inspired you to investigate karate?

I started my karate training with a man who was in the Navy, stationed in Maryland. He had previously been stationed in Japan and claimed to be a black belt in Shotokan (he was also dating my sister at the time). He would tell us stories of karate in Japan, and he offered to teach me. However, once I was exposed to real Okinawan karate I could see that he had,

---

[65] Coffman, James H. "Timeline." *S.M.O.K.A.-U.S.A.*, 2002. Web. 15 Nov. 2014. <http://www.SMOKA-U.S.A..com/timeline/timeline.html>.

in fact, very little real karate experience and most likely either attended a few classes or was just an observer. This is the reason I do not claim any *real* karate training from this man.

Q: After high school, you opted to join the Air Force. Did you find military life and boot camp difficult or shocking?

Honestly, boot camp was not all that hard for me. It was based upon hard discipline, which I was already well versed in thanks to a strict daily routine through my father. My only problem was with the Drill Instructors, "D.I.'s," and their hard-lined authority. I had a bad attitude back then as well as a real problem with authority.

Q: When you found out you were to be stationed on Okinawa, were you excited to investigate karate or were you completely focused on military activity?

When I received orders to go to Okinawa, I didn't really know what karate was. In 1960, here in the States, "karate" was a word not often heard. When someone stated they were a black belt, you took a step backwards because of the unknown mystique at that time. I knew karate had a lot of kicks, punches, and board breaking, which I picked up from my sister's boyfriend. When I reached Okinawa, I had no intentions of investigating karate; it wasn't until my exposure with Kise Fusei that I really became interested.

Q: What were some of your day-to-day military duties while stationed on Okinawa?

I was an electrician in the Air Force, so naturally I was assigned to the electrical shop. The shop foreman found out that I had a driver's license, and the customary process was to have an American assigned with an Okinawan to work together. I was assigned to work with Kise Fusei, who was a local electrician on the island. Our day-to-day duties consisted of various electrical repairs throughout the base and housing areas. At a later date, I was assigned to the Overhead Department where we worked on the electrical power transfer high-voltage.

Q: How did that repair work with Kise Sensei eventually lead to a karate relationship?

My first day on the job with Kise Sensei turned out to be one of the best things that ever happened to me. First thing in the morning, when we got to the electrical shop, Kise and I picked up our assignments for the day. The first half of the day, I don't think Kise said five words to me; he simply told me to turn right, turn left, go forward, stop here. We would get out of the truck, Kise would do the work, and I would stand by and assist or watch until the job was completed.

Mid-day or half way through the workday, we returned to the electrical shop and broke for lunch. I would go to the base chow hall and have lunch, Kise and the other Okinawans would eat their lunch that they had bought from home and then sit around either playing Hona Funa (a Japanese card game) or simply nap until the lunch break was over. During the lunch break, one of the other G.I.'s came up to me and said, "Jimmy, go over there and slap that small Okinawan." I said, "What Okinawan?" He replied, "The little guy that you work with." Now, I've been in enough fights to know that when someone tells you to go hit another person, there's a reason. I asked, "Why should I slap Kise?" He then told me that Kise Sensei was, in fact, a karate instructor. Of course, I didn't go over and slap anybody, nor was I about to just because a fellow G.I. asked me to.

After getting back in the truck and driving to our next location, I asked Kise Sensei, "Are you a karate instructor?" Kise Sensei's eyes lit up, and he said, "You like karate?" Hell, I really didn't know what karate was other than the small amount of so-called training that I had back in the States. So I said yes, and then I asked, "Can you break a brick?" Well, to make a long story short, yes — Kise did break a brick in front of me with his bare hand. Before the Air Force I had worked as a brick / block laborer, so I knew just how hard a brick really was. When I saw him break the brick, I was hooked. That evening I started taking karate with Kise Sensei at his home dojo.

Q: What made Kise Sensei's dojo stand out as one you would like to be a part of?

That's really a simple question with a simple answer. Hell, I didn't know what other schools were around, nor did I care once I had seen Kise Sensei break that brick with his bare hands. I had no desire or need to go to a different school at that time. Looking back at things now with my current knowledge and experience in karate, I know that I had made the best decision staying with Kise Sensei's dojo, which in turn led me to Soken's dojo as well.

Q: Kise Sensei's training background is diverse, spanning multiple styles. What style did he teach when you met him, and who were his primary teachers?

Yes, that is very true. Kise was well known all over the island for his karate ability, known as a hard fighter and a hard teacher. The style which he was teaching at that time in his home dojo was Shorinji Ryu. His teacher at the time was Maeshiro-San, and later I found out that he had also been taking lessons with Soken Hohan Sensei. Kise was friends with many other karate black belts around his belt level from various karate styles on the island, such as Shiokawa, who was a 5th degree at the time; Kise himself was a 4th degree and was a contemporary of others such as Odo and Oyata, just to name a few.

Q: Could you tell us more about Maeshiro Sensei?

As it turned out, Maeshiro-San lived next door to Kise Sensei. During my three and a half years training at Kise Sensei's dojo, there were only a few times that I actually saw Maeshiro Sensei attend classes and give any instruction at all. Most of the time he just sat in a chair, observed the class, and simply made comments to Kise. Of course, he was Kise's teacher, and whenever Maeshiro would enter the dojo Kise would immediately stop the class and everybody would come to attention and bow showing the proper respect. So actually Maeshiro did very little when it came to actively teaching the classes I attended.

In 1960, Kise Sensei's dojo belonged to the All Japan Karatedo League. At this time, Nakamura Shigeru Sensei of Okinawa Kenpo was the head man that represented the all Japan Karatedo League on Okinawa. Second in command was Shimabukuro Zenryo of Seibukan. Both of these great karate instructors were 10th Dans. Maeshiro Sensei, a Hachidan (8th Dan), was third in line, he was the head of the Koza City branch. So Maeshiro-San also carried a lot of weight on Okinawa.

Q: Could you describe some of the day-to-day training at Kise Sensei's dojo?

The training at Kise Sensei's dojo was very intense. It was seven days a week, a minimum of three to three and a half hours a night. Each class always started out with rudimentary and standard Shorinji Ryu exercises. Next came blocking drills, punching drills, kicking drills, etc. After all of the exercises and drills were done, we would pair up and do man-on-man street techniques, or fighting techniques. After that we would go through kata. After kata everyone worked on the makiwara, and after makiwara exercises we paired up and would do korte (body conditioning). Every class ended with full contact sparring.

James Coffman receiving his green belt certification (kneeling far left). Kise Fusei is kneeling front and center while Maeshiro Sensei sits far right.

Most people are familiar with the kendo style fighting gear known as bogu gear. The difference between the kendo gear and karate fighting gear that we wore was that the karate fighting gear that covered the chest area was not solid, it was made of fabric with wood planks sewn in separate panels. The kendo chest plate was made of a solid, hard material with no panels. We wore full face cages, karate chest gear, and padded gloves. Some of the students wore groin protectors, shin instep protectors, and even forearm protectors.

This protection allowed you to make full contact, which was encouraged by Kise Sensei, while limiting physical damage. Extreme hard contact was a must for every sparring session. I found Kise's methods of teaching and stressing aggressive contact to be very real and valuable. The Okinawan students liked to use me as a punching bag until I developed enough skill to return the physical abuse that they had given me.

For the most part, the Okinawan people did not like the Americans. We had to earn their friendship and trust; after all, we were intruders on their island, and we had money and they did not. We could purchase things that they could not afford. We were dating and sleeping with their women, which they did not approve of. By the time I reached Shodan (1st Dan) I had not only earned their respect, but had befriended all or most of my fellow students and teachers.

Q: How did you balance this tough training with daily military duties?

We simply worked five days a week on base doing the required electrical jobs from 8 a.m. to 4 pm. In the evenings, after changing clothes and having an evening meal, I took the bus to Kise's dojo. Training was always at Kise's dojo for the first year or so before we formed a karate school on my military base. So it was seven days a week (nights) training at Kise's dojo for three and a half hours or more each session. Most often students would arrive early to class and / or stay late after class and train on their own as well. Once we formed the school on Kadena Air Force Base, we (Kise and I) would teach and work out on the base for two hours per evening. Then Kise and I would go to his home dojo and work out for an additional three to three and a half hours, seven days a week.

Q: When did you first meet Soken Hohan Sensei?

I first physically met Soken Sensei in 1961, just after receiving the rank of Shodan.

Q: Could you describe that first meeting and your early impression of Soken Sensei?

During the first year and a half of my training with Kise Sensei, his students and I had been attending the various shiai (competition meets) around the island on a regular basis. One evening while we were out at a bar relaxing after class, Kise said to me, "Tomorrow we go see my teacher." At the time I was thinking he meant Maeshiro Sensei, but it wasn't to be Maeshiro at all; it was Grandmaster Soken Hohan. Now I knew that Kise was training with another Grandmaster, but I had not been privy to who it was up until now, so I was excited but did not know what to expect.

James Coffman with Kise Fusei and Soken Hohan.

Tomorrow came, we had finished work, eaten, and jumped in a cab to meet Soken Hohan Sensei. When we arrived at Soken Sensei's home, it looked just like any other Okinawan home at the time — a small wooden house with a mud courtyard and a small cinder block fence around the property. We walked up to the house and were greeted by his wife. She and Kise exchanged the customary greetings, then she escorted us into the sitting room. It's important to remember that the Okinawans were not wealthy people; the common Okinawan home consisted of two to three rooms with no running water and possibly a single light bulb in each room, if at all. Kise and I were seated on the tatami floor and awaited Soken Sensei, sipping on tea that his wife had served us. Master Soken came in the room, Kise and I stood and paid the common respect with a bow. Soken Sensei glanced over to me and I recited a very respectable greeting in Okinawan Hogan. I said, "Unjogonju yamisaeti Sensei," which translates basically into, "How are you most Honorable Sir?" Master Soken's eyes lit up and a tremendous smile came across his face. He spit out a very long sentence in Okinawan Hogan (the native language of Okinawa, also known as Uchinaguchi). Now Soken Sensei thought that I spoke Hogan because of my greeting, but he was wrong. Ha, ha. At this time I spoke enough Japanese and a mixture of Hogan to get around the island okay, but that was my limit.

Once Soken Sensei realized that I did not speak Hogan, he simply turned to Kise and directed all of his conversation, questions, and statements to him. My first impression of Soken Sensei was not really that great. Soken, as Kise, was small in stature. Soken was a frail looking older gentleman in his 70s, and to me, at the time, just another "old karate master." That is not to say I lacked proper respect for the gentleman, but I basically knew nothing about him other than that he was a Grandmaster and Kise's teacher.

Kise and Soken talked amongst themselves for a few minutes; from time to time Soken would glance over at me and then back to Kise. After a few minutes of talking, we all got up and went out to Soken's mud courtyard. Kise then directed me to do kata Seisan Shorinji. I performed the kata as he requested. He and Soken made comments to each other, then Soken Sensei requested that I do a bo kata. I asked which one he wanted, and he told me to do my best bo kata. I looked at Kise Sensei, and he said to do Bo One Shorinji.

I performed the kata, doing the hardest, fastest, and best performance I could muster. Soken Sensei acknowledged my kata as being very strong, precise, aggressive, and hard. He told Kise that he had seen me at the various shiai and knew I was a student with "great potential." Soken Sensei asked me several questions. When I did not understand the questions fully, Kise would interpret them for me. Some of the basic questions were, "Do you like Okinawa?," "Do you like karate?," "How often do you train in karate?," "Why do you want to become a student of mine?"

I gave Master Soken my answers, and he seemed to accept what I had to say. When Soken Sensei asked me how often I trained, I told him seven days a week. He then said, "One can train every day very hard and still never be good at the art of karate. If one trains wrong, or if one is being trained incorrectly, he can never obtain a high level of skill." I've never forgotten that statement and have found it to be true many, many times by seeing others that have trained for years and still have a low skill level.

Soken Sensei asked me why I wanted to train under him; I said because Kise wanted me to, and a good student always did as his teacher told him to do.

Although my first meeting with Soken Hohan was not very impressionable to me at the time, I later found out why other Okinawan masters referred to Soken Hohan as a teacher of teachers. During my time training under Soken Sensei, I witnessed several times Soken striking and hurting Kise. Now I had seen many, many people try to hurt Kise and were unable to do so. Once I saw that Soken could hurt Kise, my respect for him grew higher and higher. Watching Soken strike Kise and Kise doubling over in pain was a lesson well learned. It was a great honor to be accepted after that meeting as Soken Sensei's first American student.

Q: What was training with Soken Sensei like?

Kise Sensei and I would attend private lessons with Soken Sensei once a week, or at a minimum, two to three times a month. We would train in karate for an hour or two, but Soken Sensei really liked Okinawan weapons so we did a fair amount of weapons training each class as well. Soken Sensei spoke no English at all, but could speak Japanese, Okinawan Hogan, and was fluent in Spanish. I spoke limited Japanese and Okinawan Hogan but no Spanish, which meant Kise often acted as interpreter. Since Kise and I spent so much time together, we could communicate on a very high level of understanding. Soken Sensei's classes varied from one step street fighting, to weapons training, to kata. Soken Sensei was extremely proficient with the bo and kama, which were his favorite, although he was well-versed in nunchucku, tunfa, and sai as well.

Soken Sensei believed in the old ways of training: hard, aggressive, fast, but also patient. Soken was a true gentleman, extremely respected on Okinawa by all of the other masters and black belts that new him. Soken Sensei did not like what karate was turning into nor the modern ways that the Okinawans were moving. He did not consider his karate to be a sport, but rather considered Matsumura Seito Shorin Ryu a true art form that should not be changed. After a few months, Soken Sensei started attending the classes on Kadena Air Force Base. He would observe the classes, making comments and adjustments. This is how many of the other students that were training under Kise at the time got their exposure to Soken.

Q: Could you talk more about some of the cultural and communication barriers you encountered during your time on Okinawa?

Yes; when one gets to Okinawa for the first time and is confronted by a foreign language and new culture, it can make things difficult. When I first went to Kise's dojo, all of the students were young Okinawans, and none of them spoke English. I, of course, did not speak any Japanese or Okinawan yet, so communication was very hard.

Soken Hohan (left) and Kise Fusei (second from left) during one of their visits to Kadena Air Force Base. James Coffman is seen fourth from left.

The way Kise taught was to demonstrate an exercise or position, which I would mimick as best I could. After a while, when I would do something wrong or be in an incorrect position, Kise would simply come over and either kick or punch me and then correct my position. This was one way to learn very fast, because, let's face it, who likes to get kicked or struck? The other thing is that Kise and I were spending so much time together that we learned to communicate very quickly, almost by osmosis if you will. A person that trains seven days a week, five hours a day with another person can and will develop a very cohesive understanding with the other person. Day by day, each and every day, I was learning more and more Japanese and Okinawan Hogan. When I started taking classes at Kise's dojo located in Old Koza, there was only one other American student there. At the time Kise had maybe six students total. The American that was there before me was a green belt, and he left and rotated back to the States a month later. That left me as the only American student in the class.

Q: Did Soken Sensei ever tell any stories about Matsumura Nabe or Gokenki?

There were very few ways one could sit down and discuss various things with Soken Sensei. One way was to stick around after class and talk in a casual setting, which very few people had the opportunity to do. Another way was via the very limited interviews that he granted. What Soken and I discussed the most was his training methods. He told Kise and me how he trained balance using banana leaves, or how he did kata while balanced on a log which was floating in the water, and some other methods. He would tell of working as a farmer as a young man, and training in the mornings and / or evenings with his uncle Nabe. I never heard him mention Gokenki, but he did talk about other Okinawan greats from time to time.

Q: Were there any particularly memorable quotes or lessons from Kise Sensei or Soken Sensei that stick with you?

The most memorable thing that Soken Sensei ever said to me was, "One can train a lifetime and still never be good in the art of karate, if you train wrong." Kise's most memorable quote to me was, "It is better to be a lower rank beating a higher rank, than to be a higher rank getting beat by a lower rank." This meant that there is no power in the belt one wears or the rank one claims. Skill, ability, knowledge, and experience are what's important.

Q: When did you come back to the United States, and where did you open your first training club?

When I first returned to the states in 1964, I was stationed at Fort Bragg, North Carolina, at Pope Air Force Base which is a branch of Fort Bragg. I was ordered to assist the 101st Screaming Eagles and the 82nd Airborne divisions. After I got settled in with a normal work routine, I started a small karate class in the electrical shop open bay area. We only had three or four students at that time, and I was teaching six days a week.

Now, I had less than six months to go in the military and then my tour of duty would be up. However, I tried to teach the way that we were trained on Okinawa and found it very hard for the few G.I.'s in my class to accept that amount of aggressive contact and continuous hard training.

Q: What was the general perception of karate at that time in the United States?

Back in 1964, karate was virtually unknown as compared to today. I would say most karate schools in the U.S. were actually Korean taekwondo, so Okinawan karate was somewhat unknown at that time. There were a couple of Shotokan schools, a few Judo schools, maybe one Aikido school in my area. The Okinawan schools in the area (North Carolina and Washington D.C.) would've been one Goju Ryu and possibly one Isshin Ryu school. I did not see any Shorin Ryu schools at all yet.

Q: Did you get involved in the competition scene back in the United States?

Yes, I competed in the States for a little over 20 years in kata, fighting, and weapons, compiling a little over 300 trophies and wins. I competed mostly on the East Coast; however, we traveled as far west as Tennessee.

Q: How did you see the rise in tournament popularity affect the direction of karate training / teaching in the U.S.?

Tournaments back in the early-to-mid-60s here in the States were very different than they are today. I competed from the mid-60s to the early '90s. Back then (in the '60s) there were no weight classes, size divisions, or age divisions. No head gear or hand gear. Only the truly Okinawan tournaments required the wearing of bogozuki [bogu] fighting gear. There were a lot of cracked ribs, busted noses, and split faces back then. I had to fight black belts that were 6'2" and 230 lbs, and I was 5'7" and 140 lbs. Tournaments in the '60s overseas were basically full contact.

I feel tournaments have a purpose and are both good and bad. The good is that they allow you to compete against others that you have never met and who practice a wide variety of styles. Tournaments allow you to gain timing, distance judgment, technique application, and the opportunity to see if you are, in fact, transferring weight when you make contact where contact is allowed. The bad part is that tournaments can give a false sense of security because they are regulated fights. There are judges to stop the action if someone is too aggressive, or someone is getting hurt. On the street there are no judges to intervene. In tournaments there are rules such as no kicking to the groin, no eye strikes, and only kicks above the belt. On the street there are no such rules. There are many karate grand champions that would get their tails handed to them by a strong street or bar fighter.

In today's tournaments you see more acrobatics, "creative" kata, and supposed high ranking officials that are undeserving of judging others. I stopped going to tournaments in the '90s when I saw the direction they were headed. A lot of my students competed in tournaments, but it was never a requirement in any of my schools. I feel tournaments teach the wrong way to fight, with little or no contact, and take away the ability to use all strikes, kicks, and targets.

Q: You had a few more teaching opportunities after Fort Bragg, eventually winding up in Maryland. What kind of challenges did you experience while trying to teach in the West?

I lost my first three schools, not due to the lack of interest or enrollment but rather from the hard training methods that I was teaching. The students would not last. I started teaching in the local high schools, community centers, and churches. I opened my first commercial school in 1966-67 on Wisconsin Avenue above a bar named The Rabbits Foot. I had hooked up at that time with a fellow karateka named Gary Saluter, who had also been stationed on Okinawa. Gary was a Yondan (4th Dan) that had trained under Nakamura Shigeru Sensei on Okinawa and just happened to live in Maryland not too far from me.

Coffman Sensei engaged in spirited training with Kise Sensei. This dedication to intensity caused difficulties when teaching in the West.

We formed an alliance and opened my first commercial karate dojo. The school lasted approximately six months before we had to close due to lack of income. As it turned out I was having to put in half the rent money each month to meet the expenses in order to operate the school. So I went back to teaching at the local community centers and churches.

I guess you could say the biggest challenge at that time was finding students that were willing to take the abuse, work hard, and actually earn their rank promotions or belts. Jhoon Rhee was a big name in the Washington, D.C., metropolitan area around 1966-1967 and was promoting people to black belt within one year of enrollment. My style, Shorin Ryu, required a minimum of three and a half years to reach black belt level, so this was another reason some students left.

Q: In 1972, you reunited with both Soken Sensei and Kise Sensei. Could you describe that short trip to the U.S.A. and what it meant to you to see those individuals again?

1972 was the first and only trip to the United States for Soken Hohan, and it was the first of many for Kise Fusei. A well-known karate kata winner of tournaments, Glenn Premru, contacted Kise on Okinawa and told him that he had hundreds if not thousands of students that would sign up and become members of an association that could be formed by Soken and Kise here in the U.S.A. Glenn promised Kise a lot of potential income. He said he would pay for the round-trip tickets, hotel, and meals for both he and Soken. At this time, neither Soken nor Kise knew of or had ever heard of Glenn Premru.

In the early 1950s, Soken Hohan, along with four or five other Okinawan masters, formed an association called O.K.F., the Okinawan Karate Federation. Soken Sensei chose to close the O.K.F. on Okinawa, I believe in 1956. Even at that time in the 1950s, Soken Sensei did not like the direction in which Okinawan karate was headed. So in 1972, Soken, Kise, and Glenn Premru formed a new association here in the U.S. by the name of O.K.F. Now at that time Glenn knew of me through the various karate competitions and tournaments that I was attending. He contacted me and asked me to come to Philadelphia to be reunited with my former teachers. As it turned out, Kise had asked Glenn if he knew me, and if he could contact me and ask me to attend.

I was very excited to once again see my old teachers, so I entered the tournament to show my teachers that I had kept up with my training and was still working hard to perfect my art. During that time period, when Soken and Kise were in Philadelphia, we had several meetings to set up the new association. Since neither Soken nor Kise knew of Glenn before this time, Kise asked me to be co-head of the newly formed O.K.F. Both Kise and Soken were very pleased to see me again. They requested that I stay with them from that time on.

Now Soken and Kise had been in the States for only a few days, less than a week, before I was able to see them. When I arrived in Philadelphia and immediately went to see my teachers, I was informed by Kise that Soken was sick. I asked Glenn what he had been feeding these great men. Glenn said he was feeding them the best steaks he could find. I told Glenn that these men don't eat steak, and that they needed to be eating rice and vegetables, not big chunks of meat, so as not to disrupt their normal diet. I immediately took Soken and Kise to a Chinese restaurant and ordered them soup, rice, and vegetables. I also informed Glenn that neither Soken nor Kise lived with air conditioning. When I went to the room, they had towels and blankets placed over the A / C units. I immediately shut them off.

Soken, Kise, and I only had personal time during the late nights after the association business was concluded and whenever we went out to eat. Soken Sensei became so ill that he had to return to Okinawa a few days later. To sum up your question, it meant everything to me to once again be united with my teachers from Okinawa and was sad that it was short lived.

Q: If you were involved in Glenn Premru's O.K.F., how did that eventually turn into you creating S.M.O.K.A (Shorin Ryu Matsumura Orthodox Karate Association)?

As it turned, out Glenn was misappropriating the funds that were being paid to the O.K.F., which were supposed to be sent to Okinawa. Soken Hohan became disillusioned with the whole thing, said he could no longer trust Glenn, and told Kise he was closing the O.K.F. and wanted nothing further to do with Glenn. Now at that time Kise had probably 40 to 60 black belts located here in the States, many of whom had schools. Soken and Kise discussed forming a new association called S.M.O.K.A. They both agreed that this time I should head up the association because they knew and trusted me completely. S.M.O.K.A. was formed by me here in the States, and from that time on I would bring Kise back to the U.S.A. each year for further training and seminars.

Kise Sensei and I broke apart in 1977, which was the same year that Soken Hohan told Kise that he would no longer be his teacher and that Kise could not use the name of Soken Hohan's family system, Matsumura Seito (Orthodox). So here Kise Sensei was without a name for the system of karate he was teaching, thus the formation of his new karate system which he calls Kenshinkan. I sent notices out to all of the members of S.M.O.K.A. and informed them that I was stepping down as president and head of S.M.O.K.A. here in the United States. A few of the member schools said that Kise was not their teacher, and that all of their training was coming through me, thereby requesting that I head up S.M.O.K.A. here in the United States as a separate entity (away from Kenshinkan), of which they would become members; thus the name S.M.O.K.A.-U.S.A. came to be.

Q: As a keeper of old-style karate, what kind of methods and mindset do you try to instill in your students?

First and foremost, I stress that there has to be contact. That is not to say that it has to be full and heavy contact on each and every technique performed, but it should be hard enough to knock the wind out of the person. As an example, if an upper rank student is working with a lower rank below black belt level, the student attacking or punching the face of a lower rank should try to make contact to the forehead, not the nose or jaw. That way if the person that is blocking does not block properly, or execute a properly timed block, the worst he would get is a blow on the forehead. On the other hand, strikes to black belts should always be done with speed and intent to the right location, such as the nose. It is the black belt's job to block or avoid.

Without some contact, there is no reality in training because karate is a fighting art, not a sport. Our system of karate is a tried, tested, and proven form of self-defense. I instill in my students, some of which have been with me for over 40 years, that the kata are to remain unchanged and should be passed to the next generation as they were passed to me. I personally work with each of my students from class to class, doing the same drills, exercises, and fighting techniques of street self-defense as they do. I am not one to stand off to the side just counting and giving commands; I am an active participant. I tried to instill in my students that this art they are learning is an ancient one and one that is not to be abused. Only defend yourself when you have to or for the protection of your love ones and family.

Q: What are some unique trademarks or characteristics that you think make Matsumura Seito special?

Soken Sensei's karate was a family style and came directly from Bushi Matsumura to Nabe, and, of course, to him. It was a closely guarded version not to be taught to many others. I do not feel that he ever taught it to anyone in its entirety.

When I was stationed on Okinawa, Soken's was the only system I came across that made mention of Matsumura Seito, and I was exposed to many, many other styles while on the island. Since the vast popularity of Matsumura Seito Karate came to be known in the late 20th century, it seems a lot of Okinawan styles have made the claim that they are connected to Matsumura's lineage in some way or another, even those that do not have a Shuri-te lineage. In my mind, Arakaki, Kise Fusei, Nishihara, and a couple of others were taught the most by Soken. This, of course, is not to say they were taught the complete system by any means.

Q: How does Matsumura Seito coordinate hard striking with tuite (joint locking), kyusho (vital point striking), grappling, etc? Is one emphasized over another?

Most, if not all, Okinawan systems stress the workings of makiwara conditioning, which translates into hard strikes. Soken Sensei would tell us about when he was a young man, and the games he and others would play. They would spar using tuite-type strikes, holds, and grappling techniques. Soken emphasized point location and accuracy as all-important when fighting an opponent. If Soken Sensei emphasized any one thing to his students, it was focused, hard, constant training.

Q: Soken Sensei is known to have performed some beautiful White Crane Kata and techniques. Did he share his Hakutsuru (White Crane) form with you and other students?

Hakutsuru, as told to me, was Soken Hohan's highest and most guarded kata. That being the case, it was not taught to anyone but a very few senior students of his (Arakaki, Kise, and possibly Nishihira). No American nor other non-Okinawan ever learned this kata.

Soken believed that kata was the true path to knowledge, skill, and mastering of a system. I was never allowed to see his Hakutsuru kata in its entirety, and I never learned this kata. I believe this great kata has been lost forever because of his passing.

Q: What was your motivation for creating your autobiography entitled, *One Man's Quest for Perfection*, and what can readers expect to find in that book?

For years my students, friends, and acquaintances have said to me, you should write a book with all of your life experiences in karate and the many times that you had to use it in self-defense. Over the past 53 years I have been compiling information on various life experiences both with karate and without, so I had quite a bit of information already written in some form or another. It took me about three years to actually write the book with the help of one of my students who is a professional writer and student for over 40 years now.

The book entails some of my life experiences on Okinawa as a young man of 17 years of age as related to karate, how I met Soken Hohan and became his first American student, how I met Kise and the training that I received from him while on Okinawa. My book describes several actual physical altercations that I experienced both in Japan and Okinawa as well as here in the States. In the book, I give what I feel is justification as to why I broke away from my teacher Kise Fusei and the mindset I have about my art. Most of the readers of my book feel that it encourages them and their students to work harder and to remain true to their system of karate. I never state that there is bad karate, however I do think there are bad karate teachers.

George Alexander

Born in 1947, Alexander Sensei began his martial arts journey in the 1960s. Starting as a Judoka, Alexander Sensei quickly expanded his experience into the realms of Shorin Ryu, Goju Ryu, and Kyokushin. He ultimately ended up on Okinawa on his way to Vietnam where he served in the U.S. Marine Corps 3rd Force Reconnaissance Company. Stationed in Dong Ha, he often led teams on jungle reconnaissance and information gathering missions throughout 1967 and 1968.[66]

Interspersed with his duty in Vietnam, Alexander Sensei became a direct student of notable Okinawan instructors such as Shimabukuro Eizo, Kise Fusei, Odo Seikichi, and Kuda Yuichi. After decades of study in karate, Alexander Sensei expanded his experience into the realms of kendo and White Crane, amongst other pursuits.[67]

Alexander Sensei is responsible for some of the most important books in publication on the topic of martial arts. Two of his seminal works include *Okinawa: Island of Karate*, and *Bubishi: Martial Arts Spirit*.

Q: Alexander Sensei, how did you get your start in the martial arts, and what was the whole "scene" like at that time?

Well, I started when I was a kid. My dad had been in the Army Air Force and was teaching

---

[66] "Martial Arts Biography - George W. Alexander." *U.S.A.dojo.com*, 2006. Web. 15 Nov. 2014.
<http://www.U.S.A.dojo.com/biographies/george-alexander.htm>.
[67] "George W. Alexander - Worldbudokan." 2006. Web. 15 Nov. 2014
<http://worldbudokan.com/worlbudokanhome/about/board-of-directors/>.

something they called Combat Judo. At that time (late '50s, early '60s or so), there was no karate around. I was intrigued by Judo initially, and ultimately, I joined the military myself (United States Marine Corps 1964).

Shortly into my military career, I started studying Shorin Ryu at Camp Lejeune in North Carolina. I did that until 1967 when I was transferred to Okinawa.

George Alexander performing a sidekick while in a Marine Corps "Hooch", 1968.

Q: Is that when you started studying with Kuda Yuichi, who you cite as your primary Sensei in Shorin Ryu?

Actually, no. I didn't study with Kuda Sensei until later. I spent a good many years studying with different sensei on the island. Two you may have heard of are Shimabukuro Eizo of Shorin Ryu (later referred to as Shobayashi Ryu) and Kise Fusei of Matsumura Seito.

Q: It must have been very educational on the island where so many outstanding instructors were accessible. When did you ultimately decide to train with Kuda Sensei?

I spent a good 20 years in training before that. I think up until 1984 . . . or '85. So before that I was learning a lot about Shorin Ryu, Shotokan, Goju Ryu, and Kyokushinkai.

Q: What was training like during that era? Did you find it different than modern training trends?

I think the '70s were kind of a "macho" era. There were no kids in karate, or very few. It was a lot of young men with a lot of testosterone, so it was kind of a knock-em-around environment. Then the '80s were the decade of *The Karate Kid* with Mr. Miyagi and wax-on-wax-off. Much more contemplative. The '90s were more about sport karate, and we saw the emergence of a lot of federations. Now it seems we have come full circle, in a sense, where we have M.M.A. (mixed martial arts). These are individuals who are interested in combining all kinds of styles together, which I think is a bit more like what the original karate instructors had intended. Of course, M.M.A. is still very heavy sport-oriented, as was the influence of the '90s.

Q: Could you expand upon the idea of old-style karate and M.M.A. having similar mindsets?

The world, and the things in it, are dynamic and they're bound to change. So I always like to use the old Matsumura saying: "Change with the times." Matsumura Sokon, a fountainhead of Okinawa karate wisdom, said that to one of his students when he [Matsumura Sokon] was in his 80s. He wrote his student a letter containing that message.

Of course, that doesn't mean give up whatever martial art you're doing and do M.M.A. Actually, too much adherence to trends has resulted in some of the "factionalizing" that we see today. Every decade seems to have a trend (like ninja in the '80s), and clearly M.M.A. is this decade's hot trend. It's important to decide whether you want to pursue a martial art or martial sport.

Q: You have studied kobudo training alongside your karate training, collecting experience from a handful of reputable instructors. Would you consider yourself a collector?

Yes, I would. In fact, a lot of the early kobudo practitioners were collectors. Mabuni Kenwa was certainly a collector. Taira Shinken — he went around Okinawa collecting and codifying 40 or so different weapons kata into a system. Odo Seikichi Sensei of Okinawa Kenpo did so as well.

Alexander Sensei with noted kobudo expert Odo Seikichi of Okinawa Kenpo.

It was no different for me. I learned kata and technique here and there, but then established myself in Kuda Sensei's kobudo program. I think it's valuable to learn that way because no one person has it all. You have to interact with different sensei to get different knowledge.

Q: Speaking of gaining experience from different instructors, you studied Shorinji Ryu Jujitsu in addition to karate. What is Shorinji Ryu Jujitsu, and where did you learn it?

Shorinji Ryu Jujitsu traces its roots to Japan, but I trained under Ken Penland Hanshi. The style, more or less, came from Albert C. Church. There are 20 two-man kata, which are training drills in Jujitsu technique. Ultimately, it shares the same principles as most jujutsu styles (a wrist lock is a wrist lock, an armbar is an armbar).

Q: One of the things you are best known for is your experience in Hakutsuru (White Crane) Kenpo. Could you discuss a little bit about what that is, and why you've dug so hard to uncover and preserve the principles of Hakutsuru?

Well it actually became a sort of quest! You may recall *The Karate Kid* movie with the crane kick and all that — those techniques were perpetuated by Soken Hohan and Kuda Yuichi, which is ultimately where I came to do a lot of my training. Due to those instructors and the movies, my interest was peaked as to what the Hakutsuru techniques were all about, especially after I had studied Naihanchi, Pinan, Passai, Kusanku, etc. for so long.

Ultimately I came to ask myself, "Hmm...what else is there?" Well the Matsumura lineage has its own Hakutsuru . . . but you go past that and start to wonder where THAT came from. Eventually it leads to the fact that there were certain instructors who were teaching these White Crane concepts in Okinawa . . . and historical curiosity keeps pushing past each barrier to something deeper. I've been doing that for probably 25 years, trying to get to the bottom of White Crane.

The paths of all this study continuously led me back to China. The evidence was so powerful, in fact, that I decided to visit China myself two years ago and pursue the study even further, experiencing the area myself.

Q: That must have been an amazing trip. What did you unearth there?

Through that trip I was better able to trace the White Crane lineage, even as it jumped from China to Okinawa. What it amounts to is that the White Crane style (or southern White Crane style more specifically) is what influenced Okinawan karate the most. Southern White Crane mythology suggests that a woman started it about 350 years ago in Yong Chun village in the Fujian Province. I happened to go there and had the chance to talk and train with the masters still practicing the style in one form or another.

I actually did a documentary to help record these findings called *Yong Chun White Crane*, and another called *In Search of Shaolin*.

It was all part of a larger search. As I began putting these connections together, I noticed a strong influence of White Crane on Naha-te, more so than Shuri-te and Tomari-te, the other two major styles of the time.

Of course, there were exceptions. Soken Hohan, of my own lineage (Matsumura Shorin Ryu, which is strongly connected to Shuri-te), was known to have studied with a Chinese man named Gokenki. Gokenki was an herbalist and tea merchant, but also a traveler who visited Okinawa around 1910. He influenced many Okinawans with White Crane, including Matayoshi Shinko, Miyagi Chojun of Goju Ryu, Mabuni Kenwa of Shito-Ryu, and perhaps Uechi Kanbun as well.

Higashionna Kanryo of Naha-te, one of Miyagi Chojun's Sensei, traveled to China in the late 1800s and studied under two masters named Ryu Ru Ko and Waishinzan. He was rumored to have acquired great skill under these men and even acquainted himself with other Chinese styles during his days there.

There are a few other lineages of this nature, but you can see how the connections started to develop and how White Crane could have assimilated and mixed with Okinawan technique as these experts continued to train and seek out new approaches to their art.

One important thing to note is that Hakutsuru karate doesn't exist as a separate style on Okinawa. It was always integrated into the arts. But as I saw it fading out more and more, I decided to put extra effort into preserving it. That is why you see me offering it separately from karate like Shorin Ryu in the form of Hakutsuru Kenpo. It helps the preservation efforts, and, really, anybody can benefit as the old masters did.

Recently, the Okinawan government took note of what I was doing and actually sent me a Menkyo (teacher's license) in recognition of their approval.

Q: That's significant. Did you have to apply for something like that?

Actually, no I didn't. They just sort of heard about me. It wasn't my original intention to develop anything official. I'm just like a green belt running around out there trying to learn more stuff, and I think I'm always going to have that mentality. But over the years the recognition just kinda happened.

Q: How important do you think hojo undo (body hardening and strengthening) is in traditional training? Some people swear by it, while others find it a bit antiquated for modern society.

Alexander Sensei performing Ishi Sashi technique with modern kettlebells.

There are a few ways you can look at it. What hojo undo originally did was make you stronger. If you were stronger you could be a better fighter and would, therefore, be better at self-defense.

There's a counter argument from the modern perspective — when was the last time you actually defended yourself? Sure if you hang out in dark alleys and shady bars you may have to, but in normal day-to-day life, is it applicable? Why are we doing all this?

The whole point of hojo undo, I think, is preserving tradition and enhancing other aspects of your martial arts. Two prime examples: the first is developing a stronger martial spirit, which helps you with everyday trials and tribulations, and the other is improving your health. Kata and sparring help with cardio, but hojo undo fills in the gap with resistance training (which develops muscle tissue and bone density).

Q: Another big question for traditional karateka is how many kata to focus on (a handful, a dozen, two dozen, etc.) In your personal training, how do you handle kata diversity?

For my personal training, I tend to focus on just a few kata. You may be able to do every kata in a system all the time . . . but then that's all you do. I try to diversify, both in class and on my own, and dig deeper into kata as much as I practice the form itself.

Q: How do you see kyusho (vital point striking) factoring into overall training when compared to other elements of karate? It seems like there can be preoccupation sometimes with kyusho and the "magic touch" effects it can inflict on an opponent.

Yes, I've seen that as well. I think kyusho has to be part of a larger whole. It's kind of like saying, "I'm going to study karate, but I'm only going to focus on front kick. Front kick is all that matters." Well, no, there's round kick too! And let's not forget about down block.

Kyusho-jitsu is part of the whole picture. When I first started training in Shotokan in the '60s, there was very little focus on it. Over the years it has developed and grown in popularity. Unfortunately, as kyusho grows in complexity, it requires more and more compliant opponents. Sometimes you have to pare it back down, even though it's less impressive than some of the fancy stuff you can do with a helper standing very still right in front of you.

A lot of the basic kyusho points follow the centerline — throat, chin, nose, groin; not fancy, but effective. The Chinese say there are 108 vital points. They also integrate chi flow which follows 14 meridians, and a two-hour clock that shifts chi points. So in the heat of combat you have to remember what time it is, where the chi is, and where to hit . . . it gets complicated and technical if you let it.

Q: You are part of the current generation which is helping preserve and guide the martial arts as a whole. Where would you like to see the next few generations take the martial arts?

I think . . . the martial arts are going to continue to evolve and change. The only thing we can do is try to nurture it along, and make sure that the knowledge everyone has maintained so far gets passed along correctly. A lot of times things can get watered down and the quality suffers. So quality control is an issue. Things are getting better, I think, but its important that we all keep pushing for that.

I've also noticed that people are more open than they were in the past to learning new things. I can remember in the '60s, if you use the Bruce Lee example, the Chinese were upset with him because he was teaching non-Chinese. That racial tension existed all over the place. I see a lot less of that now. The protectionism has really diminished, and I think it's good to see people being able to learn things that were not at all attainable not so long ago.

Ronald Lindsey

Born in 1945, Ronald Lindsey grew up a fit Texas athlete with a talent for football; however, his life's path led him to military service, and eventually to Okinawa where he truly began his martial arts career. During that time, Lindsey Sensei distinguished himself through contributions to Military Police operations and martial arts.

After his service in the Army, Lindsey Sensei returned to the United States and became an influential teacher and researcher. His studies focused on the history of Okinawan Bushi (warriors), as well as the role of Hakutsuru (White Crane) in Okinawan karate. His written work culminated in a book entitled *Okinawa No Bushi No Te*, an extensive worked filled with Lindsey Sensei's thoughts, findings, and martial concepts.

Q: Lindsey Sensei, what made you decide to join the military, and where did your service take you geographically?

I was commissioned from the Cadet Corps at Texas A&M University. I could have played professional football but chose to serve Uncle Sam as an officer instead. I was in the U.S. Army Military Police and went to Okinawa, Korea, the Philippines, and so forth. I also went TDY (Temporary Duty) numerous times to South Vietnam. The years that I served as active duty military were 1968,1969,1970, and for a number of years after as a reserve officer. I was first stationed on Okinawa in 1968.

My main job while in the Army was training military dogs. At one time I had over 300 German military police dogs. We were training sentries and scouts; I actually wrote the lesson plan and carried out the program to train the first drug detection dogs ever used in the military.

Q: According to your biography, your study of martial arts began in 1963 in Shotokan. This would have been while you were still in the United States. Who did you study with and what prompted you to seek out lessons?

I was from a little town called Hallettsville, Texas. We didn't have any karate schools there. During the summers, when I was not at Texas A&M, I worked in Houston, Texas. At that time I trained in Shotokan at Japan Ways in the Southern part of Houston. The karate training was good in terms of intensity, but it was nothing compared to the football training I got during my college years. What we actually did at Texas A&M was probably the hardest football practices ever conducted in the game, and that was under Gene Stallings, a protégé of Bear Bryant. They made us literally fight against each other during the off-season program. It was not Asian fighting, but it certainly was combat training. In the end there were less than 44 boys who did not quit Gene Stallings' program out of about 140 athletes who were there when the program started. That was very rigorous training. You learned not to hesitate. This gave me an edge even when I went to Okinawa and participated in karate training, especially bogu sparring.

I don't recall who was teaching at Japan Ways at that time, but I did pick up a number of kata including the Heian and Tekki forms, so I had some familiarity with karate training when I got to Okinawa in 1968.

Q: When you heard you were going to be stationed on Okinawa, did you have karate in mind right away or were you entirely focused on military responsibilities?

The military aspect had to be my number one priority. Nevertheless, I looked for karate as soon as possible. There were two things I wanted right away when I got to Okinawa — to improve my karate, and to find a Japanese Samurai sword. I was able to accomplish the former. Actually, I only saw four Japanese swords the whole time I was there. At that time on Okinawa, you had to have written permission to even own one.

Q: You studied under a number of top tier masters over the years, but who was your first teacher on the island? What drew you to him over other options?

The very first style I studied was Uechi Ryu under Shinjo Seiyu. My wife and I lived in a little housing development called Morgan Manor near Kadena Village. To get there you had to go around the Kadena Village traffic circle. On that circle was Shinjo Sensei's dojo. As a sidenote, Shinjo Sensei was the father of the now famous Shinjo Kiyohide, a man of great martial talent.

A short time after joining Shinjo Sensei's dojo, I was on duty as the Armed Forces Police Duty Officer in Okinawa (all company grade officers in the First M.P. Group were required to serve about once per week as duty officer). One of the Duty Officer's "check points" was to check the M.P. substation in Koza. While I was at the substation, I told one of our interpreters about how I started karate with Shinjo Sensei. The interpreter said, "Oh, the person who owns the store next door also does karate." So I went over and ended up meeting Kinjo Seizan (alt. spelling: Seizen or Seisan), whose parents owned the store. Kinjo lived either on top of or behind the store at that time and was a student of Shorin Ryu Matsumura Seito under Grandmaster Soken Hohan and Master Kise Fusei.

As a result of that meeting, I started training with Kinjo Sensei. We would meet at that store and then go down a nearby alley to Kise Sensei's dojo where we would work out. At that time I was the only American in the dojo. The training was about 50% kata and 50% bogu gear fighting.

Q: Could you tell us what Kinjo Sensei was like as an individual? Was he stern, fun loving, etc?

His personality was jovial and easy to get along with. He was really strong for his size. At that time in my martial arts career, he was the type of teacher I needed. We did kata training, but it was not very strict. What he wanted to do was teach both bogu gear fighting (fighting with kendo-like armor) and then real fighting techniques. Much of what we did was called tuite (joint locking), but was different than the tuite you see nowadays.

The tuite we did on Okinawa , at least that I learned, was mostly pressure point hitting. The only major difference between our tuite and regular karate was instead of striking we used compression with our thumb or one of the knuckles of the fingers. Now it seems like a lot of modern tuite is almost like jujutsu; we didn't really do that. Encounters in those days were over in a second or two…or half a second.

Q: How did your training with Kinjo Sensei eventually lead to your studying with Soken Hohan Sensei?

Well Soken Sensei was the head of the system, so everybody drifted toward him. Especially during the summer of 1970, I would go with Kinjo Sensei and we would train in Soken's dojo.

Q: Was Soken Hohan able to practice / demonstrate / conduct class himself or had old age relegated him to the sideline?

The thing about Soken Hohan is this — he, and people of that generation, did not have formal classes. You did not have classes where you lined up, bowed in, and things like that. They did not use formal terms for a lot of things; you were expected to watch and follow and they would correct. They didn't focus on a lot of verbal bunkai discussion. Some people found Soken Sensei to be stern, but I did not think that. He was very capable for his age and he would demonstrate, counter, and so forth.

Kuda Yuichi said Soken taught 50 / 50 kata and fighting techniques. I found him to do more fighting technique training than say Odo Seikichi Sensei (Okinawa Kenpo), who focused more on kata.

Q: Did Soken Sensei have much of an issue with you as a foreigner?

No. That is the biggest falsehood that I hear about American karate is that the Okinawans didn't like us or train us. Think about it this way — I was side-by-side with Okinawans training at the same time. When did these Okinawans supposedly learn "special techniques" separate from what I learned . . . at 3 in the morning? We were there, they were there, it was all the same thing. Sometimes we had difficulty with understanding the language, but that was the only barrier.

Q: Do you feel as if the Okinawans would make character judgments of foreigners and restrict certain teachings as a result?

Not particularly. If a person came to the dojo regularly, he received training. Now, there are certain levels of absorption that have to take place before you are able to learn certain things. Some things the Okinawans tried to teach you and you may not have been capable of learning yet. Many Americans that studied on Okinawa returned to America shortly after their time there. They may have received a black belt while there, but they also may have quit practicing or may have never found another teacher.

Had they gone back and found a teacher, the second level and third level of learning may have gradually sunk in, but there is a time element involved that cannot be shortened due to the physical and mental level of absorption. On Okinawa, unless a person was a real "jerk," they received training. In some cases senior students would show us advanced stuff when the primary sensei wasn't looking.

Q: Could you describe some of the unique characteristics of Matsumura Seito? How much emphasis did Soken Sensei place on Hakutsuru forms and techniques over other methods?

Soken Hohan's style as compared to other Shorin Ryu styles is different. In Soken's style, there was not a lot of block-then-punch and there was no fighting or punching with the hand chambered on the hip; chambering the fist was mainly done only during kata. The hands were always out in front and techniques were done at one time, block and strike at the same moment. Tai sabaki, body change, was used at all times.

Soken's karate was never associated with the karate that was brought into the Okinawan public schools systems. They (my Okinawan teachers) called Soken's karate "straight karate." They meant it was a straight line from Matsumura Sokon, through Matsumura Nabe, to Soken Hohan. Other styles of karate that were being modified and put into the school systems they referred to as "school karate." Stright karate (or "village karate") like

Soken's style, was considered by my teachers to be unaltered and different from the school styles.

Soken Sensei performing nukite, thrusting with the point of the fingers.

In Soken Sensei's style, the hands were held open and the finger tips were used heavily. A lot of pressure points were used along with low kicks. For example, Soken Hohan did not have a back kick. He would just change his body 180 degrees and use a low front whipping kick. He did not bring his knee up; instead, he would cock the heel backwards slightly and then whip the foot up from the ground, using the big toe as the impact point.

Hakutsuru was seeded throughout the whole style. A lot of the village karate kept many of the techniques that were discarded in school karate.

Q: Did Soken Sensei have any anxiety about the changes going on in karate, especially in terms of modified techniques and kata in school karate?

I have a letter in my book where Chibana Chosin wrote to Soken Hohan, inviting him to the meeting in 1956 where they started the first Okinawan Karate Renmei. Soken Sensei was troubled by the idea that karate was changing. He made very few changes in his own style from what he learned when he was younger except what was needed to adapt as he got older due to body limitations and improvement in understanding.

Q: There isn't much known about Soken Hohan's teacher, Matsumura Nabe, and the other direct students of Matsumura Sokon. Did Soken Sensei ever discuss his teacher or that generation?

It's important to understand the Okinawan culture in regards to this, especially people of Grandmaster Soken's generation. They were old and it was considered disrespectful to ask questions like that. They would offer some little tidbits sometimes. One time Soken Sensei told a story of Matsumura Nabe doing his kata and Funakoshi Gichin, the father of

Japanese karate, was caught watching through a hole in the fence. Besides such stories from time to time, he didn't say much. I know he looked for Matsumura Nabe when he returned to Okinawa in 1952 from Argentina. It seems that Nabe died sometime around World War II or just prior to the War.

In regards to Matsumura Nabe — the "Nabe" was actually just a nickname. When you see his name written in Japanese it is never written in kanji; it's always in hiragana, which means it is a pronunciation instead of "picture writing." Kuda Yuichi said that Nabe was a "baby san" name. Nabe's last name might not even have been Matsumura; it could have been something else. I have some more extensive research in my book, but off hand I recall that Matsumura Nabe may also have been called Nagahama Nabi no Tanmei and maybe even Ko Ishigawa.[68]

The Okinawans often had multiple names throughout their lives. Sometimes they would use their wives maiden surnames. In the case of Nabe specifically, there was a period in his life when he was on the run from the Japanese. He supposedly hid out on Ishima for a while. He might have actively avoided the use of the name Matsumura.

There is little recorded history of Matsumura Nabe and karate in general, and even worse a lot of historic objects were destroyed during the Battle of Okinawa.

Q: How much focus did Soken Sensei place on bunkai during training?

Generally the Okinawans didn't teach bunkai. The trick was to ask them leading questions. If they showed you something you would have to tell them that it wouldn't work, then they might show you something a little more. Bunkai, as it appears today, is a non-Okinawan need. The real secret to Okinawan karate is not bunkai, it's the coordination of trying to perfect kata. That, combined with the principles of shuhari, lead to exceptional coordination and understanding. When your coordination is really good you can do many things as a reflex action; this is the last step in shuhari.

Mr. Kuda would say, "Your bunkai good, his bunkai good, everybody's bunkai good."

Q: Could you talk about when Kise Fusei began his study with Soken Sensei and what role

---

[68] Further investigation on this can be found in *Okinawa No Bushi No Te* on pg. 136-137.

Kise Sensei played in the dojo?

Kise Fusei was a senior in Soken's dojo, although he was not the only senior. Soken Sensei had what we called the "big 5" — Arakaki Seiki was his senior student. I believe Arakaki's father and Soken were boyhood friends. They both grew up in Nishihara Village. Arakaki was number one. Mitsuo Inoue was second. In addition there was Kohama Jushin, Nishihira Kosei, and Nakazato Hideo. Those five guys were from the Nishihara Village area and studied more with Soken than many others. That being said, there were others that studied too, including Kuda Yuichi, Kise Fusei, Nishimei, Takaya Yabiku, Ushiro, Saha, etc. Many people also came to Soken Sensei for specialized training, say in the sai or bo or fighting techniques. Even Taira Shinken came to him on some occasions. He had a lot of students.

Ronald Lindsey with Kise Fusei, who was one of Lindsey Sensei's early influences in Matsumura Seito.

There is often discussion regarding whether or not Kise was the direct successor to Soken

Sensei, and if Kise received a Menkyo Kaiden (scroll of direct transmission). Let's go ahead and look at that a bit. This should be read with the understanding that I studied with Kise; his skill and mastery of Matsumura Seito are not being called into question.

First of all, it would have been out of character for an Okinawan of Soken's generation to issue a Menkyo Kaiden to anyone. That was not a widely used Okinawan method of the time; it was more based in Japanese arts and only came into practice later as Japanese influence gained momentum in Okinawa. As such, I do not believe Kise Sensei received a Menko Kaiden from Soken Sensei.

Soken Hohan died in 1982. At that time Kise Sensei claimed that he was the successor to Matsumura Seito. I wrote an article back then entitled "The Last Samurai" covering that issue. After extensive research, I found no declared heir by Soken Hohan. Arakaki Sensei went directly to Kise and asked if he received a Menkyo Kaiden from Soken, and the answer was no.

Kuda Sensei also said no; that this transmission did not occur and that the successorship would go by age starting with Arakaki.

I have been told that in Kise's dojo there was / is no Menko Kaiden from Grandmaster Soken. Soken Hohan had a falling out with Kise in the late 1970s. I don't know how well they mended those fences before Soken died.

I have been told that Soken Sensei denied Kise permission to use the name Shorin Ryu Matsumura Seito, which I think was the wrong thing to do. Certainly Kise Fusei was an expert in Soken's art. I think that after a number of years went by and people started dying, including Arakaki, Kise took whatever legal action was needed to get permission to use that name. I also believe it was correct for Kise to use the name Matsumura Seito due to his hard work and dedication to the style.

Of course there is the matter of the Japanese government recognizing Kise as a progenitor of Soken's style. I don't think the Japanese government can truly take a family art and give it to another person. They can provide permission to use the name, but can the government give the style over to someone? I think not.

I could be wrong on this topic…but my research has been thorough and I have spoken with a good many Okinawans about it, all of whom were close to the situation and tend to agree with me.

Q: You've seen Matsumura Seito spread out over the course of a generation. What do you think of the developments and changes or lack thereof?

What you have to understand is that Okinawan teachers and culture did not have a longing need to preserve a style 100% as it was. Instead they follow a principle known as suhari.

Suhari (su-ha-ri) . . . "su" means that during the first time period of training (5 years, 10 years, time varies with the individual) you emulate your teacher and try to make everything exactly like him or her. Then the "ha" is another time period. During this time it is natural for you to make some changes according to what you need and can do as long as it doesn't violate the principles of the ryu. The "ri" is when everything becomes automatic and it just, boom, happens. Really suhari is the natural way of doing things.

This used to really bother me. I knew my kata were drifting from what I learned in Okinawa, which was natural since I was built different than an Okinawan. Over a period of time my kata became my kata, although I always tried to keep them like Soken Sensei, especially in principle. Anybody who says they are doing Soken Hohan's kata is not really telling the truth. They think they are, but kata drift according to what each person's body can do best. This is not to mention the age factor, which also alters the kata. When Soken Hohan died, his style died. The principles and how they can be applied are still alive, but my kata became uniquely mine and so it is with all karateka.

Q: How did you come to meet Kuda Yuichi Sensei, and did you train extensively with him?

I knew him in Okinawa and trained with him, but I really started studying under him when I got directly involved with his organization. Kuda Sensei blended Okinawa Kenpo with Shorin Ryu Matsumura Seito to found Shorin Ryu Matsumura Kenpo.

I actually switched from Kise Fusei's kata to Kuda Yuichi's kata one afternoon; my senior student Charles Tatum and I switched once we saw how Kuda was teaching and performing his kata. Kise Fusei is a brilliant tactician and his fighting techniques are very good. Kata-wise he does a bit of blending, and shortcutting, and his own "thing." On the other hand, Kuda Sensei was very precise and his teachings were very precise. He was not as flamboyant and flashy, but he had really good fighting techniques too. Kuda Sensei was a bigger physical person than Kise Sensei, which suited me well since I am also a big person.

Ronald Lindsey with Kuda Yuichi. Yuichi Sensei was one of the most important influences on Lindsey Sensei's martial arts career.

It's important to note that although there were differences between the methods of Kise and Kuda, at a high level they were executing very similar concepts. When you hear these heated arguments about small details, this way versus that, it really misses the point of what the teachers were doing. They were merely executing suhari, just as we attempt to.

One thing I think a lot of people are missing in their training is the experience of seeing the old masters train on their own. When teachers like Kuda Sensei and Kise Sensei trained on their own, it was different than when they taught classes. They would ad lib and add different timings, alter techniques, and other similar principles.

In the old days kata was a living thing, not meant to be set in concrete. It was a set of principles that could be tweaked and used to explore and teach and learn. Using the concepts of the kata, the teacher would optimize it to each individual. He would walk behind and around you and make mental drawings of your procedures and how it could be optimized to you. Their methods would make you stronger just by correcting your kata.

Q: When you returned to the United States, did you begin developing a school and association right away? If so, what were some difficulties you experienced at the time?

I noticed in the United States that there was a lot of focus on getting quick promotion. There was a big mindset (and still is) of wanting to get a one-up on someone else. The problem with a lot of organizations is that they are not really organizations . . . they are cults. I did not do that.

We had a quality standard, and I wanted people to meet that standard. Rank has a tendency to devalue over time and become worthless if there are no high standards being met. I brought Okinawan Sensei over and we held large camps to spread the cost and make it affordable for everyone involved. Not too many other people wanted to do that because they wanted extended personal time with the sensei instead of sharing that time. There was a lot of ego involved with spending time with the sensei. All of these ego trips made it difficult to teach traditional karate.

Q: Who were some of the other big players in the United States when you started your organization? Was this at the same time as men like Robert Trias and Ed Parker?

I did not personally know the people you mentioned. At first I only taught a few people and never got involved in sport karate. I did my organizational work in the late 1970s through the mid 1980s. My sole purpose was for education, which is why I started a newsletter at the same time based on what I learned on Okinawa (history, technique, and kata). I believe this predated a lot of the important works done by men like George Alexander and John Sells.

We did not advertise a whole lot. We tried to select people and ask if they wanted to get involved and train with us. Although all of us in the organization did Matsumura Seito, we still invited other people to our events because they could walk away with useful principles to add to their art.

Q: When did you meet and train with Odo Seikichi Sensei? Could you talk a bit about your experiences with him and what you were able to learn from him?

I met him when I was on Okinawa and trained with him for a while there. I got to the point where I was ready to test for Shodan in Nago (the location of Nakamura Shigeru's dojo), but I was already a black belt so I couldn't see the point in getting another one.

When I trained with Odo Sensei I wasn't so concerned about emulating his physical technique specifically, but I liked his mental attitude and the way he treated his students. He would encourage people and would always be in good spirits. He said things like, "Don't try TOO hard," or, "Take it easy." One thing he really liked to say was, "Kill him a little bit," which meant to slow down, learn the technique right, and focus on quality over raw speed or power. Sometimes too much muscular tension and effort were actually counterproductive.

Odo Sensei was a true gentleman.

Q: Could you talk about the relationships between great instructors like Odo Sensei, Kuda Sensei, etc. who all knew each other on the island?

Kise, Kuda, Odo and others were all friends and contemporaries . . . and rivals. Of course at different times they were also all enemies, depending on who was trying to woo students to make more money. If you got any one of them to yourself they would express doubt / concern about the other guys, but then when they would get together they were the best of friends. It's important to remember that the Okinawans were people, no different than anybody else. People want to better themselves financially and in terms of status. It's important not to fault them too hard or hold them up too high. Imperfect attitudes were more prevalent on Okinawa than some people would like to admit, and wasn't unique to my teachers.

Kuda Yuichi, Odo Seikichi, and Kise Fusei sharing a moment of reprieve during a karate tournament at the Schilling Community Center at Kadena Air Base.

Q: How did training on Okinawa when you were there differ from what individuals might experience nowadays?

One very key difference is the military factor. If you were in the Army, Marine Corps, or Navy in Okinawa, you had to take a combat proficiency test twice a year. You trained continuously to get ready for that test which was, of course, getting you ready for the act of combat. We started our work day way before dawn. We conducted the Army "Daily Dozen" and then finished that with a four mile run. After that we went to work for the U.S. military. At the end of our military work day we repeated the Army "Daily Dozen" and the four mile run. Then we went to karate training for a number of hours. We did this five to six days a week.

Going over to train in Okinawa now is less strenuous. Today, visiting students don't get up before dawn and undergo rigorous workouts before daylight. Their training is different from what we did some 40 to 50 years ago. We lived a Spartan lifestyle.

Okinawan G.I.'s (American Servicemen during the 1950s, 1960s, and early 1970s) were on the island at a special time. There were teachers who had trained directly with older masters, who were, in fact, Samurai (Shizoku). What was learned by them and initially passed down to us was the old art. That time is now gone. According to men like Kuda Yuichi and Nakaza Seiei, there is more old karate now in the United States than there is in Okinawa, tucked away with the G.I.'s. Many Okinawan Sensei are now focused on business and sport karate. There are just a few teaching old karate, and you'd be hard pressed to find them.

Q: In a lot of modern dojo, we often hear the term "oss" or "osu" used. Did you detect a lot of that on Okinawa?

We never heard it on Okinawa. It was not said when I was there. I asked Kuda Sensei about it one time because we had a number of Shito Ryu people at one of our camps, and they were doing a lot of oss-ing. Kuda Sensei said it was okay if they wanted to do it, and that it just meant "Hi." I also asked Shimabukuro Zenpo, Tomoyose Ryuko, and several others, all of whom said that it was not a term the Okinawan masters used.

Q: You recently released a book called *Okinawa No Bushi No Te*. Could you tell us a little bit about this work and what readers might gain from it?

I started writing the book shortly after I got back from Okinawa in 1970. I was gathering historical material while on Okinawa because I wanted to learn the history. I am somewhat of an amateur military historian as well. In my civilian job I was in the agricultural extension service, which meant I wrote thousands of newsletters and newspaper articles and pamphlets. I have written a lot of stuff over the years. Previously I had written a karate magazine called *Maishin Shorinji* which was all educational material. I tried to steer clear of politics and nay-saying because there is nothing to be gained by doing this, focusing instead on history. Of course, there will be people who disagree with my history and findings, and that's totally fine. The thing about Okinawan history is that it greatly depends on who you get it from, how they slant their history, and what they want you to know. All you can do is present the facts as best you can.

Q: What could you tell the next generation of karateka to help them preserve the essence of karate and kobudo as you have come to understand it?

In terms of passing the arts to the next generation...there are a lot of people who studied in Okinawa but have not contributed much after they left the island. They have not produced high quality students, or they have taken long extended breaks in training and then come back and want everyone to treat them with respect. Hell...they have moved back toward beginner level, not forward toward expertise! Maintaining training and contributing to the next generation is key to becoming a true karate senior.

In terms of advice, I would have to say this — you cannot learn every kata invented, so don't try. Find a school and learn the core curriculum. Knowing 25-30 kata does not mean you know 25-30 times more than a person who knows less kata. We (including myself) have made the mistake of trying to learn too many kata. Learn a few kata well instead of many halfway. Train persistently and do not quit.

Chapter 9 –
Okinawa Kenpo

Due to Okinawa's tumultuous history with conquering powers, karate and kobudo have long been intentionally obfuscated, guarded closely as a cultural treasure and last resort tools of life protection for the Okinawan people. It wasn't until the early 20th century that communication and demonstration of the art truly opened up.

In the earliest years of the 1900s, important men such as Itosu Anko made a push to integrate karate into the Okinawan school systems. This move toward public education was combined with a series of demonstrations. Many of karate's early demos were for important Japanese political figures, including Admiral Dewa of the Imperial Japanese Navy in 1912 and the Crown Prince Hirohito in 1921. Influential karateka like Funakoshi Gichin were also beginning to make their presence known in Japan itself.[69] Japan had taken a much more active role in integrating Okinawa into Japanese lifestyle and mindset, as well as conscripting Okinawans into the Japanese Army. As a result, when they saw the potential benefits of karate training for soldiers and for overall cultural hegemony, they supported and guided the growth of karate on a much larger scale.

It was in this climate of growth and integration of karate that Nakamura Shigeru was born. Nakamura's father was a man who valued education; he used his financial success to ensure that young Shigeru was accepted into the Icchu First National Okinawan Junior High School, a well known educational facility located in Shuri. Although exposed to karate as a youth, Nakamura Shigeru continued his karate journey under preeminent

---

[69] Sells, John. *Unante: The Secrets of Karate*. City of publication: WM Hawley, 1995. 70-75. Print.

masters like Hanashiro Chomo and Yabu Kentsu while in school. As he grew, he increased his exposure to other experts like Itosu Anko and Higashionna Kanryo.[70]

After his school years, Nakamura Sensei moved back to Nago in the northern part of Okinawa and was accepted as a personal student of Kuniyoshi Shinkichi, a renowned keeper of "old style" karate and an individual who traveled to China to study the roots of the art.

As a result of his decades of quality training and experience, Nakamura Sensei became a well-known and respected master on the island. Concerned about the stylistic fracturing of karate throughout the early-to-mid 1900s, Nakamura attempted to create an umbrella group for all Okinawan karateka. He named it "Okinawa Kenpo," and had the support of many influential masters of the time, including Shimabuku Zenryo and Uehara Seikichi. While the Okinawa Kenpo umbrella never succeeded in gathering all karateka, the name did stick in regards to Nakamura's own brand of karate.

A number of skilled practitioners became known for their prowess in Okinawa Kenpo, including Oyata Seiyu, Kise Fusei, and Nakamura Taketo. Upon Nakamura Sensei's passing the style was placed under the care of Odo Seikichi, one of Nakamura's most senior students and a savant of Okinawa karate and kobudo.

---

[70] Apsokardu, Matthew. *Shigeru Nakamura: A Study of the Man Responsible for Okinawa Kenpo Karate*. Place of publication: Matthew Apsokardu, 2014. *IkigaiWay*. Web. 20 Nov. 2014.

Necomedes Flores

Necomedes (Nick) Flores was born in 1943 and grew up in South Texas. Introduced to karate at a young age by his older brother, Flores Sensei later found himself learning karate from the source as he traveled to Okinawa as part of his Marine Corps duty.

Flores Sensei was an early student of Uechi Kanei and developed the potent internal strength inherent in the art. While on the island, Flores Sensei made an effort to expand his exposure to various arts; however, the bulk of his training would eventually come at the hands of Odo Seikichi, inheritor of Okinawa Kenpo. Flores Sensei has also enjoyed a lasting relationship with Nakamura Taketo, son of Nakamura Shigeru, an important Okinawa Kenpo inheritor in his own right.

Flores Sensei conducted three tours of duty in Vietnam and became a close combat instructor as well as drill instructor. He also established early Okinawa Kenpo schools back in the United States, building unique old-style training structures so that his students could feel a little of what he himself experienced on Okinawa.[71]

Q: Flores Sensei, what kind of exposure to martial arts did you have before your time in the Marine Corps?

My older brother was stationed in Okinawa, Japan, in 1945-1948. He came back to our ranch in South Texas and began teaching us karate. It was a variation of Uechi Ryu Sanchin and Naihanchi kata.

Q: What motivated you to join the Marines in 1964?

---

[71] Introductory image courtesy of Marco Garcia.

A Marine Corps recruiter visited us at high school and then our family ranch. He said, "You can go fight Nazis." No kidding. True story. So four of my brothers and I signed up.

Q: How much did you actually know about karate before arriving on Okinawa?

I learned a little from my older brother, but I also saw a Marine Sergeant and a Vietnamese individual practicing out near our first military station. It got me interested because these guys clearly knew what they were doing.

Q: What were your day-to-day duties while stationed on Okinawa before being deployed to Vietnam?

During Vietnam we were always training and doing rotations. Humping hills, weapons drills. We trained and ran around in circles.

Q: How did you come to meet Uechi Kanei in 1964?

We were told to go to karate classes before being deployed.

Q: What were your impressions of Uechi Sensei, and why did you decide to study under him?

He was the closest dojo to the base. He was right outside of Camp Foster. I literally found him because he was the closest.

Q: Could you describe what training was like under Uechi Sensei? Did he focus mostly on kata, kihon, hojo undo, sparring, etc?

Uechi Sensei focused mostly on the following:
1. Kumite (full contact)
2. Sanchin
3. Machiwara (makiwara) striking, which involved repetitious hitting of a padded wooden post
4. Agility drills like practicing running up a wall

5. Kote Kitae drills, which involved two students striking one another to toughen parts of the body

Q: You were also influenced by Goju Ryu, Shorin Ryu, and Isshin Ryu while in the Marines. Which Marine instructors did you study with and for how long?

Beginning in late 1964, I was sent to Vietnam and then back to the United States. During that time I was unable to train with Uechi Sensei personally, so I studied with other individuals who knew about karate. My main influences were as follows:

1. Hank Pharaoh - Isshin Ryu
2. Sergeant Man - Uechi Ryu
3. Dan Petaco - Shotokan
4. Sergeant Rosenberry - Shorin Ryu

Q: In 1972, you found your way back to Okinawa. At this time did you begin studying with Odo Seikichi or Nakamura Taketo (or both)? Also, how did you find out about them and meet them?

After my second tour in Vietnam, I ended up back in Okinawa. I went back to studying Uechi Ryu near Camp Foster, but then received transfer notice to Camp McTureous, near Agena. It was there that I met Odo Sensei, who was teaching in the gym. There was only Okinawa Kenpo nearby, so I started training with him and stayed with him until he passed away in 2002.

Q: What was training like under Odo Sensei? Could you discuss his focus on kata, sparring, exercises, etc?

Odo Sensei used a wide variety of exercise, punches, blocks, kicks, kata, kobudo, and kumite. I was surprised that he never changed his teaching in all the years I trained with him. Many other sensei take a different direction. I was very lucky.

Q: What was Odo Sensei like as a person? Was there something about him that inspired you to continue training with him for so long?

The initial interest was that he was different. He taught the broadest curriculum of any Okinawan teacher I knew of. No other teacher, to my knowledge, at that time had the scope of knowledge he had with kobudo, kata, kyusho . . . anything. I was on rotation back to Vietnam, so Odo Sensei taught me the bo right away. He realized that I could use bo concepts with my rifle while out on the battlefield, and he was right — I had to do just that. I am indebted to Odo Sensei for those lessons.

Flores Sensei leaps over a bo attack while training with Odo Seikichi Sensei in Okinawa.[72]

---

[72] Images of Odo Sensei with Nick Flores courtesy of Lou Protonentis.

Nick Flores and Odo Seikichi perform a two-person Tinbe Rochin combative form.

Q: You lived in an apartment above Odo Sensei's dojo from 1976-1981. Could you describe that experience? Was it difficult moving your family?

My boys were young, and they loved adventure and karate. For my wife, it was a bit harder. She began training at a time when no women were allowed to train directly under an Okinawan teacher if they were American. She constantly faced criticism from the Okinawan women (karate and non-karate) because they thought she was Okinawan and married a G.I. That was the most difficult of situations. She was able to withstand this and came out for the better.

Q: When did your wife and children begin training? Did they study with Odo Sensei, or were you their direct instructor most of the time?

They started in 1976. My older son, Gonzalo, advanced quickly. Odo Sensei realized his aptitude and began giving him private classes. Gonzo had a photographic memory. The thing I remember is that Odo Sensei would show a kata to my son a couple of times and then would watch to see if he could repeat it. By 1979, Gonzalo learned the entire curriculum, and then some, of Okinawa Kenpo. He also studied with the Gushiken brothers, Henzan Hideo, Maehara Seijiro, and Mr. Nakazato (an old student of Nakamura Shigeru). My wife trained with Odo Sensei only. She valued his teaching and kindness. She was the ambassador to many of the other Okinawan dojo as well as to many Marines, including Dean Stephens, Rick Van Meter, Vic Coffin, Richard Battle, etc.

You have to understand, this was a time when traditional Okinawan karate was on "the outs." Kise Fusei had gone to point tournament sparring. Many Okinawan dojo did this eventually. Odo Sensei and several other sensei made an effort to teach Gonzo and several other children all the kata, kobudo, and koryu training methods. When we moved back to the States, I continued teaching my wife and kids. My younger son did not take much interest but still earned his Shodan.

Q: When did you return to the United States, and were you still enlisted at that time?

I returned to the States for the last time in 1981. I retired in 1984.

Q: You made a big effort to continue teaching once back home. Could you describe the process of opening schools and some of the challenges you faced in growing them?

As I taught students they would sometimes have to move away, so I had them open up a dojo wherever they moved. Some were military, police, civilians, and so forth. I have been teaching a long time and you get a lot of students . . . about 1% go on to open a school. I always told them, "All the Okinawan Sensei have day jobs." I told them to teach what I taught and not to eliminate anything. They could add other material if they wanted, but they needed to keep the minimum of Okinawa Kenpo clear.

Q: What was the climate of martial arts like in the United States throughout the '80s?

When we moved back to the States in 1981 it was tournament this, trophy that. Everyone was a black belt, from kids to adults. Brick breaking and ice breaking were the "in thing." It was truly a circus. Luckily there were enough hot heads from other schools like Kajukenbo that would still visit for "friendly matches." Those visits tended to be brutal. It was full contact in the bogu gear, but people still had cracked ribs, busted collar bones, etc. One of the visiting schools was run by a teacher who eventually closed his school down and joined mine and ended up living with us for several years. That guy was Howard Webb, one of my most prolific and hardest working karate students. You have to remember, in the States, the other dojo(s) were not used to training this way. The majority of American karate (including Okinawan Kenpo) did not want to do the body conditioning nor the full contact kumite.

Q: You have built at least one beautiful and classical dojo that honors Asian architecture. What inspired you to undertake that project, and how long did it take you?

I wanted Okinawa closer to me. I realized I had a unique experience and most people interested in karate would never have the opportunity to go to Okinawa and train that long. I wanted to bring some of that back here. I am proud to be Okinawa Kenpo.

Q: What is your current relationship with Nakamura Taketo, and how are you working to continue spreading the art of Okinawa Kenpo?

He promoted me to red belt and "rank with no rank" several years ago. This was very kind of him to do this. I still hold 10th dan from Nakamura Taketo, but he insisted that I was beyond the ranking idea. His son Yasushi runs the dojo in Okinawa and has several sensei training with him. I am still teaching and spreading the word of Okinawa Kenpo. I hope my sons continue to do so as well.

Flores Sensei with Nakamura Taketo Sensei, son of Nakamura Shigeru.

Q: What words of advice could you provide to younger martial artists looking to improve in their art and make karate a lifelong pursuit?

Don't give up. Try all the bunkai. See what works for you. Do not change the kata. For Okinawa Kenpo specifically — keep it like Odo Sensei taught us. There is a whole world of Okinawa Kenpo people do not understand. That was Odo Sensei's greatest gift.

Ann-Marie Heilman

Ann-Marie Heilman has dedicated her life to helping individuals in need both as a martial arts instructor and as a special needs educator. Through decades of hard work and uncompromising standards, Ann-Marie has excelled as an athlete and academic, becoming a role model for a generation of young women hoping to achieve success in all areas of professionalism.

Heilman Sensei began her martial arts journey in the late 1960s, when difficult circumstances in her life led to a desire to improve her self-defense capabilities. She studied with the great American pioneer Robert Trias, and eventually with Odo Seikichi of Okinawa Kenpo.

After years of diligent training, Ann-Marie Heilman gained the respect and friendship of senior karateka in a variety of styles. As a result, she and her husband C. Bruce Heilman formed the International Karate Kobudo Federation, a multi-style organization designed to promote the sharing and preservation of karate and kobudo. Heilman Sensei is considered a rare resource for Okinawa Kenpo and a true pioneer for women in the martial arts.

Q: Heilman Sensei, when was the first time you set foot in a dojo or training environment?

I was a freshman at Albright College in Reading, PA, and Hidy Ochiai was a senior there at the time. He was offering Judo Self-Defense classes at the local Y.M.C.A. I was really interested in that, and had some personal safety concerns because one of my family members was being released from the state hospital (mental and behavioral problems). I signed up for it, hopped on a bus, and went down to the Y once a week for self-defense training. This began in 1966.

The content of the course focused on street awareness and defense techniques (where to hit, how to hit, how to throw, etc). The basis of the class was on Judo methods, which I found challenging as a smaller woman.

It was a very good experience because Ochiai Sensei had endless patience with us. He always encouraged me to continue, even when the program was coming to an end. I was never sure if his encouragement came because he saw a spark of passion in me for the martial arts or if he thought I was so bad I needed lots more extra help, hahaha.

Q: Where did your training go from there?

As I mentioned Ochiai Sensei was a senior, so after his time was up at the university I had to seek training elsewhere. One day when I was in my dorm room a friend of mine named Rick Ulrich walked in and invited to take me to a local dojo operated by George Dillman.

I had no real knowledge of what karate was, but Rick and a few other friends were involved. I remember my first class there I had to go through something called a "kata" (no clue what that was) named Taikyoku One. I remember thinking, "This is kind of . . . odd." Coming from an inner city school I had almost no experience with gym classes or sports. To do something in a coordinated and physically organized fashion like that was hard.

Q: Were you tempted to quit at first due to the difficulty and unusual nature of the exercise?

I don't think I knew at the time how hard it was for me and how bad I must have been. I didn't know that I was struggling.

Q: Could you talk a bit about the curriculum at the Dillman School?

At the very beginning I didn't realize that what we were doing was different from what other people were doing. However, over time I realized that our style of practice was connected to Isshin Ryu Karatedo. In time, the name changed to Okinawa Kenpo due to influence from Daniel K. Pai, however the content of the class didn't change. Our training consisted of Isshin Ryu forms and sparring as well as some self-defense.

Things were very tournament oriented at that time. I remember going to a national tournament in Indianapolis in 1969, which coincidentally is the first time I met one of the major figures in United States martial arts — Robert Trias.

Q: What was the climate of martial arts training like at that time?

Truthfully, it was a very macho kind of environment. Practitioners were mostly men and the martial arts were still heavily connected to the military. There were so few women that we were a sort of a novelty.

All the women I knew in training at that time were white belts. It wasn't until I attended a tournament that I actually met a black belt woman named Bobbi Snyder. She was competing in the same ring as us because there was only one ring for women (white belt through black belt and regardless of age). Bobbi took first place in our kata division, and my roommate Linda took second.

Linda and I were convinced this woman (Bobbi) was going to be standoffish and / or aggressive, but when we all met in the locker room after the competition she immediately joined us in conversation saying how glad she was to meet us. She really encouraged and supported us in our training and said how she was looking forward to watching us gain rank and skill.

She was a student of Glenn Premru at the time, a very well known karateka in his own right located in Pittsburgh.

Q: You met your eventual husband, C. Bruce Heilman, at the Dillman School. Could you talk about that meeting?

I had been training at that dojo for about a year before Bruce came to town. He was from the Pittsburgh area but was serving an internship near Reading. He was already a Shodan under Hank Talbott when he arrived, which was in a style of jujutsu / karate developed by Dewey Deavers that featured a healthy mixture of tripping, throwing, and striking methods. The Deavers system was known as a hard knocks style that integrated ideas from other methods, including karate. As such, when Bruce arrived in the Dillman School he was honored as a black belt. Of course, he had to learn the kata before being recertified in our style.

When we first started we were side-by-side students. However, he had an unusual natural gift for martial arts and it didn't take him long to become one of the instructors there. He was a savant for kata and a very good fighter.

We were married in June of 1971, only about nine months after meeting.

Ann-Marie Heilman with her husband, C. Bruce Heilman.

Q: Could you discuss how you eventually began to train under Robert Trias Sensei?

We reached out to Mr. Trias, who we had known from tournaments for a number of years, and expressed our interest in learning from him. He directed us to connect with his regional director, who, as it turns out, was Hidy Ochiai. Since Bruce was a Nidan at that time, Ochiai Sensei decided to test him and subsequently made Bruce fight all the black belts in his dojo for hours. Bruce was loving it, and afterward we all went out for dinner and had a great time. Ochiai Sensei was instrumental in helping us with our East Coast training and keeping us connected to Trias Sensei.

Bruce and I established our own school in 1972 in the Reading area. For a few years we were focused on building the school and teaching while still learning from the U.S.K.A. (Trias Sensei's organization) members in the area. It was in the late '70s and early '80s that we actually studied with Trias Sensei directly.

Ann-Marie Heilman attends an Indionapolis training seminar with Robert Trias Sensei (pictured far left). C. Bruce Heilman is seen behind Ann-Marie in the black gi.

It was also at this time that we participated in many seminars and got to meet some of the great American practitioners and pioneers of the time.

Q: Could you talk about what training was like with Trias Sensei? How was it different or similar to what you had experienced before?

It was really excellent, he was as good as his reputation suggested. Trias Sensei provided us with fantastic training and helped us understand what made karate work (or not work). He had keen insight into functionality, fighting, and kata interpretation. He was one of the best of his time.

One thing he pointed out to us fairly early was that we were not doing Okinawa Kenpo, even though that is what we were self-labeled through the Dillman School. He suggested that we travel with him to Okinawa in order to meet the headmaster of the style, Odo Seikichi. Of course we were a bit taken aback by this revelation, but Trias Sensei's honesty and knowledge were part of his value as a teacher. He was rather strict in this regard; he told us that if we wanted to keep calling ourselves Okinawa Kenpo that it was our duty to meet the head of the style and learn his ways.

It took a few years for us to gather the funds and make arrangements; in 1983 we eventually went with Trias to Okinawa, which turned out to be a huge turning point in our martial arts careers.

Q: You mentioned earlier that you, as a woman, were something of a novelty in the dojo. Could you discuss if that feeling persisted through the '70s and early '80s in the Trias organization and martial arts world in general?

Trias Sensei himself was always very giving and open and honest. He would tell you what he thought you needed to do, but not in a hurtful way. Training within that organization was something that I found to be fairly inviting with a productive mindset during training.

Q: What were some of the problems you noticed in general (perhaps not specifically things that happened to you) for women of that era?

I think one of the biggest hurdles was the mindset of martial arts being a "good 'ol boys club." It was a time when women in general were struggling to gain a foothold in the business world. It was very difficult in the martial arts to get respect . . . you had to prove yourself. The men didn't want to judge us, and there were no women allowed as judges.

One of the true stories of Bobbi Snyder was that she was very rankled by this idea of women being unable to judge. One day she walked up to a corner judge, tapped him on the shoulder, and informed him that he had an emergency phone call on the line that he needed to attend to. When he left, she promptly took the vacant judging spot. Naturally there was no phone call to be found. She ended up judging and refused to give the flags back.

Another issue was actually finding space to compete. We only ever had one ring, and often it was pushed to the side away from the regular competition near the bleachers or even under the bleachers. By the time I was nearing black belt we really had to take a firm stand to be respected. I was an innately shy person, so this was difficult for me.

It should be said that there were some really good men at this time as well, supportive and fair. I remember Ochiai Sensei was an instructor with a mindset of equality from the first time I met him, and even when I visited his dojo in later years he always had female students.

A very important matter is that gay men and women of the time had very little protection in society, so they needed to learn how to protect themselves badly. Therefore, since there was a contingent of lesbian women in the martial arts, a stereotype developed amongst men that all women martial artists were lesbian. This developed into hurtful and derogatory behavior toward women of both orientations, straight and gay alike.

Q: Could you discuss how you met Odo Seikichi Sensei of Okinawa Kenpo? What were your early impressions of him that made you decide to train under him full time?

The first time I met him was during a banquet we attended with Trias Sensei over in Okinawa. When they announced us and our style as "Okinawa Kenpo" a very small Okinawan man jumped up and yelled, "Yay! Okinawa Kenpo!," with his arms in the air. That, of course, was Odo Sensei.

That's the thing — he was always happy and joyful. Even when he was quite ill, he was always a happy, funny man, and it was easy to grow to love him. He was also an excellent teacher. We brought him over to the United States the following year and continued to train with him as much as we could until his passing.

We established a routine of going to Okinawa or bringing Odo Sensei to the United States every year. We would spend weeks and sometimes months with him in focused training. It was a great relationship, and we were blessed to have him here in our home so frequently.

Q: What did you find similar / different studying with Odo Sensei versus some of your previous instructors?

Ann-Marie Heilman with Odo Seikichi Sensei at the Heilman Karate Academy located in Reading, PA.

It was different in that he was very laid back. I'm not sure if my previous experiences were flavored with American military or Japanese martial art style, which is very very different in the dojo and very serious. While we were training and doing kata with Odo Sensei, although the training was rigorous and focused, he always taught with a smile and laughter. That was different and good for me.

Odo Sensei's training was exacting, and he had a huge emphasis on kata. That worked well for us because we could receive the kata and bunkai from Odo Sensei, but then also receive high level application, theory, fighting, etc. from Trias Sensei.

I remember early on in our studies with Odo there was no particular structure for the material. He would teach you what you were interested in or what he thought you should know. I remember attending a meeting in 1984 with a number of other senior students of his and establishing an actual hierarchy of material that students would have to learn. Once we had that scaffolding set up, everyone could then test standardized material. It was in this way that I tested up to 7th Dan directly under Odo Sensei.

Q: Odo Sensei was known for teaching in the old Okinawan manner of suiting material to the student, tweaking it as needed to make it more functional for the individual. Were there any particular ways in which Odo Sensei molded your learning to make it work better for you personally?

I think the most unique thing about my relationship with Odo Sensei was how frequently he used me as his bunkai partner. Bunkai became a very live experience for me. Before Odo Sensei I trained with a lot of tall, strong men. It was really great to learn from Odo Sensei who was much closer to me in size. That being said, Odo Sensei was very muscular and had huge hands. He was a powerful individual. I remember when we put our hands together his fingers could fold over mine.

If I watched him very carefully I could learn how a smaller individual could move, especially with weapons.

Q: Your husband C. Bruce Heilman is also a senior in Okinawa Kenpo. This fact could inevitably lead people to wonder if you were perhaps "riding his coattails" or getting free rank simply by association. Am I right in assuming this sort of thing came up, and how did you go about handling it?

Testing and receiving rank directly from Odo Sensei and NOT my husband was critical. In fact, Bruce was of the same mind and made sure that it was not him who tested or promoted me. Over the years I noticed a few women who did receive high rank simply because of who they were married to. My testing was always public and I was always sure to keep my training as transparent as possible. This is another reason I did tournaments for a while. I wanted people to see what I could do and prove that I was not just a figurine following my husband.

Q: While studying under Odo Sensei, you and Mr. Heilman were also busy building the I.K.K.F. (International Karate Kobudo Federation), which Odo Sensei approved of and even sat on the board. Could you discuss the challenges of starting something of that nature?

The organization came about because we wanted to establish a personal identity while being a branch of Odo Sensei's Shudokan. Bruce had a talent for organization and was experienced in setting up this kind of structure. He knew about getting accountants, lawyers, etc. We met a number of excellent martial artists over the years that we wanted to associate with, and also wanted to help other styles learn things like Okinawan weapons.

The growth of the federation allowed us to share our art, especially the kobudo, with people in the U.S.A. and internationally. I never would have thought it possible when I was growing up.

One of the challenges of the I.K.K.F. is the desire to maintain high standards throughout the entire organization. Sometimes our style is not ideal for individuals that want to join us, or our standards may not be attainable for a commercial school. We try to be fair while maintaining what we think is right.

I.K.K.F. Annual Training gathering hosted in 2004. Teachers sitting front row include (left to right): Victor Coffin, Bill Hayes, Nick Adler, C. Bruce Heilman, Ann-Marie Heilman, Chuck Merriman, Jody Paul, and Marilyn Fierro.

Q: While you've spent many years developing your martial arts, you've also studied and acquired degrees in special needs education. How have you found those two worlds fitting and interacting with each other?

They fit together like a glove! I'm a people watcher to begin with, but the study of psychology is extremely applicable, especially when it comes to teaching self-defense. For example, how do you take a woman who has been victimized and traumatized and make a fighter out of her? She cannot become capable of defending herself without addressing the psychological factors.

We have had many special needs students throughout the years. I recall one individual in a wheelchair who we developed material for. We've had individuals with cerebral palsy, autism, etc. At times I've had specialty classes, and other times have had individuals in a regular class with proper assistance.

I believe even limited individuals can benefit from martial arts training as long as the teacher knows how to work with the limitations.

Q: Recently you received the rare honor of being promoted to 9th Dan, Hanshi. I'm sure this was something impactful for you. Could you talk a bit about your feelings and reflections on the promotion?

I remember my husband brought up the possibility two years ago, but I was staunchly opposed to it. I wanted no parts of it and that kind of responsibility. As far as this time around, I feel right about it because I've had two years to reflect on the possibility and the things that I've done, and the amount of study I've done and still want to do. I knew that if I received it this year it would be coming in a legitimate way from teachers outside of the I.K.K.F. who are respected in their own right.

Q: As you mentioned, the title of Hanshi bears a certain amount of weight and responsibility. How do you see yourself using it for the betterment of the I.K.K.F. and the martial arts in general?

It certainly has imposed a sense of obligation on me . . . in a good way. I believe I need to take a step up in the amount of teaching and seminar instruction that I am doing. I need to be more of a "Bobbi Snyder" for the young women coming up through now, as she was for me. I need to represent the martial arts in a more visible fashion.

In the coming years I'll be taking a more active role in traveling, especially overseas. I would also like to increase the amount of writing I do. I need to find a way to balance all that with my current job of working with special needs children.

Q: When you think about your overall legacy in the arts, what do you hope your lasting impact will be?

I'd like to be remembered as a good and fair karate woman, teacher, and judge. If I can do that, and combine it with the I.K.K.F. learning materials we have already created, I would be happy. We have set up the scaffold so that people will have what we created for a long time to come.

I've never considered myself (nor was I, in truth) a natural talent at martial arts. Everything I learned was through repetition over and over and over. I would watch others get it much sooner than I could. I've had multiple injuries as well that were very debilitating. In total, my learning process has been slow, with many ups and downs.

I hope that other "non-naturals" out there can see my struggles and continue to push through, too. I would say to them, surround yourself with a good support system and never let "quit" enter your equation. As I was once told in grade school: "Aim for the moon . . . even if you miss you'll land amongst the stars."

C. Bruce Heilman

C. Bruce Heilman Sensei is one of the most well-known figures in Okinawa Kenpo, exhibiting a combination of physical skill and organizational acumen. Creator of the International Karate Kobudo Federation, Heilman Sensei is responsible for decades of sharing and growth amongst senior karateka from a variety of styles.

Mr. Heilman began his martial arts journey in 1961, studying jujutsu at first and then transitioning into karate. Heilman Sensei achieved his black belt in the mid 1960s before eventually coming to study directly under Robert Trias, founder of the United States Karate Association. Trias Sensei introduced Heilman Sensei to Odo Seikichi, inheritor of the Okinawa Kenpo style, which proved to be the beginning of a lifelong training relationship.

Heilman Sensei is a veteran tournament competitor and keeper of a large amount of kata, passed down to him by Trias Sensei and Odo Sensei. He has worked diligently to preserve and spread the ideas of old Okinawa.

Q: How did you first become interested in the martial arts, and what was the first dojo you attended?

When I was young, my mouth was larger than my physical capabilities to back it up. As you might imagine, this got me into trouble from time to time. I figured after a few incidences that I should try to keep my mouth shut, but also learn something to help me in those situations. A school opened up near my house in the Pittsburgh area called North Hills Jujutsu Karate. I happened to see a demo of it at the local North Hills Mall, and I thought it was something I'd really like to do.

I decided to pursue it, but the deal I made with my mother was that I had to take on multiple paper routes to pay my own dues. So that's what I did in order to pay for dues and equipment. This took place in the early 60s.

Q: How widespread were martial art schools at that time?

Not particularly widespread. There was an Isshin Ryu school downtown, a school in Castle Shannon, as well as another school in North Hills operated by Glenn Premru. There were maybe five or so schools in the entire Pittsburgh area at that time. In fact it was not uncommon in the early 60s to have a brown belt as the head of a school. If you had a black belt, that was considered a big deal.

Q: Do you recall much about your teacher at that first jujutsu / karate school?

Oh yes. His name was Hank Talbott. He was of French descent and was a plasterer by trade. He didn't have a neck — it just went from head right to his shoulders. His hands were like vices, which made him extremely good at close-in ranges. Many times he would be on the mat with a lit cigar and would explain how to use that cigar once he got a hold of you. His was a little different approach to say the least!

Talbott Sensei sort of took me on because my father died when I was seven. In the Talbott school there were only two kids, myself and Bill Starr's niece (Bill Starr being Talbott's business partner at the time). Starr's niece was a little more advanced than me, so she would throw me around the dojo. He [Talbott Sensei] sort of adopted me and I helped in the summers as a plasterer's assistant.

Q: Could you talk a bit about Talbott Sensei's style and how you eventually got involved with more traditional karate?

Talbott Sensei's methods came mostly from a gentleman named Dewey Deavers who opened a jujutsu school around 1938. Most of the old timers in Pittsburgh had some involvement with Mr. Deavers' program at one point or another. Mr. Joe Hederman eventually took over the Deavers' school in Castle Shannon. That school still exists and is now on Route 51 and teaches both jujutsu and karate (it follows the Chito Ryu methods now under the guidance of William Dometrich's organization). One interesting thing about Deavers was that his parents were Judo players who went around with Vaudeville acts performing various "tricks" (as techniques were called then).

C. Bruce Heilman launching a flying sidekick at a ready-and-waiting Hank Talbott.

Talbott operated a shared content school, so I was able to get Shodan grading in the late 60s in both jujutsu and karate before heading off to college. After leaving home I started a college program of my own. Between my junior and senior year I traveled to Reading, PA, due to an internship with the Berks County Planning Commission. I found the Dillman Karate Institute in the area where I continued my learning and teaching. You might say I worked during the day and "lived" in the dojo at nights. It was only after my time with George Dillman that I started with Robert Trias and the U.S.K.A. in 1970. I also met my wife, Ann-Marie, at the Dillman School, and we left the school together in 1972.

While traveling throughout the late '60s and early '70s, I maintained contact with Talbott Sensei in Pittsburgh and got back to train whenever possible. By the time I left to study with Trias Sensei, I was a Sandan in jujutsu and karate.

Q: Robert Trias Sensei is regarded as one of the founding fathers of karate in America. Could you talk a bit about him as a person and instructor? What drew you to him?

Mr. Trias had a background in both the military and Arizona police. He was a father figure for sure, but also a gruff taskmaster. He could be very demanding and at times lacked some of the finer social skills, but that was typical of that era of hard knocks teachers. He was very charismatic and pulled people together in order to create the United States Karate Association. What he was able to achieve organizationally was really unprecedented.

As a teacher, he stressed strong technical knowledge and an understanding of application. He emphasized this to people whether they were part of his style or not. His efforts in practicality and understanding helped the overall quality of karate in America, by my estimation. He would often say that there was "good karate" and "bad karate;" not all good karate was traditional and not all bad karate was traditional either. Same goes for eclectic. What made good karate, he suggested, was if it worked intelligently with the body and achieved maximum power. He would gauge both traditional and new styles on their merits, judging not purely on lineage but also on efficiency and effectiveness.

I tell people that I learned my technical understanding from Trias Sensei and my kata from Odo Seikichi Sensei. They had two different methods of teaching.

Q: You mentioned that Trias Sensei focused on good fundamentals and technical understanding. Can you talk a bit more about how sound basics are important in karate and how that relates to kata training?

Kata are high level drills that provide unique insight into an art. If you understand the basic foundation of a kata, it will provide the ability to understand how other kata and methods in the system interact. For example, you might see one fundamental concept that appears in multiple kata in slightly different ways. You can then analyze the different potential angles and ideas being expressed in the kata using the context of the other kata to inform the overall idea. You can then transfer that fundamental idea into weapons. What that gets down to is ultimately breaking away from the confines of the kata. After muscle memory and understanding is in place, you can then utilize the concept in any capacity.

Q: How did your training with Trias Sensei develop, and how did it lead to meeting Odo Seikichi Sensei of Okinawa Kenpo?

I studied with Trias Sensei into the mid '80s (about 1983) and was able to attain Rokudan through him. In '83, my wife Ann-Marie and I were selected to travel East with Trias

Sensei along with about 15 others to represent the U.S.K.A. on a tour throughout Japan, Okinawa, and Hong Kong. When we got to Okinawa, there was a big dinner gathering and one of the masters present was Odo Seikichi Sensei. When Trias Sensei introduced all the people traveling with him, he placed Ann-Marie and me under the banner of "Okinawa Kenpo." Here's why I think he did that:

A young Heilman Sensei as he transitioned through his early martial arts career in 1970.

At that time, George Dillman was teaching under the stylistic name of Okinawa Kenpo as opposed to Isshin Ryu (Dillman's original style) even though his material did not follow that of Nakamura Shigeru (the founder of Okinawa Kenpo). It's likely that Trias Sensei wanted to demonstrate his coalition's connection to Okinawa, so instead of labeling everyone as Shuri Ryu (Trias's personal style) he used some of our previous experiences. When Odo Sensei heard "Okinawa Kenpo" he jumped up with his arms in the air and yelled "Yaaaay!" He was so excited that someone else shared the style he received directly from Nakamura Sensei. The pure enthusiasm and welcoming energy of Odo Sensei immediately caught my attention.

Prior to this traveling showcase Trias Sensei told me that he wanted me to transfer completely to Shuri Ryu, his personal system. I expressed gratitude but also told him that I desired to get the real "Okinawa Kenpo" of which I had only seen a fraction of back in the U.S.A. In response, Trias Sensei told me that he would support me in whatever direction I chose to go as long as I honored my teacher and preserved the art correctly. Meeting Odo Sensei at that meeting was fortuitous, and Trias Sensei was instrumental in helping me develop a more permanent connection to Odo Sensei.

Q: Besides just the dinner event, what was it exactly about Odo Sensei that caught your attention and made you decide to commit fully to his methods?

It was his personality. You could tell immediately his love for the art. Throughout that trip with Mr. Trias we got to meet a number of senior Japanese and Okinawan instructors. As you might imagine, the Japanese instructors were quite stoic and serious while the Okinawans were a bit more welcoming. Master Odo in particular had a warmth and openness about him. I always think of him like a bright light in a dark room. He opened his arms to us, and we were very thankful for that.

In addition to his personality, he had a fantastic reputation as a practitioner. His karate was well-respected, and he was considered one of the top weapons practitioners in the world. I had always loved kobudo so this seemed like a perfect fit.

C. Bruce Heilman and Ann-Marie Heilman with Odo Seikichi Sensei during one of Odo Sensei's sponsored trips to the United States.

Q: Were weapons something you took to early on in your training and discovered you had a talent for?

I was exposed to weapons pretty early on thanks in part to Glenn Premru. As I mentioned, Premru Sensei had a school in the Pittsburgh area. There weren't many tournaments back in those days but we had inter-dojo shiai. Basically one dojo would visit another and everyone would line up across from each another. We would pair up and then fight. No points really — just winner standing and loser not. We had a number of shared events with Premru's school, and at the time Premru was really known for his kata. I was impressed by his performances, in particular Shimabuku no Sai. Another gentleman named Joe Pennywell was known for his usage of the sai. This combined with things I had seen in magazines (like a picture of Bill Hayes) really got my imagination going. I pursued kobudo thereafter.

Q: Odo Seikichi Sensei is well-known for being a pioneer of integrating kobudo with karate. Before that time, they were considered by many to be separate entities. Could you discuss Odo's motivation and methods for his integration?

Typically you had karate organizations and kobudo organizations as separate bodies. Of course that wasn't a hard-fast rule — people cross-trained and pursued both karate and kobudo, but they tended to be separated organizationally. Odo Sensei was a kata sponge and felt strongly about keeping the old kata alive. Also, he had exposure to weapons early in his life, especially that of the Matayoshi family. As Nakamura Sensei got older he did less and less teaching in the dojo, leaving much of it to Odo Sensei. Odo Sensei told me that before Nakamura died he asked Odo to integrate more weapons into the Okinawa Kenpo system.

Politically, Odo's efforts to combine the karate and kobudo aspects were not universally well received. It took some of the control away from the kobudo-specific organizations. Now, in hindsight, almost all of the major karate programs on Okinawa have some sort of kobudo contingent (so it is no longer seen as unusual).

From that point on, Odo Sensei taught weapons not just to Okinawa Kenpo people but to practitioners of many styles. Due to expanding interest he decided to create the Okinawa Kenpo Karate Kobudo Federation. Historically speaking, the O.K.K.K.F. was just the latest iteration of previous organizational attempts by Odo Sensei's instructors, such as the All Okinawa Kenpo Renmei led by Nakamura Shigeru and Shimabukuro Zenryo (who in turn branched out from the All Japan Karatedo Federation Okinawa Special District). When Nakamura and Shimabukuro both died in '69, there was a significant loss in leadership on the island and it was up to the next generation to pick up the pieces and attempt to reorganize.

It should be noted that Okinawa Kenpo was not originally developed as a style; instead it was meant to be a gathering of practitioners. Nakamura, Shimabukuro, Uehara Seikichi, Matayoshi Shinko, and others intended to bring Okinawan karate back under one umbrella. Despite these early intentions, Okinawa Kenpo eventually became connected with Nakamura's particular brand of karate and kobudo.

Heilman Sensei carefully monitoring a full contact kobudo match. The kobudo combatants use a modified version of the bogu protective gear popularized by Nakamura Shigeru Sensei.

Q: How open were the Okinawan instructors to foreigner students?

Some sectors of Okinawan karate embraced new students, even Western students. After World War II and into the Vietnam era, you had an increasing number of G.I.'s on the island. Some instructors, either for survival or family or whatever, decided they were going to open up to the Americans and teach them. Other teachers were not at all open.

The openness of these teachers ultimately affected the global growth of different styles. Isshin Ryu is a perfect example. While Isshin Ryu was a fairly small style on Okinawa, relegated to Shimabukuro Tatsuo, it has grown immensely in the United States due to the number of early military members that Tatsuo Sensei taught.

It's important to remember throughout the '50s and into the '60s and '70s there were limited sources of income on the island. Teaching karate could serve as a good source of income (potentially a great one) that could feed oneself and one's family. Nakamura Sensei himself came from a family that endured wartime with some financial stability. As such he was able to fund many karate gatherings. Others weren't so lucky.

Q: Odo Sensei stressed keeping kata as it was, preserving it as he taught. What's your take on that?

Yes, it was very important to Odo Sensei that we "keep his kata straight." Kata preservation is critical so that the forms can be passed on in the same way to future generations so they have the opportunity to explore them as intended.

A lot of what you see in modern competition is something akin to martial theater. It involves a lot of posing, acrobatics, and the like. Some excuse changes to kata as exploration or personalization, but exploration does not mean fundamentally changing the form and losing it's intended purpose. Timing, focal points, transitions, etc. are in place for particular reasons, and losing them can mean losing the kata.

Q: A lot of what you are discussing hints at both proper and improper ways of using the Shuhari concept of obeying, digressing, and then separating. Could you share more on that?

When you look at the heads of all the different systems, they each added something to their art. For example, Odo Sensei came from a background of weapons comprised of Chinen, Matayoshi, Taira, and Nakamura methods and melded those different body mechanics into Okinawa Kenpo. He kept the essence and key elements of the kata the same without losing the pattern and purpose.

When it came to karate transmission from the Okinawans to Westerners, some things got lost in translation due to cultural differences and communication problems. Many Okinawans didn't do a lot of basics drilling (like you might see in a Japanese dojo). You were expected to learn through osmosis. Some people were able to learn that way while others weren't. The Okinawans also had an aversion to "losing face" where if they saw something being done wrong they might neglect to correct it in order to stay within good manners (or with the assumption that it could be fixed slowly, non-verbally over time).

To illustrate the point — in Western culture, if you ask, "Is this okay?," and I say, "Yes, it's okay," we both generally assume that whatever is being discussed is actually okay. There is a directness in that communication. This is not necessarily the case with an Okinawan teacher. If an Okinawan teacher says, "Yes, it's okay," it might just mean that what you are doing is close enough for now or that you needn't be concerned about anything more.

This cultural quirk is something that has affected many styles. When you think about how long exposure to a teacher tended to be (a year or two for most military folks depending on tours of duty), you might never have gotten past this issue. What we are left with is perceptions, and cultural / personal backgrounds can greatly flavor those perceptions.

For me personally, Trias Sensei's focus on basics and application helped me unlock some of the things Odo Sensei was trying to express both superficially and underneath. Often he would demonstrate something and explain it; I would have to stop and say, "Okay, Sensei, but you're doing something different." He would chuckle at my noticing but then tell me that what I was doing was okay, too. I had to persist and tell him that I wanted to do it how he did it. Then he would open up and explain a little more.

Many of the Okinawans had that differentiation — they offered "baby" karate to help us grow, but if we showed we were ready for more and knew how to ask for it they would provide it. This is the difference between the notion of karate "secrets" and simply not knowing which questions to ask or what to look for.

This evolution based on inquiry was considered a natural part of the Okinawan learning process, and over generations it led to an art's growth. Exposure to other arts also helped practitioners figure out which questions to ask and how to look at their own material from new angles. Unfortunately too many folks, once they received something, figured they were done. They put a stamp on it and never questioned it again.

One thing I came to believe, thanks in part to both Odo Sensei and Trias Sensei, is the idea of being true to your art without wearing blinders. Since the first time we hosted a training gathering via the I.K.K.F., we tried to bring in practitioners from a variety of styles. I made sure they didn't get bogged down in kata differences between styles but instead shared the fundamentals and unique qualities that made their arts effective.

Q: When did you establish the Heilman Karate Academy and International Karate

Kobudo Federation? Can you describe your main goals of establishing a larger martial arts federation?

The H.K.A. began in 1972 and the I.K.K.F. in 1991. The I.K.K.F. was formed out of necessity, I feel. Odo Seikichi Sensei was a fantastic teacher, but his organizational skills were not as developed. He had an inability to say "no" at times, and this caused problems.

When I first became the U.S. Director of the Okinawa Kenpo Karate Kobudo Federation and later the International Director, I put a lot of effort into creating some structure that was becoming more and more needed as Okinawa Kenpo expanded outside of Okinawa itself. One interesting trait of Odo Seikichi Sensei was his ability to adapt to the individuals he was working with (again, great for teaching but tough for organization). Depending on the personality and skill level of the individuals he was visiting, he would tweak the content. As you might imagine, this resulted in almost mini-ryuha (style sects) across the U.S. and Okinawa as people experienced different subtle versions of Odo Sensei's art.

One of the first things we did in the O.K.K.K.F. was create a central training event around 1984. We brought everybody together so as to settle discrepancies. These annual get-togethers were challenging but valuable. I liken it to going to the dentist — you know you have to go, but you don't relish in it. There were a few times when things almost came to blows because of our differences. Each person in attendance had a good heart and motivation for keeping Odo Sensei's ways alive, but each was certain about what Odo Sensei told them. Each was correct in their own way but tried to bend others to their way of thinking, which frequently resulted in problems.

Eventually we were able to get Odo Sensei to clear up some of these issues, although ultimately due to his kind nature and fluid teaching methods (and his own personal development over time) things were never completely squared away. It took a number of years to go through this process.

The first O.K.K.K.F. Annual Training held in Reading, PA, 1984. Odo Seikichi Sensei is standing third from left in the front row.

Despite the challenges, some comradery was built along with an appreciation for the efforts of others in the style. Unfortunately, Odo Sensei did not choose to follow the structure we put in place for the O.K.K.K.F. We had some delicate checks and balances which were broken, and, once broken, were essentially impossible to repair. One of the hardest things I ever had to do in my career was choose to establish the International Karate Kobudo Federation. I felt that if I was going to continue spreading Okinawa Kenpo that there should be accountable rules and quality standards, and that those rules should apply the same to everybody involved.

Originally the I.K.K.F. was set up in coordination and cooperation with the O.K.K.K.F. I wanted to continue paying respect to Odo Sensei and had him as part of the chief advisory board for the I.K.K.F. Eventually the structure of the O.K.K.K.F. became very fluid, and there was a lot of struggle internally. It was at that time I decided it was best for the health of the system to break the connection to the O.K.K.K.F. This was the most difficult thing in my martial arts career, but in hindsight it was definitely the correct thing.

I will always love and respect Odo Sensei, but he was human. Many of the Okinawans were put in a tough situation where they had to choose between their art and their own well-being in terms of financial stability (remembering that Okinawa was a very poor place).

When seeing Western money, many instructors chose a profitable course of action, selling rank to individuals who didn't necessarily earn it. Odo Sensei fell into this trap at times. Regrettable, but like I said you have to understand the totality of the situation he and other senior Okinawans were in. Ethically I chose not to endorse this behavior — that was my choice to make just as Odo Sensei had his choices to make.

Q: As you learned about the history of Okinawa Kenpo and the different organizational efforts of gathering different styles together, how did it affect your own vision for the International Karate Kobudo Federation? Were you impacted by the ideals of the old masters to share and collaborate?

I think people in general are influenced by the environment in which they grow and development. Early on I was exposed to a combination of techniques and methods under Hank Talbott. I learned a lot about body mechanics through jujutsu and karate. However, I came to feel that I was missing the foundational structure of true traditional arts. I proceeded to take my martial arts career in more and more traditional directions, searching for what I felt was missing. I discovered that the answers were not necessarily guaranteed in a traditional style. Many traditionalists were caught in a box of rote repetition without actually understanding what they were doing or how to maximize the efficiency of the body. As such, I realized that there were no guarantees that one style had all the answers ready-made and packaged for the student. A lot of it depended on the quality of the program and the quality of the particular teacher.

Trias Sensei instilled in me early on the sense of digging deeply into whatever art I was pursuing, tearing it apart, and making sure the basics were sound. The jujutsu influence from my earlier days allowed me to see how other styles could benefit my traditional karate.

Later, as I learned more about the history of Okinawa Kenpo, I saw the ways in which old stylists worked together and shared ideas in order to make each other better. This appealed to my sensibilities and how I personally developed as a practitioner.

Q: What is your vision for the growth of the organization, and where do you see it going?

When I named the organization, I intentionally stayed away from style-specific terminology. "International Karate Kobudo Federation" is a wide umbrella and is not Okinawa Kenpo "style" specific. We have practitioners from many different styles involved in our program. By keeping it broad, everyone feels equally welcome and valued.

My vision for the organization is to maintain the level of quality we've established via members like Bill Hayes, Chuck Merriman, Jody Paul, etc. but also allow room for growth.

Q: Could you talk about the early days of getting to know other seniors in the U.S.A. and how that led to outreach via the I.K.K.F.?

Initially we all competed against each other. In the late '60s and early '70s, it was cutthroat out there. Mrs. Heilman and I both have memories competing against one of my biggest kata inspirations — Chuck Merriman. I still remember Chuck Merriman doing Seiunchin kata, and it was just excellent. Glenn Premru, George Alexander, Bill Hayes . . . really memorable competitors. Despite the fact that we were out there trying to whoop each other, we still respected each other.

I think the martial arts in this country went through a growth phase at that time. As we all learned and matured, we came to understand and appreciate more of what others were doing. Seeing the differences became a source of positive interaction rather than negative. When the traditionalists found each other during these open tournament events and recognized the skill level in each other, they tended to stay in touch. This contact was important in the early days mostly as a matter of verification. Sometimes we would have visitors showing up at our doorsteps claiming to be students / disciples of Master XYZ. We as seniors could simply call one another to verify the visitor's claims.

Eventually the World United Martial Arts Federation (W.U.M.A.F.) got a number of us together to do a tour of Europe and other locations. That evolved our relationships and got us comfortable working with each other in a more formal capacity. I started inviting these now-friends to train with us when we brought Odo Sensei over to teach. Eventually it grew so that we would have our guests teach as well, even during times when Odo Sensei wasn't in the U.S.A. Odo Sensei thought this was a great idea because it reflected his personal training under a variety of experts, and it reminded him of the philosophy of the old Okinawa Kenpo Renmei with Shimabukuro Zenryo, Uehara Seikichi, and Matayoshi Shinko.

When the O.K.K.K.F. was set up, the governing board consisted entirely of Okinawa Kenpo practitioners. When I set up the I.K.K.F. I specifically chose heads of major traditional lineages from a variety of styles. It provided a healthy variety of input streams and supplied an aspect of quality control. Each person represented a well-preserved and respected line of martial arts, and they wouldn't put their own reputations on the line for other individuals who weren't up to snuff.

One of my hopes is that this sort of cooperation and quality control can continue into future generations. I realize some commercialism is needed to keep the business doors open, but I hope we can prevent commercialism from compromising the collective value of the arts in the U.S.A.

I.K.K.F. Annual Training in 2011. This photo features a number of leaders from styles such as Goju Ryu, Shorin Ryu, Seidokan, Okinawa Kenpo, and more.

Q: What do you think about the state of martial arts in the United States?

I think we're in some trouble at this point. It's often embarrassing the amount of theatrics involved. Some of it has become far removed from what it was supposed to be and the benefits it was supposed to provide. It has become so marketing-oriented and commercialized that the programs change every few months. The goal is entirely based around making the customer happy so they continue paying dues.

People live up to the expectations you place on them, and to placate to students shortchanges them of their potential.

The other thing I think that is lost in today's martial arts is learning how to overcome failure.

During my tournament days, I heard some people express that they couldn't win with traditional kata. So they decided the solution was adding rollfalls, jump kicks, and whatever else. No, that's not it. If you aren't winning with traditional kata, then it's time to get better at your traditional kata.

Dean Stephens

Dean Stephens Sensei is a veteran of the United States Marine Corps and a noted karate historian. With a unique introduction to martial arts stemming from his childhood in Japan, Stephens Sensei was intrigued by the arts at a young age and sought out training as quickly as possible once stationed in Okinawa.

Spending years under the direct tutelage of Odo Seikichi Sensei, Mr. Stephens became a rare resource for insight into Odo Sensei's teaching methods and kata. A record keeper and note taker at heart, Stephens Sensei has helped generations of Okinawa Kenpo students by providing pictures, dates, and firsthand knowledge of martial arts events that have occurred on Okinawa and in the United States throughout the mid-to-late 20th century.

Q: Stephens Sensei, could you start us off with some basics on when / where you were born?

I was born in Eugene, Oregon, October 4, 1949.

Q: What kind of neighborhood did you grow up in?

We were a mobile military family so I had a number of neighborhoods growing up, mostly military housing. I spent time in Mountain View, Alaska; Everett, Washington; Paine Field, Washington; and departed for Tokyo, Japan, on December 8, 1956, aboard the General H. B. Freeman AP-143 and arriving in January of 1957. Tokyo was a memorable experience for me, but we left in July of 1957, bound for San Francisco, California. After that we traveled by train from San Francisco to Eugene, Oregon, and ultimately moved to Boise, Idaho, in an old green Studebaker in August of 1957.

Q: What was your first exposure to martial arts?

My first exposure to martial arts was in the streets of Tokyo, Japan, with the neighborhood boys. The oldest boy wanted to be a sumo wrestler, so we all did sumo on numerous occasions in between playing baseball and running. There were about 14 or 15 of us that hung around together. This went on for at least six months. At the time, I was seven years old.

My sister and I took the train by ourselves from where we lived in Tokyo to Tachikawa Air Force Base to attend school. I learned to love the hot soba that was brought to our house by a man riding his bike with the soba stacked high on trays.

My mother taught English to Japanese businessmen in the neighborhood. We would go with our mother to their houses and sit at their table under the blanket and warm our legs and feet by the coal heater while we waited for the lesson to be over. I also watched Japanese Samurai movies during this time. This is when I decided that I would study the martial arts when I had the chance.

Q: What were some of your earliest memories of martial arts in the United States?

It was in about 1964 or so that the first karate dojo was opened in Boise, Idaho. I asked my dad if I could join and he said, "NO!" Then I wrestled in 1965-66 at school and took "All City" in my weight class. My next exposure came when an R.O.T.C. instructor came to our school and demonstrated some techniques. This happened when I was in 10th grade at Borah High School in September, 1967.

Q: What year did you join the Marines, and what inspired you to take the leap?

I joined in October, 1967, on the delayed entry program and went into active duty in November of 1967. I went to the Marine Corps Recruit Depot in San Diego, California. I joined because the Marine Corps was considered the best and the toughest, so I accepted the challenge.

Q: Could you give us a brief timeline of your military career and where it took you?

My active duty was from November 1967 in San Diego, California until March 1990 in Seattle, Washington, when I retired from the Corps. In 1968 until 1969 (13 months), I was stationed on Okinawa, Japan. I went back for 18 months in 1972 to 1973 and again in January 1981 through March 1981. My final tour there was in 1984 through 1988 for a period of about 44 months. Over six years and six months in Okinawa I had the opportunity to study karate, sumo, Tai Chi Chuan, Hsing Yi, and Paqua.

Q: When you first arrived on Okinawa, what were your particular duties?

My first job was clerk typist in the training N.C.O. (Non-Commissioned Officer) office. Then I worked at cash sales (military uniforms for Marines).

Q: What did an average Marine day consist of?

At 0500 we did Reveille (first call), made a head call, got into formation, and ran three miles. Then we did the three S's, had breakfast, made the racks clean, then went to the barracks for second formation. After that we would go to work, go to lunch, and then back to work. We would get off work and eat dinner, get a liberty card, then go to the dojo in Futenma and do karate for three hours. After that we would return to the barracks, hit the rack, and do it all over the next day.

Q: What were some of your early impressions of Okinawa upon your arrival?

It was extremely hot and muggy, but also very lush and green. We had rainy typhoons during the season and clear ocean waters otherwise. The people were very industrious and friendly; however, racial tensions were prevalent. I was made a member of the riot platoon and received specialized training with the jo (short stick) in order to break up potential riots and conduct crowd control just in case there was an incident.

Q: Once you settled into your Marine duties, did you seek out karate right away?

I found Uechi Ryu Karate in Futenma very quickly, and started studying karate under Uechi Kanei Sensei. It cost me 10 cents a month for lessons. The dime was used to show Marine Special Services that Uechi Sensei had American students, and the Corps paid for the rest of our karate lessons.

Every class we bowed in and did kihon waza. We then broke up to work on whatever Uechi Sensei had assigned us to do, be it punches, kicks, kote kitae, circular blocks, kumite, or bunkai. During each class we went before Uechi Sensei and performed Sanchin Kata three times. Everyone did this every class. I used to do kote kitae (arm conditioning) with the black belts every class as well. They just loved trying to make me quit, but of course I'm a little stubborn; no matter how much it hurt, I never quit. Classes ran for about three hours and were held six days a week. I met James Thompson there, the most senior American student of Uechi Kanei. I also bought my first karate book by Stan Mattson.

Q: How did you eventually find Odo Seikichi Sensei of Okinawa Kenpo? Why did you decide to train with him even though you were initiated into Uechi Ryu?

I was introduced to Odo Seikichi Sensei by Necomedes Flores in 1972 when I told him that I would like to learn kobudo (I had seen Mr. Flores practicing weapons next to our barracks). Soon after, Mr. Flores took me to meet Odo Sensei at Stillwell Fieldhouse whereupon Odo Sensei accepted me as a student. He then found out that I was studying with Uechi Kanei Sensei. He told me to get in his green car and drove us to the Uechi Futenma Dojo and took me into the dojo and had a talk with Uechi Sensei. Uechi Sensei told me to go and study with Odo Seikichi Sensei, so I did from that time on.

Odo Seikichi Sensei performing a sidekick on Dean Stephens at Camp Courtney, Okinawa.

On my first day of studying Okinawa Kenpo Karate Kobudo under Odo Sensei, we did kihon waza and started learning Naihanchi Shodan and Tonfa Ichi. The first time I swung the tonfa downward I hit my knee just below the kneecap, and it hurt like the dickens. I learned early on not to use wide stances when doing kobudo. The kobudo front stance is a deeper and narrower stance than the typical Seisan Dachi.

At that time I met a young Sandan named Carlos who showed me the ropes and took an interest in my development in Okinawa Kenpo. He also helped show me how to put on bogu gear and how to fight in it. I did karate six to seven days a week when I was not on duty, twice on Saturdays, and once on Sundays.

My first actual promotion was held in Nago in Nakamura Taketo's dojo (son of Okinawa Kenpo's founder, Nakamura Shigeru). Nakaima Kenko, president of the All Okinawa Kenpo Karatedo Renmei, and Nakamura Taketo, chairman of the Promotion Board, both signed my Yonkyu Certificate. I saw Yamamoto Mamoru of Chito Ryu Karate there as well. That first promotion test consisted of kihon waza, empty hand kata, a kobudo kata, and bogu kumite. Maehara Seijiro, Kina Toshimitsu, Chibana Kenko, and others were also present.

Q: What was Odo Sensei like as a person and a teacher?

He was very polite yet very demanding. He insisted on some things very strongly, like how your belt was tied. He shook hands at the end of each class with each student that had been in class and thanked them for attending. He led each class and went through every basic and kata during each class, leading from the front. He showed students how to check stance, technique, power, etc.

Q: What made you stick with Odo Sensei as your primary instructor?

I loved the way he taught and the breadth of his kobudo knowledge. It was also his "mo ichi do" ("One more time!") and "mo ii kai" ("Ready or not!") spirit. I liked how he shook each student's hand and thanked them for attending class.

He had total dedication to karate. I saw it in little things, like when I was following his car driving down the road behind him and seeing him doing karate as he drove along. When we sat in the park, he would punch the bench he was sitting on. He helped me learn more about Okinawan culture by doing things like taking me to Okinawa bull fights.

Odo Sensei also helped open doors for me in the karate world. He introduced me to Kakazu Mitsuo Sensei at his house in Shuri and took me to Toma Seiki's house and dojo in Awase, Koza. He also took me to Matayoshi Shinpo's dojo in Naha. We attended a number of demonstrations and tournaments, which is where I met other quality Western practitioners like Kimo Wall. I first met Kimo after he did a demo for a bunch of Japanese businessmen. Odo Sensei took me there to do the demo, but Kimo was already doing it so we watched.

The Okinawa Kenpo Karate Dojo of Odo Seikichi.

Q: What were some specific things about Okinawa Kenpo that you liked?

Primarily I liked that it was / is a very practical system. Also, kobudo was done from the very first class I attended. It is a system of fighting that is full contact from the beginning and is very physically demanding. I liked that I could go to class every day and learn as much as Odo Sensei would teach me. Even though it was repetitive (or maybe because it was repetitive), I was able to internalize what I was shown. Odo Sensei would show you how to do the kata, and if you asked the right way he would show what the meaning of the form was by demonstrating it on you.

Q: What was a typical class like with Odo Sensei, and how was kata taught?

We would line up behind Odo Sensei and follow him through the kata while keeping our eyes closely on him, watching him do the kata over and over again. Then he would have us go to the back of the class and run the kata over and over again, occasionally receiving correction from senior students. As we were learning each kata, we would count out loud, "Ichi, ni, san," etc. We would also be required to measure our stances to make sure they were the correct distance in width and depth and our arms were the right height and distance from our chest.

You had to stay with Sensei in formation until you did not know the next kata, then you got out of formation and went to practice whichever kata you were currently working on. When the weapons kata started, you got back in formation and did each weapons kata, once again excusing yourself when things got passed your level.

Once the kata work was done, we would sometimes do bogu kumite, full-contact fighting with padded gear that resembled kendo equipment.

Dean Stephens performing a sidekick during a bogu kumite match.

Q: When did you return to the United States for good, and did you try to open a dojo right away?

I returned to the United States for good in 1988 and was stationed at Sand Point Naval Station, Seattle, Washington. I ran one karate class on base and one out of my condo in Federal Way, Washington. In 1989, I brought Odo Seikichi Sensei to Seattle, Washington, and conducted a seminar and several classes. Odo Sensei met Jerry Gould, James Knoblet, and Ronald Robles. I also took him to Dallas, Oregon where he met with Dennis Stocks and did a seminar.

Q: What were some of the challenges of teaching karate in the U.S.A.?

Americans are consumers by nature and want what they want, how they want it. They tend to feel that if they pay for classes they have a right to dictate what is taught. Another problem is big egos and individuals expecting to be able to punch or kick perfectly on the first go around, without hard work over many years. Getting Western students to let go of their egos was my biggest hurdle.

Q: When you look at the growth of karate in the U.S.A., do you think it is changing in positive or negative ways?

In some ways it is positive . . . but it is very negative on the tournament side of things. The kata divisions are becoming more like dance, not at all reflecting battle intensity and intent. Kobudo divisions are using very light weapons that could not be used in real situations. Gymnastics are being incorporated into the kata. Dramatic pauses are being held for far too long, or, conversely, the kata are executed at supersonic speeds. You have people doing kata they made up and winning kobudo divisions despite never having a qualified kobudo teacher in their lives. There is a distinct lack of understanding in the mechanics of weapons and why they are used in certain ways.

On the positive side, there are more resources available (like the internet) for research and contact amongst people who can share good information, translations, and techniques.

Q: What are some of the keys to preserving Okinawa Kenpo as Odo Sensei had intended?

We as students need to get together and work out with each other while leaving politics at the door. We should keep Odo Sensei's kata true to the way he taught it to each of us. He taught each of us a little differently depending on when we were with him and what backgrounds we brought with us. Each of us that were his students watched Odo Sensei and learned what we were ready to learn from him. As time went on, we might have learned something slightly different if we were ready for the next level of knowledge. As we get older, our understanding becomes wider in scope and also deeper in depth. Our skills become deeper and become a part of us.

Q: What are some of the most important lessons you've learned through long-term karate training that might benefit readers?

Awareness may be the most important lesson. Understanding that karate is a way of life — something that is applicable to daily living.

The following is a list of tenets that I think will help karate student's dive into the deeper, more meaningful aspects of training:

- Stay relaxed and calm as much as possible.
- Be aware of your surroundings.
- Look before you take any rash action.
- Before you strike, think and withhold your strike if possible.
- If mad, withhold your voice and think.
- Do not prejudge an opponent. If you do, you will find that you may have underestimated him / her and it may be too late.
- Do no harm to yourself.
- Do no technique before its time.
- Do not throw out the baby with the bath water.
- Do not discard a technique just because you don't understand it, because one day you may find out what it is for or you might find that it works with a very slight modification.
- Understand the history and background of the martial art you are studying as well as the underlying principles of the physical action you are doing.
- Understand tactics and strategy along with how to teach what it is you are doing.
- Keep up with your pursuit of knowledge. Continue to research the history.
- Continue to teach because you will learn more than the student from teaching.

Larry Isaac

Larry Isaac Sensei grew up in the American South during a time of racial unrest. Experiencing a wide variety of schools, including those "left behind" in terms of financing and attention, Isaac Sensei realized he would have to work diligently to avoid the negative path he saw others around him taking. Joining the United States Marine Corps, Isaac Sensei proved to be a standout soldier as well as martial artist. He parlayed that experience into teaching the martial arts back in the United States, influencing karate on the East Coast and in the Marine Corps itself.

Isaac Sensei is respected as someone who has found balance between operating a successful dojo, running well-respected tournaments, and keeping old traditions of training alive. His personal training experience spans multiple styles, including Golden Crane Kung Fu, Shorin Ryu, and ultimately Okinawa Kenpo, which he chose to make his lifelong pursuit.

Q: Isaac Sensei, could you tell us a little bit about when and where you were born?

I was born on August 22, 1950, in a small town called Eutaw, Alabama. If you imagine the smallest town you've ever been to . . . that's about the size of Eutaw. It had a few mom-and-pop eateries, but no Walmart, Sears, or fast food places . . . just the basics of a little town in Alabama.

Q: How would you describe your childhood? Were you the outdoor type or more of an introvert?

I think I was an eclectic type of kid growing up. My father was in the Air Force, so I did quite a bit of moving around. My mother and father always stressed the value of education, no matter where we ended up.

Early in my youth we moved to El Paso, Texas, where I went to a predominantly Hispanic school. Then we moved to Austin where I attended a black segregated school which was very poor, receiving little in the way of funding and support.

In my early teens we moved to Watertown, New York, my dad being stationed at the U.S. Air Force bomb site at Camp Drum. At the time I was probably five years behind my peers in terms of quality of education. I had to go to special ed classes to improve my reading, and also attend summer school to catch up on most of the core subjects. When I did have free time, I spent most of it in the mountains of New York (the Adirondacks and the Catskills) or playing sports like basketball, baseball, swimming, and track.

My time in New York proved to be difficult. I remember listening to the other students read and they flowed easily through the pages. When I tried, it was very slow, and hesitant, and jerky. Because there was a serious lack of flow when I was reading and my educational tools were weak, there was very little understanding. I could excel at sports and outdoor exercises . . . I was very proficient at hands-on learning. But when it came time for academic retention, I was hampered. It took a lot of time and effort to overcome those hurdles.

Looking back on those challenges I am grateful for the many valuable life lessons they provided. First, I realized that if I intended to succeed in life I would have to learn how to deal with different kinds of people. Second, I needed to understand the importance of education and that if I didn't want to be at the bottom of the social food chain of life I would need to learn how to articulate and express myself effectively. Most importantly, I had to make sure that my ethnicity and cultural background were not crutches, but sources of strength to achieve success.

I found these lessons extremely valuable when I entered the Marine Corps. In my reconnaissance unit and boot camp I was one of the few people of color in my platoons.

Q: As part of an Air Force family, what are some of your earliest memories of encountering martial arts?

Judo and wrestling were the big things when I was young. There were a few movies that highlighted Asian fighting moves, and on a few brief occasions actual Asian individuals were on screen. The basic atmosphere in American culture was that if you saw a throw of any sort, it was Judo. If you saw a chopping motion, it was karate. Martial arts in general were not a big deal to me in my youth because I was so preoccupied with outdoor mountain hiking and sports.

That being said, I was a shorter individual so from time-to-time people wanted to "punk the little kid out." A need for self-defense led to my first hands-on experience in martial arts under the instruction of a gentleman named Luke Easter. I was a teenager and signed up during the summer of 1967. Easter Sifu taught a Chinese art called Golden Crane, which was similar in execution to White Crane Kung Fu.

I stayed with Easter Sifu for about a year and also studied with a gentleman named Russell Griswall. When I trained with Griswall Sensei it was a rather typical format of, "Do as I say. Don't ask any questions." Griswall Sensei was primarily a street fighter with little structure or foundation in what he taught. In class he would use a few Japanese words, and taught stances that looked roughly like karate but lacked refinement. Training with him consisted primarily of getting beat up. If you asked questions, you got beat up. If you messed up, you got beat up.

Q: What made you decide the military was the path for you, and why did you ultimately choose the Marine Corps (considering your father was in the Air Force)?

During my junior year in high school, my dad got orders to move to the Davis-Monthan Air Force Base in Arizona. By that time I had caught up with my peers in New York in terms of academic skill. I had made the honor role during my last semester in New York, and my mom was so excited because she remembered the struggles I endured growing up.

When we got to Arizona it was a little bit of a culture shock for me because Tucson High School was very multi-cultural. It was Hispanic, black, white, Chinese, and more. Thanks to my previous efforts in studying I performed well academically there, although I didn't play as many sports.

One thing I noticed while in Tucson was that the black kids I knew had either been in reform school, jail, or some other kind of trouble. When I graduated my original plan was to go to college, probably at Arizona State or Northern Arizona University. However, I realized something. If I went to college with my friends, I would just end up getting into trouble right alongside of them. They were going to party and continue living as they had been living, and I saw the writing on the wall.

Soon thereafter I talked to a Navy recruiter. The recruiter said they would take me in about two to three months. I also talked to an Air Force recruiter and his waiting list was about six months. The Army recruiter was out when I went to visit him, but the Marine Corps recruiter had just gotten back from lunch. I said to him, "I want to join the Marine Corps. What is the fastest I can get out?" He said, "When do you want to leave?" I replied, "I need to go home and tell my parents that I'm going to join, but I'd like to leave Monday." He said, "Done deal. You'll leave Tuesday morning."

I found out that everybody in Tucson looking to join the Marines had to get on a bus and ride to Phoenix. From there we would be processed and flown to San Diego to the Marine Corps Recruit Depot (M.C.R.D.). At the time I was 17, so I had to have my parents sign off on everything. The night I met with the recruiter I went home and told my parents about my decision. My mother was crushed because she wanted me to go to college. I told her that I had to get away and join the Marine Corps or I would end up like the rest of the guys in the area. She understood.

I went down to the recruiter the next day with my mom and dad to sign all of the paperwork. That night I went home and packed some basic essentials. Saturday morning I was on a bus headed for Phoenix. A funny coincidence about that time — the Monday I left for Phoenix my dad received orders to go to Germany. Had I waited at all to enlist, I would have ended up living in Germany instead.

Q: Could you talk about your boot camp experience and if it was difficult for you?

I arrived at boot camp on July 31, 1968, at the M.C.R.D. in San Diego. Thanks to my experience in the martial arts, I was in the habit of keeping my mouth shut and sticking to my business. This was the hippy generation, full of afros and what not, but I had always kept my hair tight. I found myself right at home in boot camp; the discipline and physical fitness was up my alley. In fact, the day I arrived at the M.C.R.D. I knew I was going to make the Marines my career.

Private First Class Larry Isaac (seated left) with Private First Class Taylor in 1969. Third Recon Battalion had just finished a mission in the jungles of Vietnam.

Q: Did you continue your martial arts pursuits while in the Marines?

My introduction to the martial arts through Easter Sifu and Griswall Sensei made me very curious about the origins of karate, so I continued my research even after joining the Marines.

Back when I was with Griswall Sensei, I had once worked up the nerve to ask him where karate came from. As a result I got beat up. Eventually he said to me that karate was Japanese and had always been Japanese. I tried to do some research to learn more, but little written material was available. I was forced to take Griswall Sensei at his word for the time being.

Six or seven months later, while at Camp Pendleton in San Diego, I met an individual who trained in Tang Soo Do named Howard Jackson (nicknamed "The California Flash."). We used to go to the same barber shop in Oceanside, California. One time I approached him and asked, "I know you're a Korean stylist, but could you tell me where karate came from?" He said, "I don't know a lot about karate, but I do know it began in Okinawa. A lot of our techniques look like Okinawan martial arts and Shotokan. The Koreans who studied karate in Japan tended not to be recognized or promoted by the Japanese, so they created their own art."

I went back to my research and started digging around again, still coming up with very little. In 1969 I received orders for Vietnam, but I stopped off on Okinawa before being deployed. Of course, I realized I had arrived at the home of karate, but didn't get a chance to stay long. When I got to Vietnam I was sent to the 3rd Reconnaissance Battalion, Charlie Company, which was based at Quang Tri. We had a lot of missions that sent us into the bush, but whenever I got a chance to spend time back in the rear of the battalion I snuck in some karate training with the other Marines. That went on for about a year until I came back to the United States.

Q: Were you able to spend time on Okinawa after your tour in Vietnam, or did you come directly back to the United States? How did you continue your training?

I went back to the United States after Vietnam, reporting to A Company, First Recon Battalion, First Marine Division, at Camp Pendleton. Soon after I reported in I received temporary order to report to the Marine Corps Development and Education Command at Quantico, Virginia. While there I attended the three week Marine Corps Hand-to-Hand Close Combat Academy. I was the honor graduate from the program in March of 1971.

My karate journey then continued under the instruction of Bobby Joe Blythe, operating out of Dumfries, Virginia. He spent several tours on Okinawa and had trained with Nakamura Shigeru of Okinawa Kenpo. It was through him that I was able to receive a stable and solid foundation in traditional karate that would serve me well in later years. This training took place in 1972 until I went back to California. Unlike some of my earlier instructors, Blythe Sensei seemed open to answering questions and talking about his past training. He told me directly that I needed to get to Okinawa if I wanted to pursue karate. Also, he informed me that I should keep my eyes open for a Marine named Bill Hayes, who was one of the top Western practitioners and a direct student of Shimabukuro Eizo Sensei.

Larry Isaac with First Sargeant Saxton in front of headquarters in 1969.

Q: When did you finally get your chance to visit Okinawa long-term?

That occurred in 1973. When I arrived on the island I sought out karate as quickly as I could. I remembered the stories Bobby Joe Blythe Sensei had told me about Bill Hayes, so I figured I would look for the same teacher Bill-San had. That led me to the dojo of Shimabukuro Eizo Sensei. When I got there I saw a big bulletin board, and in the center of that board was a picture of Bill Hayes. I knew I was in the right place.

I was fortunate in that Shimabukuro Sensei accepted me as a student, and my assignment on Okinawa allowed for ample training time. I practiced seven days a week for a full year. On Saturdays and Sundays I attended special classes with sensei where I benefited from a lot of one-on-one attention. I trained from 1pm-3:30pm on those weekends. On weekdays I attended the regular classes at 6:30pm-8:30pm, after which I would stay until about 11pm, training on my own. There were many occasions when sensei came into the dojo and told me, "I-zack [Isaac], you go base now. Need go to sleep. Sensei go chicken farm early."

I was able to keep such a rigorous schedule because I was a Sergeant and I ran the fitness center for Camp Hansen. I had four other Marines working for me, which allowed me to work during the day and delegate responsibilities in the evening. I was blessed in that, due to sheer training hours, I was getting years' worth of martial arts experience in mere months.

Q: Could you talk more about Shimabukuro Sensei's teaching style? What did he like to focus on and how did he balance kata, bunkai, etc.?

Shimabukuro Sensei loved kata, no doubt about it. I made the mistake one time early on of trying to spar in the dojo. Sensei stopped me and said, "No. No understand kata, no can fight." One day at our weekend class I was working out, doing kata with Shimabukuro Sensei watching. Halfway through he stopped me and said, "Too much speed. No understand. One speed fast kata, not good. Little fast, little slow, strong here but not here. Kata like fighting, so fight like kata."

I didn't quite understand, so he demonstrated for me. After watching I thought, "Wow. What did he just do?" So I asked, "Sensei, one more time please. You show me." He said, "No. More better this — you punch me." He wasn't joking around, so I went in to blast him. Next thing I know I was on my backside looking up at the ceiling and praying that nothing was broken.

He helped me up slowly, telling me it was okay. At that time I was in peak condition, not only as a Marine but as the operator of the Camp Hansen Fitness Center. Yet there I was, knees wobbling, eyes watering, hurting bad. He said to me, "Japanese say bunkai. Okinawans, tichiki."

A few weeks down the road I was working on kata during an evening class, running Naihanchi Shodan and Seisan repeatedly. I must have done them 50 times each and there was a big puddle of sweat on the tile floor. I was getting close to passing out so Sensei stopped me and began discussing parts of the Naihanchi kata. He explained that a technique we normally accepted as a block was, in fact, a strike. I was struggling to understand how something could be both a block and strike at the same time, so to clarify he demonstrated the technique on me. I grabbed at him but before I knew it I was down on my knees in pain. I asked him to please show it again slowly, and he said, "I already do slow, you no see!"

After class that day, I went back to the barracks feeling pretty beat up and confused. I didn't want to go to the evening class, but something inside me kept prodding to ask more questions about what I had seen that day. While at the barracks I met up with one of the Corporals that worked for me. He was a big bodybuilder type, so I said to him, "Grab my hand." He said, "No! You're gonna try some of that karate stuff on me." I said, "No, no, I just want to see something."

He refused to grab my hand, but instead grabbed my collar . . . figuring it would adequately defuse my plans. I recreated the movement that Shimabukuro Sensei did to me and the Corporal ended up in the floor. After spitting out some bad words, he told me that I wasn't going to do any more of that stuff on him. Once was enough — I was glad for the opportunity to try because I was able to see the value of what I had been taught earlier.

That evening I went to class and trained in kihon, kata, and yokusoku kumite (pre-arranged fighting drills). All night I was thinking, "kata, kata, kata," even during the fighting drills. When Sunday came around I was able to study kata with Shimabukuro Sensei again, and I noticed he was grinning at me slyly. I thought, "Oh no. He's getting ready to do something to me." Instead he just said, "Jouzu. Jouzu Arimasen. Good, good." That small confirmation that I was beginning to understand his methods was a huge moment.

Q: Seeing as how you had an introduction to Okinawa Kenpo via Bobby Joe Blythe, were you tempted to look around at other schools, namely Okinawa Kenpo, while studying with Shimabukuro Sensei?

I wanted to, yes. In fact, a good friend of mine at Shimabukuro Sensei's dojo, a gentleman named Joseph Bunch, went to Henoko to visit Maehara Seijiro Sensei's dojo. Once Mr. Bunch got stationed further north on the island at Camp Schwab, he decided to continue his study in Okinawa Kenpo with Maehara Sensei full-time. I was tempted to go train with him, but I quickly realized there was too much to learn with Shimabukuro Sensei and that I couldn't afford to split my efforts and time.

Q: Did you continue your training when you returned to the U.S.A. in 1974?

Yes. I was stationed at Camp Lejeune, located in North Carolina. Interestingly, I returned to the U.S.A. as a Godan (5th degree black belt), courtesy of Shimabukuro Sensei. Obviously my time in Okinawa was rather short to receive such high rank, even considering my earlier training in the U.S.A. and Vietnam. Shimabukuro Sensei didn't have set time intervals for giving rank, and instead based it on performance for me. I defeated all of the other students at our dojo in kumite-shiai (sparring competition) and had won numerous other island competitions . . . so Sensei awarded me the rank. In July of 1974, I won the Island Championship held on Kadena Air Force Base and was given the "Best Fighter Award" by renowned master Soken Hohan Sensei and Kise Fusei Sensei.

Once I arrived back in the States I started training at Camp Geiger, which was a satellite facility of Camp Lejeune. I began training routinely with Mr. Richard Gonzalez, who was a Nidan (2nd degree black belt) in Okinawa Kenpo. Neither of us really cared about the specifics of rank. We just considered ourselves two black belts that wanted to work out. Unfortunately, I found that the kata of Okinawa Kenpo and Shorin Ryu were quite similar but with subtle differences; as a result I began getting them confused. I made the decision to switch my efforts over to Okinawa Kenpo Karate and Kobudo full-time.

In 1974 I also found out that Bill Hayes Sensei was stationed at Cherry Point, not terribly far from Camp Lejeune. I made a specific effort to go visit him. Although I had begun studying Okinawa Kenpo again in earnest, I knew Bill-San was someone I wanted to meet and gain insight from. When I visited Cherry Point to meet up with him, I entered the training hall where class was being held. I saw Bill-San in the back wearing a white belt, presumably to mess with everyone. The class started off with 100 sit ups, 100 kicks each leg, 100 punches, and so on. I enjoyed the hard work but was really there to meet Bill-San, so, as quickly as I could, I got him alone and introduced myself. We've been friends ever since. In fact, Bill-San and another Shorin Ryu Great, Marine Doug Perry, became like big brothers and mentors to me.

Q: Could you talk more about your efforts to organize training sessions at Camp Geiger?

Richard Gonzalez Sensei and I had an open door policy at our Geiger classes. I made a decision to help spread the word about our training by going on the tournament circuit. In those days there was a lot of taekwondo; kung fu was becoming popular as well thanks to the movies. I wanted to show some traditional karate and make our mark.

For the first year and a half I went to every tournament I possibly could. In 1975, I went to Greensboro, North Carolina, and attended a taekwondo event that was billed as full-contact. So I went to fight and got paired up with the local, hometown hero — a big, long-haired, blonde taekwondo fighter who stood at 6'2" and weighed 290 lbs. I knocked him out and got disqualified for it. I was surprised because the tournament was supposed to allow for that. The crowd was also surprised at the result of the fight since I was only 5'9" and weighed 150 lbs.

My large, blonde opponent moved on in the tournament and I was left to watch. Unfortunately for the taekwondo fighter, he faced a gentleman named Vic Coffin next. In short order Mr. Coffin knocked him out also. That was the beginning of a long friendship between Vic and I, but more importantly, an intense rivalry. At my invitation, Coffin Sensei started coming to my training sessions with Gonzalez Sensei. Whenever we went to the same tournament, we did our absolute best to beat each other. It turned out to be great motivation for us both. As the saying goes, "Two warriors, steel sharpening steel."

Q: When was your next opportunity to return to Okinawa?

In 1980 I got a lucky break and the Marine Corps sent me back to Okinawa, stationed at the 3rd Marine Division Headquarters at Camp Courtney. I was a Staff Sergeant and was selected for Gunnery Sergeant. I had 999 Marines to oversee. The Sergeant Major told me, "If you can be a Company Gunny over at Headquarters Company, Headquarters Battalion you can be Company Gunny anywhere in the Marine Corps." It turned out he was right because my next command was 1st Battalion 6th Marines with 200 troops, which was nothing in comparison.

Q: When you got to Okinawa in 1980, was that your first chance to meet and train with Odo Seikichi Sensei of Okinawa Kenpo?

I had trained with Odo Sensei before, actually. In 1979 we brought him over to the U.S., which was the first time he had come to the States. Richard Gonzalez, Vic Coffin, Al Louis, and myself picked up Odo Sensei at the airport and had some great training. That being said, getting to spend extensive time with Odo Sensei on Okinawa was very valuable for my development.

Q: Could you talk more about Odo Sensei and his teaching methods?

Odo Sensei had a great love for kata, and it showed in his teaching. He was a collector and had an extensive repertoire of weapons, which was one of the things that prompted me to train with him full-time. Like most of the teachers of his generation, Odo Sensei focused on kihon and strong fundamentals. He also integrated limited sparring in the dojo with the padding that Nakamura Sensei favored. Undoubtedly, kata and kobudo was the backbone of his training and teaching.

Isaac Sensei performing an Eku posture from Odo Seikichi's kobudo curriculum.

I remember Odo Sensei used to love to do the breathing kata he received from his Goju Ryu background. Tensho was his favorite, and one time when I saw him working on it he said to me, "Used to do all the time." Then he switched over to practicing Sanchin. I noticed that he did Sanchin in an older fashion, with hands open throughout. He had received the kata from Nakamura Shigeru Sensei, who did it in the style of Higaonna Kanryo as opposed to Miyagi Chojun, who adapted the kata to a closed hand method. Later, Odo Sensei taught the kata in a more modern way, adopting the common closed hand method.

It's important to note that Odo Sensei, like many instructors, experienced evolution within himself over time. If we were to look at students who were with him during different eras, we would notice subtle differences in their performance and understanding. This is a result of Odo Sensei's teaching preferences and his habit of adjusting to each student's specific body type and disposition. Even Odo Sensei's own understanding of kata and bunkai changed over time, which is why there is no one right way or one correct explanation for the practice of Okinawa Kenpo.

Q: Why do you think Odo Sensei was hesitant to teach things like kyusho and tuite?

Nakamura Shigeru Sensei had a number of other prominent students besides Odo Sensei, including Oyata Seiyu Sensei, Kise Fusei Sensei, Maehara Seijiro Sensei, etc. Whenever I would see them doing techniques like vital point striking (kyusho) or joint manipulations (tuite), I would ask Odo Sensei, "Do you do? Why no teach?" Odo Sensei would respond, "G.I. no like. Too much hurt. More better do kata." Luckily I had my background with Shimabukuro Sensei to fill in some of the gaps, otherwise I might not have known enough to ask questions of Odo Sensei regarding deeper matters of karate's execution.

One time when I asked about kyusho, Odo Sensei said to me, "Maybe talk about Udundi." This was an old term for the palace hand as taught by Uehara Seikichi. Uehara Sensei, Nakaima Sensei, Shimabukuro Zenryo Sensei, and others were all in an organization with Nakamura Shigeru Sensei. They had trained together and shared information, of which Odo Sensei was privy but often didn't teach in more modern times.

Q: Did any other instructors significantly affect your training? What can you tell us about them?

At one point there were some complications in the politics and organization of Okinawa Kenpo, so in order to steer clear of it I started training with Kise Fusei Sensei, who was experienced in Okinawa Kenpo as well as Matsumura Seito. Years later I met Nitta Seifuku Sensei, who was a practitioner of Matsumura Seito as well as Seidokan under Toma Seiki. I liked Nitta Sensei right away and spent a lot of time training with him.

I felt through these experiences I was improving the diversity of my training while still keeping to what Odo Sensei taught me. This is the same method Odo Sensei himself used to become the great master he was. As we know, Odo Sensei was one of the senior students of Nakamura Shigeru. However, he also spent a lot of time at the Higa Seiko Goju Ryu Dojo, the Shimabukuro Zenryo Dojo, the Shimabukuro Tatsuo Dojo, and others. Kimo Wall Sensei, a student at the Higa Seiko Dojo, has confirmed that Odo Sensei trained there extensively.

Kakazu Mitsuo Sensei in 1985. Kakazu Sensei was a significant influence on Odo Seikichi Sensei's kobudo.

It is also important to note that Odo Sensei's kobudo was heavily influenced by Kakazu Mitsuo, who in turn introduced Odo Sensei to Matayoshi Shinko. At the time, Odo Sensei and Matayoshi Shinpo (Shinko's son) were dojo-mates in those kobudo classes with Kakazu Sensei. It is a fact, at one point Matayoshi Shinpo Sensei (the son) traveled to Japan and spent significant time there. When he returned to Okinawa he needed help remembering a number of kata and turned to his sister for assistance. Although she was not on the dojo floor, she was in the dojo every day with their dad. She remembered all the kata well and practiced Ryukyu Buyo, traditional Okinawan dance, which is closely connected with the practice of "Ti", or karate.

Q: As you continued your own karate education you also became an influential instructor, both in the Marines and the private sector. Could you talk about some of those early teaching experiences?

Two of my first black belts were Mr. George Epps and Mr. Charles Mann. Both went on to become world championship competitors. Mr. Ron Donvito, Mr. Cardo Urso, and Mr. Leon Wright were early black belts as well (all of whom influenced the direction of the hand-to-hand combat program in the Marine Corps). I've always been very proud of these gentlemen as well as my other accomplished students, but I do not claim their achievements as my own. They worked hard and stepped forward to make a difference in saving many lives in all the branches of our military and law enforcement.

Q: You've managed to preserve a lot of old style of training while also achieving commercial success as a dojo owner. How have you balanced the two and not sacrificed quality for quantity?

First, I have a strong spiritual base for my training and leading. I've had several surgeries and health complications, some of which were due to my time in Vietnam. I do not dwell on those things or burden others with them. In fact, one time while teaching a seminar I started experiencing brain bleeding. I technically died while the paramedics transported me to the hospital. I was brought back to life and was given a chance to see "the sun rise twice." All of that has given me some perspective on what is important in the martial arts.

When people come to study with me I let them know that I train the old way. If they also want to train that way, fine. If not, I do not hesitate to recommend other schools to them. While I've seen other schools and franchises make hundreds of thousands of dollars, I have never been motivated by financial gain. Karate is part of my survival, pure and simple. I was given tools by my teachers that have helped me stay alive, and now I want to share those tools with others.

One of the things I try to stress to students and those I train with is the power of choice. Every person has the choice to train or not to train, just the same as they have the choice to be a good citizen or a criminal. Through martial arts the student can learn the power of making good choices, even when those choices aren't easy.

Q: Having gone through the growth and maturation process of a lifetime of martial arts training, what do you think the next few generations need to do in order to preserve karate as it was intended?

I really think all lifelong karateka need to make a trip to Okinawa at some point in their lives. It's a matter of feeling the air, meeting the people, and training on the soil.

Also, there is a lot of talk about avoiding ego in the martial arts . . . but the loudest voices condemning ego tend to be the most pompous individuals. People find weird ways of trying to show how egoless they are, all while bragging and posturing. The key to preserving karate the right way is in understanding the mindset and spirit of karate without falling into those traps of "look at me."

Future karateka should understand that rank is a combination of skill, time, and effort. High karate rank is often a result of the impact a person has made on a karate style. Many individuals wonder why high rank never comes to them, but miss the fact that they have done nothing substantial to spread their art or improve the lives of other martial artists.

Self actualization is going to be the key in overcoming the hurdles of modern karate. While some karate has been well-preserved, much of it has passed quickly from hand to hand, becoming altered and watered down for consumer purposes. The karateka of the future will need to study hard and dig deeper to find resources that will enhance their training and answer questions that their primary art has not addressed. It's going to take intestinal fortitude to look honestly at their own training and endure criticism as they break out of their watered down habits . . . but greatness often comes from the willingness to take chances, stand out (many times alone), and excel.

Chapter 10 –
Oyata Shin Shu Ho

Oyata Seiyu ("Taika") is one of the most well-known masters to have ever lived in the United States. Renowned for his high skill level, depth of knowledge, and combative prowess, Oyata Sensei's reputation preceded him in later years as demand for seminars grew.

Oyata Sensei's journey in the martial arts was not typical of his generation. Conscripted into the Japanese Army during his teenage years, Oyata Sensei was moved into the Kaiten Suicide Torpedo Program, which consisted of torpedo attacks operated by a pilot from inside the torpedo itself.[73] Fortunately, World War II ended before Oyata Sensei completed his mission and he was able to survive.

During his time in the military, Oyata met two old Okinawan Bushi (warriors) by the names of Uhugushiku no Tan Mei and Wakinaguri no Tan Mei[74]. Connected to the royal court, these men were able to teach old methods of ti (karate) to Oyata Sensei before they passed away.[75] Oyata Sensei later improved and diversified his skill set by training under Nakamura Shigeru of Okinawa Kenpo, becoming one of the most well-known champions of the style.

In 1968, Oyata Sensei made his first trip to the United States, opening a dojo and giving

---

[73] "History - RyuTe" 2014. 31 Dec. 2014 <http://www.ryute.com/html/history.html>.
[74] "Tan Mei" was a traditional title as opposed to an actual name.
[75] Sells, John. *Unante: The Secrets of Karate*. WM Hawley, 1995. 193. Print.

Americans early exposure to his art. He returned to Okinawa shortly after, teaching military members on the island. Oyata Sensei returned to the U.S. in 1977, this time to stay. It was after he moved west for good that his reputation began to grow thanks to consistent teaching and seminars. It was during this time that Oyata Sensei exposed the West to the terms "tuite jutsu" and "kyusho jutsu," the arts of joint locking and vital point striking, both of which are key in the understanding of old style karate.

Oyata Sensei developed the stylistic term "Oyata Shin Shu Ho" to recognize his top tier students, and to honor their efforts in preserving his teachings.

Greg Lindquist

Lindquist Sensei's martial arts journey began by being in the right place at the right time. While working in a small Kansas gas station, Mr. Lindquist came face to face with one of the most formidable martial artists in the world. This stern looking Okinawan gentleman — Oyata Sensei — had opened up a dojo in town and was taking on new students.

Lindquist Sensei had the foresight to pursue karate with Oyata Sensei and managed to survive the difficult training. When Oyata Sensei traveled back to Okinawa, Mr. Lindquist proved vital in the continued communication between Okinawa and America. Upon Oyata Sensei's return to the U.S., Lindquist Sensei was instrumental in helping establish schools, an organization, and seminar tours.

Lindquist Sensei is highly regarded for his loyalty to Oyata Sensei and for the depth of his karate and kobudo knowledge.

Q: Lindquist Sensei, what was your earliest experience with the martial arts?

Around 1968, I noticed that posters for a dojo had been put up around town, advertising a new school. One of the flyers had been placed in the gas station where I worked. The instructor, Oyata Seiyu, lived one block away from the gas station and would pass by as he went shopping at the local corner convenience store. One day on the way back he stopped at the gas station. We met, and without much conversation he said, "You come dojo," and pointed to the poster already hanging in the window.

I thought about it and said to myself, "What harm can it do?," and went that same day.

I worked out with other people in other systems over the years between 1969 and 1977 (the interim where Taika Oyata returned to Okinawa due to a family medical emergency), but I never accepted another individual as a full-time instructor. Oyata Sensei was my one and only instructor.

Q: Were you involved with the military at any time, and in what capacity?

Due to a medical condition, I was declared 4F when I got examined for military duty. This made my training with Taika for all these years all the more satisfying, proving people with medical issues can still practice martial arts and be proficient.

Q: What was it about Oyata Sensei that impressed you and made you decide to stick with him as an instructor?

Number one impressive feature: Taika had limitless knowledge regarding martial arts, technique, teaching methods, and more. Oyata Sensei was given incredible gifts in the training he received from his two instructors, and he enhanced it all the more by training with other instructors like Nakamura Shigeru and Uehara Seikichi, as well as contemporaries like Toma Shian, Odo Seikichi, Kisei Fusei, and more. He was always learning and developing his understanding of martial arts right up until his passing.

An equally important feature was Oyata Sensei's sincerity. Upon meeting Taika, I felt he was authentic and original with good credentials lending to credibility, and he also maintained a sense of Asian culture from his homeland.

I knew from the start if Taika said something, a) he meant it, b) he could and would do it, and c) if he told you to do something, you could bank on it working. A student of mine made a remark, having met Taika years ago, that he only became a student because when he met Taika and called him "Master," Taika slapped him on the head and said, "I no master; I instructor," and walked away. This was what Taika was like; no putting on airs or arrogance, but making it clear that if he said or did something, it would work and work well. This made training with him very grounded and a solid foundation to grow from.

Q: What was Oyata Sensei like as a teacher in the early days?

At first, he was very stern and strict in teaching. It was his way or the highway (a phrase he used for years), explaining that optimal results were only possible if students did the technique or kata exactly as he did. As time went on, he relaxed and became kinder and more thoughtful, sharing more with us as we proved our dedication to his system and teachings.

Q: What was the material Oyata Sensei liked to cover (kata, sparring, weapons, basics, etc.)?

My first class with Taika involved him acting as referee while his student Nicky Nicholson and I put on bogu kumite gear, followed by me soundly getting my head busted. I remember it was a very painful and "trial by fire" class, getting beat up not just by Nicky, but also Taika himself at certain points.

After demonstrating what a real fight can be like in that first class, Oyata Sensei then moved into teaching kata and weapons in following classes. Since he taught seven days a week for hours at a time, he was able to change up the routine pretty well, getting across a wealth of knowledge in short order.

Q: Were you tempted to quit during the early stages of your training? Surely you would have had second thoughts with that kind of treatment?

Quitting was not an option. I was infatuated with the idea of training, especially with someone so skilled and authentic. The idea of giving up was never a consideration for me.

Q: How early in your training did Oyata Sensei introduce the ideas of tuite (joint manipulation) and kyusho (vital point striking)? Was bunkai (kata analysis) a big part of his teaching?

How did Taika introduce tuite and kyusho . . . first answer is "painfully." The purpose was for us to understand the pain and weakness of the body. He explained that kata had very deep instruction, including but not limited to kyusho and tuite. Although this kind of training started for me in 1968, the first real titled "tuite and kyusho" training was introduced in 1977 after he returned to the U.S.A. for good.

Oyata Sensei performing a tuite technique during a seminar in the 1980s, located at Wood Jr. High School in Davenport, Iowa. Greg Lindquist emcees in the background.[76]

Q: As you mentioned, Oyata Sensei went back to Okinawa a year or two after you started your training. Did you manage to stay in contact with him after that? If so, how?

---

[76] Davenport images courtesy of Peter Ryan.

Oyata Sensei received word of a family emergency in Okinawa, requiring his return in early 1969. Until he traveled back to the U.S.A. in 1977, I continued training and building schools here in the U.S. with some other students, and wrote letters to Taika in Okinawa. These letters, known nowadays as "snail mail," are how I came to know Jim Logue, Taika's new American student in Okinawa, and Taika's only other original and lifelong student. Jim would translate our letters to Taika, then draft Taika's responses and send them to me. This continued until Jim's return to the States in 1971.

We continued to write to Oyata Sensei throughout the early 1970s, but less frequently as we began to build an American organization between Jim, myself ,and a handful of others, which took up a lot of time and effort. We were working on raising money to send one of us to Okinawa to train with Taika, and bring back that training for the rest of us to learn. However, those plans changed when we received a letter in 1977 stating that Taika himself was returning to the U.S.

Q: Right after Oyata Sensei left in 1969, was it difficult starting a program based on your limited experience? Were you worried about "not knowing enough"?

Of course I was worried about not knowing enough! At this time, I was one student among a small group in the area. However, the enthusiasm we had for training did not give us time to allow this anxiety to settle in and stop us. And the best way to beat out a negative thought is to "train, train, and train some more!"

Q: Could you discuss your time with Oyata Sensei while in Okinawa? How did you get to the island, and what was Oyata Sensei's dojo like?

I went to Okinawa in 1975 to meet up with Taika after his absence from my life in 1969. This first trip was by airplane, in connection with the Heart of Japan-American Association based in Kansas City, MO. Over the following years, I made several more trips to Okinawa, each one opening up more and more about Taika and his culture for me to appreciate. He introduced me to several of his students and his family, but I trained more with him at his house rather than a regular school. At this time, it was common for dojo(s) to be built into the family house itself, rather than a separate "storefront" location.

I have been to Okinawa five separate times over the years, meeting with people like Uehara Sensei, Nagamine Sensei, Arigaki Sensei, Yoshizato, Toma, Odo, Senaga, Miyahira,

Miyazato, Hokama and Nagamine Takashi. Every time was an education in culture and the arts.

Over the years, Taika led association-driven group trips to Okinawa. On these trips, we would train at the various sites like Nakagushuku Castle and Katsuren Castle.

When Oyata Sensei came to live in the U.S., I enjoyed all that Okinawa had to offer being with my instructor. I did not really have a need to go to Okinawa as much since Okinawa came to me.

Q: Could you talk a bit more about the Okinawan traditions and ways of teaching you experienced? How is it different from more modern models?

The Okinawan methods are less regimented, with smoother motion, more simultaneous attacks and defenses than most other systems. The Okinawan bushi (warrior) ways of teaching were created in response to actual attacks, so whatever did not work was not kept or taught.

Q: Did Oyata Sensei ever tell stories about his old instructors Uhugushuku and Wakinaguri? If so, can you share some of that with us?

In order for us to understand the importance of his training, Taika told us of his instructors over the years. Some points he made were how Uhugushuku was the descendant of a legendary Okinawa warrior "Uni" Uhugushuku, and Wakinaguri had fingers that were "all the same length" from constant pumice stone pounding practice. He emphasized the value of the concepts and traditions each one taught him.

I remember that Taika used to stress that martial arts were for all ages. Taika was in his late teens and early 20's when he trained with his early instructors, both men over the age of 90 at the time. Taika was very adamant about how his younger age should have made him a challenge to these old men, but their training was so complete that they showed him time and again that he was only a beginner.

Q: Did Oyata Sensei ever discuss Nakamura Shigeru Sensei (of Okinawa Kenpo)? What did he share about him?

Nakamura Sensei was well-known as a punch technician. Taika had a large amount of respect for Nakamura Sensei, explaining how anyone who trained with Nakamura learned very good punching method.

Q: Could you describe some of your experiences with bogu kumite and visiting other schools for shiai (competitive gatherings)?

After 1968, I made a few friends who were teachers in other systems. These friends would come to bogu fight with me in order to change up their own routines and form some good fighting technique foundation, but bogu is very difficult and I had trouble finding people to practice with on a long-term basis.

Greg Lindquist (left) and Oyata Seiyu (right) engaging in bogu kumite.

After Taika's return in 1977, we set up bogu tournaments in Kansas City, MO, and other parts of the country, to help spread the practice. This opened up new venues to train, but there was a marked difference between the point-sparring most were used to and bogu.

One difficulty in teaching bogu is getting people to understand how to penetrate with their strikes through the armor, to "move" their opponent. Most point-sparring allows for light touches that "could" damage the fighter; bogu armor calls for far more power to be demonstrated to count as a point.

Q: What kind of emphasis did Oyata Sensei put on kobudo? Did he have a preferred weapon, and did you have a preferred weapon?

Oyata Sensei put strong emphasis on kobudo. For weapons training, please understand, one does not choose the weapon; the weapon chooses the student. It has nothing to do with personal preference or, "I like how that looks / moves," but has to do with the comfort of the movement of the weapon in the hands of the practitioner. I have seen several people over the years try to be the "expert" with several weapons simultaneously, only to see become very frustrated and, in turn, give up weapons training altogether.

Taika's favorite weapon was the bo (six foot long wooden stick). He would demonstrate fighting techniques with the bo quite often, and, unfortunately, quite often on me.

Oyata Sensei performing a jo-vs-bo joint manipulation and disarm.

My personal weapon is the kama (sickles). They come in a pair, and there is a precise method of cutting and the techniques require a high-quality weapon that matches the practitioner. With live blades, the "comfort of motion" becomes of paramount concern in short order.

Oyata Sensei made it clear that his weapons training was very important. It was taught to him by Uhugushuku and was considered the treasure of the Uhugushuku family. Taika was the recipient of this training — the last person to be taught by the family teacher and continue the family tradition — and I am a proud descendant of this line through my personal training with Taika.

Q: When did you open your first dojo in the United States? What were some of the challenges and successes of that undertaking?

My first commercial dojo was opened in 1984. Prior to this, we trained wherever we could, be it a park or, more often, someone's basement or garage. We did not care where we trained, so long as we did.

Some challenges for the commercial schools I opened included locations with reasonable rent, keeping up with the come-and-go students, and even local legislation.

There was an issue at one point where a city ordinance was put in place against "bludgeon weapons," categorizing all manner of our weaponry under this new definition, making it so we could not practice in public. I went to the City Council, presented my case, and ended up getting the law changed to allow us to carry our weaponry to and from the school in a public forum.

In all my years of teaching, I have always done so on a part-time basis. I never worked to make my living as a karate teacher. I felt what Taika taught me, what he wanted all of his true students to do, was to help the community and the world by teaching good quality technique, not water it down to make it a fast-food martial arts mentality. This required me to keep my day job.

Q: You were in close communication with fellow senior students Jim Logue, Albert Geraldi, and Bill Wiswell, starting an organization in 1977. What was the goal of that organizational effort?

The goal we had was to start up an American organization so we could continue our training. We saw that if we had a good group here, bringing in money and having quality students, we could get our teacher to visit and teach us more or send one of us over to him.

This became even more important when Taika chose to come back in 1977; now our organization was no longer to "bring him here," but to help him make a life in the U.S. and continue our studies.

Q: According to some documentation and accounts, Oyata Sensei experienced difficulties here in the United States with unapproved usage of his art's name (Ryukyu Kempo) and also his methods of kyusho. Could you describe how this affected him and what efforts he took to resolve the situation?

First off, Taika was incredibly hurt and angry about those events. He felt there was very little honor or respect shown in this country to another person's knowledge and teaching ability. This led us to work on developing a name for our system that we could trademark and handle in a more legal fashion, as the customary Okinawan etiquette and courtesy was not being held to.

Q: How did your contact with Oyata Sensei continue throughout the '80s, '90s, and '00s? How did Oyata Sensei's art grow during that time?

I was there to pick up Oyata Sensei at the airport in 1977, and basically my life was no longer my own at that point. I accompanied Taika to seminars and training all over the country, oftentimes driving him from Point A to B, in addition to my teaching classes in my own schools. I helped introduce him to new students, provide for his (and his family's) needs, and always tried to ensure that Taika was not put in a bad position. As time went on and the association began to grow with people we could trust, I was able to back off a little. At that point he could travel on his own, which led to a number of phone calls discussing how the seminars went and what needed to be fixed, what should be done about certain schools or problems, arranging future events, etc.

Taika always wanted quality students, not quantity. Over this time period, Oyata Sensei received several offers for large schools, hundreds of students, big associations with large payrolls . . . he wanted none of it. He was all about having students who would train properly, learn what he taught as he had learned from his instructors, and keep the quality and art alive even if it was via a handful versus thousands.

Q: What do you think Oyata Sensei's vision was for the continued growth of his art?

It was always his wish that his students continue on the ways of the Okinawan bushi warriors, to be his "handprints and footprints on the world," to always strive to be warriors for a peaceful and free world by using what he taught us in defense of ourselves and others.

Q: What is your goal with your current organization in preserving the art? How do you carry on the kata, bunkai, and weapons of the system?

My goal is the same as my instructor's. He wanted his students to improve and grow by training, staying true to the proper art through kata, bunkai and kobudo, but also to be examples to other systems of what can truly be accomplished by studying earnestly in the ancient ways.

Q: When you observe the growth of karate in America, how would you like to see it develop in order to carry on the ways of the Okinawans?

I would like to see us go back to the old way of training. A major part of what Oyata Sensei brought to us was the traditions, culture, and context of what his instructors taught and showed him. It is this history and custom that has not been emphasized in the American karate scene, partly because most American martial arts groups were started by people who did not have access to this culture.

I feel the historical element enhances and accentuates what we know, helping us better understand our kata, bunkai, and weapons because it provides us with the reason why we train so hard. This was a way of life on Okinawa, not a hobby. Being a way of life calls for the history and culture to be learned so the karateka can lead a balanced way, not giving up on some of our training because of the unknown. This reason, this motivation, is part of the gift Taika showed me.

Q: Could you provide some words of caution and advice for individuals looking to pursue kyusho in their training?

People do not understand enough about kyusho to know all the implications of its use. Kyusho looks like it is a one-point knockout blow, but actually the techniques involve total control of your opponent. A kyusho expert understands how the body reacts, the strong and weak points of the body, and even how to tell the timing of the person's body functions (pulse, inhaling and exhaling, and blinking) and how these are affected by techniques. Kyusho affects the body's balance, posture, and weight and allows the expert to use these features to their best advantage.

Taika said kyusho was "vital points technique," meaning it affected a person's body in damaging and possibly lethal ways. A trained practitioner has a rough enough time keeping the control needed to do "only enough and no more." Anyone who does not invest in proper training can very easily hurt someone unintentionally.

Q: Are there safety or healing measures associated with extensive kyusho and tuite training?

Oyata Sensei performing a kyusho knockout technique on Peter Ryan. Greg Lindquist stands far left.[77]

There are some healing methods we use, but they are not used or taught exclusively. We

---

[77] Image and knockout courtesy of Peter Ryan.

use these methods to undo or reverse the technique just performed in order to stimulate other vital points for the person. What we do is "instant pain," like a stone in the shoe, but when you remove the pain the person should return to normal without wanting to continue the fight.

Q: Do you have any final words of wisdom you'd like to give to karateka looking to make karate part of their lives?

To anyone considering studying martial arts, seriously train to understand what it is that you are actually doing. Keep an open mind, and do not become too proud of what you do. Stay humble at all times. No single system has all the answers, so show respect to all and try to understand what the other systems are doing and why. Staying true to your own technique and methods will give you a sense of confidence, but only if you study earnestly and learn to understand why something works one way, but not another. Accept this same mindset when dealing with others.

James Logue

Inducted into the Army in 1968, James ("Jim") Logue Sensei was one of the first Westerners to study with Oyata Seiyu for a prolonged period of time. At first Logue Sensei was just another student, but in short order he proved himself a capable practitioner, demonstrator, and emcee of events. Oyata Sensei came to rely on the young man to appeal to new Western students, and eventually Logue Sensei became one of the most senior and trusted proteges of the great master.

Logue Sensei passed away in 2011 — a loss that was felt deeply by the martial arts community. He was an extremely talented martial artist, and an enjoyable personality. Many relied on him as a key element for the future growth and dissemination of Oyata Sensei's art (including Oyata Sensei himself), a task which Logue Sensei's few primary students now endeavor to continue.[78]

Q: Logue Sensei, could you discuss your earliest experiences with martial arts? What were your first motivations to study?

In my early teens I was in the boy scouts, and a new scoutmaster, George Lawson, came into our troop and introduced us to Judo and boxing. George was a former Marine and held a black belt in Judo. I trained with him, mostly as an uke (recipient of technique), for about two years. I often helped him out when he taught other teenage groups. He was a large-frame man, and it was easier for the participants to throw me around than him.

A childhood friend, Gary Shull, had been accosted by older teens when he was a pre-teen,

---

[78] Images acquired from James Logue Sensei prior to his passing, with posthumous permission to print from the Logue family.

and his mother asked if I could help him overcome this trauma. So, I introduced him to what I knew and we began to seek any kind of martial arts knowledge that we could. Our sources were limited, so we found books and an occasional student who would help us. However, most of what we did, we did on our own.

Q: I understand that in 1969 you were stationed in Makiminato, Okinawa. Could you describe a little of your military background and how it brought you to the island?

On July 3, 1968, I was inducted into the United States Army. This was at the height of the Vietnam War, and everything was geared toward support of that. After completing basic and advanced training, I received orders for Okinawa. This was a bit unusual because most of the troops were sent to Vietnam or Germany.

To me, this was an act of fate. I truly wanted to find some place to learn martial arts and now I was being sent to the birthplace of karate. Ninety percent of all those completing advanced training at Fort Jackson, SC, were sent to Germany or Vietnam. In my class, we had two that went to Korea and four that went to Okinawa.

I arrived in Okinawa on December 24,1968, and was stationed at the 2nd Logistics Command, the largest supply depot for the Army in the pacific theater. The U.S. Air Force also had the largest air base in support of Vietnam at Kadena where B52 bombers flew their missions to Vietnam daily. The Marines were located mostly in the Northern part of the island, except for Futenma Marine Station located just north of Makiminato.

At the time I was stationed in Okinawa, it was still under American administration and the overall command of the local government was under the U.S. commissioner. All monetary exchange was in U.S. dollars, and the road system and electricity were the same as in the U.S.

Q: Did you study at multiple schools on Okinawa, or did you find Oyata Seiyu Sensei right away? What was your first meeting with Oyata Sensei like?

After arriving in Okinawa, I immediately set out to find a dojo. The base where I worked was just outside of Naha (Okinawa's capital). By cab, it only took 15 or 20 minutes to get down town, so I began my search there.

I first came across Nagamine Shoshin's dojo in Naha. I stopped in for a visit, but even though by today's standards it wasn't that far away, my meager Army salary didn't afford me enough money to pay for cabs to and from the dojo.

Nakazato Shugoro's dojo located in Aji was a little closer to the base, but I had brought my wife Sherry over and we were living on the opposite side of the base. Again, the expense of the cab rides precluded me from training there.

One day during lunch break at work, I went outside to play catch with some of the local workers who all loved baseball. I noticed a fellow serviceman practicing a kata. I asked him where he was training, hoping that we could perhaps share the cab fare. He explained that he walked from the base to the dojo and pointed in the direction that I lived.

I met up with him again that night, and he took me to Oyata Sensei's dojo. As it turned out, the dojo was in the village next to where I was living . . . literally two blocks away!

James Logue standing outside of Oyata Sensei's school. Sign reads: "Karate Dojo".

The small cinder block building could have been easily overlooked except for a sign in front. It was written in Japanese but I easily recognized the characters for "karate."

The class consisted of several other G.I.'s, some dependent teenagers, and some Okinawan students. I was approached by the dependent teenagers, who were part Okinawan and part American. They were fluent in both Japanese and English. Oyata Sensei spoke to me through them.

I was invited to come in and sit to watch a class. After a few minutes, I asked about the fees and class schedule. As explained to me, classes were every day, seven days a week. I could come every day or as often as I would like for a fee of six dollars a month. I could not get my wallet out fast enough to pay my first dues.

My first class the next day consisted of standing in a horse stance doing a blocking and punching drill. Oyata Sensei had one of his Okinawan black belt students teach me. Neither of us could communicate verbally since I didn't speak Japanese and he didn't speak English. I had to visually follow his instruction.

This type of instruction continued for several weeks, and then I was introduced to bogu kumite. I was much taller than anyone else in the dojo, so I was chosen by all of the Okinawans to spar. Of course, I didn't fair too well against them, but I was learning a lot through this experience.

After about a month of training, I was told there would be a demonstration on the base where I worked. Through the translator, I was told to emcee the demonstration since I didn't have enough experience to be a part of the demo. This seemed really strange to me as there were many others with much more insight into the art who would do a better job.

As the dojo practiced for the demo, Oyata Sensei began to explain to me in broken English and through his translators what he wanted me to describe during the demo. He also instructed me to buy and wear a brown belt during the demo. He didn't think a white belt would be well-received as a spokesman for the dojo.

Oyata Seiyu Sensei (seated center) leads a bogu kumite class. James Logue is seen crouching far left.

The day after the demo was as different as night and day for me. Suddenly, Oyata Sensei was talking to me directly, no longer using the translators, and also began teaching me directly. I guess this must have been some sort of test and that I had done well enough for him to trust me.

Q: When you started your training, was Oyata Sensei still a member of the Okinawa Kenpo Renmei? Could you describe how that affiliation transitioned into the creation of Ryukyu Kempo and subsequent styles?

Oyata Sensei was brought to the U.S. by a former student in the beginning of 1968. During this time, he was still affiliated with the Okinawa Kenpo Renmei. While he was in the States, internal politics from younger students caused a rift among the Renmei members. When Oyata Sensei returned to Okinawa after six months in the U.S., most of the seniors (except for Odo Seikichi Sensei) had left the Okinawa Kenpo Renmei.

Oyata Sensei and Toma Shian Sensei formed an alliance with Uehara Seikichi Sensei, establishing the Ryukyu Karatedo League. When I began training in February 1969, Oyata Sensei was no longer a member with Nakamura Shigeru Sensei. Shortly after I began training at Oyata's dojo, Nakamura Sensei passed away.

In 1977, several of Oyata's Sensei's American students — Albert Geraldi, Bill Wiswell, Greg Lindquist, and I — formed the American Federation of Ryukyu Kempo and brought Oyata Sensei back to the United States where he decided to live.

Nakamura Sensei had wanted all Okinawan karate to be united under one banner in order to give Okinawa credit for karate. This dream continued with Oyata Sensei as he called his art Ryukyu Kempo; however, in the mid 1980s, after he had introduced tuite and kyusho jutsu to the general martial arts public, others tried to ride his coat tails and began using Ryukyu Kempo as the name of their art also.

Since Ryukyu Kempo is really a generic term for karate, Oyata Sensei could do nothing about others using this name . . . so he decided to combine the words Ryukyu Karate or Ryukyu Te into an acronym of sorts, affecting the same dream of giving Okinawa full credit for karate, thus he formed the term Ryu Te.

Advised by his students to prevent someone else from stealing the name, he formally had the Ryu Te name, kanji, and patch design registered as a trademark. This proved to be a wise move as there have been several occasions where others tried to use this term in association with what they were teaching. They were advised through legal counsel that they were in violation of federal trademark laws and were subject to fines or worse.

Nakamura Shigeru Sensei of Okinawa Kenpo (seated far left) with Oyata Seiyu next to him. Kise Fusei is seen seated fourth from left.

Q: It is recorded that Oyata Sensei studied with two very unique individuals: Uhugushuku no Tan Mei and Wakinaguri no Tan Mei. Could you describe that training?

After WWII, Oyata Sensei worked for the U.S. Army delivering food and supplies to the outer islands on the east coast of Okinawa. He traveled to six different islands using an amphibious vehicle, visiting an island each day. His route took him through the seaside town of Teruma where he noticed an old man groveling for fish in small pockets of the coral reef during low tide. This man was very unusual because he still wore a warrior's top knot.

After asking some of the local villagers, Oyata Sensei found that this was Uhugushiku, a retired warrior whose family had a long relation to the nobility of Okinawa. Since Oyata

Sensei's job was dangerous, he thought that maybe this man could teach him some martial arts should he be robbed of his supplies. Although he had received martial arts training in the military, there was no in-depth study.

He befriended Uhugushiku by offering to take him to the deeper waters in his amphibious vehicle to catch bigger fish. After learning that Oyata Sensei's ancestors were also from the warrior class, Uhugushiku agreed to teach him.

The Uhugushiku family was noted for their skills in weapons, and Oyata's Sensei's first lessons consisted of learning the bo. He eventually learned many weapons from Uhugushiku in addition to the bo — sai, kama, nunchaku, jo, tonfa, chizikun bo, tan bo, manji sai, surichin and nunti bo. He was taught kata, concepts, and fighting techniques. There were also discussions about history, language, and culture so that he could better understand the arts of life-protection.

Uhugushiku also introduced Oyata Sensei to Wakinaguri, a large man of Chinese descent. Wakinaguri's family dates back to the original 36 Chinese families sent to Okinawa as emissaries. Wakinaguri was the sixth generation to receive his family art and, having no immediate family, he agreed to teach the young Oyata.

Lessons with Wakinaguri consisted of concepts and principles rather than repetition of drills. He learned how to make technique more effective and how to use this knowledge to read kata and decipher the code hidden within. As part of his training, Uhugushiku introduced him to the family scroll, much like the Bubishi, but in greater detail. This scroll is more than 20 feet in length and contains hundreds of pictures depicting many techniques and concepts. Just before Wakinaguri's death, Oyata Sensei was presented with a copy of this scroll.

Q: Speaking of training methods, what was your personal training like in Okinawa?

The training in Okinawa was a mix of a lot of things. First, there were drills aimed at teaching proper defensive covers. Then came kata training. A heavy kick bag was used for kicking and punching. There was makiwara training and occasional exercise to develop strength and speed. Everyday training included bogu fighting. Usually, before the night was over, you fought everyone in the dojo.

Sometimes, after most of the class left, I was asked by Sensei to stay a little longer. He worked with me privately on weapons fighting and finer points of kata. I wasn't sure if he was treating me special or that he just needed someone to practice his techniques on.

At least once a month on the weekends, we'd travel to other dojo(s) or they would come to ours for bogu fighting. It became a highlight of training for those of us who liked that sort of thing. We also held belt tests in conjunction with Toma Sensei's dojo and would travel to Koza where they trained. There, Uehara Sensei, Toma Sensei, and Oyata Sensei all sat on the testing board. We were called individually to perform a kata or two and then paired for bogu.

Q: Were there many cultural barriers to overcome in order to integrate into Okinawa (and dojo life in general)?

At the time I was in Okinawa, it was still under American administration and many of the locals worked on the bases. Most of them could speak English and were used to the Americans. There was a large number of military and U.S. civilian workers in Okinawa, so the locals were used to that.

When I first started in the dojo, Sensei didn't speak much English and some of the Okinawa students didn't, but as I stated before, several dependent kids were fluent in both languages and there was no problem with communication. After a month or so there, I began to learn a little Japanese and Sensei began to speak English to me directly.

I suppose it was probably more of an advantage than disadvantage that my first lessons were in Japanese. I had to use my eyes to visually understand what I was being taught rather than having to hear the words and try to watch at the same time.

Q: Could you share an interesting or funny anecdote that reveals a sense of Oyata Sensei that people might not have heard before?

We did several demonstrations while I was stationed in Okinawa, and they all included breaking. As I had observed during my first demonstration as emcee, the breaking was a little different than I had witnessed or read about. Boards were broken across the outstretched arm, leg, stomach, or back rather than breaking a stack of boards.

Sensei and I were doing a series of demos for a company in Koza that was selling timeshares in Florida to American servicemen. As part of the presentation, they hired Sensei to do a karate demo a couple of times a week.

So, after class, we'd drive to Koza and he and I would do the demo. Sometimes he asked me to do an empty hand kata or weapons kata. He also threw me around with some self-defense, and then we'd do the breaking. He would break a two by two across my outstretched arm, leg, back, and stomach. One particular night, he was breaking one across my right arm. *Smack*, it didn't break. He tried again to no avail, then he tried the left arm, my back, my stomach and then my leg, still the board did not give.

Oyata Seiyu Sensei breaking a board over the outstretched arm of James Logue.

His face began to redden in anger and he placed the board against the wall and kicked it only to have it push him back. Without saying a word, he walked outside and broke the board across the corner of the building. I believe that I could feel the building shake under the power of this strike.

He walked back in smiling and laughing. "Sometimes board no break." As we drove back to the dojo, we laughed about it as he explained, "It's okay board not break. If it break every time, everybody think fake!"

Q: When you returned to the United States in 1971 and ultimately opened your first dojo in 1973, what kind of challenges did you face at that time? What was the general perception of karate, and how did it manifest itself through the students you first attracted?

When I returned from Okinawa, most of the local dojo(s) were either taekwondo or American Freestyle. I wasn't used to this concept, so I kept to myself. I found a few dojo(s) to visit and was seeking others to spar using bogu; however, this was when the "safety chop

/ kick" was in vogue and no one was interested in really getting hit.

I noticed there were not very many people doing weapons except for nunchaku popularized by the Bruce Lee movies. I tried to garner some interest in the weapons, but it was so foreign to most everyone that, again, no one was interested.

On one of my trips home to see my parents, I noticed a dojo advertising Okinawan karate. This turned out to be Ridgely Abele, and he invited me to come teach at one of his camps in the mountains of North Carolina. There I was, back in my environment where I met many others who trained in Okinawan karate. Through those seminars I met others such as Doug Perry Sensei, Bill Hayes Sensei, Phil Koeppel Sensei, Kimo Wall Sensei, and many other influential Okinawan karate practitioners.

Q: How did you manage to maintain an active relationship with Oyata Sensei after you came to the States? Was it difficult continuing your learning?

After I returned to the States, I was stationed at Fort Hood, Texas, until I got discharged. At that time, I was corresponding with Albert Geraldi, Bill Wiswell, and Greg Lindquist as we worked on forming the American Federation of Ryukyu Kempo.

We maintained some contact with Oyata Sensei, but could not train directly with him. From 1972 until 1977 (when he [Oyata Sensei] returned to the U.S.), training was on my own except for an occasional meeting with the former students mentioned above. When Oyata Sensei was in the States, his students made an 8mm film with all the basic empty hand kata that we used as a guide for our continued training.

When Oyata Sensei returned to the U.S., he spent a couple of weeks with me refreshing what I had been taught in Okinawa and introducing me to new concepts. My students and I traveled to Kansas, where he lived, staying a couple of weeks each time. He also drove to South Carolina a few times for more personal training.

In 1981, I hosted a seminar at my dojo and invited several friends I had made from other Okinawan systems. This set off a wave of seminars for Oyata Sensei, and we also began to hold summer and fall camps.

Q: Were you surprised when kyusho became such a focal point surrounding Oyata Sensei?

Karate in the U.S. had become stagnate; there was nowhere for it to go. The only emphasis was on the sporting side of karate, and it was moving further away from the old ways of life-protection. The introduction of tuite and kyusho jutsu has been good for karate overall, in that it has sparked a new interest in finding the meaning behind kata other than the kick / punch definition that most have.

Unfortunately, some have found a way to "fool" everyone into false knowledge through "magic" tricks. It hasn't changed the real meaning of tuite or kyusho jitsu, but has hurt in that people try to associate themselves with Oyata Sensei, saying they learned his "secrets." People are really gullible believing that a lifetime of study can be learned by attending a few seminars. There is no magic button as people think, and those that teach these things are no more than snake oil salesmen.

Q: What emphasis is placed on weapons in your style? Is it seen as a companion to karate? When is it introduced to students?

Oyata Sensei's first lesson with Uhugushiku consisted of training with the bo and other weapons. It's my belief that weapons and empty hand go together. The same principles and concepts apply as far as footwork, angles, shifting, etc. If you watch the way the hands move using the weapon and imagine using only the hands, you can see no difference in empty hand.

There are differences in how each type of weapon is used. For example, bo and eiku are used differently even though they are both long weapons. Just as a fork and knife are used differently to eat, so go the weapons. Of course, as with any tool, the weapon multiplies the strength and power of a blow.

Q: It seems as if you have maintained Nakamura Shigeru's tradition of contact sparring with kendo-inspired bogu gear. What is your sense on the importance of sparring, and why have you chosen to continue the use of the original equipment?

Sparring and pulling punches is like target shooting using blanks. Your technique might be good, but you don't know if you really hit the target. Likewise, getting hit with a full power blow lets you know, without injury, how it feels to really get hit.

There are limitations to any type of sparring: gear confinement, limiting strikes to "point zones," etc. However, being able to move at full speed without limitation (and reacting to the same) trains the reflexes much better than never being hit or never being able to hit.

I know some say, "We do full-contact, but don't need the protection of the gear. We can take a full power punch or kick." Over my years of training, I've run across many who say such things. It has been my experience that after they receive properly placed kicks or punches, they quickly change their mind about that.

Like kendo is to sword fighting, so bogu is to kumite. No one wants to be cut with a live blade, and no one wants their ribs broken from a punch or kick.

Q: If you had to list just a few highlight moments or accomplishments regarding your propagation of karate in the U.S., what would you include?

I think helping Oyata Sensei with his seminars and conducting seminars of my own. It's surprising how much you learn about what you're teaching when you have to teach others. Teaching beginners is much different than teaching experienced martial artists. Beginners are a clean slate, and you teach from the bottom up. With experienced practitioners, you often have to overcome built-in prejudices in order to get them to overcome preset ideas.

I find you have to be a little more diplomatic and "politically correct" when you teach experienced people. You can't tell them they are wrong about their approach to a particular technique or they will not listen. You must approach it such that you get your point across, and then they decide whether it makes sense to them or not.

I learn as I teach. I watch how people move and how they approach a technique. I'm not trying to learn what they do, but better understand what I do. I think by sharing these ideas we all gain further knowledge into that which we study.

Q: What is your vision for karate's continued expansion? How do you think current generations can help keep the old ways alive while avoiding modern trappings that move us away from the core principles of the arts?

Unfortunately, I believe that the "old ways" are being lost. The generation that was close to the "old ways" (Oyata's generation) is getting old. Many are already gone, and those left to propagate these arts have been caught up in monetary gains.

M.M.A., American Freestyle, and all sorts of made up and combined systems are movements away from the old ways of karate; however, there are a few of us out there that try to adhere to the old ways. Those that trained in Okinawa in the 1960s and early 1970s were exposed to these methods. The training was for training, not for money or to see how many trophies you could win.

I've often talked to Perry Sensei, Hayes Sensei, Wall Sensei, and others who trained directly in Okinawa about how we are the last of a generation. It's a scary thought to know that this knowledge and experience lies with us.

Hopefully, we've instilled in our students the same sense of duty and obligation to keep the art as pure as possible. It is my desire that this experience, history, and spirit will remain for many generations.

Greg Lindquist and James Logue.

Chapter 11 –
Seibukan

Born in 1870, Kyan Chotoku was one of the most prominent karate masters of his time. Kyan Sensei was small and sickly as a youth, but thanks to the relatively high status of his family, he also had access to some of the best karate instructors on the island. Among his influences were Matsumura Sokon of Shuri Te and Matsumora Kotaku of Tomari Te. From these luminaries, and a handful of other legends, Kyan gained a healthful vigor and became one of the most deadly and knowledgeable practitioners on the island.

Kyan Sensei traveled to Japan and Taiwan during the 1920s, but eventually returned to Okinawa and moved to the village of Kadena.[79] Once settled, he took on a small number of students for long-term training. One of those students was Shimabukuro Zenryo. Shimabukuro Sensei was small in stature, much like Kyan Sensei, but had a great spirit and manner about him. Kyan Sensei spent a significant amount of time training the young Shimabukuro at his home in Kadena. In time, Shimabukuro Sensei became one of the most senior students of Kyan and worked diligently to preserve his art.

Kyan Sensei passed away in 1945, shortly after the conclusion of World War II. Shimabukuro Sensei waited until 1947 to begin teaching on his own, which he did to ensure the continuation and refinement of his own skills.[80] As American occupation increased, Shimabukuro Sensei eventually began teaching Westerners, often from the 503rd Airborne paratroopers. It was through that arrangement with the American military that

---

[79] "FightingArts.com - Kyan, Chotoku (1870-1945)." 2004. 31 Dec. 2014 <http://www.fightingarts.com/reading/article.php?id=106>.

[80] Bishop, Mark. *Okinawan Karate: Teachers, Styles and Secret Techniques*. Tuttle Publishing, 1999. 80. Print.

Zenryo and his talented son Zenpo first began their influence on karate in the West. Their specific line of karate is now referred to as Seibukan, but was also known as Sukunaihayashi Ryu ("Small Pine Forest" Style).

Walter Dailey

Walter Dailey is an Army veteran and one of the most senior Seibukan practitioners in the world. Dailey Sensei was trained as an Army paratrooper and arrived on Okinawa in 1960. One of the first beneficiaries of the cooperation between Shimabukuro Zenryo and the U.S. Military, Dailey Sensei grew very close to the Shimabukuro family and spent significant time training with both father (Zenryo) and son (Zenpo).

Dailey Sensei was the first individual to open a Seibukan karate school in the United States and was integral in long-term visitations by Shimabukuro Zenpo to the country. It was through Dailey's early efforts that Seibukan grew on the American East Coast, allowing a whole new generation of practitioners to experience the art for themselves.[81]

Q: Dailey Sensei, could you tell us when and where you were born? Do you remember hearing about any martial arts when you were young?

I was born in Philadelphia, 1940. The only martial art I ever heard about early on was Judo. They used to have a program at the Y.M.C.A. near where I lived, although I never attended a class. In terms of karate, the only thing I had ever seen was a book called *What is Karate?*, by Oyama Masutatsu. That book kicked off my interest in karate and stuck with

---

[81] Images courtesy of Walter Dailey and Angel Lemus.

me as I grew up, inspiring me to seek out Okinawa and pursue my training.

Q: As a youngster, were you an athlete, a troublemaker, a quiet introvert . . . how would you describe yourself?

Well we'll just skip the trouble part! Hahaha. I was interested in gymnastics and had joined the gym team in high school. We participated in the kinds of events you might see in the Olympics. I actually had joined gymnastics because I was crazy about the underwater demolition teams (U.D.T.) being developed by the Navy. My interest was piqued in demolitions even before high school, all the way back to grade school. I started writing letters to them, inquiring about what they do. They corresponded with me, sending pictures and information.

At the beginning of high school I realized it would be incredibly difficult to get into the demolition program. They required a high level of fitness, at the very least. So I got into competitive weight lifting, working out in various ways, and eventually joined gymnastics.

Q: It's interesting how early on you knew what direction you wanted to go after school!

Yes, it was a real love of mine. I tried my best to increase my chances of success both physically and academically.

Q: So did you go straight into the military after high school?

I actually worked for one year at an electronics firm. One of my buddies in the firm had an uncle that was an ex-paratrooper from the Second World War As we worked together, my buddy would constantly tell stories about his uncle's missions and the high level of skill needed to be a paratrooper. At that time paratroopers were cutting edge, and the military was still experimenting with different drop techniques.

We decided that the excitement of skydiving and the challenge of jumping was something we wanted to be a part of. Despite my years of thinking about the Navy and the U.D.T.'s, I ultimately enlisted in the Army Airborne with my buddy. This took place in early 1959.

Q: Were you taken by surprise at all by boot camp and the military lifestyle?

Not so much. During basic training I was able to take a physical exam with representatives from Fort Bragg (home of the 82nd Airborne). During that examination period the Army had selected me and my buddy for O.C.S. (Officer Candidate School). We had heard that officers were called "90 day wonders," and weren't renowned as the toughest guys in the military. Also, we had met a few officers who we didn't think were up to snuff. We didn't want any part of it and continued to pursue our dream of becoming paratroopers.

After basic training I was sent to electronics school to pursue electronic technician training, then I went to jump school. After that I was accepted into the 82nd Airborne, 2nd / 501st. I was one of the last groups to get sent to Fort Bragg for jump training. Later groups would go to Fort Benning, Georgia, where they had towers set up specifically for paratrooper training. The tower would hook on to your shoot and lift you straight up. When you got to the top the hook would release and you would chute down.

Q: Could you talk a little about what paratrooper-specific training was like?

Sure. As I mentioned, Bragg didn't have towers so we went right to airplanes for our training. As jumpers we were eligible for hazardous duty pay, which was an extra $55 a month. To qualify you had to make sure you jumped at least once every three months. I didn't have any problem meeting that quota, and in fact I had 82 total jumps throughout my time at Bragg and on Okinawa.

One interesting thing about those jumps is that Fort Bragg had drop zones (landing areas) made out of soft dirt or sand surrounded by pine trees. When I got to Okinawa I realized they didn't have as much square footage of clear landing areas, so we ended up dropping onto a golf course. The officers weren't too keen on that because we kept ripping up the neatly trimmed grass.

As a result, they moved our drops to an old Japanese airport. The airport was used during World War II to launch and house Zeroes (Japanese fighter planes). The problem with that airport was that three sides of the drop zone were covered in high tension wire, with the fourth side facing a steep cliff drop-off and the ocean. The drop zone itself contained concrete from runways and dirt patches which the Okinawans had converted into sweet potato patches. Landings were rarely as light and smooth as they appear in the movies, so we usually opted to drop down into the sweet potato patches. A safe landing was definitely not guaranteed; I saw one soldier get tangled in the high tension wires.

Q: After you finished your training at Fort Bragg, were you immediately shipped off to Okinawa?

No, I was at Bragg for a little while. One day I saw a notice on our company bulletin board asking for volunteers to go to Okinawa. That was right down my alley because I had known about Judo and karate previously. I was even teaching myself as best I could from Oyama's book. I definitely wanted to go, so I volunteered. As it turned out, I was the only volunteer so I got the go-ahead quickly.

Q: Most bases on Okinawa were Air Force and Marine. Did you have to switch branches or were you able to stay with the Army?

I didn't have to switch. The Army had an Airborne unit called the 2nd / 503rd Rock. It was listed as a combat team even though at that time there were no combat teams in the Army.

2nd / 503rd Infantry Combat Team in 1960. Shimabukuro Zenryo OSensei seated third from left.

Q: When you arrived on Okinawa, which camp were you based out of? What kind of duties did you have?

In 1960, I arrived and was assigned to a Howitzer group in Machinato, which was halfway between Naha and the Sukiran Army Base (more modernly known as Stilwell). Strangely enough, I wasn't assigned to work in my M.O.S. (Military Occupational Specialty). I was trained as an electronics technician, but they put me in a Howitzer gun group. I had no idea why that happened, but I guessed they were already filled with technicians so they just put me on the gun group due to my previous experience with a mortar team. The work was alright, but I was just happy to be in Okinawa.

Q: Speaking of being happy to be there, what were some of your earliest impressions of Okinawa and its people?

I loved it, plain and simple. When I got off the airplane in Naha they had a guy in my outfit come and pick me up. He loved to go into town and have fun (typical G.I. stuff). On our way back to the base he asked if I would like to see the town and I said, "Yea, absolutely!" So we were cruising down the streets of these little towns where the roads were just big enough for two or three people to walk abreast. I thought we were going to get arrested for sure and that I was going to get in trouble my first day on the island. Thankfully nothing came of it, and he showed me a lot of what the towns had to offer.

I wasn't that familiar with the Okinawan people in general before arriving on the island. My only exposure to karate was through Oyama, who was a Korean gentleman. However, I found the native populace to be very kind — I grew to love them very quickly.

I held off joining a karate school for about a month or so because I wanted to see what the night life was like. Sukiran had a gym that had activities like shooting, boxing, Judo, etc. That was the extent of the "entertainment" G.I.'s were offered on base, which often led to soldiers going into town. I realized pretty quickly that karate was something I was ready to pursue.

Q: How were the towns set up to receive the military personnel? Did you feel any racial or ethnic tensions?

Many towns were filled with bars, and they welcomed U.S. Military members readily. A bar would be no bigger than a single car garage, but there were many of them lining the streets. You'd have a bar inside, and a couple of tables, but that was it.

In terms of tensions, I met a number of people who had lived on the island during the second World War, many of whom had to flee to the North of Okinawa to survive. Fortunately, the American soldiers on the island during World War II were really decent to the Okinawans, even in the face of violent battles. Most of the Americans sympathized with the plight of the Okinawans getting caught in the middle. At that time many of the Japanese soldiers were lying to the Okinawans about Westerners, saying that if the native residents were caught by the Americans they would be eaten or worse. A lot of Okinawans were forced to hide in caves and often decided to commit suicide rather than get rescued.

Over time, exposure to the Americans helped remove that fear. When I got there the relationship was much improved.

Q: Could you talk about your search for a dojo?

Once I settled into my military outfit and had a sense of the island, I started talking to guys around base that were taking karate. They trained in vacant military buildings, little nooks and crannies here and there, or just outside in nature. I found out they were being taught by an individual named Shimabukuro Zenpo, son of Shimabukuro Zenryo OSensei (founder of Seibukan). I decided that I was going to see what it was all about.

At the time, Zenpo Sensei was sharing a recreational room on base with the Judo people. The Sergeant Major at the base was involved in Shimabukuro karate and had helped facilitate the teaching of it at the Stilwell Gym. Unfortunately for us, the Judo class was growing so large that they needed the facility every night and we got kicked out. There we were, wanting to hold classes, but having no place to work out. Subsequently, I was invited by Zenpo Sensei to go over to his house to train. I jumped at the chance.

Right behind Zenpo Sensei's house was a tomb. Tombs on Okinawa tended to be caves or holes built into mountain sides and often had cinder block fronts with arches. They also had concrete platforms that extended outward, surrounded by walls. The walls, which were about three feet high, left an opening in the front so you could enter. We would frequently train on that concrete platform by the tomb behind Zenpo Sensei's house.

After talking about the lack of training space on base with some of the students as well as the Sergeant Major, we got permission to hold classes occasionally in vacant dormitories when the weather outside was cold or hostile. During the summer we were allowed to train on the front lawns of the dormitories. None of the lawns were flat. They were mostly built on top of mounds which could reach 30-40 feet high, sloping downward toward the roadways in order to prevent flooding out. We could work out on the hills, which was fine until it started raining and we began slipping and sliding all over the place. Inside the dorms, we had to move all the beds and what-not to the side so as to clear space. In the kitchen areas, we had to watch out for pipes sticking up out of the ground so that no one busted a foot or fell on their face during training.

Training at the barracks in Machinado with Shimabuku Zenryo, 1961. Equipment and beds often had to be moved to the side before training commenced.

Q: Was there a language barrier during your training?

There was, except when Zenpo Sensei was around. He had been taking English in high school and was getting very good at it. His English was broken and we had to talk slowly with each other, but it worked. Most importantly, Zenpo Sensei was able to translate lessons to us in detail rather than us having to follow along and guess.

As a teacher, Zenpo Sensei was a total natural. Of course, he had been training since he could walk. We became great friends, and to this day I consider him my brother. On Saturdays I would take him to the movies, watching cowboys and Indians films or whatever else was available. The Shimabukuro house was about an hour bus ride from the base, so sometimes, when I wasn't due back, Zenryo OSensei and Zenpo Sensei invited me to stay over for the evening.

I remember many occasions sitting with Zenryo OSensei in his home and conversing with him. Of course, his English was limited, but we were able to communicate nonetheless. They say when people are of the same heart and mind most communication is done non-verbally. You see it a lot in marriages, police partnerships, and things of that nature. I felt OSensei and I enjoyed a relationship such as that.

Q: Did you ever acquire a formal dojo training space? If so, how?

In 1961, Zenryo OSensei was able to secure a small piece of land near the house and started to build a dojo. On weekends I would go down and help with the construction, digging ditches and laying foundation. Every time we dug the ditches we would have to take water out of them as the ground was very saturated and rains would often occur in-between construction days. It was a real pain! But it was also a joy because we were excited at the thought of having our own place to train.

After the foundation was built, we put in wood floors that Shimabukuro OSensei had acquired, but they weren't the normal treated floorboards you might imagine. After about six months of training the boards started to move a little bit, raising, shifting, and warping. We ended up with serious calluses on our feet, which would in turn get ripped off when we caught the edge of a shifted board.

Zenpo Sensei and I helped the workers on Saturdays during the dojo construction, which is also why I often found myself staying over at the house on weekends.

Q: It must have been a special time when the dojo finally opened.

It really was! Zenryo OSensei threw a big party and had a lot of the karate heads there to celebrate. All the G.I. students came as well, and the guest karate instructors brought their senior students. We had a blast. Some of the individuals that attended included Nakamura Shigeru Sensei, Chibana Chosin Sensei, and Nakama Chozo Sensei. I remember a story about a martial arts senior who was a Christian during the Second World War. He met with the G.I.'s and informed them that there were a bunch of Okinawans that were stranded, and led the G.I.'s to rescuing them. That individual was named Kina Shosei, who was also in attendance that night.

Kyan Shinei and Kina Shosei. Shosei Kina Sensei was the Christian karate master who spoke to the first wave of American G.I.'s sweeping his village during the Battle of Okinawa. A G.I. saw that Kina Sensei had a pair of tonfa hanging on his wall, positioned so that the handles were facing away from each other. The G.I. thought it was a Christian cross and called an Okinawan interpreter working for the U.S. military. This interpreter turned out to be a student of Kina Sensei.

Opening day ceremonies at the Seibukan Dojo in 1962. Starting third from left: Nakama Chozo, Nakamura Shigeru, Chibana Chosin, Shimabukuro Zenryo, Nakazato Joen.

Kampai Party at the Seibukan Dojo after opening ceremonies in 1962. Back row starting 2nd from left:
Walter Dailey, Shimabukuro Zenryo, Nakamura Shigeru.

Q: Could you discuss the teaching methods of Shimabukuro Zenryo OSensei and what kind of content he liked to focus on (kata, sparring, basics, etc.)?

I think Zenryo OSensei was well-rounded. As far as the G.I.'s were concerned, most of them didn't like kata as much as kumite (fighting). They figured that if you were going to do the "dances" (kata), they wanted to see the practicality in it. I liked both. I felt that kata was just as important as kumite.

In Zenryo OSensei's class, we all did basics and stretching together. After that people would go into their own independent training, but you never saw anyone standing around. Sensei would then walk around and make small physical adjustments as people trained.

Q: What was it about Shimabukuru OSensei that kept you coming back for more?

It was who he was as a person that impressed me tremendously. He was a gentleman's gentleman and never put on airs. His demeanor made everything he did special, if you can understand what I mean. I'm no judge, but I saw other instructors on the island acting in a way that I thought was not suitable for karate seniors. This is why I was so impressed with Shimabukuro OSensei.

He used to work as a tax collector for his village, Jagaru. Sometimes people didn't have the tax money due to the high poverty on the island. OSensei would help them out, even sometimes without them realizing it. When they did know, he would say, "If you tell anyone I am helping you, I will not be able to help you again." Shimabukuro Sensei realized that if word got out that he was helping those in need he might be in trouble and that other inscrutable characters might try to take advantage of his kindness.

He himself was not a rich man. He began as a tatami mat maker. After that he was a baker, even going to Japan in order to attend culinary school. It was only later that he secured a job as a tax collector.

Q: Between the training, dojo construction, and weekends at the house, it sounds like you got to know both Shimabukuro Zenryo and Zenpo quite well. Could you talk more about your relationship with them?

I got very close with the family. You have to understand the way they lived. Their house consisted of one room. There was a little shed connected to that room which housed the cooking stove and was only a tiny space for one person to get into. There were sliding windows on two sides of the main room, and the back wall was solid with sliding doors. There was no bathroom in the house. You had to go outside to the outhouse. The main room is where you ate, slept, partied, and so on. The living quarters were no more than 15x15 foot. When I slept over on weekends, I slept alongside the family in the main room. Zenryo Sensei became like a second father to me. What he said, went. Period. He wouldn't want me to go out drinking, so instead he'd have me train or would take me out to the movies.

Toward the end of my initial tour on Okinawa, Zenryo OSensei was generous enough to give me a family name. You see, all the men's names in that family start with "Zen," which could also be said "Yoshi." Zenryo, Zenpo, etc. The name OSensei provided me was "Zenshu." I was honored at the time, but honored moreso as time went on and I realized what a gesture that was.

Q: We're fortunate to have video of Zenpo Sensei teaching and doing kata. His power, precision, and speed are evident. Was Zenryo OSensei the same way?

Zenpo Sensei's personality comes out when you watch him perform. That flash of power and speed suits him. Zenryo OSensei was more reserved, gentle, and compassionate . . . not to say that Zenpo Sensei is none of those things, but it exuded in a unique way with Zenryo OSensei. You could see there was power in his technique, but there wasn't any overt body action to it. It was a high level of refinement that had an appearance of simplicity.

As students we often spent a lot of excess time and energy winding up our techniques, trying to put everything we had in them. We would see in Zenryo OSensei techniques that could hit like a truck without revealing they were going to be thrown.

Zenryo Sensei wearing a suit and his favorite hat. Zenpo Sensei is standing by his side.

Q: With Zenpo Sensei as an aid for translation, did Zenryo OSensei ever tell stories about Kyan Chotoku?

Yes, certainly. One time Zenryo OSensei explained that Kyan was being interviewed by some newspaper people. They were saying, "Sensei, we were told that you could punch the bark off of a tree!" Kyan looked at them and laughed. He said, "What idiot would want to punch trees . . . or punch the bark off of them? That's ridiculous!"

Kyan Sensei used to love to go cock fighting. He had a favorite chicken that he would bring. So he would go into town, put his chicken into fights, have a good old time, and then head back home. One time, three ruffians decided that they were going to take his winning chicken. He had been drinking that night, so when he tucked the chicken under his arm and left, the three men followed him. On Okinawa at that time there were no streetlights, so when you got away from town it was moonlight or nothing — we're talking black outside. These guys got ahead and waited for Kyan Sensei at a pass. They thought he was duck soup because he was only 4'10," give or take. After the encounter, let's just say that the ruffians never tried that stunt again. Kyan handled them, chicken in arm, and then went about his business, singing some drunken tunes as he walked down the road.

Kyan Sensei was the type of guy that, when he drank, he wouldn't go looking for trouble. Some people get nasty and angry while drinking, but Kyan wasn't so. Shimabukuro Zenryo would have a social beer with you, but I never saw him drink two. In a lot of ways he had a personality opposite of Kyan. But of course Zenryo OSensei wasn't perfect either. His favorite cigarette was Pall Mall, and I used to go to the PX (Post Exchange) and buy him a carton of cigarettes every payday.

Q: Did Zenryo OSensei's dojo participate in tournaments and events across the island?

Yes, we were involved in a number of events. I remember one time we went up to Nago and visited Nakamura Shigeru's place. I don't recall if it was his personal dojo or just one in his network, but it was definitely affiliated with him. It was a small room, and the floor was constructed out of the wooden slats used to ship fruit. The slats were not sanded or anything . . . just rough wood, and I was surprised that these guys were training on something like this (and thankful for it to boot). Here I was complaining about our uneven floorboards, but that was nothing compared to this.

I recall that Nakamura Sensei had a belief in strength. "What good was karate if you can't out-and-out fight?," was his thought. My instructor felt similarly. So when we would meet up at his schools, we would always have sparring bouts.

Nakamura Shigeru and Shimabukuro Zenryo lead a moment of etiquette before the beginning of a demonstration in Nago. Both dojo(s) would participate in many events and conduct intramural bogu tournaments. Walter Dailey shown in the back row second from right.

Q: Was there anyone else besides Shimabukuro Zenryo OSensei who you would consider an influence on you while you were on the island?

No other mentors per se. I had a number of good friends and fellow students, and I considered Zenpo Sensei my primary friend, inspiration, and nemesis. We would fight all the time. When we were at the dojo, he would look at me and I would look at him after we got our gi's on and he would say, "I'm gonna break your bones!" That would start us off.

Q: Toward the end of 1962, after three years on the island, you were sent back to the U.S.A. Did your military career continue after that? How did you continue your martial arts upon your return?

My time on active duty ended after I got back to the U.S. While I was still on Okinawa, I had dreamed of starting my own dojo and talked to Zenryo OSensei about it. He supported the idea. I also asked Zenpo Sensei if he would like to come to the United States with me. Of course he jumped at the chance, but there was a problem. Zenpo Sensei was the only son of Zenryo OSensei. I was asking to have Zenpo Sensei go 10-12 thousand miles away to a new land with minimal communication. Zenryo OSensei was worried at first, but in short order decided to allow it. This gesture and trust made me feel very good and only entrenched my loyalty to the family further.

When I got back to the U.S., I started up a school and got busy with immigration, trying to figure out how to get Zenpo Sensei over. I found out that the waiting list for people coming from Okinawa was close to ten years. I wasn't too keen on that, so I went and got a plane ticket for him and instructed him to get a visa. I sent for him, and then when he got over here I applied for permanent residency for him.

Q: Where was the first dojo you established, and what did you call it?

The dojo was in Norwood, Pennsylvania, which is a suburb of Philadelphia. It was opened shortly after I arrived back in the U.S. Civilian life didn't have a lot of demand for a former member of a gun crew, so the dojo was a singular focus for me. I called it simply "Seibukan Karate School" because this was the first Seibukan school in the United States.

It's important to note that I was operating my school under the "Seibukan Zenshu-ha" heading. As I mentioned, Zenshu was the name Zenryo OSensei had given me before my departure. He had also approved my opening of a branch in the United States. A style head such as OSensei had the ability to designate specific, approved branches of his art. Those recognized branches became known as "ha." As such, Zenshu-ha was my specific branch.

Q: Were there any particular challenges with starting the school and developing a student body?

Yes. Nowadays everybody is totally familiar with karate. You don't have to explain what it is. Back then no one knew what it was; there weren't any movies about it or anything like that. There was a school down in Philadelphia at that time on 48th Street led by Okazaki Teruyuki of Shotokan. He had been operating for a few years before I got going, but he was the only one I knew about in the area.

Getting students in the school was difficult because no one knew about it. I wanted to get students in, but I didn't know how to do it! My solution at the time was to give as many demonstrations as I could. Gradually I started to get some students. Zenpo Sensei came in October of 1963, and thankfully we were up and running by then.

First Seibukan school in the U.S.A. The All Japan Karatedo Federation symbol is featured on the front of the dojo. 1962.

One of the first real boosts in attention we got occurred when the movie "Billy Jack" came out. This was one of the first movies that really showed technique in the form of Korean kicking. There were some other movies and shows before that, but on the East Coast "Billy Jack" made a real splash. After that there was a lot more importing of Chinese kung fu movies, and the popularity of martial arts on film increased. In fact, we saw such a trend that we decided to advertise our school at the local drive-in theater.

Q: Did having Zenpo Sensei over help to attract students?

Walter Dailey and Shimabukuro Zenpo in 1965.

Certainly, he was a great demonstrator and teacher. He wanted to see the school grow as well, so he worked hard for it. We never had arguments . . . plenty of "fighting," but never arguments.

Q: Throughout the 1950s and '60s, Okinawans, Japanese, and Americans were all trying to figure out how to handle rank. How did Zenryo OSensei like to handle it?

He worked basically on kyus. He had white belt, two kyus of green, two kyus of brown, and then black belt. That was it. He worked me through those ranks before I returned to the U.S.A.

Q: You had Zenpo Sensei with you in the U.S., but did you get a chance to revisit Okinawa any time after your return to the States?

Yes, my next trip back was in 1965. I was a little smarter during my second visit and had more freedom to practice. I trained from 7am-11am, had a light lunch, and then trained from 1pm-4pm. I relaxed after that until regular class started at 7pm-11pm.

After about seven months of training, I got sick. I went to a doctor and he said, "It's probably one of two things. Either you have Leukemia or you have Hodgkins Disease." I said, "Oh . . . that's great." So I quickly made plans to come home in order to get into an American hospital.

I came home and went into the hospital. They did biopsies and all that. The doctors there ended up telling me that I had four or five different Asiatic diseases. They pumped me full of antibiotics, and I ended up fine. I realized afterward that during my time on Okinawa I had been drinking this yogurt-like liquid regularly, hoping to benefit from the added vitamins and minerals. Unfortunately, I had picked up so much bacteria from that yogurt that the Okinawan doctor didn't know how to diagnose me.

Q: Did you continue to grow your Norwood dojo throughout the '70s and '80s?

I kept the Norwood school open for a while, but eventually the land owner wanted to sell the building. He was decent with me, always very fair, and asked if I would leave so that he could make the sale. I said okay. I went into a V.F.W. (Veterans of Foreign Wars) building and began teaching there. After that I decided we could open another independent school, and some of the students wanted to go in on it as well. So we opened a school in Edgmont, PA, around 1971. That turned out to be the largest school I ever had, well over 3,000 square feet for workout space.

After that I opened a school in Marcus Hook, PA, and also started a program in Villanova University as well as in Lansdale, PA. It was a great time of growth, but I was also drinking like crazy. In the end I decided to give the school in Edgmont over to my students. I made a decision . . . that was it — I couldn't continue in the martial arts.

In 1976, I had a car accident. I was working for a security company, in charge of their security patrol. I used to have to go out at nights in Philadelphia around Diamond Street, which was not a great part of town. I was traveling toward the airport to give a guard a hat (he had forgotten his). I got on the Schuylkill Expressway and got into a serious accident, which landed me in the hospital. I started looking at what the heck I was doing with my life and realized that I didn't like myself too much. I lost my way during that time because of drinking.

Q: Did the drinking come from the stress of owning schools or the trauma from military experience? Or are you unsure why it happened? How did you rebound out of that time in your life?

I think it was more personal problems than anything external like schools or military. My rebound I attribute to Jesus Christ. I was able to find my way back on a stable path and everything has been fine since.

Q: Have you continued your karate training since your recovery? How has your training matured with you?

Yes, I resumed training, but today I'm of the age that I can't jump around the way the young guys do. My philosophy has changed in that I won't be throwing roundhouse kicks and things of that nature.

Walter Dailey executing a flying kick toward Kimon Digenakis in 1965, Newark, Deleware.

When I was young, I was very focused on the physical aspect of things. I trained from an early age to get into the U.D.T.'s, and that kind of focus continued throughout my younger years. I didn't want anyone to get in my way. What I found from studying karate was that there is no goal that is important enough to step on people. If you don't know who you are, and ultimately what you are, you will find yourself encountering problems even if you aren't going out and looking for them.

Q: What do you think makes a good karate instructor?

A good karate instructor has compassion, and hasn't forgotten where he came from and how hard it was to get where he is. When I ran my schools, they were very difficult. I wasn't looking to build large schools with hundreds of students. I was only interested in having enough numbers to pay the rent and electricity. In all the years I've been in karate, I have only promoted about 15 people to black belt.

The training was difficult, and I taught the same way I was taught on Okinawa. I realized there was a method to the madness of doing something like this. How can you have a tough school and try to make money? It's difficult because people tend not to put up with it.

I think there is an important distinction between being an "instructor" and a "teacher." An instructor is able to organize classes and conduct repetitions of techniques. They can correct movements and teach the patterns of kata. A teacher can do those things but also knows how to feed concepts into the students so that they gradually understand, grab ahold of, and use them in original ways. This is not to cut down instructors, because they probably had instructors as well and they are carrying on their tradition to the letter.

Q: How did you balance kata, basics, sparring, and other content in your classes?

Normally we did stretching and strengthening exercises first. I considered these important because in order to get the most out of the techniques you had to be in better condition than an average person. We would then go into the basic blocks, punches, and kicks. After that we did kata (which we did a lot of).

We focused a lot on kata because there are different ways of doing the forms which will elicit different benefits. For instance, when you put your hand against a wall and tighten your muscles like you are going to try to push the wall away from you but not move your body . . . there are ways of doing kata to simulate that feeling, which results in a tremendous strengthening of physical memory. There are also speed kata and other performance methods. This keeps training from getting boring for the students yet still focuses on the proper use of the movements and their execution.

Walter Dailey at the Shimabukuro Hombu (main dojo) practicing Kusanku Kata. 1961.

I noticed when teaching that one of the biggest problems students were having was a "stopping of the mind." By that I mean, when we block or punch we have a tendency to watch and see the end result of that technique. In doing so, we are stopping the mind from moving passed the technique and onto the next one. In karate the mind is not supposed to stop at all. The block you make is history even as you are doing it. The punch is history while you are throwing it. You are not to be concentrating on that any more. The mind needs to be fluid in order to pick up anything and everything. When the mind stops it cannot be fluid, and when it is not fluid it is vulnerable in terms of reaction time and awareness.

My big question to myself was, how do I get the students to understand this and work passed it? One of my solutions was to play a little game. All the students would make a circle. Any one of the students in that circle could attack any other student at any time. That means you could attack someone on the other side of the circle or right next to you.

Likewise, you could be attacked just as randomly. There were no limitations, so two or even three people could end up attacking you at the same time.

If you did not block an attack successfully during this drill, you had to drop and do ten pushups. On the surface this seemed like an easy enough task — blocking an attack. However, if the student becomes fixated on the first block, another attack would inevitably come from a different direction. Before they knew it, they had to drop and do another set of ten pushups. To be successful in the game, the students' minds had to be fluid and aware, blocking but moving on even as the block was completing.

Once the students started getting the hang of this game, I would increase the stakes by requiring a counterattack after the block. If the initial attacker was successfully counterattacked, THEY would have to do ten pushups instead of the defender. This created a real incentive not to miss a block or get sloppy on attacks, but it also made it harder not to get fixated on one specific attacker. If a student got too absorbed in an exchange, they ended up getting hit from a different direction and having to do ten pushups anyway. This created a paradox of learning where the student needed to be efficient against one attacker while fluidly mindful of their surroundings.

The multiple attacker game is just one example of trying to create scenarios in which the student can expand their mental sharpness and understanding along with their technique. When teaching with many students in a class, it is impossible to give each and every one your undivided attention. However, by understanding how to access the principles of a style, you can set up learning so that each person is challenged and given the tools to progress.

At times it probably seemed as if I was being unusual in my demands of students. For example, I never let students wipe sweat away from their eyes. I would also have them run outside barefoot in the snow. I wasn't doing this as a pointless form of "spirit testing" which amounted to little more than, "Can you deal with my punishment?" No, everything I did had a tactical purpose. By not allowing the students to wipe the sweat from their eyes, they got into the habit of continuing to fight even if their vision was obstructed. Soon they realized a simple blink did the job or, worst case scenario, they had a little stinging from the salt which they could push through. Before long they were used to visual obstructions and it barely hindered them. I never punished students just for the sake of "survival" or spirit strengthening — I consider that a habit of masochistic or egotistic instruction.

Q: Do you have any advice or insight for future generations on how to preserve karate as it was intended?

You are going to get out of karate what you put into it. There is no way to get around that. There are no shortcuts. You pay for everything that you get . . . sometimes more dearly than other times.

You have to train as if every movement is for real. If it is not done that way, the movement isn't going to be there when you really need it. If every move is practiced in earnest, it will become instinct so that you no longer have to think about it and the mind will cease stopping. Training this way will not always be entertaining, and it will often be hard. It will not be popular. But for students it is critical for growth, and for teachers it is required to set the right example.

Walter Dailey with Russel Bennefield and Shimabukuro Zenryo in 1961. Zenryo Sensei was a powerful man despite his small stature. Photographer credit to Larry Hall.

Dan Smith

Dan Smith Sensei has distinguished himself through tireless efforts to help explore the history of Seibukan and Shorin Ryu, as well as facilitate visits by Shimabukuro Zenpo Sensei and other masters to the United States. Smith Sensei is an expert organizer and intelligent businessman as well as a skilled practitioner.

Beginning his martial career as a Judo and Shotokan practitioner, it wasn't until 1968 when Smith Sensei arrived in Okinawa that he began to explore Seibukan. Enjoying the rigors and demand of Shotokan, Smith Sensei found similar challenges in the Seibukan Dojo and endeavored to learn as much about the art as he could. Since his original tour on Okinawa, Smith Sensei has returned to the island many times and continues to share his knowledge with senior students and seminar participants.

Q: Smith Sensei, could you give us an account of your earliest experiences with Judo and karate?

I began Judo with Charlie Morris Sensei in 1962. Morris Sensei had returned to my home town, Jackson, Mississippi, after serving in the U.S. Navy. He was stationed in Japan for four years and studied Kodokan Judo where he achieved the rank of Sandan (3rd degree black belt). We were exposed to excellent Judo through Morris Sensei as he was a national Judo champion and was close friends with Major Phil Porter and Robby Reed.

In 1964, the year I graduated from high school, Shotokan Karate arrived in Jackson, MS.

Dr. Robert Parkes introduced Shotokan to our city, and Morris Sensei began teaching Shotokan one night a week along with Kodokan Judo. Akuzawa Takeshi Sensei lived in Memphis, TN, and visited us often until he moved to Miami in 1966. Morris Sensei had been attending law school at night and upon his graduation left the police department and moved to Gulfport, MS. After Akuzawa Sensei's departure, Mikami Takayuki Sensei moved to New Orleans and became our focus for Shotokan.

As far was we knew, there was no other karate in America other than Shotokan. The All-American Karate Federation was the guide for all karate activity that we were exposed to.

I graduated from college in 1968 and departed for Okinawa as an officer in the U.S. Army. I returned from Okinawa in 1972.

Q: You had a chance to meet a number of high ranking Shotokan practitioners during your time in that style. What are some of the most memorable things about them in terms of something they did or character traits they possessed?

Akuzawa of Kenkojuku Ocano style Shotokan — Steel character and tough to the bones. No edge given to any student. Excellent technician of the Japanese style.

Mikami Sensei — the model example of a gentleman and technician. Open to all styles and people. His demonstration was to spar against the grand champion of a tournament. I saw him beat many of the big name competitors of the late '60s and mid '70s. Mikami has continued today to epitomize the Shotokan persona.

Nishiyama Sensei — One-minded and not relenting.

Koyama Sensei — I met Koyama Sensei when I was stationed at Ft. Bliss, TX. I was at the Quad Fifty Artillery Unit prior to shipping overseas. Koyama Sensei welcomed me into his dojo for the few weeks I was stationed in Texas. He was cordial and outgoing. First Shotokan teacher I had met this way.

Tom Myslinski Sensei — The first non-Japanese to complete the J.K.A. Instructor's Course in Japan in 1967. He was my sempai [senior], and when I first arrived on Okinawa we trained together since we could not find Funakoshi Gichin, founder of Shotokan. My sempai was moved off temporary duty on Okinawa back to mainland Japan.

Coincidentally, if that hadn't happened, I may have never gotten off the base to find the Seibukan Dojo. Myslinski Sempai had flawless Shotokan technical ability but with an American vision of karate. A number years after I had returned from Okinawa, he commented to me in a phone call that it was best that I chose the way of Seibukan. He had come to believe that the cultural differences between Okinawa and Japan were vitally important to our long term health.

Q: How much emphasis was placed on tournaments and competition in those early days of Shotokan? Could you describe the tournament experience and how it might compare / contrast to modern tournaments?

Dan Smith performing a jump spinning back kick in 1967. Photo taken at Hattiesburg Shotokan.

All of the training was directed toward jiyu kumite (free sparring). Eighty percent or higher of dojo members competed in tournament sparring and kata.

The jiyu kumite techniques at that time were built on the use of basics. The reverse punch, rear leg kick, and block with counter punching was the extent of the jiyu kumite techniques that would score. The training was created this way, and the basics changed from the methods on Okinawa to the methods of jiyu kumite. Kata was practiced . . . but the kata had been changed to reflect the jiyu kumite basics. The distance and timing of the kata was the same as the jiyu kumite. It was not until I got to Okinawa that I realized there was a distance of fighting in the kata other than "middle." Perhaps it was due to the dojo I was training in, but it seemed to me that all Shotokan schools in the U.S. and the teachers who came from Japan trained this way.

In regards to old tournaments versus modern tournaments, they are quite different. Old events were tougher and contact was brutal. Modern competitors are more talented / multi-dimensional. Kata are now 30% longer in duration due to the gymnastic performance. I am not complaining, just explaining the differences. The current physical skills are on another level.

Q: Could you describe when and how you first arrived on Okinawa? What were your day-to-day military duties?

I was an officer in the Army. My day-to-day activities were impacted by the fact that there were over 250,000 Americans on Okinawa going to or returning from Vietnam. The Americans had plenty of time on their hands as it was policy to keep the details and training to a minimum. American soldiers filled the Okinawa dojo(s) to find outlets for their excess time and desire to learn an exotic martial art. I was free during the day to leave my job and go to the gym. The duty day was from 7am to 3:30pm. The focus was keeping the troops' minds occupied and out of trouble. Karate was an important outlet for their free time and frustrations.

Q: What were some of the dojo(s) you visited early on, and what kind of training did you find there?

I landed on Okinawa looking for Shotokan and Funakoshi Gichin Sensei. I was surprised to find no Shotokan available and realized the history of karate was much different than portrayed in the U.S.A. at that time. I visited many dojo but the three I can remember before finding the Seibukan Dojo were the Nagamine, Uechi, and Miyazato dojo(s). For someone who had never seen Sanchin or high stances before, this was quite a shock. I didn't train at these schools in the beginning. I found the Seibukan Dojo and then went out to these other schools after I had a better understanding of Okinawa. Shimabukuro Zenryo Sensei was very kind to me to send me to these dojo with an invitation so I could learn more about Okinawan karate. He knew I loved karate and wanted to give me a good view of Okinawa. He never thought I would return to Okinawa for training after my initial military tour and wanted to expand my understanding.

Q: In the early 1960s and 1970s, rank was distributed quickly, both to Okinawan Sensei and their students. Did you see that kind of behavior, and what was your reaction?

I do not criticize anyone for the irrational ranking that was given out, but I don't excuse it either. Many of the Ryukyuan instructors did not understand grading and how to manage it. Grading was relatively new to the island, only being introduced a few years prior and not entirely accepted by various karate circles. Some teachers' first grade was a 9th or 10th dan . . . so they had to ask themselves, what is the difference between a Shodan (1st degree) and Kudan (9th degree)? Even after the Americans started teaching in the U.S. with inflated rank, the Okinawan instructors continued with less-than-ideal rank practices.

Personally, I went from Nidan in Shotokan to a Yondan by 1975 which was less than seven years of training. Then it took me another 41 years to go from 4th to 9th (which is still too quick). Now, upon reflection, I can see that a lot of the Okinawan teachers and students, as well as we Americans, mishandled rank as we all tried to figure out how to manage it.

Unfortunately ego played into a lot of the rank troubles as well. The trap some individuals fell into was that they believed they were skilled and knowledgeable karate men. I do not see how anyone, in just a year or two, can gain the knowledge required to come back to the U.S.A. and create a karate organization. After I returned to the U.S.A. in 1972, I felt very inadequate and returned to Okinawa as a civilian in 1975 even though I had six years of Shotokan experience before arriving on Okinawa. The depth of knowledge required to lead continues to be a concern I have. I go to Okinawa once or twice a year (38 times in the last 20 years), and I feel that I continue to "wake up" on some subjects every day. I think it takes a minimum of 10 years on a daily basis with qualified Okinawan teachers to begin to adequately understand Okinawa karate. At my rate of ten days per year, I have no chance.

Q: When you found the Seibukan Dojo, what was it that impressed you about it? Could you describe what you saw on your first visit?

I saw the closest training to Shotokan in terms of discipline and class structure that I could find on Okinawa. It ended my search based on my familiarity with their training and movements. My goal was not to leave Shotokan but to get to the roots.

Q: How large was the Seibukan Dojo, what did it look like, and how many students were in an average class? Also, what did day-to-day training consist of?

The Seibukan Dojo was one of the largest dojo facilities on Okinawa due to Zenryo and Zenpo Sensei's vision for karate. The Americans that had been in the dojo (40 to 50) before I arrived were gone. On Zenpo Sensei's return from living in the U.S.A., he urged his father to provide the same training and grading to the Americans as Okinawans (which is to say, challenging). The enrollment of the Americans dropped quickly. The entire time I was in the dojo, there were never more than two Americans other than me in the dojo. Then Zenryo Sensei died October 14, 1969, and the dojo attendance dropped very low. Most of the senior Okinawan students left and opened their own dojo. Zenpo Sensei was only 25 and I was 23.

The day-to-day training was basics, kata, and body building. We did some form of kumite every day. We ran every night during the middle of class (about a 5k). I attended training Monday through Friday morning with Zenryo Sensei until he passed away. The evening training was Monday through Saturday night for about three hours. Of course, we trained with the makiwara and heavy bag along with body toughening.

Q: What was Zenryo Sensei like as an instructor and a person?

Zenryo Sensei did not really run classes; instead he used the Okinawa traditional way. He came into the dojo and observed students training. He would make corrections and give new movements where he thought necessary. He gave corrections by demonstrating what the fist (ti chi ki) was for. He never counted exercises or kata. Everyone practiced by themselves. He would come and go so you never knew where he was. It was a lesson in learning to motivate yourself and discipline yourself to work. This was very valuable to me.

Zenryo Sensei was a great gentleman. No matter who you spoke to concerning Zenryo Sensei, the first statement referenced what a gentleman he was. He had a deep knowledge of karate. It was part of his every movement. He was teaching by the way he moved, sat, etc. He was karate. It was a great loss for Zenpo Sensei and all others to lose Zenryo at 61 years old. I went to the dojo on the Monday evening he was to return from Japan. We were all devastated when he did not return. Zenpo Sensei lived through this, and then when I returned to the U.S.A. I lost my father. Our family friendship has taken the place of relationships we lost.

Q: In contrast (or comparison) to his father, how was Zenpo Sensei as an instructor? Did he focus on different content?

Dan Smith with Shimabukuro Zenpo in 1975.

Zenpo Sensei focused on training the body. A shared goal between father and son was to create the body required for Kyan's karate. In terms of actual content, Zenpo Sensei and I recently created a book entitled *Shorin Ryu Seibukan: Kyan's Karate* which could answer that question in more suitable detail.

Q: When Shimabukuro Zenryo Sensei passed away, was Zenpo Sensei named the next style head or was there a splintering of senior students as a result of no head being named?

There was no splintering or division between students of Zenryo Sensei. Some of the senior students of Zenryo Sensei had their own dojo when he passed away and a couple of others eventually opened their own dojo, but not for the purpose of leaving the Shimabukuro family. These men continued to support Zenpo Sensei and often visited the dojo.

After Zenryo Sensei passed away, there was no immediate change in rank or title for Zenpo Sensei. He became a member of the Okinawa Federation, and after time he was given rank by the senior members of the Okinawa karate community. He did not take any ranking from his own group and did not progress in rank quickly. He was a 5th Dan when his father died and stayed at each rank level for approximately eight years, which is the way of the traditional organizations on Okinawa. His students followed the same pattern if they remained active.

Q: How did Seibukan handle organizational matters with other styles? Was there a lot of interactivity with groups like the All-Okinawan Karatedo Federation or Okinawa Kenpo Renmei?

From my experience, Zenryo Sensei was very active with other Okinawa karate men. As an example, Zenpo Sensei was elected the president of the Rengokai this past July. It is the first father and son combination where both have been elected president of a major all-style Okinawa karate organization.

Q: Was there an emphasis on tournament competition while on Okinawa? What were those events like, and can you relay any memorable moments?

Not a big emphasis. There was one big tournament a year. The most memorable is when I competed and received a broken wrist with full bogu. The tournament was very rough. The bogu created a lack of technique and more of a knock out or knock down mentality.

Q: Shimabukuro Zenpo Sensei is well-known for the speed and snap of his techniques. What type of mechanics does Seibukan stress to help deliver that kind of explosive power?

The power of Zenpo Sensei and his father came from "gamaku" (the small muscles attaching the torso to the legs). The "whipping" action is generated from the waist and hips. All techniques of Seibukan Shorin Ryu are based on the utilization of this mechanical movement.

Q: When did you return to the United States, and did you attempt to establish a school right away?

I did not attempt to establish a school on my return. I had a dojo when I was in college, and one of my students had kept it going. It was still a Shotokan school, and he did not want to change to Shorin Ryu. He and I were childhood friends and I left the dojo to him.

I trained at various dojo(s), including an Isshin Ryu school, for almost two years before creating a dojo for a few students. We did not put up a sign or advertise. It was a private school. It was not until Zenpo Sensei was planning to come for a visit in 1975 that I opened a dojo to the public. My goal was not to teach, but to train. As such, I have never had a large dojo. My current school is approximately 50 yards from my home, and we have no sign nor advertisement. I am fortunate to have a large number of senior students who have been with me for long periods of time, but I do not attempt to expand things or build notoriety.

Smith Sensei after a tournament victory in 1973, holding his son Alan.

Q: How did you manage to stay connected to Zenpo Sensei as you developed your school in the West? How important was maintaining that connection to you?

My students are Zenpo Sensei's students. We are all one family. If I quit training and studying karate today, I would still go visit Zenpo Sensei and my many other Okinawa friends. This is about relationships and family. Without the relationship with your teacher, I do not see how deep knowledge concerning kata can be shared.

Q: How often have you been able to return to Okinawa? Have you met other interesting seniors while there?

I have made more than 40 trips to Okinawa. I have met numerous seniors by the grace of my teachers. I believe I have more close friends on Okinawa than I do in my own community. I am 67 years old now and am thinking of slowing down my trips to once a year. Zenpo Sensei still plans visits to the United States as well.

Q: How ingrained is the mindset of sport karate in modern Okinawa?

I think the sport mindset is now fully engaged in Okinawa. I do not have a problem with sport karate when it is displayed on the level of the Okinawa women's kata team and the 2012 Okinawa men's kata team. While the kata are not executed as the traditional methods, their skill level cannot go unnoticed or unappreciated.

Q: If looking for old style training in Okinawa or the United States, what advice could you give students to help them find it?

In the U.S.A. it will be a challenge to find . . . but look for someone who has a strong background with Okinawan teachers. Over a 50-year period of time, only a handful of Americans could have been produced that have attained a high level. Start by identifying someone that has more than ten years directly with their instructor. That will reduce the list quickly. I do not mean that they had access once every couple of years. I do not fit that requirement as the most number of days I receive a year is ten to twelve.

If you cannot find the teacher I am describing, find one as close as you can and understand that you will be limited. This does not mean you cannot learn a great deal, but it will be difficult.

Q: How has long-term karate training affected your physical and mental health? Are there any mistakes in training you've made that you would advise students against?

My long term health at 67 appears to be in good shape, but I am not satisfied due to my weight and too much ballistic training I did in my early days. I should have retired from kumite competition under 30 rather than 40. I have only got a glimpse at some of the real issues of training that were brought on by not following the Okinawa methods.

I advise my students to stretch more, keep their weight low, and to continue walking every day.

Q: When teaching nowadays, what kind of content do you like to focus on? Do you integrate jiyu kumite and tournament competition?

I do not push competition anymore. I have some seniors who are much better at that now than I am. I do not refer to what I do as "teach." I lead training and I train with my seniors. I prefer to reference what I do as sharing. I end up learning more than those I share with.

Q: What is your vision for the growth of your style and for karate worldwide?

I wish to see all of Okinawan karate / kobudo growing and prospering. Zenpo Sensei and I have learned over the years that by putting Okinawa first, Seibukan is moved by the rising tide of all vessels in the harbor.

Chapter 12 –
Shobayashi Ryu

Known worldwide as a master of Shorin Ryu, Shimabukuro Eizo Sensei is one of the individuals responsible for carrying on the ways of Kyan Chotoku. In addition to his Shorin Ryu experience, Shimabukuro Sensei gained significant skill in Goju Ryu and Motobu Ryu (of the Motobu Choki line). Shimabukuro Eizo Sensei also studied with his older brother, Tatsuo, of Isshin Ryu fame.[82] As a result, Eizo Sensei became one of the most effective and knowledgeable martial artists of his era.

Although noteworthy for many reasons, one of the most remarkable aspects of Shimabukuro Sensei's life came from his interactions with Toyama Kanken, a man responsible for organization and communication of karate between Okinawa and Japan. As a result of Shimabukuro Sensei's willingness to work with Toyama, combined with his extreme skill and impressive resume, Toyama granted the rank of 10th Dan to Shimabukuro Sensei in 1959 at the young age of 34.[83]

As a student of Okinawan history, and a military veteran himself, Shimabukuro Sensei felt a kinship with the American military members traveling to Okinawa after World War II and during the Vietnam War. He opened his classes to Marines and other military personnel near Camp Hansen.

---

[82] Bishop, Mark. *Okinawan karate: Teachers, Styles and Secret Techniques*. Tuttle Publishing, 1999. 85. Print.
[83] "Martial Arts Biography - Eizo Shimabukuro - U.S.A.dojo.com." 2006. 31 Dec. 2014
<http://www.usadojo.com/biographies/eizo-shimabukuro.htm>.

Paul Durso

Paul Durso distinguished himself at a young age as one of the finest athletes in the country. Excelling in multiple sports and physical endeavors, Durso Sensei saw a great opportunity to improve himself via the dynamic art of Judo. After graduating high school and joining the Marines, Durso Sensei traveled halfway across the globe to Okinawa, and, once there, encountered Shimabukuro Eizo of Shorin Ryu.

Shimabukuro Sensei's physical prowess and technical skill impressed the high performing

Durso, who in turn opted to study full time under the sensei. While on Okinawa, Durso Sensei became not just a skilled karateka, but also an important touchstone between American and Okinawan culture.

Throughout his life, Durso Sensei has achieved success in the fields of education, business, music, martial arts, and more. He was in the middle of the tournament scene in California as karate grew in popularity, and spearheaded concepts of cross-training karate with Judo, wrestling, and more. Durso Sensei is a unique character in the world of martial arts, and is considered a "hidden gem" by some of the earliest pioneers of karate in America.

Q: Durso Sensei, could you start by describing when and where you were born?

I've always identified with the New York metropolitan area, but I'm originally from Bayonne, New Jersey. Most people don't really know where that is, but it is right behind the Statue of Liberty in New York Bay.

I'm a result of the World War II era and growing up in the eastern part of the U.S.A. was a lot of fun. We had baseball — Yankees, Dodgers, and Giants. It was the beginning of integrated baseball — Jackie Robinson, Willie Mays, and the legendary play of Joe Dimaggio, Mickey Mantle, Duke Snyder . . . I am a product of that environment.

Q: Did you have a distinct need for self-defense growing up in New Jersey / New York?

No, not particularly. I was a part of the Police Athletic League, known to the locals as the P.A.L. Sports was my calling and I was active in gymnastics early on. A Bayonne policeman, Gene Kelleher, trained me, and that was to affect me for the rest of my life. Fortunately, for me, there were no particular problems in the way of getting into trouble.

That being said, the mystery of martial arts did start to come up sooner rather than later. What was jujutsu, this 'Judo' thing that people were whispering about? My Uncle Lou once said, "Hey Paulie, I heard you could break a man in two with that karate!" No doubt any young man / athlete would be strained to answer that kind of query . . . that had my attention.

Q: Did you get to see anything specific either in pop culture or via local demonstrations regarding martial arts?

Very few individuals were touring and teaching that early on. The first wave of pioneer martial artists was just settling in when my attention sprung up. I generally connect myself with that first wave, but toward the end of it. I was probably somewhere between the end of the first wave and the beginning of the second wave.

In September 1958, during my first year of high school, I went to the Bayonne Naval Station after seeing an announcement for a Judo class. It caught my eye and that was the beginning. The first instructor there was a Staff Sergeant of the United States Marine Corps, a Marine recruiter named Bill Miller.

Q: Was that Judo class open to anyone or were they only accepting military personnel as students?

They were pretty open. It was a good recruiting technique of Bill Miller to open his programs to the public and not have anything too secret or closed. I came in with some background in gymnastics. Of course, I tried to tie in my athletic ability to learn the techniques of the martial arts (specifically in this case, grappling), but I learned quickly that I had to reinvent some of my existing athletic skills in order to adapt.

I joined the program full-time as soon as I could. I found that it was my role to start learning a technique called "ukemi," or "how-to-fall." As you might imagine, this was not how I thought of myself starting my martial arts journey.

As beginners, we usually come into a dojo (work out area) with our imagination and our

Paul Durso executing a parallel bar handstand. Durso Sensei's background in gymnastics would serve as a vital tool for cross-training fitness.

fascination. We think, "Oh, I'm going to pick up a guy and throw him across the room." But no, first you learn how to survive by being thrown onto the floor. There were many lessons to be learned from that and it was the first true insight into that mysterious spirit of the Orient. One comes to understand defeat, how to handle a letdown, then, how to handle a breakdown / fall. If you learn how to fall, you learn how to survive it.

Q: It seems your initial experience with Judo didn't match your expectations. You had to endure a lot of falling and getting thrown. Were you tempted to quit as a result?

No, and I think that was mostly about my character. Some people just have a love of discipline and they have a weird reaction to obstacles. For example, when getting thrown I had a tendency to ask my partner to see the technique again. I was driven by the curiosity of how instructors made it work.

Q: Did you have support in this endeavor from parents and friends, or did everyone think you were a bit crazy?

There was little support because there was very little understanding. I lost my father at a young age. I didn't realize at the time that my instructors, the Marine Corps, the martial arts . . . all became kind of a father replacement.

I didn't even tell my mother about the training. If she knew about the throwing, the hitting the floor . . . mothers get heart attacks over these things. There was nothing for other people to compare it to. I was doing something that my peers were not. Some of them were in a boxing ring exchanging fists. In other high schools they were wrestling. I was doing something different and maybe that helped hold my interest even more and helped me to continue on.

Q: What was the training environment like with Bill Miller? Was it a military gym and were there crash pads of any sort?

Yes, it was a military environment at the Bayonne Naval Base and there was one mat, no extra pads. We had a diverse group of people with interest in finding out what Judo was really about. The students were mostly young men with a few military students mixed in. On average we would have about 10-15 individuals per session, which is a decent size. We pulled from the active military base as well as the general public.

Bill Miller had some insight into how to draw people's attention, seeing as how he was the main recruiter for the Bayonne area. He understood public relations and press releases and things of that nature. He knew how to intrigue the mind of the young man.

Bill Miller (left) and Paul Durso (right) are congratulated by Gary Alexander after finishing a full marathon.

Q: Speaking of Bill Miller — where did his training come from and what was he like as a teacher?

Bill was a product of the first wave and was stationed primarily in Bangkok, Thailand, assigned to embassy duty. Whenever he went off base he wouldn't look for bars or social events, he would immediately ask "where's the dojo?" In this way he was able to collect the techniques and skills of Judo. He never mentioned the names of specific teachers, but he had the opportunity to travel around the Far East and advance his study. Later on, as a Marine Gunnery Sergeant, he instructed basic hand-to-hand combat to Marines and young recruits.

Bill Miller was one of the architects of early hand-to-hand combat instruction for the United States Marine Corps in the 1950s. He was asked by the "powers that be" to upgrade the hand-to-hand combat manual. Here the military started to combine jujutsu, Judo, and a broader table of interests to achieve effective results. This would serve as my entry into mixing basic kicks, punches, and the foundation of sport Judo (the conception of "M.M.A." mixed martial arts).

Bill's efforts served as a precursor to the eventual development of the Marine Corps Martial Arts Program (M.C.M.A.P.) which would come later.

Q: You've mentioned the importance of character in how a martial artist approaches his / her training. It sounds like Bill Miller had the character to take risks and explore martial arts in unknown places. Is that an accurate assessment?

Pretty much so, yes. Bill was born in Jersey City, New Jersey. He joined the Marine Corps at age 15 by altering a birth certificate. He was a warrior, a fighter, and he matured young. He had discipline and adventure to boldly explore what few men before him had experienced culturally, athletically, and professionally as a Marine. As a result, he helped contribute quite a bit.

Q: How would you describe his teaching method?

He had a blend of the warrior spirit, Bushido attitude, politeness, and a gentlemanly manner. His training was basic: learn how to fall, learn how to throw . . . be a gentleman. Do not brag but keep a competitive spirit. It was a combination of military effort blended with manners and seasoned with the mystique of Asian martial arts philosophy.

Q: Sometimes one hears of early karate and Judo programs that required students to "survive" the instructor in order to prove dedication and loyalty, essentially enduring extreme hardship to the point of serious bodily risk. Did Bill Miller participate in that kind of training mindset?

No, Bill focused on building character and instilling a warrior spirit. If you were weak he made you stronger. If you were insecure he would encourage self-confidence through competition. As far as weeding out and such — no. I especially never felt that myself. Due to my interest in physical fitness and other endeavors, Bill encouraged me in more areas than just martial arts.

Q: Did your participation in gymnastics and Judo lead you to other sports and physical endeavors?

Yes, in fact the gym, Judo, and other sports would become the building blocks for who I would eventually become as a martial artist. You see, in the Post-World War II period, President Eisenhower was advised that the physical fitness level of American youth had deteriorated. The military warriors had already returned from World War II and Korea. The softness of American fitness was beginning to set in.

Our youth were out of shape. So our high schools decided to take the image of what the United States Marine Corps was all about and blend it with Marine boot camp training methods. They then introduced Marine Corps fitness testing as an experiment in the New York Metropolitan Area (Connecticut, Pennsylvania, New Jersey, New York). They said, "Give this physical fitness test to your students. After that we'll create a competition." Based on individual fitness scores, the high schools came up with the top five individuals from each school and met at Randals Island, New York City, for the first Marine Corps High School Physical Fitness Meet held in May 1960.

It's important to remember that these were not sport-specific activities; instead, they were methods of training and fitness. The schools offered to challenge students of all backgrounds and athletic pursuits to take this test. The five best students from each high school qualified for the bigger athletic competition. I won that event, becoming the first Marine Corps High School Physical Fitness Champion.

The Bayonne High School Fitness Team, coached by Marine Recruiter Bill Miller, won the overall team title. We had the #1 placed finisher in myself but also the #2 and #7 winners. As a result we won an invitation to visit Washington, D.C. and were set to meet with the President of the United States. Unfortunately, we were not able to keep that appointment, but we did meet the Commandant of the Marine Corps, General David Shoup, and the Speaker of the House, Sam Rayburn. It was a wonderful, patriotic experience.

Paul Durso receiving his first place trophy at the 1st Marine Corps High School Physical Fitness Meet.

The Bayonne High School Fitness Team receiving their 1st place award.

Q: After your one and a half years with Bill Miller and your success with the Marine Corps Fitness Challenge, was it obvious that the Marine Corps was the path for you?

It may have looked obvious; however, I had long been influenced by my family and friends. My uncles had served in the military and my older brother Andy, whom I considered my personal hero, was a Marine.

Bill Miller was a part of that development but he was transferred before I was eligible to be recruited. In his place came a Judo brown belt instructor by the name of Al Wilongowski (aka Al Williams). He was a middleweight boxing competitor as well as a Judo man. This guy worked during the day lifting garbage cans and then at night he would squeeze my neck and throw me around like I was a garbage can. His training and conditioning would prove integral to my personal development, much like that of Bill Miller.

Al Williams throwing student Paul Durso during Judo training.

When I finally went into the Marines I felt mentally, emotionally, and physically prepared. I felt like I had already been through boot camp before I had even gotten into boot camp.

Q: What time frame was your service in the Marine Corps? Also, did you get shipped to Okinawa immediately or were you introduced to karate here in the States first?

I entered the Marine Corps on September 4th, 1962. I was immediately stationed locally as part of the 2nd Marine Division, Camp Lejeune, North Carolina. This was an interesting time in history that is largely considered a turning point for our nation as a whole. I was jogging to the hum of a drill instructor's chant, and the rhyme went, "Cuba, Cuba, Here We Come . . . Castro, Castro, You Better Run!" Had Russia not pulled back, allowing us to get a handle on that situation, I assure you I wouldn't be here discussing the first wave of martial art history in America. I would have been part of the first wave to hit the beach in Cuba.

In October, the situation seemed mostly rectified although we stayed on alert. I was at Camp Lejeune, NC, and continued my martial arts training on base. While the martial arts teachers were few and far between, I did get a chance to meet a Marine Sergeant named Sam Pearson, a black belt from Shimabuku Eizo, Hanshi of Shorin Ryu.

Up until that point most of my personal experience was in Judo prior to my Marine training. However, thanks to the connections of Bill Miller, I was able to do a number of demonstrations alongside one of the true pioneers of Isshin Ryu Karate, Don Nagle. The connection was right there in Jersey City, NJ. I managed to find myself at Don Nagle's studio many times and got to meet some of his senior black belts, including a man who would become a good friend, Gary Alexander. Gary, a former Marine, did not have the opportunity to train on Okinawa, thus he studied under Don Nagle. At the time he was a brown belt and soon won the first Canadian Karate Championship sponsored by Mas Tsuruoka. Soon after, he started and hosted the longest annual running karate tournament on record.

My early exposure to karate was in Isshin Ryu, although I wasn't a direct student. Meeting and training with Sam Pearson of Shorin Ryu helped me practice karate further. In the meantime I had already networked with a number of Marines regarding my interest in martial arts, so I was leaning in the direction of traveling to where I might learn more.

Q: Did you find it challenging switching from non-striking arts like Judo to striking arts like karate? Was there a reason you wanted both in your répertoire?

One of my athletic endeavors prior to joining the Marines was playing handball. I learned at the P.A.L. from a policeman, Gene Kelleher. I had achieved some success in that sport as the Bayonne Jr. and Sr. Singles and Doubles Champion, and later, while in the Marines, the 11th Naval District Singles Handball Champion in 1965. As you might imagine, the skills needed to strike a ball with an empty hand are not terribly different from that of striking a person, except that the ball moves much faster. As such, those skills played into my overall martial arts transition.

Picture Left: Paul Durso (center) observes the second place doubles trophy after winning the singles championship in handball.
Picture Right: Durso using handball as a cross training tool for martial arts development.

I think of my early skills in the arts and fitness as a training diet. You cannot just live on steak and expect to be completely healthy. You can't just live on water either. You need a nutritious diet, and I was building a nutritious athletic diet. Not that I had all the answers, but I had good, diverse training and was developing those different skill sets.

One day I was playing handball with a Marine Officer at Camp Lejeune, NC. After the match I had mentioned my desire to get to Okinawa. I can't be sure but to this day I suspect that Major did something for me or made a call because shortly after, my transfer orders were made to Okinawa. For me . . . a dream assignment had come true.

In the infantry they had wanted me for recon but I was also in the Marine band and when I came back from a trip to New Orleans I was told that I was going to Okinawa. I was very surprised because in the Marine Corps you don't just go where you want to go. There should never be a seduction of expectations. Marine Corps life is about duty to God, Country, and Corps, and not at all about what you personally "want to do." The fact that this transfer to Okinawa worked out for me was unusual and why I am suspiciously thankful to that Major.

Q: What was your motivation for being in the band?

The band was an ability to reach down into myself. When people have abilities, talents, etc., the Marine Corps wants to use them. There's a misconception that if you aren't driving a tank or blowing up a bridge you aren't a warrior. Not true, everybody contributes their part. We, in the band, were trained to do everything a Marine Infantryman had to do, then play an instrument on top of that. From my old band officer, Chief Warrant Officer Andrew Olesak, "We are trained to do what they do . . . they cannot do what we do."

I was trained from a young age to play the trumpet and later (while on Okinawa) I was trained to play upright string bass and fender bass. While attending California State University at Fullerton and graduate school, I always worked as a musician toward supplementing my college education.

Q: Upon arrival on Okinawa which base were you stationed at and what were your duties? Did you set out to find karate right away?

I was already indoctrinated with the study of karate and couldn't wait to get over there. I could barely eat, sleep, or even unpack because I was so taken with the idea of finding a dojo. However, I was helping in the opening of a new Marine base called Camp Courtney in Tengan. It was the new Marine Headquarters of the 3rd Marine Division and we (the band) were one of the first to occupy it.

When I got to Okinawa I began to network and communicate with a few other Marine martial artists who were training and they were to guide me around some dojo(s) on the island. It took me nearly 30 days of searching and interviewing before I made up my mind. It was in my nature to be loyal, so I wanted to be sure before I made my decision.

Q: Outside of trying to find a dojo, could you describe the setting of Okinawa itself? At that time wouldn't it have been a mix of idyllic tropical environment with economic strife?

What I noticed is that there were ample opportunities to drink and go out. There were entire sections of town dedicated to socializing, which was heaven to a lot of the Marines. During my time there I had martial artists come to me and say "I just can't train anymore." It was because they were having such a good time off base. They were beaten by the lack of discipline caused by all the fun so easily and readily available.

It's important to remember that this was a collection of young men, far from home and lonely, who experimented with the temptations of excessive drinking and what nature calls young men to do. It was difficult to be amongst all that temptation and still stay focused, disciplined, and say, "I'm going to study the martial arts."

Q: How did you finally settle on a dojo?

I first met Shimabuku Tatsuo of Isshin Ryu, and was advised by him to meet his younger brother Eizo. Shimabuku Eizo was born in 1925 and had just been awarded a Grandmaster title by Toyama Kanken shortly before I arrived. He was, at the time, one of the youngest 10th Dan's on the island and one of the senior representatives of Shorin Ryu.

It was a difficult decision for me to make, but I had a chance to converse with Eizo Sensei personally. At one point he invited me into his home where he picked up a floorboard and said to me, "you see . . . I worked with my brother Tatsuo." I noticed there was kanji written on it but at the time I had no understanding what it had said. I supposed it was some sort of proof. I would only learn later the breadth, depth, and years of experience Eizo Sensei actually had.

I made the decision to emotionally contract my life, my martial arts soul, to Eizo Sensei. That was a benchmark decision, after which I never questioned.

Q: Could you talk more about what impressed you about Eizo Sensei and why you decided to commit to him?

As a person who was already into training and fitness I was amazed at how a person who was five-foot-nothing could jump on your back like a mosquito and rip your ears right off.

There I am looking at him and in the blink of an eye, in one motion, he grabbed my forearm and jumped right on top of my neck.

He was old enough to be mature and yet young enough to still be athletic. As his student, that caught and held my attention.

Q: What was the dojo and training atmosphere like? Who were some of the people you got to train next to?

We had a diverse group. Sometimes we had an even split of Okinawans and Marines, other times it leaned more heavily Okinawan. I worked frequently with one of my favorite fellow students, Eizo's son, Eiko. We had a core group that knitted and stayed together and were very close at that time: John Korab, Joe Lewis, Herbert Wong, and Henry Chai. The Americans that were present brought in a diverse set of backgrounds. Many were military, some were civilians, some were top tier athletes, while others were average.

Some of us might be considered "nuts" compared to regular folks. I remember running around in bare feet over rocks with Eiko. We never showed up to class on time, instead we arrived one hour early. We knew that we wouldn't spend much time in class hitting makiwara and doing conditioning. Shimabuku Sensei figured we could do that on our own time, so we did.

It was interesting to note the differences in the students at the dojo because even though we all trained in the same "zip code" we were all of different character and background. Not everybody went the same direction or became the same person.

Q: In terms of Shimabuku Sensei's specific training, how did he like to split his time between kata, sparring, basics, weapons, etc.?

Well, he involved himself in all of those aspects. He always believed in stretching and warmups. The Okinawans didn't have the clinical understanding of physical fitness we have today, but they certainly had effective methods of knowing and understanding how the body works. At the time I just did what I was told and then later began to realize that they had this stuff down pat.

There were always basics in class, a tradition passed down from Mr. Itosu and Mr. Kyan. The idea was to stay clean, stay basic, and slow down. There were times when some Westerners would get impatient with advancement because they were leaving in six months. Eizo Sensei would roll his eyes a bit and carry on, sometimes skipping ahead. Of course when I finally got my black belt Eizo Sensei turned to me and said, "Now I will teach you karate." I thought, "What? I had already made black belt! What the hell had I been doing?" Then he said, "Now I will teach you kata." Again I thought, "What?"

His philosophy was simple and direct; he didn't attend college or analyze Freudian theories of behavior. His explanation into the meaning of this, "karate", was emotional and from his own experiences during World War II and as a karate student. In his broken English he'd chant, "This karate meaning . . . more better no push!" This explanation, to me, had deep meaning and took time to understand the depth of his feeling. He understood a person could easily get hurt, even killed, in a fight. It was better to avoid the fight, not to back down but to resist pushing and try not to abuse this weapon, this karate thing!

There was no hard science to his methods, but he was a great instructor. He inherited gifts from his teachers and realized that he was running a kind of behavioral school. He didn't really care about belt colors, but he saw that people wanted them so he went along with the program. He gave away some black belts very quickly. These were issues at the time and he had to figure it all out as he was teaching.

Shimabuku Sensei liked to branch out of the dojo as well. Sometimes we went to the beach to train (water resistance training was awesome), and it certainly wasn't about getting a sun tan. We went out to competitions and tournaments too. Nature training and Sanchin were favorites of his. Weapons were taught later on for the more advanced students.

Shimabuku Eizo Sensei performing a takedown and finishing technique on Paul Durso while on the beach.

I think, overall, Shimabuku Sensei had a very strong core martial arts / karate curriculum, not only for karate but for fitness training methods as well.

Q: While on Okinawa you made an impact of a different nature, establishing an entertainment troupe named "The Kichi Gai Trio." How did that come about and how did it affect your overall Okinawa experience?

The Kichi Gai Trio consisted of three young Marines, John D. Riordan, Michael J. Johnston, and myself. While out in the villages we connected with the people. The Okinawans are musical by nature and often sang both in Japanese and Uchinaguchi (the native Okinawan language). We had picked up a few of these songs and started singing them whenever we were together. Eventually we started getting a little reputation with the locals. If we showed up at the local laundromat, for example, they would ask us to sing since it was such a novelty having us Westerners singing their traditional songs.

Paul Durso (center) on stage with Michael Johnston (left) and John Riordan (right) as the Kichi Gai Trio. The troupe featured both comedy and music during their televised showcases.

Eventually word got out and we were interviewed by a local television station and ultimately became radio and television personalities. It impacted the Okinawan people in such a way that we were performing at events and winning competitions, etc. It got to the point where we had to be careful how much we won and how visible we became in order to preserve the delicate relationship between Marines and native Okinawans.

The Kichi Gai Trio (Paul Durso in center) during their last performance, a TV special "sayonara" show, the only show performed in civilian attire.

I think the real impact was that we were there performing on TV in Marine Corps uniform and singing in Japanese. We were making an effort to bridge the gap with humor and song on an international human level. Of course, my instructor, Shimabuku Sensei, was proud of my TV success. Interviewers were always intrigued that I did karate too. Half the time they would try to speak to me in broken English and I would reply in Japanese.

Due to the prominence of The Kichi Gai Trio I was never assigned to Vietnam. The Marine Corps had decided that we could do more for America and the Okinawan people by staying with the reserve band than by going to Vietnam.

Q: Even during your karate training, Marine work, and Kichi Gai Trio efforts you maintained your practice in Judo. Why didn't you abandon Judo during that time and could you talk about the competitions you attended?

I'm a loyalist in that way. As a young student I didn't realize in name what I was doing, but I was building a healthy mixture of martial art influences. The arts were very segregated at that time. If you were a boxer, you used your hands and that was it. If you were a Judo player you grappled. I had to study under those rules so when I did Judo I played by Judo rules, and the like. In karate there was some crossover in terms of techniques, but it still had its own rules.

I was selected to be on the Marine Corps Far East Judo Team while on Okinawa. The team attended a number of events, but in 1965 we participated in the Far East Inter-Service Judo Tournament held in Sasebo, Japan. I was the Far East Judo Champion in my weight division and our Marine team won 2nd place overall.

During that time I looked at karate as my specialty and true focus with Judo mixed in as an auxiliary passion. Of course, later on we would see this kind of cross-training become a bigger part of our martial arts culture, but I felt a need for it even early on. I was getting barraged with questions like, "What if you went up against a fighter who . . . ," or, "What happens if a guy grabs you and then . . ." I needed to be able to answer those questions or better yet, have the person step on the mat so I could show them.

Eventually, when I got back to the States, there weren't a lot of traditional martial arts near university campuses, so I went around and wrestled. The wrestlers would wonder, "What's this?", when I showed up wearing a Judo gi (jacket). I often had them put it on so they could experience what it was about. Some of my best workouts turned out to be with college wrestlers.

Q: Did Shimabuku Sensei ever have a problem with you cross-training in martial arts or sharing time with Judo?

No. That sort of thing was never a problem with him. You have to understand that the Okinawans were already mixing things up. "Mixed" martial arts was not a new concept. Shimabuku Sensei's personal background was in Goju Ryu, Shorin Ryu, Isshin Ryu, and more.

Developing and expanding experience causes growth. With growth comes change. With growth comes some movement away from classic purity. Growth can enhance or change things depending on the person growing.

Q: Could you provide a little timeline for how long you stayed in the Marines?

I had a traditional one hitch commitment to the Marines which was September, 1962 until September, 1966. Toward the end I had the choice to stay in the Marines, but I felt compelled to go to college. My desire to improve my education was brought into focus one day while playing handball. The officers on base were playing on their own court and I literally climbed a wall to get over to play with them. At first nothing was suspicious because we were all in gym clothes, so there were no clear indicators of rank.

Surprisingly, as I was playing, an officer came over to me and said, "Hey Marine, you look familiar. Where are you from?" I tried to dodge his questions as politely as I could, hoping not to draw attention to myself and get back to the game. He eventually said, "Wait, aren't you the guy that won the Marine Corps High School Physical Fitness Meet? . . . Durso?" I had to admit that I was. Then he asked, "So when did you get your Officer's Commission?"

Of course, I didn't have an Officer's Commission, so I weaved around the question, telling him I really needed to get back to the game as my partner was waiting. As soon as that game was done I high-tailed it out of there in order to avoid further questions.

That officer's inquiry made me realize that people were recognizing my accomplishments, but were also expecting more of me. I felt just then that I was lagging behind what I was capable of. As a result, I resolved to finish my duty in the Marines and push myself to acquire a formal education once I was finished. I was dead-set on attending college, which proved to be a benchmark decision in my life.

Q: When you got back to the States did you establish a karate dojo right away and did you manage to stay in contact with Shimabuku Sensei?

When I left Okinawa, I never said goodbye. I felt that I would come back, even though I didn't know exactly how or when. I had left so much there: memories, shows, martial arts, people, and culture. When pulling away from the island I was with John and Michael from

The Kichi Gai Trio, and it was very emotional. Even though I was physically leaving the island, I felt I never really left.

Back in the U.S.A. I was assigned to the Marine Corps Recruit Depot, San Diego, California. I started a dojo within minutes . . . seconds . . . of landing. It was a natural thing to do. I didn't have a plan where I sat down and figured out the details. At the time I was focused on developing my methods of training and fighting; teaching enhanced that effort. My first club was only for military personnel and the people around me. I did not go off base or solicit with advertisements for a club.

During that time, people asked to train with me. I would often not encourage them. That became their first lesson. How do you handle "no"? When I started learning Judo, my first lesson was how to fall. Did I get to throw someone right away? No, I had to learn how to fall.

I ran my classes through the gym on base and eventually word got out to a number of Marines that there was a fighter back from Okinawa. So I garnered some students, taught, and trained with them. Later on in college I initiated an all open sparring (fighting) workout. A sort of fighter's club. A place where students and black belts were invited to discuss and exchange training methods as well as test their fighting skills. I knew success as a fighter / tournament player improved with experience against different styles. Many came — few came back! This was not a teaching class, but more of a fighting experience for participants. I was always cautious not to give too much advice or over-explain my training methods — only if I was asked directly by the student. I did this out of respect to their styles and instructors.

Q: Did you experience a lot of challenge matches being the 'karate guy' back from Okinawa?

No, but it was mostly because I never gave them the chance to challenge. I didn't wait around until they found out about me; I found out about them first. I always made sure I was as polite and humble as possible when visiting schools in the area, but I wasn't really there to talk. I wanted to line up the students, train, and fight with them.

I always respected and was sensitive to the instructors because I knew what they were trying to accomplish. I wasn't there to win fame, fortune, or students. So, to maintain my edge, I practiced with the students and if the instructor wanted to spar (fight with me) afterward that was fine — it was his decision to participate or not. Generally the instructor would not volunteer, which was fine and I made no show of it. Sometimes I would take them to the side and say, "Send the students home. Let them go and then you and I can go at it."

Q: You mentioned you competed after settling into your California setting. Could you describe what the tournament scene was like at the time and did you reconnect with fellow Shorin Ryu student Joe Lewis?

Joe Lewis and I spent time together with Shimabuku Sensei on Okinawa, but Joe was sent off to Vietnam and I remained on Okinawa. After Joe's time in Vietnam he ended up back at Camp Lejeune in North Carolina and eventually I wound up in San Diego, California. We were separated for over a year.

Luckily, Lewis was stationed with John Korab, one of the other senior students of Shimabuku. I was a little more alone on the West Coast. The tournament circuit didn't really pick up until around 1965 when Mike Stone won the Nationals and Joe Lewis won in 1966. Shortly after that Lewis reached out to me and said, "I'm coming to California." I asked, "Coming for what?" He said, "The movies!"

He came out to California and once he arrived we were back together and had a lot of fun.

Q: Did you ever get to fight with Joe Lewis and how would you describe his skill level?

Of course we fought! What . . . you think karate brothers in training didn't spar?

Pictured from left to right: Joe Lewis, Chuck Norris, Paul Durso, Mike Stone.

Pictured from left to right: Henry Choi, Joe Lewis, John Korab, and Paul Durso.

I was always happy when people interviewed Joe because he would attribute his allegiance back to his teacher Shimabuku Eizo and his secret weapon, John Korab. When two high quality people from the same 'womb' train together it's like a knife and a razor sharpening each other. Lewis and Korab became a whetstone for each other's improvement. Lewis came out so sharp from that he went ahead and won the Nationals.

Despite Joe's busy tournament schedule I did get many chances to work with him and spar with him. I used to say "Joe, what do you think you are, 140lbs? You're as fast as I am with heavyweight muscle and power!" Joe, John Korab, and I all developed a slipping side kick with Eizo Sensei that could take a cigarette out of your mouth. I was also part of the grand opening of Joe and Bob Wall's first karate studio in Sherman Oaks, California.

Paul Durso during an exhibition match with Joe Lewis. Mike Stone refereeing.

Q: While you were pursuing martial arts, you were also achieving success in your musical and professional life. Did your success in business help grow your martial arts or were the two distinctly separate?

No, no — it's the opposite. The martial arts were the tool and transition implement for my career and character. It is easy in martial arts and life to experience some success but then lose touch with the wiring that got you there. Soon you can experience failure, depression, bad judgment . . . all of these things. I was certainly not immune — no one is. But it's martial arts training that kept me connected with the D-word: DISCIPLINE, which kept me on track and helped me persevere in my other pursuits.

The discipline of training is bigger than punching and kicking. It helps you understand how to develop and change (because change is inevitable). Your body will start to change sooner or later. The body can be built for the better but will also deteriorate on the microscopic level. Athletes, particularly like sprinters, tend to notice deterioration a lot sooner as their high performance deteriorates. Non-athletes notice it eventually when they have trouble getting out of bed in the morning. Martial artists tend to notice it when they are fighting. With that said, it was the martial arts that helped me understand the completeness of a lifestyle not dependent on external things like competition victories, ego entrapments, etc.

Q: Were you able to revisit Shimabuku Sensei and continue your training with him as time went on?

Oh yes. It was not even a year upon my return to the U.S. that my desire to revisit Okinawa became very strong. With my discharge on the horizon I realized that I had leave-time on the books. I felt this was an opportunity to make a very emotional and very needed return to the island. Most people thought to take the time off, go home, see their families, friends, and girlfriends. But not me. I had to go back to Okinawa.

I marched into the band officer's office. This was not a normal request. After all, I was contemplating leaving the United States. The band officer, Chief Warrant Officer Andy Olesak, understood my motives. We were just recently together on Okinawa. He oversaw and administered the success of The Kichi Gai Trio. His cooperation was there and he understood fully my passion to return to Okinawa.

I remember his answer, "Sure Durso, go ahead, make your plans." Beyond that I had to get permission from Marine Corps Headquarters in Washington D.C. as I was taking an outside leave. I nervously awaited their approval. After receiving that approval, I made plans to stay with my Sensei and on the military Marine base for 30 days. I shipped out and made the journey back to Okinawa, finding quite a surprise waiting for me. Imagine my shock when I learned that, at least as far as the Okinawans were concerned . . . I had died!

War leaves trauma, confusion, distraction, and rumor. Rumor had it that The Kichi Gai Trio (one of us, two of us, or all three of us) had died in Vietnam. I walked into Shimabuku Sensei's dojo not knowing this and my Sensei stood up straight. He could never say my name quite right, struggling with the R. So he said as best he could, "Look . . . Dooso no die!" Everyone in the dojo stopped, stared, and looked at me as if I were a "white ghost"!

I would walk the villages and streets of Okinawa where the Okinawans looked at me, stared, and wondered. They were hesitant, shy, and afraid to approach me and ask, "Are you Paul Durso from The Kichi Gai Trio?" I even contacted my friend and Kichi Gai Trio partner John Riordan, and humorously told him we had passed away. Without missing a beat he asked, "How did we die?" I knew John had wished that he was with me on Okinawa so that he could play with this idea of us being pronounced dead but instead making a return, alive and well.

After that trip it would be 40+ years before I would return to Okinawa in 2008; however, in 1982 my teacher came to California and visited me at my home. One day he rang my doorbell and there he was, standing proudly at 5'0", bowing to me. I bowed to him, but he just bowed further to me, so (in the Japanese manner) I bowed so deep I just about hit the floor.

Our conversations were energetic and exciting. They led him to ask, "How many students do you have? How many dojos?" These questions were not my focus in the arts and I was surprised by them. What was he really asking? I sensed and knew that Shimabuku Sensei had been taken advantage of, as many Okinawan teachers had been. Some students from the West had come over, taken their teacher's name, taken their kata, and then taken off. They returned to the U.S.A. and started selling it all to the world for a price. This sad reality affected how Shimabuku Sensei would handle his students in the future, even the ones that were with him in the early days. This led to the surprising questions he asked me and re-channeled from then on a different kind of relationship and understanding. My loyalty never wavered, but I knew the old Okinawan karate spirit would be different from times past.

My return to Okinawa in 2008 came with deep feelings of where I had been as a young man. I now came back with different eyes, different feelings, and different kinds of excitement. I was a special guest of the President of the Ryukyu Broadcasting Corporation and his staff. They welcomed me with full news media coverage, interview, and a dinner. I was a special guest of Radio Okinawa where I aired a live interview and sang an Okinawan song with my teacher together for all Okinawa to hear. I knew I would be leaving shortly, but this was Shimabuku Sensei's island, his home, his people, his culture. I wanted him to have full honors.

Paul Durso in Okinawa, accompanied by Shimabuku Eizo (seated left) and Josephine Durso (seated right). Durso Sensei received honors and media coverage due to his positive impact as a member of The Kichi Gai Trio. TV Director Kuroshima (standing left) and Ryukyu Broadcasting Corporation President Zayashu Hiroshi (standing right).

Accompanied by my wife, Josephine, and my instructor, Shimabuku Sensei, I met with the Consul General of the United States, the Honorable Kevin K. Maher. I had extended news coverage from the Okinawan media as well as the American military Stars and Stripes newspaper. I was a special guest of the United States 3rd Marine Expeditionary Forces

Band, hosted by Band Officer, Chief Warrant Officer Forrest Q. Brown. My teacher, Shimabuku Sensei, was also a guest there, as well as the director of my original television show with The Kichi Gai Trio, Mr. Akio Kuroshima. What a presentation and event it was for me personally when the Band Officer handed me the baton to lead the band and give some words of advice and counsel to the band members.

I am grateful to Retired Marine Dick Jones and his wife Sachiko (residents of Okinawa), who were with me daily and drove me to all of my meetings along with my teacher. Without them my story could not have been completed.

It was from this experience, filled with so much emotion, that I would return home with a mission to share my story with family, friends, fellow martial artists, and future researchers . . . not only about the martial arts, but also by producing a film documentary of The Kichi Gai Trio experience.

Q: As the '80s and '90s progressed was there anyone in America who became a second mentor to you?

I feel that my personal experiences became my 'mentor,' although I certainly developed peers here in the United States. With peers you can rub against each other much like Joe Lewis and John Korab did at Camp Lejeune, NC., and later like Joe and I did in California. Joe and I may have been considered to be, at the time, among the elite of karate in Los Angeles. Joe wanted to be in the movies, and while on his way to Bruce Lee's house he asked me, "Do you wanna come?" At that time I was a fulltime student in college. I had homework and class assignments always due. I said, "Nah! You go and check him out." We both knew of Bruce Lee, who had already made an impact on TV. Except for Bruce Lee's public kung fu demonstrations, he was not that active on the tournament circuit.

I also recall vividly visiting one of Chuck Norris' schools and how overworked and tired he had become in teaching Tang Soo Do (a Korean variation of karate). That soon changed upon his media discovery and TV / movie success that elevated him to star prominence. I was happy for both Chuck Norris and Joe Lewis. I felt their success; their success was my success. Did I regret not going to Bruce Lee's house? . . . Of course! I can only look back and think of all the "What if I had gone?" scenarios. I recall how Joe's Sherman Oaks Karate School partner (Bob Wall) acted in one of Bruce Lee's movies ("Enter the Dragon"). Bob Wall admitted to me that Joe was the karate brawn and he (Bob) was the business and operations brawn of the school. And yet, in "Enter the Dragon", Bob wore the black beard and scar, and let Bruce Lee kick him across the screen — he had played the bad guy role to a tee. We, as tournament fighters and instructors, supported each other as best we could. I've helped many instructors and will always be thankful to Mike Stone, Chuck Norris, and Joe Lewis who supported me in my presentation of karate in California. This was more about respect, and unmentioned brotherhood. Unknown to us at the time, we were each other's mentors and teachers.

With that discovery I found that as a teacher you can often become a student of your own students. I will always recall how one of my first instructors, Al Williams (who was strong, athletic, and able), said to me, "one day you'll be my teacher," and it went right over my head at the time. But when I got back from Okinawa after the first time he said to me, "You know, I've always wanted to learn nunchaku. Can you help me?" His proverb and philosophy and forward thinking came true. I never forgot that.

Q: What do you hope your personal legacy will be? What message do you want people to come away with when thinking about your impact on the arts?

I'd like people to think of me as a complete martial arts student who was always training as a way of life. Someone who never quit until after he was dead . . . after all, isn't that what one's legacy is about, the continuum after death?

I believe in the future and I believe in physical science. With the right people and the right mindset, hopefully the best could be yet to come.

The legacy I would hope to leave isn't in a particular format or particular move. I think a legacy I would want to leave is an emotion, but you can't really leave an emotion. I would want to leave values. I think perhaps the details of my legacy are still in development because I am still trying to improve on them. That in itself might be the kind of mindset and values I hope to impart.

Today, I no longer wear a black belt. When I informed my teacher that I would no longer wear a black belt he said to me, "This is your idea?" I pointed up over his head and there were pictures of the legends looking down on us, Mr. Kyan, Mr. Motobu, Mr. Miyagi, Mr. Itosu. None of them wore a black belt. As one of my own teachers would say, "A belt just holds the gi together."

A black belt becomes synonymous with strength, character, victory . . . like a title in the sports world. Shimabuku Sensei personally issued to me (in 2008) a signed letter of recognition that was worth more to me than any rank. While I was with Shimabuku Sensei on Okinawa he took me to where he was to be buried and shared with me his family crypt. I was very honored, but in the letter he wrote to me he requested I inform him of whomever I promote and that I was his true student, a descendant of what he had inherited. I felt recognized as a Grandmaster Emeritus of status, not of rank.

It is my hope that we are able to understand and come full circle and become each other's mentors and teachers. I've always had issues with rank. I learned early that it would be better to be a very good brown belt student than an undeserving or unprepared black belt. We are a media species, inclined to want to brag, show off, and promote our own abilities. To me, this is not the character, humbleness, or philosophy of what defines a true martial artist.

These ideals and philosophies are hopefully what have and will continue to fuse us together. We are martial artists and work to promote a brotherhood. We should come to understand, respect, and talk to each other for the betterment of each other as instructors and to pass on our knowledge to future generations of students.

My reputation and experiences as a competitive martial artist stands pat. Success is a deeper understanding, by being able to come full circle, with the ability to look back and recognize achievement. To review the basics and principles of martial arts training for future students and researchers to develop. To that end, I am at peace with myself. I look back with no regrets except that I wish I had done more and given back sooner. I'm not one to retire or stop training. I feel I have much more to do. I am older, slower, not as strong . . . but I've learned to understand life and be mentally confident, careful to judge, cautious with my decisions, and better able to advise others.

To that end, I am just turning another page and hopefully more will be yet to come.

Shimabuku Eizo with Paul Durso in 2008 at Shimabuku Sensei's home / dojo in Okinawa.

Bill Hayes

Major William (Bill) Hayes enlisted in the Marines in 1964. Serving tours of duty that took him to Japan, Okinawa, Korea, and Vietnam, Hayes Sensei became well-known for his exceptional abilities as a soldier and leader. While in the East, Major Hayes began his study of Shorin Ryu directly under Shimabukuro Eizo Sensei. Throughout his tours and return trips to Okinawa, Hayes Sensei became a trusted senior student of Shimabukuro Sensei, helping spread the art of Shobayashi Ryu in the United States at Shimabukuro Sensei's request.

Hayes Sensei has garnered a sterling reputation due to his high level of technical skill and in-depth knowledge of Okinawan history, culture, and martial methods. He is considered a "teacher of teachers," helping guide practitioners of many styles and ranks into the deeper aspects of old-style karate. Hayes Sensei often emphasizes the importance of wellness and character in addition to technique and kata.

Q: Hayes Sensei, could you provide some background on how you got introduced to the martial arts?

My father was a semi-professional light heavyweight boxer in New York, where I was born and raised. He taught my younger brother and I boxing so that we could take care of ourselves on the street — that was my first organized exposure to the "martial arts" side of life.

My father also worked with the 103rd Precinct in New York. They had a youth boxing program in which my brother and I fought. My interest in "something else" came about after noticing that even after winning a bout I still had bruises, black eyes, and sore ribs. I became intrigued with the notion of better self-defense and, as a result, I began taking lessons in karate on Long Island in 1960.

Q: How did you eventually find yourself on Okinawa?

I first set foot on Okinawa in 1966 as a young Marine on my way to South Vietnam for my first of two tours of duty there. Okinawa was the final staging and training area before deploying to Vietnam. It was where one stored uniforms and personal items and prepared tactically and mentally for what would be a thirteen month tour "in Country." I made it through my first tour in Vietnam, and the Marine Corps saw fit to then station me on Okinawa at a base called Camp Hansen, next to Kin Village. As it turned out, Grandmaster Shimabukuro (known as Shimabuku at the time, without the honorific "ro" at the end) Eizo's main dojo was about 400 yards from Camp Hansen's main gate. Some Marines dreaded the thought of being stationed on Okinawa; however, I was a 2nd Dan even before I reached Okinawa and relished the thought of perhaps being able to study with one of the island's best known martial artists. My life was completely changed by what I experienced on Okinawa during that and subsequent tours of duty there.

Q: Was Shimabukuro Eizo Sensei's dojo the only place you explored when you began your studies on the island, or were there others you considered?

As it turned out, the bus that drove us from Kadena Air Base to Camp Hansen in 1966 passed right by Shimabukuro Sensei's dojo. The dojo was on the right as the bus drove past parts of Kin-Cho, and I couldn't help but notice a sign stating, "Rendokan Dojo." Shimabukuro Sensei's name was also on the sign. I'd previously heard of his reputation, and I thought to myself, "If I manage to I survive Vietnam, it would be great to try and study with him."

When I returned to Okinawa in August of 1967, I did not seek out any other dojo as the thought of possibly training with Shimabukuro Sensei was still very strong in my mind; the Rendokan Hombu Dojo was the place I hoped I would be allowed to train. Of course, in the fullness of time, I did visit other dojo out of respect and curiosity — I saw great karate in all of them. It didn't matter what style of Okinawan karatedo you chose to study back then — the teachers were magnificent and the students hard-working.

Q: Was there any heated contention amongst Marines about who the best karate instructor was or who the toughest group was?

Not so much. The contention was that — well, Marines just loved to fight — especially after just returning from Vietnam. We were young, had a little money in our pockets, and probably had less supervision and maturity than we should have had.

On Okinawa, most of the Grandmasters and other senior instructors I came across were very open and sharing. Different Marines came to like the methods or charisma of a certain instructor and stuck with them. It was not uncommon for us to visit each other's dojo(s), sometimes socially and sometimes with our gi to engage in workouts. We had pride in our teachers and the styles we studied, but it was not a divisive pride as came to be seen too often outside of Okinawa. I met some of my best lifelong friends through such visits.

Q: In regards to Shimabukuro Sensei's background, it is recorded that he was a prisoner during World War II. Did that affect the way that he interacted with incoming Marines, or was he able to compartmentalize that?

Shimabukuro Sensei had indeed been a prisoner of war. Even after the war he was held as a P.O.W. for a while and worked near what is now Marine Corps Base, Camp Courtney, along the Tengan Pier area. He helped load and offload supplies and earned what was called B-Yen Script which he traded in for foodstuffs to help feed his family.

In regards to how he treated us, he realized the big picture: the Marines needed to be there on Okinawa for the Japanese to NOT be there. He, like many Okinawans, was somewhat sympathetic to the Japanese Emperor who was seen as a god-like figure at that time, but my sensei was also aware that the brutality the Japanese military demonstrated so often was immoral, unnecessary, and often inhumane. He knew the history of his own country when it came to the Japanese, so he held no animosity towards the Americans who had traveled so far from their own country in order to free him and his fellow Okinawans. He never forgot the sacrifices American military forces made during the Battle of Okinawa, one of the bloodiest battles of the Pacific War.

Q: Shimabukuro Sensei's experience, in terms of his own teachers, was very high level. He often personally lists Kyan Chotoku Sensei, Miyagi Chojun Sensei, Shimabukuro Tatsuo Sensei, Motobu Choki Sensei, and others as influences of his. Did he ever mention what specifically he was able to capture from those instructors or perhaps what those instructors excelled at?

He did. Sensei not only mentioned what he had learned, he demonstrated some of those things whenever we were in class. More importantly, whenever other senior Okinawan instructors visited his home, the few of us students who hung around after class were treated to what amounted to "post-graduate tutorials" and practicums in the old methods of the Okinawan arts. Afterwards, perhaps the next day or next week, we would question Sensei about what we thought we saw, and he would do his best to help us understand things by referring to skills his earlier instructors possessed.

Shimabukuro Eizo Sensei in 1968.

We probed my sensei on these things quite a bit. He would sometimes compare the different body types of his Marine students to those of his teachers and earlier training partners and express who the Marines reminded him most of. Mr. Kyan Chotoku had a very slight build and excellent kicking skills. Shimabukuro Sensei also developed superior kicking abilities. I recall actually trying to see the motion of his kicks in the "Sky Dojo" and finding it almost impossible due to his extraordinary speed. Miyagi Chojun Sensei had a heavy build and was known for his great power and breathing dynamics as well as his courtesy. Motobu Choki Sensei, also strongly built, was more of a brawler and validated much of what he learned through real encounters. My sensei saw some of that same behavior in a few of his Marine students.

Shimabukuro Sensei discussed each of his teacher's physical traits and also their character traits. Each one had a different personality. Motobu Sensei was a bit outgoing while Kyan Sensei was extremely reticent, even amongst other Okinawans. There is a record of a meeting in 1936 where a number of important issues related to the Okinawan arts were discussed. A number of senior Okinawans were present, including Mr. Kyan. Despite the need for discussion, it is said that Mr. Kyan did not speak a word during the meeting —

his demeanor was sufficient to express his opinions.

Q: The bulk of your training came directly under Shimabukuro Sensei, but are there any other individuals you would consider a direct sensei to you?

As I respond to your questions, I'm mindful that I've trained for nearly 54 years; one meets, trains with, and is influenced by a lot of folks during that length of time. However, one, if he or she is fortunate, always has only one sensei. For me that will always be Shimabukuro Eizo Sensei. That does not mean that I have forgotten any of those who helped me along my journey. Quite to the contrary — I will never forget them and can never thank them enough for adding to whatever it is I may eventually become.

I think it's important to remember that we're always learning, at least hopefully that's the case, and so we will always need helpers and facilitators along "the way." Our early years are the formative years during which we learn the "martial science" of a particular system, even though we think we are "martial artists" from the very beginning of our studies. Later, as our training and the influences which impact us broaden and mature, we come to understand the actual "art" of what we are studying as well as its greater true social and philosophical purposes. During this process, our sensei (the one who is our PRIMARY guide) helps us to step ahead a little further from time to time. That happens even if he or she is no longer physically present in our lives. The results of that process also empowers each of us to help others with their journeys from "martial science" to "martial arts."

Q: The Okinawans must have been truly skillful to convince tough, confident Marines to become students and deal with so much bruising training in addition to demanding military living.

True, their skills were impressive. Marines loved to train, and fight, and many saw unique challenges in the exotic thing that karate represented. Was this "karate" something we could do? Would learning it make a more effective Marine?

Some Marines did not capitalize on the real opportunities right in front of them — the social, cultural, and life protection benefits of what was being given. Some wanted to take the path of least resistance ending in a colored belt of some sort. A few studied sporadically with instructors on the various bases, again with the thought of getting a colored belt. The Okinawans I saw always taught at a high level in their dojo, even if we didn't "see" or understand that level. Their arts were impeccable. You could feel them generating and transmitting high levels of power while moving with sophisticated grace. In my book, *My Journey with the Grandmaster*, I write about that phenomenon. When you add to that the good nature and happy lifestyle of the Uchina-jin (Okinawan people), you experience the charisma that attracted us to the dojo.

Q: Your military career took you to Okinawa multiple times, but it also had you traveling to countries like Japan and Korea. Could you provide a little bit of a timeline for those events, and where you actually operated dojo(s) while traveling?

Well, in early 1965, I held classes in the corner of a recreation room in a barracks at Marine Corps Air Station Cherry Point, N.C. I wasn't authorized to teach or promote, but I had a few students and we trained in fundamentals. During my first tour of duty in Vietnam, 1966-1967, I had the chance, from time to time, to train and teach at a place called Red Beach, not far from Danang. Following that tour, I was stationed on Okinawa during 1967-68 where I was a student of Grandmaster Shimabukuro. That was a profound tour for me as he personally taught me each of the 23 kata in his system and deepened that instruction with detailed conversations, allowing me to make precise notes, etc. Towards the end of my tour on Okinawa, Shimabukuro-sama also allowed me to help with some of the classes at both his headquarters dojo in Kin Village and one of his other dojo in Henoko Village, near Nago City in the northeastern part of Okinawa. The Henoko dojo was run by a great instructor - Nobuyuki Sensei — with whom I became good friends. He was a ferocious fighter.

From there I was ordered to join Force Troops at Camp Lejeune, North Carolina. I was a Staff Sergeant by then, and I taught in the 8th Marine Regiment area while there and competed frequently in local tournaments to help demonstrate my teacher's relatively unknown style of Shorin Ryu. I didn't stay at Camp Lejeune very long due to the troubling racial atmosphere on and around the base. After nine months there I requested to be sent back to Vietnam — and the Corps said yes. I stopped in Okinawa again on my way to Vietnam and was reunited with my sensei and his family. Of course I also received instruction from my teacher during my brief stay. He was especially interested in helping me understand how bladed weapons could be defended against using the principles of Shobayashi Ryu. My sensei had picked up some unusual bayonet techniques during the 1940s.

During a portion of the time I was in Vietnam for my second tour, I was assigned to a unit of the Republic of Korea (R.O.K.) Marine Corps — the "Blue Dragons." I was sent to Quang Ngai City, about 13 miles from Chu Lai, South Vietnam. There I joined an R.O.K. martial arts demonstration team. We trained together on a compound in Quang Ngai, patrolled together outside of the compound, and traveled to different areas to demonstrate martial arts. We also instructed several hundred South Vietnamese youths in Quang Ngai City itself. We taught them on an old abandoned French soccer field. Our instruction was part of a program geared towards helping some of those youths lead their country one day. However, because of the way the war ended, the goals of that program were not met.

Afterwards, in mid-1970, I received orders to report to Marine Corps Air Station, Iwakuni, Japan, in Yamaguchi Prefecture. I had a great tour there for a number of reasons (one being that one of my best friends was also stationed there at the time). Don Bohan Sensei, a first-generation student of my teacher's older brother, Shimabukuro Tatsuo, the founder of Isshin Ryu Karatedo, was billeted right next door to me. He was one of the true pillars of Isshin Ryu Karate.

Don-San taught near our billeting area while I taught in the base gymnasium some distance away next to a Japanese Shotokan (J.K.A.) 7th Dan whose last name was Hakayama. As it turned out, I also got to see Nakayama Masatoshi Sensei, the J.K.A.'s Chief Instructor and a direct student of Funakoshi Gichin. While at Iwakuni I also met, befriended, and trained with Nomura Gensho Sensei, a superb technician in Seigokan Goju Ryu. Seigokan was the brainchild of Seigo Tada Sensei, a now deceased senior student of Yamaguchi Gogen Sensei, who was himself a student of Miyagi Chojun, founder of Goju Ryu.

I returned to Cherry Point in late 1970 and started another dojo there. I remained at Cherry Point for almost four years during which time, I have to say, I was blessed with the benefits of a very austere dojo and very dedicated students. That combination produced some excellent martial artists.

In early 1974, I went off to Marine Corps Base, Quantico, Virginia, to become a Marine Warrant Officer. After Officer Candidate School, The Basic School, and Naval Justice School, I was assigned back to Cherry Point where I continued to instruct until ordered to Okinawa in the summer of 1976. On Okinawa, I, of course, paid an early visit to my sensei and his family and resumed my status as a direct student of his. Shimabukuro Sensei permitted me to have my own dojo aboard Marine Corps Base Camp McTureous, and I taught classes in an unused Quonset hut until I was transferred in late 1977. I had several Marines as well as Okinawan security guards as students and was honored to be allowed to represent my sensei while living in his homeland. During this, my second tour on the island, my sensei provided answers and demonstrated methods which further changed my understanding of all I had previously studied.

Bill Hayes demonstrating a sidekick inside the Cherry Point dojo in 1974. The training floor was partially matted, partially concrete. Holes in the rear wall can be seen as a result of intense training.

I headed back to Cherry Point, North Carolina, in 1977 and re-established my dojo there until I was transferred to Quantico, Virginia, in 1982. Now a Captain of Marines, I started classes in Quantico's Larson's Gymnasium, in the same general area where Captain John Carria Sensei, of Uechi Ryu fame, was also teaching. John-San was a student of Uechi Kanei Sensei, son of the founder of that art. Carria Sensei and I have been friends ever since the day we met.

In 1986, I was selected for duty as Aide-de-Camp to the Commanding General, Marine Corps Combat Development Command (a three-star General). So, while I continued to train, I did not have the time to operate a dojo for the remainder of my time at Quantico. In 1988, with the retirement of the General, I asked to be sent to Okinawa and once again the Corps said yes. I was stationed on the island from 1988 until late 1990 when I left Okinawa in order to retire. During that last tour, my duties as a Marine Major left me limited time to study with my teacher and no time to operate a dojo. Nevertheless, sensei again kindly shared a number of principles, applications, mindsets, insights, and other "precious gems" which have kept me inspired ever since. I returned to the States in late September of 1990 and retired from the Marines on 1 October, 1990, thus ending my military career timeline.

Q: Did you feel any racial discrimination or resistance as a Westerner when opening schools in Okinawa and Japan?

When I was stationed in Iwakuni, Japan, and teaching next to a senior J.K.A. Shotokan instructor — Hakayama Sensei — he was clearly resentful of the fact that an American was teaching karate in "his" gym. We had a few words, and eventually a friendly "exchange," after which he came to understand that the gym he was standing in and the base it was situated on were United States Marine Corps property by virtue of the fact that America had defeated Japan in World War II. I believe it also became clear that ethnicity had nothing to do with one's ability to fight.

On Okinawa I never felt any such resentment from other Sensei. In fact, the Okinawan students I trained in my teacher's two dojo and those I trained in my own dojo aboard Camp McTureous were very receptive and very respectful, especially after learning who my instructor was.

Q: As time moves forward, Okinawa is adapting and evolving, as any country would. How have you seen it evolve, and how has that affected the growth and availability of old-style karate?

Population growth on the island, social trends associated with such growth, the need for continuing economic development, the politics of hosting a large U. S. military presence on Okinawa, the evolution of the Okinawan dojo itself, and the focus on the "World Tournament" held on the island have all impacted the survival of old-style karate.

Okinawa is the poorest of Japan's 47 prefectures and has few natural with which to develop the increasing streams of revenue needed to support its growing population. There is a great need to reclaim the large tracts of land the U. S. military sits on — land needed to build homes, schools, commercial enterprises, etc. Such issues take away from the heavy personal investment required for the pursuit of preserving the old style of Okinawan karate — the classical arts designed for life protection. Dojo(s) where masters pass on the old ways are few in number and hard to find these days. They are being crowded out by the more numerous dojo that cater to tournament karate and the changing lifestyles of the Okinawan people themselves.

Many dojo on Okinawa are no longer recognizable to students of the earlier arts. In my Sensei's "Sky Dojo" in Kin-Cho there were no walls or ceiling, no A / C, no heating, and no windows. We trained on a concrete roof with only a six-inch high lip around its edge to keep us from falling off. We had one fluorescent light for evening training. My teacher's other dojo(s) were also austere — even the indoor ones.

That environment helped develop a certain kind of student, one who transitioned easily to the older methods. Nowadays, it is not uncommon to see dojo with nice shiny floors, air conditioned locker rooms, etc. These dojo are designed for the science of karatedo, not the art of karatedo. Accordingly, training regimens have changed as well. Hojo Undo (body conditioning) implements are still found in many dojo, but not enough of them to indicate a serious devotion to using the old instruments to protect the body against the types of techniques associated with the classical arts.

Since the intense effectiveness of classical arts are not being taught, there is no need for students to develop themselves in ways that would protect against old style attacks - a classic example of circular reasoning which has as its end result the loss of Okinawa's true heritage. Simplified bunkai has replaced the old "Ti Chi Ki" ("What the Hand is Doing") and the visual beauty of a form is valued over its practical life protection essence. Additionally, for all its other benefits, the focus on the "World Tournament" seems to be commerce. Competitors travel to Okinawa from around the world to win an award — a title — not to pursue the origins of their particular style. While on Okinawa competitors rent hotel rooms, rent vehicles, purchase retail wares, eat in restaurants, snorkel, visit Shuri Gushuku, the aquarium, the zoo, the karate museum, the bars, etc. All of this generates needed revenue; however, none of it preserves the classical arts of Okinawa, per se.

Q: In regards to tournaments — you used to participate from time to time. Is that something you still do, or have you phased that out of your personal life?

Competition was always a less important phase in our system — something to be engaged in, temporarily, during one's youth. Even so, several of my Sensei's more prominent students did extremely well in competition. It was fun and sometimes instructive to compete, but I never for a moment confused tournament fighting with the lethal life protection my Sensei demonstrated on Okinawa.

As an analogy, during my time in the Marine Corps I was a member of the 2nd Marine Aircraft Wing's Rifle and Pistol Team. I shot well and even set a range record one year. Nevertheless, I never confused competitive shooting at a target from a known distance, in good weather, using match ammunition, shooting gloves, shooting glasses, a leather sling, a fiberglass-packed stock, etc., with what was taught to some of my friends who became Marine Scout / Snipers. I and my sniper friends all practiced "marksmanship," but there was a world of difference between hitting a paper bullseye at 500 yards and putting a bullet through the head of a living human being at 1,000 yards in order to protect a village of innocent people.

Q: Clearly you took effectiveness both with your hands and with weapons very seriously. Did this lead you to your interest in the sai (Okinawan metal truncheon)?

What drew me to the Sai was my teacher's expertise with it. It was an excellent weapon which taught both defense and offense (and it also strengthened the body). You were holding two hefty metal truncheons, one in each hand and one tucked in your obi. Using them helped with conditioning. It was a classical weapon on Okinawa that some suggest was introduced from Malaysia. Even if that was the case, the Okinawans certainly tweaked it and made it their own. As such, it is tied directly to Okinawan culture.

One of the reasons I chose to demonstrate the sai during my tournament years was because not many seemed to understand what it was at the time or how it was properly used.

Shimabukuro Eizo Sensei demonstrating the sai to Bill Hayes. Class took place on the roof of the Sky Dojo in Kin Village, 1967.

Q: One of the other impacts you had was on the Marine Corps Martial Arts Program during its early development. How exactly were you involved in that, and what ideas did you bring from your background?

Well, I was living near Marine Corps Base Quantico in the early 1990s and one day I received a call from a senior Marine Staff Non-Commissioned Officer by the name of Cardo Urso. Cardo-San was a Master Sergeant at the time but would eventually be promoted to the highest enlisted grade of Master Gunnery Sergeant and receive the Legion of Merit for his work on what became the Marine Corps Martial Arts Program (M.C.M.A.P.). He told me he'd been tasked by the Commandant of the Marine Corps to put together a team of "subject matter experts" for the purpose of developing a truly effective martial arts program for the Corps. One that would be taught to all Marines, officers and enlisted, male and female, active duty and reserve. One which would be sustained progressively over the course of a Marine's career and one involving not only a physical component but also a mental component and a character component.

I'd heard similar ideas in the past and wasn't so sure this one would go anywhere; however, I knew Cardo-San to be a serious martial artist and a fine Marine Artilleryman so I agreed to help out as best I could. In short order a panel of martial artists got together along with representatives from the Corps' Training and Education Command, and we managed to cobble together a very effective, combat-oriented system which was eventually approved by the Commandant and named "M.C.M.A.P." We brought in excellent martial artists from numerous disciplines (Judo, taekwondo, jujutsu, Sambo, karate, bladed weapons, hoplology, boxing, combat shooting, and more). M.C.M.A.P. is now a comprehensive, legacy program in the Corps and is a requirement for every Marine in the Corps. It's been battlefield tested and is itself the center of moral excellence in the Corps. I was honored to have been one of the founders of M.C.M.A.P., and I continue to have tangential contact with the program.

Q: Could you describe the differences between bunkai, oyo bunkai, and ti chi ki?

"Bunkai" generally translates as "analysis," and its regular use constitutes the standard interpretation of a given kata within a given style. "Oyo Bunkai" is a more personally insightful, creative, less restrictive form of technical analysis. It allows for additional room, so to speak, to explore kata and to use techniques within kata according to one's body type. "Ti Chi Ki," on the other hand, is an old Uchina-guchi term which translates as, "what the hand is doing." While both bunkai and oyo bunkai represent different levels of the technical and scientific expression of karate methods, ti chi ki represents the height of the artistic expression of the life protection principles contained in one's art. Ti Chi Ki is based on more than the mere sequential techniques seen in bunkai.

Concepts such as "stealing time" are integral in ti chi ki. Stealing time involves changing your timing to get ahead of the opponent's technique, attacking the "cues" which precede his attack and thereby change the meaning and effect of your own technique which in turn changes the duration and outcome of the engagement.

Q: Perhaps related to oyo bunkai and ti chi ki is the term "hacho," which is an "allowable difference." Could you explain your view on hacho, and do you have any specific examples of when you utilized hacho in your training with Shimabukuro Sensei?

I saw hacho often on Okinawa because of differences in physique and age of various practitioners. My Sensei is about 5'1" and most of the students in his dojo at the time I lived on Okinawa were around 6' tall. Accordingly, over time, sensei had to be something of a "master tailor." Consider it this way — when we all show up at a dojo, what we are given during our first few years of training amounts to a "First Communion Suit" (or dress). Something designed for us to wear for a limited amount of time. Something we would look ridiculous trying to squeeze into 35 years later! What good sensei(s) do is constantly adjust and tailor the science, and most especially the art, to the practitioner over time as he or she changes / ages so that a practitioner can continue to be appropriately "clothed" during one's martial arts lifetime.

I noticed hacho even among Okinawan sensei themselves when they visited my teacher. For instance, I watched as one senior did Chinto kata without performing the usually seen double jump kick. When I asked my Sensei about that later, thinking it was a different version of the kata, he said, "No, kata same-same, maybe 55-60 no more jump okay." I got it!

In my opinion, one of the greatest mistakes in our training is in *not* tailoring kata as time goes by. My Sensei was very specific about performing Sanchin kata "maybe half tight" once you're past 45-50 years of age. It was the smartest way to prevent high blood pressure problems and intestinal disorders. After all, performing your system's kata should not become a suicide pact. Remember, Okinawan karate was always meant to extend both our lifespans and our health spans.

Q: When it came to writing your book, *My Journey with the Grandmaster*, you shared some very unique and personal experiences. Was it a difficult emotional process creating this book, and did you ever have second thoughts about publishing it?

Well, the book was not written initially for the public. It was intended as a series of connected notes for some of my students who might not have had the opportunity to go to Okinawa. What I wanted to do with those notes was give them some sense of what I had experienced on Okinawa in my Sensei's dojo and with his family. In addition to the martial arts concepts, I wanted to make sure to mention the racial issues of that era, the treatment of Okinawans by the Japanese, the brutality of the Battle of Okinawa, the role of Marines on the island, and how the character of the Okinawans themselves helped them rise above adversity.

Bill Hayes Sensei in 1996 with Shimabukuro Eizo Sensei (right) and Shimabukuro Eiko Sensei (left). Eiko-Sama was the son of Eizo Sensei and a senior in Shobayashi Ryu under his father.

Q: Speaking of Okinawan character, one of the terms you use is, "hinkaku," which is a special dignity that only comes after significant study. Could you talk about what that is and perhaps provide an example of how you saw it in senior practitioners on Okinawa?

The senior martial artists I saw in the '60s and '70s were gentlemen who had survived a terrible war. They had seen the worst of life. They were on the receiving end of extreme, undeserved brutality. They had seen much of their culture erased during the Battle of Okinawa. Afterward, they had to come up with something of a "reset" point, one that came from the inside. That's where hinkaku starts. The Okinawans had to reach inside and reconstruct their own religion, history, and art because so much of it had been destroyed. What we found were repositories of such things in the gentlemen and gentlewomen who also happened to be martial artists. They became walking cultural centers, and they dispensed their culture through the dignity and propriety of their daily lives, which included their teaching skills.

On Okinawa the role of seniors is very interesting. My teacher wasn't considered only a karate expert. People would come to him and ask him to decide on a name for their children, when to plant their crops, etc. He was a very special individual in the village, and his judgment was trusted. Thus he developed a certain dignity to accompany his many martial arts-related and non-martial-related responsibilities.

Aside from my sensei and several other seniors, I specifically recall seeing hinkaku expressed by Miyahira Katsuya Hanshi. He'd been a student of the legendary Chibana Chosin Hanshi. I watched him perform Passai Dai kata in late 1967. From the very beginning he had been sitting quietly in a chair off to the side of a demonstration area. A number of other seniors came out and performed magnificently. But the moment Miyahira Sensei stood up it was almost as if the room became charged with energy. He took a few steps, looked around, and even though the arena was filled, it was as though he was looking at an empty sugar cane field one hundred years in the past in which a lethal engagement was about to take place. He took a few seconds to gather himself. I always wondered what gentlemen like him thought in those moments, and I personally believe he was contemplating Okinawa's ruined castles, the destroyed villages . . . all the pain and hurt suffered by his countrymen. His thoughts may have been, "How can I overcome this? By doing Passai Dai."

His immense dignity, his hinkaku, expressed itself during the performance, and it was like watching a true king of the martial arts. His timing was such that you could see what was taking place in the fight he was mentally engaged in. You could "see" the effects his movements were having on the enemy who had attacked him and his countrymen. You could also "see" the outcome of those effects. At the end of the kata he bowed slowly, not to anyone in the audience but to his enemy who now lay fallen in that empty sugar cane field. He turned and walked off the stage, his energy being re-absorbed into him as he did so. Amazing. We had all just seen something very special.

Q: How important do you feel the connection to nature and training outdoors is in regards to karate?

I think it's very important. My teacher would remind us that during his youth the most likely place for getting attacked was outside while walking from village to village. We were told that Kyan Chotoku Sensei used to make it a point to not only walk between villages where thugs were known to lay in wait for passers-by, but he carried a chicken under each arm to make himself more attractive as a target for thieves. By defeating such thieves with his kicking skills and driving them away, he protected those who lived in the villages at each end of the trail. By training outside, Mr. Kyan and others became more familiar with the conditions under which they might have to use life protection techniques. Outdoor training teaches us to vary our techniques as needed. There are early films of my teacher which show him training in the sand of an old Marine tank trail near Camp Hansen, Okinawa, and also training on the concrete roof of his Sky Dojo. In both instances his footwork is noticeably different. The sand required him to lift and move his feet in a way different from the tsugi ashi (one foot moving up to the other) and suri ashi (foot sliding forward) used on concrete, wooden, or tiled surfaces.

Q: Another part of the natural aspect of training is understanding wellness. Could you describe how food was integrated with your training to restore the body and what Western corollaries you have found?

We first have to understand that "warrior wellness" was always a part of classical martial arts training. The Bubishi itself, in clearly written language, notes the link between diet and martial skill. I am fond of reminding folks during our seminars that the second most important person in the Shaolin monasteries was the cook! A similar circumstance prevailed in my teacher's dojo. He was the most important person in the dojo and his Okusan, Mrs. Shimabukuro, the chef of the house, was the second most important person there (and not *just* because she was the great cook she was).

When it came to feeding those of us who remained after class to eat with OSensei, she often prepared foods designed to balance or increase our energy before or after training — foods to help us recover and repair our bodies. On Okinawa, you'll hear the old term, "Nuchi Gusui." It means "Food is medicine," and that's how good teachers once used food. You'll also hear the phrase, "Hara hachi bu," or, "Eat until you are 80% full." In other words, don't stuff yourself — you may have to fight later.

My sensei and his wife always made sure we were properly hydrated with both water and green tea (the tea was occasionally sweetened with sugar cane, not processed sugar.) Mama-San was careful that the various soups and dishes she created were both light and nutritious, and contained ingredients such as goya (a bitter, warty, cucumber-like vegetable packed with what we now call antioxidants, zedoary (which has the same properties of turmeric), and lots of shima tofu (island tofu curd) for soy isoflavones. Animal protein was added by way of lean beef or pork.

By the way, the water on Okinawa contains the now popular supplement "coral calcium" since water on Okinawa is naturally filtered through coral (coral makes up the bulk of the island's composition). The diet on Okinawa was designed to not only lengthen lifespan but also extend health span — something forgotten here in America where promotion ceremonies are more often than not punctuated by the delivery of a dozen high fat, high cholesterol, pizza pies.

In Shobayashi Ryu, we are forever mindful of the "circle of training," depicted by a circle containing four quadrants: kata, application, ethos, and wellness. On Okinawa, you could experience the full "circle" just by living there and training in a good dojo. Once you left the island you almost always had difficulty holding onto the wellness quadrant, and many suffered as a consequence. Because it's so difficult to maintain an Okinawan diet while living outside of Okinawa, I heartily recommend quality supplements to help maintain the integrity of the "circle of training."

Q: You spend a lot of time traveling and helping others understand some of the old methods of karate, but what does your personal training look like these days?

Well, I'm a senior citizen now so I do what I want to do! Haha. No, of course I follow the dictates of Shobayashi Ryu when it comes to training. I have a daily training regimen; however, it is one that varies depending on the "cycle of training" I'm in. The cycle of training consists of four elements: kata, applications, kobudo, and hojo undo. Each element is emphasized during a three month period throughout the year so that by year's end you will have focused on and strengthened each of them. You continue to train in each element all during the entire year but, again, you *emphasize* a particular element for a three month period during the year to give it special polish.

Frankly, kata are at the heart of my training, sometimes for aerobic purposes but always for the research and application of their principles. I do a great deal of junbi undo (initial preparatory exercises) as well as stretching and speed drills. I also do a good deal of "combat toughening" using methods I brought back from Okinawa, some of which I just don't see too much of these days since my Sensei teaches differently now (as he should). In the end, I remain inspired to train by the model I saw on Okinawa in the 1960s when my teacher was in his prime. As a 10th Dan he set the pace for all of his students, and remember, most of his students were hard-charging Marines and other service personnel. OSensei's power, speed, energy, life protection abilities, and daily cheerfulness cannot be adequately described in an interview; however, I try to keep that model in mind when I train.

Q: With your particular Shobayashi-Kan organization, what is your goal and how would you like to see it grow?

The highest goal I have for the Shobayashi-Kan is to engender and support a deeper appreciation for and understanding of the classical Okinawan life protection arts. Our training group (kenkyu-kai) uses Shobayashi Ryu kata as vehicles for understanding the principles of the Okinawan arts. I believe we are seeing too many systems in which folks are trained only in "omote" (surface techniques) with some movement and a limited, style-centric analysis of that movement. Aside from that, I hope the Shobayashi-Kan will help individuals inculcate and incorporate integrity in all they do. We try to tie together warrior wellness, combative skills, character, and a happy, respectful attitude towards life and all other people. I am especially committed to the Shobayashi-Kan doing all it can to stay away from corrosive "karate politics" and hyper-commercialism, neither of which has a role in the classical arts of Okinawa.

Chapter 13 –
Shorinkan

Matsumura Sokon, the "father" of Shorin Ryu, passed his art on to multiple senior students, one of whom was Itosu Anko. Itosu Sensei was famous for his physical toughness but also for his impact on the organization of karate in Okinawa and the art's integration into Japanese physical education. One of Itosu's senior students was Chibana Chosin, a man who proved to be a critical bridge of martial knowledge between pre-and-post World War II Okinawa.[84]

Chibana Sensei was a skilled Shorin Ryu practitioner and thought leader on the island. In 1930, he began referring to his art as Kobayashi Ryu ("Young Forest" Style), helping to distinguish it from the growing number of Shorin Ryu branches. He also served on a number of organizational boards, relied upon by many Okinawan karateka to provide guidance and support.

Among the students of Chibana Sensei was Nakazato Shuguro, a young man who had studied karate in Japan but had returned to Okinawa at the conclusion of World War II. Nakazato proved to be an apt and loyal student, becoming Chibana Sensei's primary assistant over time. Upon Chibana Sensei's passing, Nakazato Sensei took on a leadership role, operating primarily out of his Shorinkan Dojo. It was in this dojo, and later at branch locations and via travel seminars, that Nakazato Sensei opened his doors to western students.

---

[84] Alexander, George W. *Okinawa, Island of Karate*. Place of publication: Yamazato Publications, 1991. 66. Print.

Eddie Bethea

Eddie Bethea Sensei is a Vietnam War veteran and senior practitioner of Shorin Ryu Shorinkan. Bethea Sensei has distinguished himself over the course of decades as a successful tournament competitor, diligent traditionalist, and source of wisdom and insight for many practitioners. His positive attitude and insights have helped many individuals during their karate journeys.

Bethea Sensei grew up during a time of racial unrest in North Carolina. Experiencing prejudice personally, Bethea Sensei had to discover a sense of self-worth and esteem while traveling in the military, eventually utilizing karate as a means of physical, emotional, and philosophical development. Since his first tour of duty on Okinawa in the 1960s, Bethea Sensei has been a loyal student of Nakazato Shuguro and maintains an active connection with his teacher and the Shorinkan organization.

Q: Bethea Sensei, can you begin by telling us when and where you were born?

I was born in Wilmington, North Carolina, on December 20, 1943.

Q: Was there anything in your childhood that might have led you to the martial arts?

The men coming back from World War II and Korea were a big influence on me. I heard them speak of Judo and I was infatuated with just the word because I had never seen or heard of anything like it. When I grew up and entered the military I knew it was something I wanted to get involved with, even though I had never even seen it.

Q: In your area of North Carolina, were there any martial arts programs that you could find throughout the '40s and '50s?

In terms of karate, there was none to speak of in the '40s. Master Robert Trias got things off the ground around 1946, and if there were pockets of karate around before him I didn't know about them. There were no martial arts at all that I was able to determine in my area.

Q: When you were coming up through high school did you already know you were going to join the military?

My desire to join came to me mostly toward the end of high school. One of my earliest dreams was to become a preacher, but then I decided I wanted to become an airplane pilot. That desire led me to the Air Force. My parents couldn't afford to send me to college, even with a few small scholarship offers. I chose the military instead.

Q: What year did you end up joining the military?

I went into the Air Force in 1961. My parents had to sign off on it because I was only 17.

Q: Were you surprised by the difficulty of boot camp and military life?

Compared to the discipline I lived with at home, the military was a piece of cake. We didn't have a lot growing up and my parents kept a strict household. In addition, when you are talking about the '40s and '50s, you are talking about a segregated society. You had to be disciplined all the time.

Q: Did you feel any of that racial tension in the Air Force?

I did at times, but I think it started to change around 1968-1969. I was born and raised in North Carolina and my first assignment was in Montgomery, Alabama for basic training. I was there during the Selma to Montgomery March, which took place in 1965. That march began in Selma, Alabama with a speech by Dr. Martin Luther King and was motivated by the idea of registering black voters. As the protesters marched they were met with some violence but achieved their goal of reaching Montgomery.

Extra troops were brought into Maxwell Air Force Base and we had to make sure we were all ready to deploy if needed. My particular unit was the 305th Transportation Squadron.

It can be difficult to understand the climate of the times without having lived through it. These days we are better able to decide our own destiny than in times past.

Q: How long did you spend on active duty in the U.S. before receiving orders to report to Okinawa?

I went into the service July of 1961 and didn't get to Okinawa until June of 1966. My service was conducted at Maxwell during that period of time. In 1961 we had to be "at the ready" for the Bay of Pigs Invasion related to the crisis in Cuba. President Dwight D. Eisenhower had directed the 101st Airborne down to Maxwell Air Force Base. My duties involved transportation so we supported the troops who came down and kept them in a state of readiness to deploy.

Q: When you were shipped out to Okinawa had you hoped for deployment there or was it a matter of coincidence?

It was a matter of coincidence. I didn't"t get to pick and choose where I was deployed, but if I had my way I probably would have selected France or something like that. I took French in high school and it seemed like a natural choice. Even though Okinawa came up randomly, it was the best thing that could have happened to me.

Q: Was karate on your radar at all before you were deployed?

It was on my radar because in 1965 the show "Wild Wild West" had started airing on TV. Robert Conrad would occasionally do karate techniques, which really caught my attention. I tried to make sure to watch every time it was on. We had a couple of guys in my squadron who had come back from Korea and had gotten their black belts. We were all excited to see what they could do. They were supposed to have been really good; unfortunately, I never once saw those guys put on their gi(s) and work out.

Q: When you first arrived on Okinawa could you describe your initial impressions of the island and also what your military duties were?

I was stationed at Naha Airbase. When I arrived on Okinawa it was late at night and we had to transfer from the northern end of the island to the southern end. I sat on the right side of the bus and despite the late hour I was wide awake. I had never been out of the country and had never seen some of the things I was seeing out of my window, even in the night's darkness.

While we were driving I saw a sign that said "Karate Gym". I placed that location in the back of my mind. I also saw a group of Okinawans on the docks and couldn't figure out what they were doing. They were all dressed alike though . . . I noticed that much.

I processed into Naha Airbase and on the 14th I got my first pay. I went out and caught a taxi and went to the karate gym I had seen on my first bus ride. Once I got to the dojo I found out it was $6 for the first month of training and $5 for each month thereafter.

Q: Did you see any leftover effects from World War II in terms of poverty, or in the way the Okinawans lived and behaved toward Westerners?

Yes, you could definitely see some poverty. However, the American military had been in occupation for some time when I arrived and the economy was operating on American money. The strength of the military bases were having an overall positive impact on the poverty level of the island.

In terms of behavior from the Okinawans — they have always been a very kindhearted people and they will open up to you and treat you well, as long as you act accordingly. One of the things that I always detested about some of the American behavior over there is that they would call the Okinawans names and treat them disrespectfully. We were on their territory and yet we were calling them names and insulting them.

That bad treatment of Okinawans reminded me somewhat of where I had come from, back in the American South. The same kinds of names and treatment the Okinawans were getting, I used to get.

Q: Did you ask around at all about different karate styles or did you just aim for that first dojo you saw?

At that point not many Westerners knew about different styles, especially me who was new to the island. I had seen the karate gym on my way in and figured it was as good a place as any to start. It turned out to be the dojo of Nakazato Shugoro Sensei who was a senior student of Chibana Chosin.

Q: Not having a lot of pre-existing experience in karate, and not knowing what to expect, what was your first day of training like?

The first day I was there Nakazato Sensei had an interpreter who explained some things to me. There was not a lot of verbal communication between Nakazato Sensei and the students. With this language barrier you had to pay very close attention and follow along diligently.

Q: What was the general mix in terms of student body between Okinawans and American military?

I thought it was a very pleasant mix. There were generally more Okinawans than Americans, but the Americans that were there seemed devoted to the training.

Q: What was Nakazato Sensei like as an instructor?

You couldn't beat him as a teacher. He was very dedicated to the art and very dedicated to his students. He always had his own subtle way of pushing you to max out your energies and your efforts. I think Sensei understood more English than most of us realized but he used that barrier to maximize the training and focus.

Nakazato Shuguro Sensei, a senior student of Chibana Chosin and instructor to Eddie Bethea.

When he watched you he was really gauging what your interest level in training was. Based on that, he would match his response and push you accordingly. He had an eye for picking out which students would become dedicated, long-term students and which would likely fall by the wayside.

Q: What do you think Nakazato Sensei's motivations were in terms of opening his school to Westerners?

I know he wanted to be a provider for his family. Karate was a means to do that and American income helped to that end. His other motivation was to share his art and his teacher's art with the world.

Q: How did Nakazato Sensei like to split up the content of his class in terms of kata, bunkai, basics, sparring, etc.?

Kata went on pretty much every class, but sparring could be going on too. Bunkai tended to be reserved for Fridays. Back in those days I didn't study weapons much, even though it was going on in the dojo. I felt that, as a serviceman with the likelihood of going to Vietnam, I should focus on hand-to-hand combat.

Even though the dojo was relatively small, Nakazato Sensei would often have little groups of folks doing different things. Some students may have been working on makiwara while others did kata. A handful of people could also be sparring in the back of the dojo.

There were no separate sparring classes. You had to integrate sparring during or after class. There were no protective pads or even mouth pieces. I wore a lot of fat lips from those times and I think it would have been nice to have some protective equipment. Sensei emphasized control, but when you have two opposing forces coming at each other full speed sometimes people get hit. On the other hand, an over-reliance on pads can cause carelessness.

Q: How did the study of karate help you improve mentally and / or philosophically?

I definitely had some insecurities and attitude problems as a result of my early life experiences. I came out of the segregated South and I have a dark complexion. Even within black culture there is segregation based on the lightness or darkness of skin. So there I was, poor and dark skinned, which bred some inferiority in me.

My self-esteem was bad. It got to the point where if I was standing in public and a nearby group started looking and laughing in my direction (not at me, just in my direction) I assumed they were laughing at me. Once I got into karate and started to progress, my mindset started to change. I felt like I was becoming somebody, and realized that I *was* somebody. Occasionally Nakazato Sensei would bring his son into the dojo and say to me, "Eddie-san. My son, you teach." It was a great honor to be trusted with Sensei's son and helped me feel valued and skilled.

Eddie Bethea Sensei pictured with Nakazato Shuguro Sensei in 2014, a strong relationship that was started on Okinawa in the 1960s.

Q: Did you have any tours in Vietnam that interrupted your training?

I had two tours in Vietnam but managed to continue training and even teaching during that time. My first tour was in 1969 with some time spent in Thailand in 1970. In 1971 I was assigned to Grissom Air Force Base in Bunker Hill, Indiana.

During my 1969 tour I took some taekwondo for a little bit with the Roaring Tiger Division, which was a Korean group. They had an American teaching the class. When I went into the class I told him that I was 4th Dan in karate but I would be happy to start fresh and do whatever he asked me to do.

This teacher proceeded to pick on me, and pick on me, and pick on me. Finally I invited him to spar, at which time I bested him. Some time later that man's instructor came down to our area and wanted to spar me as well. I sparred with him and showed him a few techniques he wasn't quite ready for. He said, "In taekwondo we don't do that." To which I responded, "In karate we do." That was my last experience with that class. I decided it wasn't for me.

Q: When you were on Okinawa the idea of rank was still fairly new. How quickly did you gain rank and what is your perspective on how it was managed at the time?

I achieved my 4th Dan in 18 months, along with a certificate giving me the right to teach. Nakazato Sensei was looking to expand his organization and was closely watching for individuals that he felt were capable and dedicated. The instructor's certificate was his personal endorsement and permission for the recipient to teach karate.

At the time there was not that much karate in the United States, especially of high rank. As a result, my credentials were not often questioned. In fact, people look at it more today than they did back in those days.

Q: Speaking of the U.S. and teaching, when did you start opening up your own classes in America?

In 1971 I started my first class at Grissom Air Force Base in Indiana. That first class was short lived though; by the beginning of 1972 I was shipped back to Vietnam. While in Vietnam I taught a class, and then when I came back to Indiana in 1973 I started a class once again. I did not open my own dojo until 1976.

Q: In those early days of teaching classes and eventually starting your own school, what were some of the challenges you faced?

In the '70s everyone who came in wanted to be tough. They wanted to do kumite (sparring) and be able to defend themselves. They were looking for confidence and courage. However, toward the end of the '80s, instructors started getting sued a lot more.

Into the '90s and even 2000s the laws changed to prevent abuse of kids in environments like schools and the home, but the downside was that it became difficult for parents to discipline their children. This hindered what martial arts instructors could do as well.

Q: Throughout your martial arts career in the United States did you get involved much in competition?

I competed in my first tournament in Indianapolis in 1973 and I didn't place. I competed on the tournament circuit for about five years and never once placed. During that time I felt myself slipping back into the same kind of inferiority mindset that I had worked to overcome in previous years.

In 1979 I went to a tournament and got first place in breaking bricks. I hadn't even practiced breaking all that much and I was unhappy that the only thing I could place in was something that didn't mean anything to me. In 1981 I received a military assignment to go to North Dakota. That assignment actually helped make my decision to retire from the military — I thought it was cold enough in Indiana, and the idea of weathering North Dakota did not appeal to me. At that point I told my senior student, Tom Ward, "We've been going tournaments and we've just been a number in the crowd. I want you and I to start working so that when we perform people look, and when we speak people listen."

We both went to work, and that's when the change started to come around. Since I had retired from the military, I had more opportunity to get out there and mix it up with other schools and events. I had the opportunity to visit some high quality competitors like Glenn Keeney in order to learn and develop. Mr. Keeney taught me how to adapt to tournament fighting in the West. A few other people that helped point me in the right direction included Robert A. Trias, Robert Bowles, Parker Shelton, Herb Johnson, Bill Wallace, Phillip Koeppel, John Benson, and Woodrow Fairbanks. Of course there were others, but it is impossible to list them all!

Bethea Sensei, an accomplished tournament competitor and teacher.[85]

I try to emphasize to students today that your teacher can show you the path, but you have to put in the hard work yourself to learn, develop, and achieve your goals.

Q: Throughout the '70s and '80s did you get a chance to revisit Okinawa and Nakazato Sensei at your old dojo?

I revisited Okinawa and Nakazato Sensei in 1972 when Okinawa was reverting back to Japanese control. It was a long spell after that, not getting a chance to see Nakazato Sensei until 1992. Starting in 1999, I've gotten to see and train with Nakazato Sensei almost every year. Sensei always seemed to appreciate the fact that I had continued to train and develop between our times together.

Q: What do you think are some of the most important mental or physical aspects of Nakazato Sensei's art that students should be aware of?

One of the things Sensei always stressed was the health one would gain from kata training. Sensei himself, even in his 90s, maintains a certain vigor which you'll notice if you shake hands with him. Part of that is good, clean living.

---

[85] Image courtesy of Joseph Haynes.

I remember him saying, "Everything you do in kata has a reason." He was always very detailed in how you do the kata, making sure it was done the correct way.

Q: As you've trained in karate and followed Nakazato Sensei, are there any health or wellness habits that you have developed that you think other martial artists should know about?

There was a four year period in my life where I drank alcohol. However, I started karate in June of 1966 and stopped drinking in August of 1966. That was probably the healthiest thing I have ever done. Gaining discipline was another important step. I can discipline myself to do just about anything that I want to do. I don't need anyone to prompt me; I just do it.

Q: After having trained and taught for so many years, what keeps you motivated to go out to seminars, tournaments, etc.? How do you keep the fire alive for training?

There is a thing called passion, and karate is my passion. I've been married for decades, but I told my wife even before we were married, "I'm going to be doing karate until I die. If that's a problem, let's not get married." She has been very supportive of me all this time. In terms of maintaining training, it's as the old saying goes, "Choose a job you love, and you will never have to work a day in your life." That's where I am with my karate.

For me, it has always been important to have faith. Without God I have no karate, and it is God that has allowed me to grow as I have grown.

Q: As a senior karateka in the United States, are there any pieces of advice you could give to martial artists for keeping karate alive in the spirit it was intended?

I'm going to do a recitation for you, and I feel it is all in there:
I will train until a firm, unshaking spirit has been developed.
I will pursue the true meaning of karatedo so that my senses will become and remain alert.
With true vigor, I will seek to cultivate a spirit of self-denial.
I will observe the rule of courtesy, respect my superiors and other members, and refrain from violence.
I will seek divine spiritual dignity and never forget the true virtue of humility.
I will aspire to wisdom and strength all of my life.

Through the discipline of karate I will seek to fulfill the true meaning of karatedo.

The second recitation is as follows:

The ideal of karate is to cultivate character and conduct and the virtues of modesty and courtesy. Karate is the military art of self-defense to protect and preserve your life and never to attack others on your own initiative. Perseverance is the root of all conduct. True patience lies in bearing what is unbearable. Put back your hands when you are prone to fight and retract your fight when your hands itch to deal a blow. Softness is unity, strength is unity. The ultimate objective of human beings should be coexistence and co-prosperity in peace. All human actions, softness and strength, should be united in peace. Avoid fights and quarrels even if you are dared.

The latter recitation is part of Nakazato Sensei's morality code as posted in his dojo. The former I came across while doing some reading a long time ago, adopted in part from Oyama Masutatsu's Kyokushinkai.

Robert Herten

Martial arts books were few and far between in the 1950s and early '60s. Bruce Tegner was among the first to publish on the topics of jujutsu and self-defense, intriguing the minds of young Americans with the potential effectiveness of mysterious Asian arts. One of the young men reading Tegner's work was Robert Herten, a gentleman who would go on to become one of the senior Shorin Ryu practitioners in the United States.

Herten traveled to Okinawa via the Air Force and connected with Nakazato Shuguro Sensei while stationed there. He studied Shorin Ryu Shorinkan diligently for decades, eventually expanding his experience by becoming a student of Iha Seikichi, who was a senior practitioner under Miyahira Katsuya (Miyahira Sensei was a disciple of Chibana Chosin, just like Nakazato Sensei). It is through his diverse understanding of Shorinkan, and Kobayashi Ryu in general, that Herten Sensei became a respected figure in the Shorin Ryu community.

Q: Herten Sensei, could you tell us when and where you were born? What kind of neighborhood did you grow up in?

I was born in Fair Lawn, New Jersey, on August 1, 1945. Fair Lawn was a small middle class borough in Northern New Jersey about twenty minutes from New York City. My mother was a school teacher and my dad was a machinist. I attended Catholic school for both elementary school and high school. My dad died when I was 14, at which time I began attending Fair Lawn High School, graduating in June of 1963.

Q: Your journey in the martial arts started when you were young, pursuing jujutsu in high school. What intrigued you about martial arts at that point, and how did you get started in your jujutsu training?

While in Fair Lawn High School, a classmate of mine told me he was learning jujutsu. I went to his house and he showed me a Bruce Tegner self-defense book that he was teaching himself from. I thought it would be cool to learn, so I started joining him every afternoon for about three months. I never had formal training while in high school.

Q: What made you decide to take the leap into military life in 1963? Why was the Air Force your branch of choice?

In 1963, most kids either went to college or the military after high school. I chose the military, the Air Force specifically, because I wanted to learn to how to work on aircraft and become a mechanic.

Q: You were exposed to taekwondo early in your Air Force career. Who trained you, and what were sessions like?

After Air Force Technical School, I was briefly stationed in Rome, New York. While there, an airman came over from Korea and started a small club on base. I went to check it out and began taking classes. They were very unorganized, and we just stretched out and fought. I did not stay long.

Q: When did the Air Force transfer you to Okinawa? Did you know about karate before this time, and were you excited about the prospect of training on the island?

I volunteered for a mission called Operation Limelight and went to Ohio for cross training in B52s, C130s, and other aircraft. From there we went to Okinawa in 1965. I knew that karate was a big thing in Okinawa, but I didn't volunteer for Limelight just to train. Training was something I got into after I arrived.

Q: What were your day-to-day duties like?

While on Okinawa, I was assigned to a corrosion control unit. We brought planes in from all over the Pacific; after they arrived, we would inspect the plane for corrosion and then the specialists would repair those sections. After they were through, we would re-inspect the plane and put it back together.

Robert Herten posing with his sister during his early days in the Air Force.

Q: How did your early search for a dojo go? Did you find any social tension with the Okinawans due to previous military encounters such as The Battle of Okinawa?

Upon my arrival on Okinawa, I started looking for a dojo almost right away. I visited a few schools teaching Goju Ryu, Uechi Ryu, and Nagamine Sensei's Matsubayashi Ryu. I had a man who lived next door to me in the barracks named Frank Hargrove who also worked with me on the flight line. Frank was already training and offered to take me to his sensei's dojo and introduce me. Quite a few of the dojo I visited still were reluctant to train Americans. When Hargrove Sensei took me to Nakazato's dojo, I signed up that night.

As for the island itself — there was much damage still from the war. Not in Naha City itself, but outside the city. The Shuri Castle was destroyed. The villages were divided. Some were friendly and some were off limits for American servicemen, marked with signs on poles.

Q: What was it about Nakazato Sensei and his dojo that made you choose to train long-term there?

Nakazato Sensei was a very strict teacher and very strong. I liked that. After fooling around with jujutsu and taekwondo in the past, I was ready to train seriously. Nakazato had day classes and evening classes and he ran them all. The dojo was small and a little hard to find. Sensei was also one of the few teachers who wasn't afraid to teach Americans.

Q: What did the dojo look like, and who were some of the individuals you trained with?

The dojo was a small single room made of wood. The floor was wood and very smooth from all the training that went on there. The neighbors' homes were so close that you could reach out the window and touch them. That's why we did not kiai, out of respect for the neighbors. The people that I trained with were Shiroma Jiro, Frank Hargrove, Gibu, Kakinohana, Gibo, Nakaza, Sid Campbell, Noel Smith, and Eddie Bethea. Yamashita Tadashi Sensei was already here in the U.S.A.

Robert Herten (right) training with Eddie Bethea (left) in 1967 at the Nakazato Hombu. It was Herten Sensei's first night wearing a black belt.

Q: What content did Nakazato Sensei like to focus on (kata, sparring, basics, weapons, etc.)?

The focus of training was on basics and kata. When not doing kata, you were allowed to go outside and hit the makiwara or spar. Sparring was not supervised; sensei would just come back to you and point at you and another student and say "spa" (meaning spar). After making brown belt, I was asked if I wanted to begin kobudo. I did, and those classes were every Friday.

Q: How long did you train while on Okinawa? Did you participate in any competitions or demonstrations while there?

I trained for three years on Okinawa. I never competed, but Sensei took me with a group of Okinawan students to an August moon festival in Aza Village.

Q: Did Nakazato Sensei ever discuss Chibana Chosin Sensei? What is some of the info he shared that readers and future generations may be interested to know?

Nakazato Sensei never talked much with me since I didn't speak much Japanese and he spoke no English. So I never heard much about Chibana Sensei. Most of what I learned about history and traditions I learned after I returned to the U.S.A. On my trips back to Okinawa, I now make it my business to visit places that have important cultural and martial meaning.

Q: In 1969 you opened your first school back in the United States, located in Totowa, New Jersey. Was this done at the request of Nakazato Sensei, or was it your own idea? What were some of the early challenges with opening a program in the U.S.A.?

Nakazato Sensei performing a sai technique.

I opened my dojo in September of 1969. Nakazato Sensei encouraged me to open a dojo if I could (and to keep training).

Opening a dojo in the late '60s in the U.S.A. had many challenges. First, when I found a space to open in New Jersey, the town council never heard of karate and they didn't have anything on their laws to allow that type of business. I had to prove to them it was similar to an exercise studio or dance school. Even then it took renting a different space from a council member to get open. The students I got were mostly young adults. We had very few children until the early '80s.

Q: Did you attend many of the tournaments and competitions of that time? Could you describe what tournaments were like in those days?

I attended many tournaments trying to establish a name for my school and personally competed in kata and kumite. Most of the tournaments of the day were held in New York City. For 18 months, Aaron Banks held a tournament a month in Sunnyside Gardens in Queens, NY. We competed in every one. Tournaments were rough at the time. They started late, ran long, and were very hard fighting with little or no equipment available. The kumite was mostly bare knuckle fighting. I made many good friends then including Peter Urban, Don Nagle, Donald Bohan, Ed McGrath, Dale Jenkins, Jerry Thomson, Gary Alexander, and more.

Robert Herten Sensei exchanging technique with Nakazato Sensei at a tournament in 1973, held in honor of Nakazato Sensei.

Q: In 1990 you decided to establish a relationship with Iha Seikichi Sensei, a senior Chibana Style Shorin Ryu practitioner. What motivated you to take this step, and how did you reach out to Iha Sensei?

There was some political turmoil in the Shorinkan Association in 1990 and I was given some very bad advice by one of my students who was a lawyer, and I resigned from Nakazato Sensei's Association.

I knew about Iha Sensei from a friend — Ernest Estrada. I reached out to Iha Sensei and asked him if I could come and watch classes at his dojo and talk to him about becoming a new student. I went to Michigan and sat and watched with his permission for three days. After the third day, he asked me to come upstairs and talk. We went up to an apartment that was above his dojo and had tea. One of his senior students sat with us and never left us alone. They continued to always have a black belt with us at all times for the entire first year that I trained with him. He was very protected, and I was looked at with a lot of skepticism. I really had to prove that I was sincere.

Q: What was it about Iha Sensei that made you interested in learning from him? Was his teaching method different from that of Nakazato Sensei?

Iha Sensei spoke very good English and could really explain things that Nakazato Sensei could not. Iha Sensei is a technical genius when it comes to technique and taught much more tai sabaki (body shifting) with his karate. He was also really into teaching the bunkai to all the kata, something that Nakazato Sensei was not willing to do.

My training with Iha Sensei was at his dojo and at my home. I went every other month for one year and stayed one week every time to learn his methods. He was a student of Miyahira Katsuya Sensei, who, like Nakazato Sensei, was a senior student of Chibana Chosin Sensei. Their methods were similar, but Iha also trained for four years with Gusakuma Shinpan from 1950 to 1954 when Gusakuma died. At that time, he began with Miyahira. So Iha mixed some of his two teachers' training methods together when he came to the U.S.A. in 1975.

Q: How was your personal Shorin Ryu developing and maturing as you continued to learn throughout the '80s, '90s, and '00s?

My style of Shorin Ryu was beginning to become what I teach now, which is a mix of Nakazato's hard style and Iha's style of body shifting and softer blocking (nagashi uke). During the '80s, I was still very hard like Nakazato Sensei.

Q: Did you ever return to Okinawa after your original tour? Did you see the island change in any way during your return trips?

I have returned to Okinawa many times since the late '60s. I would like to go every year if I could afford it. The island has grown up since the '60s, featuring new modern buildings and using karate as an attraction to bring many visitors.

Q: What do you think are some of the key elements in preserving Shorin Ryu as Chibana Sensei intended it?

I think the key elements of continuing Chibana's teachings is to make sure that students understand that basics are the most important part of training, and kata is part of those basics. Strong basics will make strong kata and strong kata will make strong karateka.

Q: If you could give advice to future generations on how to preserve the true spirit of karate, what would you tell them?

Competition karate has its place as a sport only and can not be taught as self-defense. Way-of-life karate must be taught!

Noel Smith

From 1940 to 1973, the United States utilized a military draft to fill its ranks when voluntary means fell short. As a result, a number of men from that era were conscripted into service and fought in World War II, the Vietnam War, and other conflicts. Noel Smith was one such individual, and his conscription saw him shipped to Okinawa in 1966.

Upon arriving on Okinawa, Smith Sensei already had an active interest in the martial arts and sought out instruction as quickly as possible. He found Nakazato Sensei and took a liking to his teaching style. Ever since that first tour, Smith Sensei has been pursuing the ways of Shorinkan and is considered a senior practitioner of the art in the United States.

Q: Smith Sensei, what was your earliest experience with martial arts?

I first started training when I arrived on Okinawa in 1966.

Q: What inspired you to join the military in your youth? Which branch did you serve under and for how many years?

I was drafted into the Army. I was in for two years. I already had a career with Ford Motor Company.

Q: When arriving on Okinawa, did you know about karate ahead of time or did you stumble across it once there?

I knew of it and was actively looking for a place to study.

Q: Did you discover Nakazato Shugoro Sensei right away, or did you train under other individuals first?

Nakazato Sensei's dojo was the first and only dojo I went to.

Q: What was military life like for you on the island?

I enjoyed my time in the service. I was one of 11 individuals who loaded and back loaded all the Roll On + Roll Off ships.

Q: How did you first meet Nakazato Sensei?

Nakazato Sensei at his Hombu school.

I had no pre-existing knowledge of Nakazato Sensei and met him when I decided to visit his school, but it was not with the intention of seeking him out due to prior knowledge.

Q: What was day-to-day training like with Nakazato Sensei? Could you discuss the different focuses on kata, kihon, bunkai, sparring, etc.?

When I studied, Sensei had two classes Monday through Friday at 12pm-1:30pm and 5pm-8pm and on Saturday 1pm-2:30pm. It was also possible to arrive early and stay late. If you made both classes, you could study five to six hours a day. I would study on average 30 hours a week. In addition to karate, Sensei would teach kobudo one or two nights a week.

Day to day, Sensei would start off with kata. We did each kata two to four times. When you reached the end of your known kata, you could work on makiwara or fight (if you were at the appropriate level). Sensei would watch everyone on the floor and correct wrong movements.

Noel Smith Sensei performing kata at the dojo of Nakazato Sensei.

Kata took up about 60% of the class time, kumite taking up about 20-25%. Kihon (basics) would be done at the start or finish of class. Bunkai was shared between students unless we were preparing for a demonstration or festival. Nakazato Sensei would share knowledge of bunkai and technique, but the student had to show interest. With proper dedication and inquiry, Sensei would fill you up with knowledge.

Q: Which dojo classmates did you train with routinely? Are there any Westerners or native Okinawans you came to know well?

I studied along with Sid Campbell, Frank Hargrove, Bob Herten, and Eddie Bethea. There were also three Special Forces individuals as well as an Air Force Airman. The Okinawans included Gibu, Yamashita, Shoroma, Kinjo, and many others . . . however I cannot remember all of their names.

Q: What were some of Nakazato Sensei's unique qualities as a karate practitioner? Do you remember any of his favorite kata or training methods?

Nakazato Sensei had his own unique movement. He always executed with speed and power. My favorite training methods that he shared with us were wrist and punching exercises.

Q: What was Nakazato Sensei like as a person?

I recall that he was always business first and social matters second.

Q: Did you get a chance to meet any other karate luminaries while on the island?

I had a chance to spend time with Chibana Sensei, Shimabukuro Zenryo Sensei, Shimabukuro Eizo Sensei, and a number of fellow karate students.

Q: When you came back to the United States, what was the karate scene like?

There was still a mystique about karate. This came from a general lack of knowledge regarding karate's origins and the methods of the Okinawans. In the United States, there was mostly taekwondo, Shotokan Karate via the Japan Karate Association, and the Ed Parker brand of Kenpo. Shorin Ryu was also growing with about half a dozen dojo(s).

Q: What were some of the challenges in growing your program in the early days?

It was difficult helping people to learn the vast amount of knowledge needed to understand karate. They did not know the depths to which karate can enhance a person mentally, physically, and spiritually.

Q: Could you discuss your time as a coach for the U.S.A. Team? How did they choose you, where did you have to travel, etc.?

The head of A.A.U. (Amateur Athletic Union) karate, Caylor Adkins, asked me to coach a U.S.A. team on a European tour. We went to France, Sweden, Germany, England, and Scotland.

Noel Smith Sensei with Nakazato Sensei at the Hombu.

Q: What are some of the differences you notice in modern karate styles and organizations that differ from what you experienced in Okinawa?

I've noticed that there has been a shortness of knowledge for years, which inevitably leads to a shortness in teaching knowledge.

Q: Do you think karate is growing in a healthy / unhealthy direction? If you could provide advice to instructors and organizations for staying true to old-style karate, what would you say?

I think there has been positive growth, for the most part. Karate has been around since B.C., although it may have been called something different in times past. As for advice — most people judge martial arts on logic and reality, if they have any. I believe we must make sure to keep touch with that logic and reality.

Q: How has your personal training changed / adapted as you've grown older?

I do not work out as much or as hard as I once did, but I still teach the methods that were taught to me the way it was intended.

Q: For individuals looking to make karate a lifelong endeavor, what words of wisdom could you provide to help them grow and mature as artists?

Your students are a product of yourself. If they become great, you become great.

Doug Perry

In 1946, Doug Perry began his boxing career at the age of nine. This marked the beginning of a long and distinguished career in the fighting arts as well as the military. Perry Sensei survived multiple tours in Vietnam as a Marine and distinguished himself by demonstrating uncommon bravery and fortitude in the line of duty.

Although Perry Sensei is one of the senior-most representatives of Nakazato Shuguro Sensei, he is truly a collective product of multiple martial arts experiences. While on Okinawa he studied under a handful of premiere masters, including Shimabukuro Tatsuo of Isshin Ryu and Uechi Kanei of Uechi Ryu. Perry Sensei was also fortunate enough to learn some of the Takemyoshi Family Style, a very rare and old art which preserves much of the deeper aspects of kata training.

Perry Sensei continued his karate learning while rotating between the U.S.A. and Okinawa, broadening his experience and becoming a rare resource with an unusual depth of knowledge. It was this depth (along with his training experience under Shiroma Jiro Sensei) that led Perry Sensei to study directly with Nakazato Sensei, becoming a trusted and senior pupil.

Q: Perry Sensei, you were introduced to the fighting arts at an early age. Could you talk about your youth and what made you join boxing so early?

I think it's important to know that I was adopted by elderly parents. My mother was 56 years old when I was born in 1937, and they adopted me when I was eight months old. My dad could not read or write. He was a garbage man and earned $12 a week. I grew up in a depressed section of Charlotte, North Carolina, in an area called Highland Park Mills. As an only child, I often got into scuffles with other kids. If I was outnumbered or overmatched, I would run . . . and when the opportunity presented itself, I would throw rocks at them.

I started boxing in 1946 and had my first official match at nine years old. Back in those days, everyone wore black tennis shoes and brown short pants. We didn't have boxing trunks, jockstraps, headgear, mouthpieces, or even protective cups. When my first match started I had no real boxing skills, so I just lowered my head and started flailing away. About 30 seconds into the first round, my britches fell off and I had nothing on under them. I just stepped out of them and kept swinging. My dad (who was in attendance that night) and I both remember that the referee grabbed me and helped me get my britches back on, ran tape through the loops, and resumed the fight. That was how my boxing career started. I actually won the match by decision, but I guess it was a little much for my dad who never opted to attend my fights after that night!

A young Doug Perry with trainer Leo Johnson in 1953, Golden Gloves Tournament, Charlotte SC.

During my boxing career, I had 147 fights. After 1946, I started fighting regularly and got to National Golden Gloves level in 1950. Tournaments in those days would go for three or four days, and we would compete from Wednesday or Thursday through to Saturday night finals. Depending on the number of competitors, we would have two or three fights per day. You got a small trophy if you went far enough, which was about four to five inches tall . . . a far cry from the six foot modern-day trophies.

I continued to fight competitively until entering the Marine Corps in 1956.

Q: Speaking of the Marine Corps, could you describe some of your time there and how boxing followed you into the military?

Boxing was big in the military in the '50s. My dad took me down to the Marine Corps Recruiting Office when I was 18 years old. I really didn't want to join, but my dad was fully aware that many of the boys in our neighborhood were getting into trouble with the law, and opportunities for decent employment and personal betterment were limited. The Recruiting Sergeant told my dad that I was too small to join, but my dad responded that I had over 100 amateur boxing matches and was a multiple Golden Gloves Champion. The sergeant called his Officer-in-Charge and ultimately I was granted a waiver, after which I enlisted. I believe one of the reasons I was accepted was that Charlie Brown (his real name) was the top flyweight at that time. Unfortunately, Charlie could no longer make the 112 pound weight division. So it was figured that I would have a decent shot at replacing Charlie who would move up to Bantamweight (118 lbs).

On the day of graduating boot camp, I was hospitalized with a case of double pneumonia. I was in sickbay for two to three weeks before being returned to Casual Company. I then went to the Lyceum on Parris Island and started training with the Marine boxing team. While working out I noticed a few guys in the corner kicking and throwing each other. Keep in mind this was in 1956 and very few people had ever heard the word "karate" before, including me.

I went over and asked them what they were doing. They said they were studying karate and Judo. I asked, "What's that?," and they told me about the connection back to Japan and Okinawa. They also explained how you used your hands and feet for striking and throwing. I said that I would love to try it!

They were a good group of guys, but I think I spent a half hour looking up at the ceiling. They were sweeping my feet out from under me, executing throws on me . . . it was a real eye-opener. When it was all over I asked to join them. This occurred in October of 1956, which marks the real start of my interest in karate and other foreign fighting arts.

Q: Do you know what style they were practicing in karate?

They were Isshin Ryu guys, but they studied Judo as well.

Q: Where did your training and military service take you next?

I ended up transferring from Parris Island to Camp Lejuene, continuing my training when I could find someone to practice with. There were a couple guys who had been able to train in Okinawa, post-World War II. It was a conglomeration, but primarily what you found was Isshin Ryu.

In 1956, I was transferred to Marine Corps Air Station (M.C.A.S.) Cherry Point and assigned to a special weapons training unit. During 1956-57 I was a member of a small detachment escorting classified gear to Okinawa. The guys at Cherry Point told me that Shimabukuro Tatsuo Sensei had a dojo in Agena. I went down to Agena, got lost, but finally found it and went in. I only got to train for a short time, but continued to train with the Isshin Ryu guys back in the States. At that point I was training hard and decided that I had to make a singular commitment, so I gave up competitive boxing in 1959. Ultimately, I felt that I was a fighter more than a boxer, so I did my best to keep up my karate training.

In 1964 I was ordered to Vietnam and, like many, staged in Okinawa before heading into the war zone. I returned to Shimabukuro Sensei's dojo in Agena. At that time it cost me $1 to train there. I paid $1 to the Marine Corps Special Services, and I think they in turn paid sensei about $20 a month to teach us.

Q: That must have been a really significant amount of money for Tatsuo Sensei at the time.

That was big bucks. A lot of my training at the Agena dojo was makiwara training, a habit which I continue to this day. In addition, we did lots of Seisan and Sanchin kata. Sensei spoke very little English at that time, and I spoke no Japanese. When I was doing something wrong (I tended to throw my punches from the shoulder like a boxer), he would just hit me. From there I had to figure out what the heck I had done wrong.

402 Tales from the Western Generation

There were no counts for kata, so we would just learn sections of the kata and work on them for a while. After Sensei would retire for the evening we would all practice kumite (fighting), which is really what most of us wanted to do anyway.

Q: Do you remember who made up the student body at that time?

It was about half Okinawans where I trained. Sensei's son, Kichiro, was in the dojo. John Bartusevics primarily trained at the Hamada dojo. He was something else. There was a joke about Bartusevics Sensei that when he connected with a Yoko Geri (side kick), the only thing left of you was dust. He was, and still is, an astounding martial artist as well as a fine Marine.

The guys that I trained with were mostly transient. They were on their way into or out of Vietnam. I was personally held back from the war zone due to my security clearance and nuclear background for about two to three months. I trained with Shimabukuro Sensei until early 1965 when I went to 'Nam. During my first tour "in Country" I had three to four different assignments, partially because I had a high level of security clearance. On occasion I had to fly back to Okinawa for the C.G. III M.A.F. (Commanding General of the III Marine Amphibious Force) to deliver classified documents and gear. Whenever I was able to get back to Okinawa, I tried to get some time at the dojo. After that I would fly back to war.

During my tour in Vietnam I was able to train as operational time permitted. We studied karate and Judo. At one point we went down and stole a mat off of the Army guys so that we didn't have to bite dust or mud all the time.

When I came back through to Okinawa in 1966, I got my Shodan certificate, which was about the size of a driver's license and had Shimabukuro Sensei's symbol, the grade, and date. After training for a short time in 1966, I was transferred to H.Q.M.C. (Headquarters Marine Corps) and assigned duties with the Joint Staff in the Pentagon. I studied karate and also had the honor of training in Judo with Jan Vandersluis, the Armed Forces Judo Association President at that time.

I did a bit of competing once I got back home, mostly in karate but a little in Judo too. Sometimes at the Judo competitions we would do karate demonstrations. Afterward, I would change into my Judo gi and compete. Unfortunately, my Judo competition career was short-lived as my Judo contained a few too many karate techniques for the referees . . . resulting in constant fouls and disqualifications.

In 1970, I was transferred to M.C.A.S. Cherry Point. Shortly thereafter, I met Bill Hayes Sensei. Hayes Sensei came up with the idea of getting those of us at Cherry Point with experience together for some training. The first black belt meeting of that club took place in a little shed. About 13-14 guys showed up. Hayes Sensei was a little leery about the background and experience of some of the black belts. He closed the door to this little room, took us through opening drills and then started up jiyu kumite. The next time we all got together only five or six people showed up.

Doug Perry in Sanchin stance while at M.C.A.S. Cherry Point North Carolina Dojo. 1970.

There were some good practitioners around our area at that time: Bill Hayes, Don Bohan, Larry Isaac, Kazuo Hovey, Vic Coffin, Danny Glover, "Doc" Stroud, Sam Pearson . . . we all competed against each other and were friends in training. At tournaments we would sit around shooting the bull. One person would get called up, go do their kata or kobudo, and come back. It was a time of great friendships and a sharing of knowledge.

Doug Perry at a tournament at Camp Lejeune, NC, 1970. Image features (from left to right): Jody Paul, Kazuo Hovey, Doug Perry, and Sam Pearson.

Q: When you started studying Shobayashi Ryu, did you notice any significant differences between that style's execution and your previous experience in Isshin Ryu?

Yes. The fist in Isshin Ryu was done by Tatsuo's method (vertical), but Shobayashi used the iron fist. If you form a regular fist by curling all the fingers your index finger will press right near the base of the thumb. With the iron fist you don't curl the index finger; you point it straight down and secure it with the thumb. This alleviates the pressure area near the base of the thumb. When thinking about styles, it's important to remember that back in the old days karate training involved two or three students max. It was a very individualistic activity. Each student was taught in their own way because each student brought a unique body type and skillset. A tall lanky individual can't pretend to fight like a short stocky guy. When your life depended on it, this tailoring was critical. Nowadays, in some circles, there is a push for too much conformity. Individual instruction and ability to help students grow is what distinguishes the quality of a teacher and style.

Q: So after Cherry Point, where did you end up?

In 1974, I went back to Okinawa and I couldn't get to Shimabukuro Eizo Sensei's dojo (Eizo being Bill Hayes's teacher and the head of Shobayashi Ryu). At that time I was a Captain, so I had a squadron to look after. To travel in Okinawa you either bought a car or rode the bus (or walked), but I was at Futenma so it was about a two hour bus ride to Kin Village where Shimabukuro Eizo Sensei taught. In addition to training with Bill Hayes, I had the opportunity to train with Shimabukuro Eizo Sensei a couple of times when he was in the States and was hoping to train directly with him . . . but couldn't make it happen with my Commanding Officer, who was concerned about me being away from the command.

After realizing that training in Kin Village wasn't going to happen, I wandered around looking for a place to learn. I joined a group of Motobu Ryu practitioners and also had a chance to study with Uechi Kanei Sensei in Futenma Town. While walking back to base one night, I saw a dojo off to the left not 150 yards from the Futenma front gate. It was a Shorinkan dojo, the head of which was Shiroma Jiro. He was one of Nakazato Joen's senior students. I walked in and watched, liked what he was doing, and asked if I could train with him. Some of the Marines in the dojo that night knew who I was, and I believe their vouching for me helped me get accepted as a student.

Shiroma Sensei was a little guy but a heck of a fighter, and a demanding sensei. I had a great time training there and really enjoyed a true Okinawan karate experience. We all developed reputations as tough fighters, going to schools like Kise Fusei's dojo and performing well against our opponents.

Sometimes we had guys wander into our dojo, declaring some sort of high rank and lineage or whatever. Shiroma Sensei would pick one us for the new guy to work with, and we would all be volunteering to "welcome him aboard". Humility was an important character trait on Okinawa, and it had a way of enforcing itself in the dojo.

I trained consistently there until I was ordered to participate in a military operation. Afterward, I came back and continued training with Shiroma Sensei. I met Nakazato Sensei and trained with him, but never consistently studied under him until after I retired from the military. Shiroma Sensei was my teacher and was very special to me.

Q: Before settling into your training with Shiroma Sensei, you mentioned you spent time with Uechi Kanei. What was he like?

I had collateral duties on Futenma Base that I didn't even realize were mine right away. Apparently some of the Okinawans that worked on the Futenma Base worked for me. While in Futenma Town one day, I noticed a Uechi Ryu dojo and went in. There was a Sergeant there who recognized me and asked me if I wanted to work out. I couldn't do their kata (although I eventually picked up Sanseiru). When the kumite started though, I was right at home. Those guys trained hard and were extremely good fighters.

Once Uechi Sensei found out about my connection with the Okinawans working on our military base, he talked to me quite a bit. I got a lot of value from his karate knowledge and have fond memories of those times.

One of the interesting things Uechi Sensei shared with me was about fighting. He noticed that I liked to get inside and fight rather than stay outside. He said that a lot of karate fighting techniques he saw around the island were based on fighting from the outside. Kata, at a basic and intermediate level, focused on that outside level. Unfortunately, some of the Sensei he knew tended to stay on that outside level and never taught beyond that concept. Over his many years of study, Uechi Sensei came to believe that most fights happened close to the opponent. Although fighting from the outside might be desirable, especially in kumite or competition, reality and experience dictate that fights are brutal, quick, and inside. This nature of fighting is a true test of a man's fighting abilities. Years later, during the Okinawan Masters Tour of the U. S. in 1999, I had the opportunity to spend quite a bit of time with Tomoyose Ryuko Sensei . . . a true gentleman and amazing karate practitioner. He confirmed Uechi Sensei's foregoing comments and shared considerable insight on his personal theories and training methods. It was an honor and experience I will always treasure.

Q: One of the other instructors you spent time with while on Okinawa was Takemyoshi Sensei, who is a lesser known figure in Okinawan karate. Can you tell us a bit about him?

Takemyoshi Sensei's uncle lived in the Napunja area. Because of some family tragedies during WWII, for which he blamed the Americans, he would not have anything to do with Americans. They had a family system, and thanks in part to my duties in Industrial Relations, I had the opportunity to meet Takemyoshi Sensei, who was about 45 years old at that time (I was 38 yrs old). Takemyoshi Sensei worked at Futenma and one day we got to talking about training. He invited me to train with him, and we went out the back gate to a nearby cane field.

We worked on understanding the deeper meanings of kata. He had me start Naihanchi and after the first few moves he stopped me and asked, "Now what does that mean?". His English was quite good. I told him that I thought the technique involved tuite (joint locking). He said, "Yes, but go beyond that." He told me to punch him, so I did and he threw me about ten feet in that damn cane field. I'm glad I had some background in Judo in order to take the fall.

We trained together two times a week and then we would go to Kitomae to have a meal and talk. I had recommended one of his kinfolk for a job at the base so that made our relationship stronger. Takemyoshi's uncle was an associate of Hohan Soken and had also studied in China. I learned my Hakutsuru from Takemyoshi Sensei and have noticed some concepts similar to other crane forms that are from southern China and practiced on Okinawa. Unfortunately this is about all I know of the family style's background.

Takemyoshi Sensei was very knowledgeable about weapons, and one of the ideas he stressed was that once you learn something it should become yours and eventually it should become you. He stressed attitude to express intention and emotion without theatrics. The kata Hakutsuru, he said, allowed you to explore the range and motion of your body . . . and allow you to perfect each technique.

Q: You got to see tournaments in the U.S.A. throughout the '60s and '70s. How had karate changed or evolved over that time period?

In my area, guys like Don Bohan, Bill Hayes, Jim Logue, Larry Isaac, Danny Glover, and Vic Coffin were still teaching the old school ways. Elsewhere, guys like Bruce Lee and Chuck Norris were becoming popular. Tournaments were becoming much more commercialized and high profile. People were starting to care about things like how many students you had, how much money you were making, etc. Karate had really done some evolving into sport. I think the '70s was when I started seeing a lot of this behavior. One other thing I noticed was a big push toward people associating with only one style. In the Marines, we didn't care what background people had. If they wanted to train, they could just train without specific affiliation.

In 1978, I got transferred to Marine Corps Development and Education Command in Quantico as the Command Adjutant. When I got to Quantico, I started a little dojo and one of the first people to walk through the door was the Commanding General (a three star general). He asked if he could start training and I thought . . . what am I going to say? I'm a Major and he's a three star General! "Yes sir," was the answer. Our dojo had some guys from the Officer Candidate School, a couple of middleweight full contact fighters, my eldest son Jason, John Carria (an Uechi Ryu practitioner who I would exchange ideas with), and some others. Eventually, the General (who had eight children) couldn't maintain the schedule of training and had to drop out. I was more than a little relieved.

I retired from the Marine Corps in 1981 and moved down to Hendersonville, North Carolina, and started teaching at the Y.M.C.A. I taught there for about three months, but eventually couldn't fit the students inside the facility anymore. I chose to rent a modest unit in a shopping center . . . and we are still there today.

Q: Why do you think your Y.M.C.A. program grew so fast?

When I came to Hendersonville there were some other commercial schools in the area, but no one was teaching classical karate. My dojo was growing, and the funny thing is that I was still teaching as if I were in the Marine Corps. It was tough. One of my students who is still with me remembers his first night in the dojo from those early days. He's about 6'2," 200 lbs, and the first night I had him out for some kumite. While we were fighting, I punched him square in the thigh and he said, "Hey you're hitting below the belt!" I said to him, "You're 6'2" and I'm 5'6," where do you think I'm going to hit?"

In 1991, I started my Shorinkan training camps. A close friend of mine, Jim Logue, found out about it and asked if he could attend one. I said sure, no problem. As the years went by, more and more people started coming. Gentlemen like Bill Hayes, Vic Coffin, Kimo Wall, Phil Koeppel . . . even R.W. Smith (famous author of books like *Martial Musings*). Before I knew it these welcome "aliens" (folks from other styles) almost outnumbered us in the Shorinkan at our own event, and I couldn't have been happier about it. Isshin Ryu, Shobayashi Ryu, Kobayashi Ryu, Ryute, Goju Ryu, Uechi Ryu . . . all coming together. Bill Hayes coined the nickname "Little Okinawa" for the event.

Q: You touched upon your relationship with Nakazato Sensei earlier, but could you expand on when you spent time with him and how you became a direct student of his?

My relationship with him began in 1974, but I was training with Shiroma Sensei as my primary teacher. Once I retired from the Marine Corps, we were able to arrange trips for Nakazato to come over to the U.S.A. and I was able to go to Okinawa to study with him.

Nakazato Sensei was something of a quiet and reserved gentleman (most of the time). A lot of men from his generation seriously trained in karate as a "life protection" art, and so continued in many ways to treat their art very personally and held it close. That being said, sensei was also very jovial and outgoing.

Perry Sensei receiving correction from Nakazato Shuguro Sensei in 1985.

Q: Could you describe some of the challenges you encountered while trying to grow your school and organization throughout the '80s, '90s, '00s, and into today?

I believe I grew personally alongside my dojo. I did not teach anyone to go out and win a tournament. In the first few years it was brutal military style stuff. Eventually I realized that I needed to change some of my methods . . . but I have never changed my philosophy. I've also tried to respect people's trust and privacy. Individuals know that if they need to come to me that it will stay "inside the office," so to speak. I'm happy to say I've had students whose children I taught, and even some of *their* children. I've kept dojo training fees extremely reasonable. I want students to know that it's not about the money; it's about training the right way for the right reasons. Sometimes my senior students will come to me and offer business or money management advice because I just don't pay attention to those details.

Q: Are there any specific lessons you like to pass on to students that readers might also benefit from?

Even in my advanced age, I still train with my students. I try to stress that one of the keys to good fighting is relaxation. It can be difficult to get people to relax, especially the bigger and stronger they are. A 250 lb bricklayer will possess manufactured power, but there is something else called "natural power." Through dedicated kata training and study, and especially proper makiwara training, a serious karate practitioner can develop this natural power.

We have to become more efficient. This becomes more important as a person ages. It may not be critical to understand at a young age, but the sooner a person realizes it, the better. Karate is a life protection art . . . train like your life depends on it . . . and pray it never does!

Chapter 14 –
Shotokan

One of the most popular and widespread styles of karate in the world, Shotokan has played an important role in the growth of karate in America. Skilled Shotokan instructors were some of the earliest to begin traveling overseas in order to demonstrate their art in the Western world. They were also some of the most organized practitioners, developing early models of karate structure that are still in use today.

Funakoshi Gichin, the father of Shotokan and "modern karate," was born in 1868 to a family with a moderate amount privilege and rank. As a result, Funakoshi had access to some of the finest karate teachers on the island, including (but not limited to) Itosu Azato, Itosu Anko, and Higashionna Kanryo.[86] As Funakoshi grew, he developed both his physique and his intellect, becoming a respected karateka in addition to scholar and schoolteacher.

Funakoshi's teacher, Itosu Anko, was one of the most pivotal characters in the public dissemination of karate, pushing for its integration in both Okinawan and Japanese school systems. To help him demonstrate and eloquate his plans, Itosu needed a man of refinement that was literate, technically skillful, and considerate of history and etiquette. Funakoshi Gichin Sensei was the man for the job.

Participating in a number of demonstrations throughout the early 1900s, Funakoshi Sensei became a well-known karate commodity. This came to a head in 1922 when the Japanese

---

[86] Sells, John. *Unante: The Secrets of Karate*. Publisher location: WM Hawley, 1995. 76. Print.

Ministry of Education held its First Athletic Exhibition in Ochanomizu, Tokyo.[87] The ministry looked favorably upon the physical fitness potential of karate, persuading Funakoshi to stay in Japan and travel to help spread the idea of karate to Japanese universities. It was during this time that Funakoshi Sensei met Jigoro Kano Sensei, the founder of Judo, and began cementing ideas for the modernization of karate. Funakoshi was keen on Kano's ranking system, as well as his ability to organize and create a streamlined system with consistent requirements.

Funakoshi Sensei's karate experienced quite a bit of change throughout this era in order to meet the desires of the Japanese government. However, it also achieved consistent adoption in the university system and cultivated many dedicated practitioners. A handful of exceptional students studied with Funakoshi directly and eventually spawned systems of their own, including Ohtsuka Hironori of Wado Ryu, Konishi Yasuhiro of Shindo Jinen Ryu, and Oyama Masutatsu of Kyokushin. In 1949, Shotokan seniors gathered to form a more cohesive organization. Obata Isao, Nakayama Masatoshi, and Nishiyama Hidetaka were integral in this development. The new organization was named the Japan Karate Association, and would serve as the hub of Shotokan training throughout the following decades, spawning multiple branch organizations over time.

Of the many students who remained loyal to Shotokan throughout their lives, a few courageous individuals were integral in the spread of the art to the United States. Oyama Masutatsu was perhaps the earliest karateka to make a large-scale impact in the U.S.A. — an interesting quirk of history considering that Oyama Sensei was a Korean gentleman studying a Japanese version of an Okinawan art. His American tours began around 1952 and contained impressive feats of skill and strength, including challenge matches against boxers and wrestlers and demonstrations of breaking for which he would become famous.

In 1955, Ohshima Tsutomu began a small karate group at the Konko Shinto Church, located in Los Angeles. The following year he opened a public program and founded the Southern California Karate Association, which later became Shotokan Karate of America. In 1961, senior practitioner Nishiyama Hidetaka moved to Los Angeles via arrangements with Oshima Sensei, starting the All American Karate Federation branch of the J.K.A. in short order. That same year, Okazaki Teruyuki moved to Philadelphia and became a primary force of karate development on the East Coast. Okazaki Sensei would go on to

---

[87] Alexander, George W. *Okinawa, Island of Karate*. Publisher location: Yamazato Publications, 1991. 56. Print.

form the International Shotokan Karate Federation (I.S.K.F.), a widespread organization in the U.S.A. and abroad.[88]

Nishiyama Sensei had begun teaching Westerners in Japan around 1952, primarily via the Strategic Air Command of the U.S. Military. Okazaki Sensei was integral in the development of the J.K.A. Instructor Program, a prestigious group with high standards designed to create Shotokan senior instructors. Both men, along with a number of others, helped launch Shotokan in the U.S. and spread a culture of physical fitness and tournament competition throughout the karate scene.

---

[88] Corcoran, John, Emil Farkas, and Stuart Sobel. *The original martial arts encyclopedia: tradition, history, pioneers.* Publisher location: Pro-Action Pub., 1993. 244. Print.

Maynard Miner

After World War II, the U.S.A. constructed a number of military bases throughout Japan in order to maintain peace and disarmament. Occupation of those bases continued throughout the 1950s, during which time Maynard Miner found himself called overseas as part of the U.S. Army. While traveling, Miner Sensei heard about karate from some of the other servicemen and decided to investigate it once settled in Japan.

Through chance and dedicated investigation, Miner Sensei found himself training in Shotokan with the likes of Mori Masataka Sensei and Kanazawa Hirokazu Sensei. When he returned from his overseas duties, Miner Sensei continued his training with Okazaki Sensei in Philadelphia and became a source of Shotokan knowledge on the East Coast.

Q: Miner Sensei, did you have any exposure to martial arts early in your childhood and teens? What motivated you to seek it out?

When I was young, I wanted to be able to walk down the street and not be afraid. I grew up in Brooklyn. It was a rough area, I suppose, but I had a big brother, so I didn't have much to worry about. I thought if I could get as strong as my brother, I might be able to handle myself. I noticed he was very strong but also very arrogant.

I joined the Golden Gloves and got the hell kicked out of me. I had the bloodiest uniform in the group (they said I had a glass nose). So that wasn't a very good experience. I went into Judo and Aikido shortly after. This was before my time in the military. I didn't particularly like getting thrown down over and over again, so I decided not to stay there too long.

Q: At what age did you decide the military was the path for you? What inspired that decision?

I chose the Army when I was about 22. All of my friends were joining at that time, so I wanted to follow them. I found boot camp to be very humbling. The sergeants were aggressive and they intimidated you all the time.

Q: Did you feel any extra attention or aggression at the time being an African American, or was it basically the same treatment for everybody?

From my perspective it was about the same for everybody.

Q: Did you get shipped out to Japan immediately?

I did my first eight weeks at Camp Dix which was essentially basic training, then did my second eight at Fort Gordon, Georgia. The second eight was a little more intense. I didn't make any special requests to go to Japan, I just happened to end up there. After basic training I shipped out for Korea, but while there they called my name out for service to Japan. At first I thought this was terrible because in Japan you had to do three years while in Korea you only had to do 24 months. Once I was in Japan, though, I was glad. I arrived January of 1955 and stayed until 1958 sometime around July.

Q: You were in Japan about ten years after the end of World War II. What was the primary role of the Army there at that time?

Mainly occupying I think, in case the Japanese wanted to go backwards. I was personally in communications, teletype, and telegraph stuff. It involved mostly standing in front of a machine that spit out tape. I had to learn how to read the tape, make hard copies, and then move it around as needed. It was a good job as it was 9 to 5, so I had all the rest of the time off to go down to Tokyo.

Q: Did you experience any tension between yourself, your military mates, and the native Japanese?

Not really, but I think it was because the Japanese weren't used to black people at that time. They used to turn my hand over and over because it was light on one side and black on the other. They thought I was pretty tall, too (even though my height is average for an American). I weight lifted back then as well so I was somewhat muscular.

Q: What were some of your initial impressions of Japan when you arrived?

I noticed that the people were very poor. They regarded me as rich.

Q: Did you know what karate was before your military time?

I didn't know about it until I got on my assigned ship headed for Korea and ultimately Japan. One of the guys with me in the squadron was saying, "They have this new thing in Japan called karate." He was going to take it up, so I decided to take it up too. I was there for about a month before beginning my search. I asked around and heard the best place for me to find karate would be in Tokyo. Unfortunately I was stationed in Kosaka-machi, north of Tokyo by a stretch. I decided to try anyway.

I traveled to Tokyo and started asking around. Someone told me that there was a karate school up a nearby alley, so I went there. While I was walking I started hearing this shouting (kiai). I thought, "Oh no, I think I might be getting myself into something I shouldn't be getting into."

I went in to watch the class, and it looked like they were trying to kill each other.

Afterward I went into the office and they asked if I wanted to join. I asked how much it was, and they said some ridiculously low number like a dollar. So I said okay. I came back the next week and they put me in the beginners group. So that's how I started.

Q: Were you surprised that the Japanese allowed you into the dojo as a Westerner and foreigner?

Yea, I was. I think maybe they let me in because they wanted to show me up. They all came after me, and I thought they were trying to hurt me. I defended myself as best I could, which meant we usually ended up wrestling. Of course, that's not Shotokan. I didn't care about that, I was just defending myself.

Q: Do you think your size and strength surprised them somewhat?

I think so. I was fighting with strength rather than with technique. They were shorter than I was so I was able to stand high over them.

Q: Did they provide you with a uniform?

I had to go out and buy one. Since they were in Japanese size, they fit me like knickers.

Q: What was training like on a day-to-day basis?

It was mostly kihon. Basics over and over again. They stressed stance, stance, stance. Then blocks over and over again. I studied primarily with Mr. Mori, Mr. Makami, Mr. Asai, and Mr. Kanazawa. Mr. Yaguchi was there, but he was very young (they treated him like a boy).

In terms of technique, they wanted your front toe bent a little to the inside, and the edge of the foot straight. They would come up and stand on your back leg to see if your stance was strong. They would also kick your front foot from the side to see if you would fall down. I kept my eyes open for these tests and was able to avoid falling. Some of the smaller students would get knocked down, get back up, and then get knocked down again. The teachers would yell and scream at them. They never yelled at me because I wouldn't have understood what they were saying anyway.

Sometimes I would attend the morning class, but I preferred the evening class. In the evening you would get all the roughriders . . . the street kids. They came and all they wanted to do was spar.

Maynard Miner at the J.K.A. headquarters while stationed in Japan in 1957. Shoji Sensei is seen standing far left while Kenazawa Sensei squats in the front.[89]

Q: With as challenging and negative as the atmosphere could be, did you ever have a desire to quit?

There were plenty of times that I wanted to quit. I thought that if I could make it to green belt I would get out after that. When I made green belt I said to myself, "Well I'll try to make purple belt, but then I am gone." Every step was harder and the students were faster

---

[89] Images and identification courtesy of Maynard Miner, acquired via the assistance of Ronald Johnson.

and stronger . . . but I stayed. I remember there were times when I could barely walk after class. My feet felt like wood blocks.

Q: Could you describe the dojo itself, the interior, and how it was maintained?

It was poor, but also very clean. The floor was the most important thing. We worked the floor at the beginning of class by getting pails of water with rags. We went up and down on all fours cleaning, so it was very well-maintained. The dojo was small; whenever there was a test and all the classes came together, we had no room.

Q: What were tests like when everyone got together?

They were very similar to the way I still hold them today. Basics, or kihon, were the start. Then we would do kata and sparring. During my first test, I did my kata and ended up facing the wrong way when I finished. Mr. Okazaki was there smiling. But I ended the kata and stayed focused throughout, which is what they liked to see. No quit. When it came to the sparring, I was a little bit too aggressive. I was pulling guys around and doing more wrestling than fighting. We didn't have padding (they frowned on that). They wanted control, but I thought the other guys were really trying to hit me. Despite the flaws in my test, I ended up passing.

Q: Were there serious communication barriers during your training?

Some of the guys in class could speak English. That was their subject in school. The sensei in the dojo taught mainly in Japanese, but that was ok because after you hear something once or twice you know what they are going to do. Of course, because of the language barrier I didn't get the same criticism the others were getting. While the instructors were criticizing others, I would try to pay attention to what they were correcting and fix myself.

Back then they didn't like a lot of questions, especially from an American. Often they would say "Just practice," or if you asked about a technique they would simply hit you with it.

Q: Did Okazaki Sensei teach day-to-day classes or was he more reserved for special events?

Mr. Okazaki didn't get involved much with the daily teaching. He was part of the yudansha, the high black belts. He was highly respected, it was easy to see. Whenever Okazaki Sensei put on a sparring clinic, everyone would line up with Mr. Okazaki at front. He would toss people around like apples.

Q: What kind of lasting lessons did you receive that still stick with you today?

I remember that Mr. Mori, even though being a slight fellow, could take on even the biggest guys. If we had someone brand new coming into the dojo, Mr. Mori would be sent out to show what high level fighting felt like. Mori Sensei would put the guy all over the floor.

Mr. Mori was a great mentor . . . and I greatly admired Mr. Kanazawa as well. Kanazawa Sensei would often take me to the side and correct me. I used to pull my head back when trying to block strikes to my face. I remember one time he put my back up against the wall and started punching toward my face. He told me not to pull back but to drop down. That really helped me.

Q: Did you participate in tournaments or demos while in Japan?

I attended a couple of exhibitions. During demonstrations they would often want to bring me out since I was a Westerner. Everything was choreographed for those demos, and we never sparred.

Q: Did you ever teach karate to people back on your military base?

No, I didn't. Sometimes I would go to the gymnasium with my friend and spar, but I never really taught. The funny thing is, they never taught sparring in my dojo. They would *let* you spar, but they wouldn't teach strategy or anything like that. "Try anything," they would say, but then would say, "No, no wrestling," when I would grab my opponent and wind up on the ground. It was kinda limiting.

Q: After your tour of duty was over in 1958, did you come straight back to America or did you have tours elsewhere?

I came straight back, although I wish I hadn't. I think I should have stayed and learned more.

When I was leaving, they made out my rank certificate. In the main office, Mr. Nakayama got a pen and sat the certificate out on the desk, wrote on it, and handed it to me. The students thought that was very unusual and figured I was being honored by Mr. Nakayama. Sometime earlier he had asked me if I wanted to go back to the United States and open a franchise. I never answered that question. I wasn't taking karate to open a franchise, I was taking it to try to become the best in the world and teach what I knew. However, I thought I had grabbed the essence of it while in Japan and wanted to share it.

From left to right: Maynard Miner, Orito Sensei of Wado Ryu, Nakayama Sensei, Okazaki Sensei, Wado Ryu Assistant.

When I came back to the United States, I was still enlisted, but was ready to be discharged. My motivation now was more training and teaching, and I wanted to focus on that. There weren't many schools around in the U.S.; I knew about some Goju Ryu, but that wasn't the same as what I was doing. Peter Urban was running the biggest dojo I knew of at that time. I heard the name Robert Trias, too, but I never met him. When I came back I was stationed at Fort Dix until I was discharged, and then I went to Brooklyn.

Q: What was it like opening your first dojo in the United States?

I didn't actually get to open a studio right away. I would go to St. John's Recreation Center in Brooklyn to practice kata. That's when I met George Cofield (around 1959). He had put on a black belt and was trying to teach (he had a pretty good group together, too). Then he saw me training and asked if I could help him in his class. So what he ended up doing was putting all of his students up against me for sparring. None of his students knew much about sparring and they had very poor basics, so it wasn't a problem.

After that, Mr. Cofield let me take over the class. A little while later we opened up a program operating out of a basement. The classes continued to grow and grow. At one time I had 60 people on the floor in a space that couldn't hold more than 15. It was too crowded.

Long Island University J.K.A. touring event in 1978. From left to right: Nakayama Sensei, Ito Sensei, Maynard Miner Sensei , George Cofield Sensei.

Q: What was the general perception of karate from the students you encountered at that time?

karate was still somewhat mysterious. They thought they were going to learn how to climb up walls and walk across the ceiling. Especially the kids. They wanted to see me do backflips and that kind of thing.

Q: As you were growing your school, did you manage to stay in touch with your instructors back in Japan? Was it difficult staying organized with them?

I was on my own for quite a few years, but I don't think it was their fault. I never reached back to try to contact anybody. But then I met Orito Hiroshi Sensei of Wado Ryu. I was looking to further my training and I thought he looked pretty good, especially his basics and kicks. I decided to pursue training with him.

During one of our first training sessions, he pulled me on to the floor and said, "Now I'm going to show you what a *real* black belt looks like." The way he said it . . . I took it as a slur against me as a Westerner and as a black man. He tried to bang me around and he was good, but every time he tried to hit me I tried as hard as I could to knock him down. As a result, he backed off a bit.

Orito Sensei liked to hang out downstairs from the dojo and drink beer with me. He would say, "Let's go out and find a dojo and kick some people around." I didn't think that was a good idea. Despite our early conflicts, we turned into friends.

One unfortunate thing about Orito Sensei is that he had a racial problem. Most of the people of color in his class ended up finding out where I was teaching so they could come to my class. Orito would say things in class about people of different races, and at first the students didn't realize it since Orito wasn't speaking English. He would say that people of different races could never really learn karate.

Orito Sensei eventually helped me connect back to my sensei in Japan. He was making deals, and Mr. Okazaki wanted to come over to the United States. He needed someone in the States to sponsor him, and Orito Sensei volunteered. So Mr. Okazaki was able to come over and they started an organization that became a part of the Japan Karate Association.

From that point forward, Mr. Okazaki took over testing responsibilities for our style. I was able to join back up with Mr. Okazaki and keep training. When sensei taught here it was much the same as I had experienced in Japan, sticking heavily with basics and stance.

Q: Did Okazaki Sensei continue to test and promote you as well?

Yes. It was about seven or eight years since my time in Japan when Okazaki Sensei approached me and said, "You must take test." I went down to Philadelphia where Okazaki was located, and they had a big event going. He made me spar Leslie Safar which I believe was his way of testing my level.

Okazaki Sensei and Miner Sensei conducting a kyu test in Brooklyn NY, 1977.

Q: Could you explain how you viewed tournaments and sparring while building your program?

Mr. Okazaki would say that tournaments were just like training . . . you do your best. We were allowed to spar in the dojo to prepare for competition, but it was never taught to us. No strategy or methods were shared with us, so we would often lose to the direct Japanese students of the senior instructors. Mr. Okazaki would say, "Just keep training."

My students felt discouraged and wanted to quit or at least avoid tournaments. I encouraged them to keep entering. "We have to try," I would say. At times I felt like we weren't being taught everything, or that we were being taught backwards.

In time I started teaching my own strategy and tactics, and we improved. In fact, we won some championships. I tried to help students with the theory of what we were doing, building a foundation of understanding, instead of just, "Do this, do that," with no explanation.

Q: What kind of advice and methods would you use to improve the sparring of your students?

I would teach them not to stand and wait for things to happen. A better method was to create a scenario and draw the opponent in. When I was teaching strategy and fighting methods I would adjust the basics too, letting the stances be higher and more mobile.

Miner Sensei performing a dynamic jumping sidekick into a heavy bag.

Q: Outside of the tournament arena, how did you see karate begin to affect your students in terms of maturity and development?

It seemed in every class I had at least one tough guy or someone going down the wrong road. Drugs, or whatever. Karate would change them. I'm not always sure why, but it would change them. They wanted to "live" in the dojo, and they became better people.

Q: Did you ever have other schools come in and challenge your school to fight?

No, but I did have a number of individuals come in to challenge me personally. They would ask if I could show them a little bit of sparring, and then they would come at me and try to half kill me.

Q: Could you talk more about how you guided your organization and infused your own ideas into your teaching?

I think a lot of the Japanese instructors were surprised when they came over and found my students comparable to their own. They never taught us beyond the basics, but I was able to grasp what they were doing and share it with my students. I realized that the low stances could get you killed, and even though they trained us in it all the time it wasn't always right to do. I taught the importance of agility as much as rooting. Orito Sensei said I was putting boxing into karate, but I knew it was just good movement and basics.

Receiving the best attacks and effort from my opponents in Japan and America allowed me to see firsthand what was working and what wasn't. I have passed that on as best I can, and now I want to see my students pass that on as well.

These days we still start off with the low stances and traditional Shotokan fundamentals but we don't limit ourselves, especially as students grow in understanding. Our goal is to understand what the basics do, when they work, and when there are drawbacks. We want students to understand the art so well that they can find their own stance.

Q: What kind of philosophy, spirit, and heart do you want your students and teachers to exhibit?

I think they should have strong discipline, know what they're doing, understand the philosophy of Shotokan, and train hard. One thing that students need is hard training and challenge. When they don't get it, they quit. When they do get it, they complain but they stay. That's how you know it's what they want and need.

Q: Do you have any words of wisdom for students as they develop in their training?

One thing I have noticed is that some people always want to learn more things instead of polishing what they already have. Also, I noticed that a lot of people wanted to be exactly like Mr. Okazaki. But I found it better to figure out what kind of "equipment" each student had in order to make things work for them instead of trying to make them look like someone else.

I think Shotokan is a very strong style, but to do it right you need speed and focus. You also need to understand the techniques from the inside out. Whatever you're doing has to come from inside you. Train hard.

Cathy Cline

Cathy Cline's martial arts journey began in a unique way. After moving to the Denver area in the early 1970s, Cline Sensei found herself employed near one of the earliest karate schools in the state. After a chance meeting with a member of the dojo, Cline built up the courage to investigate karate further — a decision which she never regretted or abandoned.

Cline Sensei's dojo was operated by Yaguchi Yutaka, a graduate of the J.K.A. Instructor Training Program and a senior student of Nakayama Masatoshi Sensei. Yaguchi Sensei was a pioneer for karate in the American Midwest and creator of a regional branch of the I.S.K.F. (Okazaki Teruyuki's organization). As a student of Yaguchi Sensei and later Okazaki Sensei, Cathy Cline became one of the most prominent Shotokan instructors in the U.S.A., and a pioneer for female martial artists everywhere.

Q: Cline Sensei, what was your earliest introduction to the martial arts? Was there anything that happened in your youth that made you think martial arts may be an area of interest to you?

David Carradine and the *Kung Fu* television series initially sparked my interest in Southeast Asia and the martial arts. Japan especially fascinated me as it seemed to offer a very different culture and way of life. My fascination with Japan and the Orient prompted me to write book reports, create art projects, and conduct research centered on Japanese history, the Emperor, and their unmistakable architecture.

Then, when I was a freshman in college, I was walking back to my dormitory one evening and was taken completely by surprise when a man came out of an alley and grabbed me from behind. I had been looking down at the sidewalk as I was walking and this posture had put me in a vulnerable position. I pulled away and ran. I wasn't physically injured, but my pride was bruised and I was ashamed that I never saw it coming. It seemed that with some awareness training and self-defense I could have avoided that assault. Karate or some form of self-defense was what I looked for soon thereafter.

Q: How did you first find out about Yaguchi Yutaka Sensei and Shotokan in the Denver area? What was your first visit like to his program, and what were your early impressions of karate?

I found out about Yaguchi Sensei and his dojo completely by accident. After I moved to Denver in 1973, I found employment at Grand Prix Management. Grand Prix owned and managed the dojo property and was located right across the street from the dojo itself. Each month Yaguchi Sensei walked over to pay the rent, and I would write him a receipt. I smiled and spoke to him, but we never carried on a conversation. His English was still quite broken, and I was embarrassed because I couldn't understand him.

One time the dojo president came to pay the rent and I was able to ask him questions about the school. The club name on the check read "Colorado Karate Association," which interested me because I knew they were practicing a martial art. The fact that the school was right across from my job seemed like destiny. I asked about the training, how difficult it was to learn a martial art, and if any women were practicing. I was encouraged to come watch a class to see what it was all about. I did watch, and observed only one woman training in the daytime class, but she was a black belt. I thought maybe I could do it too, so

I signed up for classes the next day.

My first evening lesson was a one-on-one session with a young black belt man who was very good, very fast, and very strong. He demonstrated his kata for me, which included a jump and turn in the air, and a landing on all fours; I remember being impressed. The beauty of the movements and his strength and speed were beautiful, and it made me hope I would be able to learn those same moves. I came back the next night and every night after that. I was hooked. Once I had learned the basic blocks, stances, body shifts, and punches I was allowed to train in the beginner's class with Yaguchi Sensei. It was within weeks that I realized I had found the dojo, and the martial art, that would hold my interest for a long, long time.

Q: Was Yaguchi Sensei hesitant at all accepting you as a student since you were a young female?

Yaguchi Sensei did not hesitate to accept me as a student in his dojo. He sincerely believed that karate was designed for everyone, regardless of gender. When I first came to his dojo in 1973, classes were predominantly male. The women who did train seemed engaged, but did not fit my image of how a karate practitioner should look or train. Those women wore make-up, had fancy hairdos, and grew their fingernails so long that it was difficult to make a fist. After observing them, I knew I could do karate. That was the early '70s, when many people were trying out the martial arts. It was different, unlike any American sport, and everyone was watching *Kung Fu* on TV. Like most fads or crazes, it didn't take long to separate the casual practitioners from the serious karateka.

Q: What was day-to-day training like with Yaguchi Sensei? What kind of material did he focus on?

Day-to-day training at the Denver dojo was interesting, challenging, and exciting. Every class we learned a new combination and worked on variations of that combination with a partner. We learned to shift and move our bodies in different ways to block and parry attacks from our partners. These creative drills kept us on our toes and captured our attention. I didn't always feel the movements were natural for me, but Yaguchi Sensei explained that you never knew where, or under what circumstances, you would find yourself when attacked. This had already happened to me in college, so I knew I had to be prepared for any situation. Each time we practiced with a partner, we improved our distancing, timing, and target accuracy.

Following the combination drills, we would work on kata. When Yaguchi Sensei introduced us to a new kata, he would have us sit down along the sides of the dojo and he would perform the kata; first slowly, then medium speed, then full speed. Each time he did this, he would remind us to look for different things — first, how to make a correct technique, then how to use the technique through combinations of movements, and finally rhythm and timing. It was a wonderful way to learn a new kata, providing an accurate picture of how the kata should look.

Training six days a week wasn't enough for me, and on Sunday, our day off, I was already looking forward to Monday and the start of a new week of training and learning. After about a year of training, Yaguchi Sensei would work with me on slow, free sparring. He would spar with each of us to ensure that no one ever got hurt. When we were with him he used to say that black belts should act as "human punching bags." Black belts were supposed to exhibit control, and by following this method of slow, controlled sparring, we all avoided injury and were able to react to unannounced techniques.

Cathy Cline during kata training in 1981.

Q: Could you describe Yaguchi Sensei as a teacher in terms of personality and methods?

Yaguchi Sensei's classes were always challenging and exciting. I loved to see what new and different combinations he had created to challenge our minds and bodies. I consider him a "master of combinations," as well as a "master of shifting." Although it is easy to learn techniques and execute them, it is not easy to execute a technique while you are shifting. He could move his body smoothly and quickly at the last moment, so you could never catch him with your punch or kick. He could see the technique coming and was gone before you finished the attack.

Yaguchi Sensei's personality and teaching style made it fun to train. He was very personable, always joking, and very well-liked. I trained very hard with serious intent, but somehow he made it fun and enjoyable. He would make us laugh when we were struggling with a technique or a kata, always keeping things in perspective. It is easier to learn when you are relaxed, not afraid, and not under too much pressure.

Q: Did you meet other Shotokan seniors while studying with Yaguchi Sensei? What were your impressions of them?

We met many different instructors in the 1970s. Yaguchi Sensei believed it was important to meet and train with instructors from both inside and outside the United States. In 1974, we were honored to have Master Nakayama visit the Denver dojo. He was very good at demonstrating and explaining technique. Sometimes he would remove his gi top to expose his arms and chest to point out the muscles involved in a particular block or punch. Those seminars and demonstrations make an impression and stay with you. In his honor, we hosted a welcome tournament that ran late into the night. We also met Master Sugiura Motokuni who, ten years later, would become the Chief Instructor of the J.K.A. following Master Nakayama's death.

During a visit to Japan in 1975, Yaguchi Sensei took a small group of us to watch the All Japan Karate Championship at the Budokan. This was a dream come true. There I met Sensei's Kanazawa, Tanaka, Mori, Ueki, Shoji and many of the other competitors, judges, and officials who participated in the tournament. While in Tokyo, we trained at the honbu dojo and were given permission to watch an Instructor Trainee Class. I watched each instructor, but was most proud of Yaguchi Sensei who seemed to have boundless energy and seemed to run circles around the younger Japanese trainees.

One year, Yaguchi Sensei brought Master Okazaki for a visit from Philadelphia. We had heard many stories about how Okazaki Sensei exhibited amazing technique, and we had all seen his photos in magazines and the karate reference books. He stressed the importance of basics and kata in his clinics and loved to tell stories of his interactions with Master Funakoshi. Those stories gave us a glimpse of his love and dedication to Master Funakoshi and the martial arts. He would eventually become the Chairman and Chief Instructor of the I.S.K.F. (International Shotokan Karate Federation) in 1977.

We also trained with Tanaka Masahiko, whom I had the opportunity to spar with at the Denver dojo. Being a naïve green belt, I was too ignorant to be afraid, so I had a good time with our match (which ended with both of us on the floor). We met and trained with several great American instructors like Greer Golden, Ray Dalke, Frank Smith, and James Field. As a beginner powering through my first decade of karate training, it was a thrill to meet and train with these karate legends.

Cathy Cline (center in sunglasses) in 1977 with the I.S.K.F. group. Okazaki Sensei, Yaguchi Sensei, and Frank Smith Sensei are also pictured.

Q: Did you get involved with helping other women break into the martial arts?

As soon as I was a brown belt, I asked Yaguchi Sensei if I could teach an eight week self-defense class for women. With his approval, I brought in 12-15 women, including friends, neighbors, co-workers, my sister, and my sister's friends. All of them were excited to learn something new and different. Several of them stayed and trained in the regular karate classes after the self-defense course ended.

We were all in our 20's, so the social aspect was important to us and our interaction extended beyond the dojo. The school really began to grow, and our membership rose from 60 to 120 students. With this influx of students, the ratio of women to men became 40:60. It was a boom time for the martial arts, and the enthusiastic and endearing nature of Yaguchi Sensei helped keep the dojo full. We were all young, holding on to dreams of travel and adventure through karate training and competition. This trend continued as students soon recognized the benefits of self-confidence, self-defense, and purposeful physical exercise. They spread the word about karate training to their friends, family, and co-workers.

Q: Did you partake in competition at this time? What were those early tournaments like, and how well-defined were the women's brackets?

Yes, I was very competitive and I entered both kata and kumite divisions. We drove or flew with Yaguchi Sensei from Denver to Arizona and California in order to compete in tournaments hosted by Koyama Sensei and Dalke Sensei. These tournaments prepared us for the national tournaments that we would eventually compete in after we formed the I.S.K.F. in 1977. We traveled all over the United States for our nationals.

Cline Sensei throwing a powerful front kick during competition.

It was a struggle in the '70s and throughout the '80s to maintain women's kumite as a division in the national tournaments. One year it would be offered, and the next year it wouldn't. If it was offered, the host would bracket brown belt women together with black belt women. It was difficult for me to understand why black and brown belts were in the same division, and why women were not allowed to spar at every competition. It seemed for every step we took forward, we took two steps back.

I realized that the level of women's sparring had to be raised, and the number of women competing had to increase if we were to have a consistent presence in competition. To be taken seriously, we needed to exercise good control, demonstrate good technique, and avoid injuries. If we did that, eventually women's sparring would have to be accepted in every competition; but it took almost two decades for that to happen.

Q: When did your time in Colorado end, and what took you to Philadelphia?

I moved from Colorado to New York City in August of 1980 to attend graduate school at Long Island University in Brooklyn. While taking classes in New York during the week, I would drive the 90 miles to Philadelphia each weekend to train at the I.S.K.F. headquarters under Okazaki Sensei. I earned my Master's Degree in Exercise Physiology at L.I.U., and while there I worked as a counselor and a Teaching Fellow under the tutelage of Dr. Stricevic, who co-authored the *Textbook of Modern Karate* with Okazaki Sensei.

In 1981, a breakthrough happened for women in Shotokan when we were allowed to officially enroll in the Instructor Trainee Program. Prior to that, women were restricted to auditing the courses and we did not get credit for the classes we participated in. This changed and the policy was reversed, allowing four of us to enter the program in September, 1981.

Upon completion of graduate school in 1982, I moved from NYC to Philadelphia to continue the instructor classes, train for competition, find employment, and work as the International Secretary for the I.S.K.F. at the headquarters office.

The opportunity to move to the East Coast and attend graduate school was a mixed blessing . . . leaving Denver and Yaguchi Sensei was very difficult. I missed him, I missed training at his dojo, and I missed my friends . . . but I knew I wanted to take advantage of an opportunity to better my education, participate in the Instructor Program, and study under Okazaki Sensei. It was very exciting but also bittersweet.

Q: What was day-to-day training like with Okazaki Sensei? Were there any notable differences in content or method from your time with Yaguchi Sensei?

Training in Philadelphia was very different from training in Denver. In Philly, there was a strong emphasis on basics and repetition. The standard class began with hundreds of repetitions of punches and kicks from the right side and then the left. This was very different from the creative and complex combinations and shifting patterns I had been accustomed to with Yaguchi Sensei. Basic katas were emphasized and practiced every class, as well as basic three-step and one-step sparring. I eventually got used to this style of training and realized that my techniques were becoming more polished. My body began to feel and understand the true and direct line of every movement.

Besides the different training style I experienced in Philadelphia, I also had to learn the Japanese terminology for all techniques, movements, and stances. We had mostly used English in Denver, so I was scrambling to learn the terms in Japanese. I would stand just behind the students on either side of me, so I could quickly imitate what they were doing. Finally I learned the terms and they became second nature, but it was about a six month period of adjustment before I felt comfortable and part of the dojo.

Q: Could you describe Okazaki Sensei as a teacher and individual?

Okazaki Sensei was completely grounded in, and committed to, the principles of basic techniques. His instruction demanded perfection through repetition and regular training. I came as close as possible to achieving my best while training with him. Classes were well-attended and intense and we were consistently pushed to our limits, both mentally and physically. Basic techniques and basic sparring were practiced with maximum power, speed, and intensity. It was exhilarating, if not intimidating.

As an individual, Okazaki Sensei was a perfect gentleman. He was quite shy, with polished manners and a friendly demeanor . . . but we all knew he could decimate an opponent in the blink of an eye. His power, when he did demonstrate, was palpable. However, because of his humility, you would never know his legendary status.

Q: In your mind, what were some of the most important tenants of Shotokan expressed by your instructors?

Yaguchi Sensei taught me to "never give up." I was accustomed to trying something once or twice and if it didn't work out, moving on to the next thing. The lesson of staying with something and not giving up, even if it was difficult, was a concept that I needed to learn at a young age. Sports and physical endeavors usually came easy to me, so knowing that I had certain shortcomings in karate that challenged my highest expectations was a challenge that I needed to tackle. The ability to see and go beyond my roadblocks and eventually reach my goal meant that I had to endeavor.

Yaguchi Sensei also taught me the importance of being generous and extending that generosity to others. I found that the act of being generous to others, expecting nothing in return, has a way of coming back into your life.

Cline Sensei training with Yaguchi Sensei in 2013.

Okazaki Sensei taught me how the second principle of the Dojo Kun, "be faithful," can put meaning and continuity into one's life. Following this principle, which extols loyalty and unwavering dedication, provides a stable foundation upon which to build. Okazaki Sensei's unwavering dedication and loyalty to Master Funakoshi's principles is a model for all of us, one that has made a significant impression on me and one that I try to live by every day of my life.

Q: Could you describe what your tests were like as you progressed into 6th, 7th, and 8th degree black belt?

All black belt examinations for 6th degree and above required a technical paper that had to be submitted two months prior to the practical examination. The technical paper could explain, for example, a specific technique or group of techniques, the physical principles of training using kinesiology, anatomy and physiology, neurophysiology, etc. The papers were read and graded before the practical exam and counted as one third of your grade. The 6th, 7th, and 8th Dan examinations are only administered at Master Camp in Pennsylvania in June, or at the national tournament usually held in November.

The examinee is not asked to perform kihon because they should already be proficient in the basic techniques. The practical test begins with kata. The examinee performs his / her individual kata, and then the examiner asks for a second kata. The second kata is selected from the list of intermediate and advanced Shotokan kata and the examinee does not know beforehand which kata that will be. It is important to be familiar with all the kata.

Following kata performance the examinee then spars, or chooses between free sparring and self-defense if they are 45 years of age and over. Self-defense includes attacks from the front, sides, and back. You must demonstrate that you are able to free yourself, counter attack, and then flee. I chose free sparring for my 6th Dan test, but didn't pass. I realized my body reactions were not as fast as during my competitive years, and self-defense was a more realistic choice. On a subsequent attempt, I chose self-defense and passed my 6th Dan.

Besides writing a technical paper, performing kata(s), and demonstrating self-defense, I was asked questions about teaching and technical principles when I took my 7th and 8th Dan examinations. The Shihan-kai (governing body) wanted to be sure I understood the basic principles of training.

Finally, it should be noted that there is a minimum age requirement for each dan rank. The rationale is that life experience, which comes with age, is usually accompanied by maturity and wisdom; if you are too young you do not possess the maturity and wisdom needed to fulfill the higher ranks.

Q: Have you expanded your training into other martial arts or styles of karate?

Over the past three years, I have expanded my interests to include Tai Chi Chuan. The slow "soft style" of Tai Chi is a wonderful complement to the fast "hard style" of Shotokan Karate. Tai Chi concentrates on breath control as well as movement and transmission of energy. Energy, or ki, comes from the center of the body and moves outward toward your opponent. I find that Tai Chi aids the Shotokan practitioner with power control. It is a great balance to the sharp, focused techniques we practice in karate. Although it is soft and slow, it provides a significant workout and is easier on the joints.

Q: You are the highest ranking woman in the I.S.K.F. and the first to receive 8th Dan. What does this honor mean to you, and what kind of responsibility do you feel as a senior role model?

Yes, I am the first woman in the I.S.K.F. to achieve the rank of 8th Dan. I give the credit for this achievement to my instructors, Master Yaguchi and Master Okazaki. Without these two men, I would not have achieved this rank. Their extraordinary teaching ability and their personal charisma drove me to train harder. They both understood my character and took the time to help me press on when I needed encouragement.

I am, of course, very honored to hold this rank; but the most important thing I want others to know is, if I can do it, you can do it. Perseverance, sacrifice, and never giving up is what it takes. I hope that by reaching this goal I have set an example for other women and men within the organization, spurring them on to see that there is much "beneath the surface" of their karate training. The physical training is finite, we all age and begin to lose speed, strength, and flexibility; but the mental and spiritual training is infinite. That is the beauty of martial arts training, "seeing" and "knowing" that which is unspoken. I cannot imagine myself without this art and the benefits I have derived from it.

Q: What are some of the most important benefits karate has brought to you in your life? Are there mistakes you made in your training that you might recommend students avoid?

Karate has given me the confidence to do things I would not have done and go places I would not have gone. Standing before a group of people, speaking or demonstrating, was impossible for me prior to karate training. Extending myself to help others rather than standing back and watching has become second nature. Understanding that internal peace, spreading to the outside as we seek to perfect our character, is our goal and what the martial arts is all about. Karate changes you.

Physically, one of the greatest benefits karate exercise has brought to my life is the ability to sleep. Before training, I suffered from insomnia. My mind would race and I couldn't stop the constant stream of thoughts that prevented me from getting a decent night's sleep. After an evening of training, I am able to fall asleep soon after my head hits the pillow, which makes me feel refreshed and alert the next day. Ironically, I also find I can better control my thoughts during the day. I am able to keep my mind on work, school, karate, family, or personal life without them running together or overlapping.

In addition, I have become healthier. As my lungs got stronger from strenuous training and were able to take in more oxygen, small physical ailments fell by the wayside. Karate has been a wonderful, all around tonic.

Mentally, karate's great benefit is a sense of peace and calm that can be tapped into whenever needed. A sense of well-being coming from self-confidence is a by-product of regular and purposeful training.

Mistakes to avoid: Never say never!

Q: What is your vision for the future of Shotokan? How would you like to see it grow with the next few generations?

I see the future of I.S.K.F. Shotokan Karate to be bright, successful, and full of hope. The foundation that has been laid by Master Funakoshi and Master Okazaki is very strong because it is based on the solid precepts of the Dojo Kun and the Niju Kun. The next generation has also committed to these principles and has the ability and drive to evolve and keep pace with the 21st century while keeping us on track. Decades of training and the usual ups and downs of life may be a roadblock for some, but when things get too easy, they are not worth pursuing. Challenges, followed by successes and failures, build individual character.

The Millennials, or Generation Y, have grown up with computers and the internet, causing them to seek instant gratification. Training for decades to achieve a certain rank or status would be hard for them to imagine. How will this generation take to a traditional martial art like Shotokan Karate? Our style of karate is definitely not for those looking for "instant gratification." However, the fact that we are always learning, and will continue to learn as long as we train, may keep the interest of this young, intelligent generation. The future leaders of our organization will face unique challenges, and I hope they work hard to tackle them head on.

James Field

James Field Sensei has developed a unique understanding and appreciation of Shotokan thanks to decades of dedicated training under multiple high level instructors. Field Sensei's influences include Nishiyama Hidetaka Sensei, Okazaki Teruyuki Sensei, and Yaguchi Yutaka Sensei. Each instructor brought value to Field Sensei's training, making him a highly sought after practitioner in his own right.

Besides his credentials as a teacher, Field Sensei also distinguished himself as a competitor. After winning multiple championships on the collegiate and national level, Field Sensei became the U.S. Representative to the Olympic Games in Mexico and a medalist in the 1976 World Tournament.[90] He was one of the first four Westerners to graduate from the prestigious J.K.A. Instructor Training Program, a feat once thought closed to anyone besides the Japanese themselves.

Q: Field Sensei, when did you meet Okazaki Teruyuki Sensei? How did that meeting come about?

I first saw him in 1965 at a special training during a tournament where there was a team from Japan. I next saw him in 1967 when he visited Nishiyama Sensei's dojo where he was helping to give dan exams (at that time, 3rd Dan was the highest rank in the U.S.A.). I didn't personally meet him at first; instead, he was introduced to the class. He first spoke to me in 1968 after a tournament, at which time he told me I needed to practice more.

Q: When did you begin competing in tournaments? Was competition an emphasis in

[90] "An Interview with Sensei James Field - The Shotokan Way." 2007. 31 Dec. 2014
<http://www.theshotokanway.com/jamesfieldinterview.html>.

Nishiyama Hidetaka Sensei's dojo?

I began competing in 1964 or '65. Competition was not emphasized in the dojo. However, I trained on a special competition team. You had to be invited to train on the team by all the other members. They were the only people allowed to spar in the dojo. We trained specially for competition (plus five days of basic classes per week).

Q: When did you come to meet Yaguchi Yutaka Sensei? How did this meeting come about?

He came from Japan to teach. I met him on June 5, 1965. I'll never forget it. He changed my whole life. He came to Nishiyama Sensei's dojo and I met him there. I was ready to quit. But that day I saw him moving across the floor, so smooth . . . like a cat. He didn't run you down. He would just spring and suddenly be there. I was so impressed. I'd been around fighting my entire life and had never seen anything like that.

Q: How did training with Yaguchi Sensei differ from Nishiyama and Okazaki?

Mr. Yaguchi was more explosive, and moved more like a feather in the wind — hard to catch. When he attacked, there was pretty much nothing you could do about it. He was so fast. He would attack before you could block it or move. Mr. Nishiyama stressed strength, saying, "You must block when someone attacks." But Mr. Yaguchi would say, "When you kick, you must be in and out before your opponent's arms can block you." This style suited me better. Mr. Okazaki also emphasizes speed and quickness. Master Nakayama also stated to me, the three most important things in karate technique are: 1. Speed, 2.Speed, and 3. Speed.

Q: How was application of techniques handled by your instructors? How early would they introduce "bunkai" into your kata training (after weeks, months, years of practicing the form)?

Yaguchi Sensei taught me the applications as he taught me the kata. He was pretty much the only one to do this, except for Master Nakayama, who demonstrated bunkai for complicated techniques. I don't know if Yaguchi Sensei did this for everyone.

Q: Shotokan is known for deep-rooted stances and big movements. How much of this is for body development versus effective technique development?

It is to develop the body so that it can deliver effective techniques. You develop strong muscles so that you can move faster and deliver maximum power to the target at the moment of impact. When free sparring, your stance is necessarily higher for faster, freer movement, but training the body rigorously in deep stances enables you to snap more easily into the longer stance at the moment of impact with the target. The stances have been scientifically proven to be the most effective means to deliver maximum power to the target, but other factors such as correct course of techniques and timing when striking the target, and the combination of either hip rotation, stepping in, or hip vibration are also crucial.

Q: When did you first travel to Japan in order to pursue your training? Was it difficult managing the finances of travel and uncertainty of residing in a new country?

I first went in 1967 or '68 to train. I resided in new countries when I was in the military, so I was used to adjusting to new cultures, so that was not a problem.

Q: In Japan you undertook training for the J.K.A. Instructor's Course. How did training differ in this course from your previous experiences?

The instructor's training course isn't for everyone; you had to be selected. You had to win X amount of tournaments, or be outstanding in some way and recommended by a senior instructor, such as Master Okazaki (non-trainees were not even allowed to watch instructor training). Everyone there was already "the best" so they weren't teaching you to do techniques, instead focusing on refining them.

We trained morning, afternoon, and evening. It was difficult as it was important to know how to do everything the most correct way possible, as we would have to demonstrate and explain techniques properly. We were responsible for passing on the art correctly. The instructors really focused on kata, but every class had basics, kata and kumite.

Q: You were one of the first four Americans certified as a Japan Karate Association Instructor. Who were the others, and what was the process for achieving this status?

Mr. Greer Golden, Mr. Ray Dalke, and Mr. Lester Ingber were the other three. To graduate from the program they say it takes one year, full time, but it really takes three years to finish. You had to attend EVERY class, or you were dropped. We also had to give lectures and write many papers.

Q: What was the J.K.A.'s motivation for teaching Westerners and increasing Shotokan's presence in the U.S.?

That was Master Nakayama's decision. I do not know his thinking on this.

Q: When did you open your first dojo? What were some of the challenges you faced during your early days as a teacher?

I opened my dojo on Sept. 22, 1972. Beside the challenge of paying the rent (still a challenge), I had to learn to put my students first. Therefore, I stopped competing and focused on helping them.

Q: How have you tried to grow your students both technically and philosophically over the years? What characteristics of Shotokan do you stress as most important?

All characteristics of Shotokan are equally important. I teach like I was taught. I don't favor one over the other.

Q: Experiencing multiple perspectives from different Shotokan instructors helped in your personal development as a martial artist. Do you think others should experience multiple teachers or styles as well?

That's up to the individual. I was taught that you don't mix anything until you've mastered what you're trying. Loyalty to one's instructor is very important. The only reason I ever trained with other instructors was because my sensei sent me to train with them. It is very much frowned upon to hop from teacher to teacher, or dojo to dojo. I suggest that to experience different instructors in Shotokan one should attend the annual Master Camp organized by Master Okazaki. All the instructors are from the same "tree" of Shotokan, just different branches.

Robin Rielly

Robin Rielly has carved out a reputation for himself as both technically skillful and well-researched. As the author of numerous martial arts and military history books, Rielly Sensei has helped preserve many teachings of Shotokan throughout its global growth.

Rielly Sensei was introduced to Judo and karate before joining the Marines, eventually finding himself stationed in Japan. Once there, he began training in a style known as Shin Kage Ryu, distinct from the sword style of the same name and influenced by Shotokan.

After that he began his direct Shotokan training in earnest, eventually becoming a senior disciple of Okazaki Teruyuki Sensei.

Q: Your journey in the martial arts began in 1959 while in college. Could you tell us which college you attended, and how you were first introduced to Judo and karate?

I entered Fairleigh Dickinson University, Madison, New Jersey Campus in Fall of 1959, having just turned 17. Fairleigh had a wrestling team and I was interested in joining. On the team was a student from Indonesia named Sophjan Rophy, and we became close friends. Sophjan had practiced Judo in Indonesia and was a brown belt. After wrestling practice he would show me Judo moves, and within a few weeks we had a club going. Since we were also wrestling and lifting weights, we were in good condition. He also knew some karate, and, using Nishiyama Hidetaka's book *Karate: The Art of Empty Hand Fighting* as a guide, we also practiced the basics. I actually preferred Judo at first, but in time my interest in karate overtook it.

Q: What was your academic focus in college, and what made you decide to leave your studies in order to join the United States Marine Corps?

As with many college students, I did not have a focus for my studies. Basically, I was a bit immature and probably should have worked for a year or two before attending. In addition to my athletic interests, I was also an avid spear fisherman. My spear gun and wet suit were always in the trunk of my car. If the striped bass were running, I headed for the beach and skipped classes. None of this contributed to academic achievement.

By the end of two years, I was doing poorly and in danger of flunking out. Some of the individuals I knew from spearfishing were ex-Navy U.D.T. (Underwater Dive Team) men and encouraged me to go into the Navy to join the U.D.T. So in the spring of 1961, I went to visit the Navy recruiter. He informed me that U.D.T. was a voluntary outfit and that even if I volunteered I might not get a chance to try out. I told him I would have to think about that, and began to leave his office. A Marine staff sergeant in the next office had overheard the conversation and said, "Say, son, we have frogmen in the Marine Corps. We call them Force Recon. I guarantee you'll get a chance if you join."

So, being very naïve and only 19, I joined the U.S.M.C. I did well at Parris Island and had a meritorious promotion to Private First Class and headed off to Infantry Training Regiment at Camp Geiger, North Carolina. My drill instructor had told me to see the 1st Sergeant there and tell him of my interest in Force Recon. My encounter with the 1st Sergeant was a disappointment as he told me my orders had already been cut and I was going to Japan.

Q: Could you tell us where you were stationed in Japan, when you arrived, and what your duties were?

From Camp Geiger we were transported across country to El Toro Marine Air Base near Los Angeles, California, to await transport to Japan. We were there a couple of weeks, and during that time I met Don McNatt, who had also done some martial arts training. We began to work out together in our off hours and met Gunnery Sergeant Edwards, who had trained in Japan in Wado Ryu. He had come back to California and took up Shotokan with Nishiyama Sensei, who had just moved there. We trained with him a couple of times and within a week or so found ourselves on a troop transport, heading from San Diego to Yokosuka, with stops at Hawaii, Guam, and Okinawa. I arrived in Japan in early March 1962 and, after landing at Yokosuka, was transported to East Camp, Atsugi Naval Air Base. Our duties in the Provost Marshall's Office were varied. We guarded the facilities, buildings, flight line and aircraft, radar installations, bank, and various parts of our area. We chased prisoners (escorted them back and forth from the brig to work details) and also rode shotgun for the payroll officer.

Atsugi is about one half hour by train from Yokohama. It is located on the Kanto Plain about halfway between Tokyo Bay and the mountains. Each morning we could get up, look to the west, and see Mount Fuji. Tokyo is about one and one half hours away by train, with a change of train in Yokohama. We took occasional trips to Tokyo, but Yokohama had a number of dojo(s), so there was no need to go farther. After I had been there for a few months, I bought a small Honda motorcycle from a departing Marine and had a lot more flexibility for traveling on my time off.

Q: How quickly did you set off to find a dojo once in Japan? What was your process for looking, and how did you finally choose a location?

We arrived on base and within two days had liberty. Don McNatt and I headed to the nearby town of Yamato in search of a dojo. We saw a police officer and asked him where to find a karate school. He told us to get on the train and go to Yokohama. We arrived in Yokohama central train station and asked another police officer where we might find a dojo. He told us to get on the trolley and head for Chinatown. Chinatown in Yokohama is in a rough port area and is filled with bars and transient merchant seamen from the ships. The trolley let us off and we walked a few blocks to the center of the area. Once again we asked advice of the first police officer we found, and he told us to go around the corner and we would find a dojo there. As you can see, it was not a very scientific approach. On the other hand, we had little knowledge of various styles — karate was karate and we had no idea of any differences between schools.

We went around the block and found a walled in compound which was the Chinese Association of Yokohama. It was rectangular in shape with several buildings and businesses on each side. Facing the opening to the enclosed area was the dojo. In large Japanese and English letters it proclaimed itself the Kobukan Judo and Karate School.

Don and I stood outside the dojo and listened to the sounds of some hard training from within. Kiais and crashing into the walls seemed to dominate. We finally decided to enter the front door, and observed about a dozen men sparring. Periodically one or another would be thrown against the wall resulting in the shaking of the entire building (which was only one story and framed in wood). Overall it was not a very sturdy structure, with basic planking over frames.

We stood at attention in the foyer as class continued. The focus at the moment was freestyle sparring and we were greatly impressed. It was the first real karate class I had ever seen. Within a few minutes the instructor, Nagaoka Fumio Sensei, came over and asked us what we wanted. I replied that we wanted to learn karate. He told us that he didn't teach karate, but karate jujutsu. We learned later that the style was Shin Kage Ryu. This is a very old name in Japanese martial arts and usually identified as a famous sword school. However, Shin Kage Ryu at the Kobukan had no connection with it and, in fact, used different Japanese characters and had a different meaning than those used in the school of swordsmanship.

The origin of the style Nagaoka Sensei taught is unknown to me. However, one evening when I was not there, his teacher, Nagai Sensei, came to visit. My friends told me he was very old, probably in his 80s, which would have made him active in the early part of the century when Funakoshi Sensei was introducing karate to Japan proper. My guess is that

Shin Kage Ryu was probably developed at that time from an older jujutsu school that adopted the new karate techniques. I think that many styles evolved in the early 20th century in that manner. We see a similar transformation today both in Japan and the United States as new styles and organizations are formed with great frequency.

Nagaoka Sensei told us that there was an initiation fee, a monthly fee, and that we would have to buy a gi. The exchange rate at that time was 360 yen to the dollar. Even though we weren't paid a great deal in the Marine Corps, it was still a lot more than the average Japanese worker at the time. We handed over our money and he told us to come the next day at 6 pm. We thanked him and left.

The following day we showed up at the Kobukan ready to train. As we had no gi(s) we brought workout clothing. There were some dirty gis hanging on an overhead rod and we were given those to wear. Our first evening of training consisted of standing in kiba dachi for extended periods of time and punching. Nagaoka Sensei stood in front of us correcting us. Frequent kicks to the stomach ensured that we tensed our muscles at the end of each punch. Slaps to arms to correct position were also frequent. We left there after two hours convinced that he was trying to rough us up to discourage us. In typical Marine fashion we vowed that he would not be able to do that, muttering to ourselves that if he kept trying to weed us out we'd roll a hand grenade into the place.

Nagaoka Fumio Sensei, Chief Instructor of the Kobukan, shown in 1963.

So you can see that our choice of schools was based solely on chance and circumstance. We could have just as easily found our way to a local Shito Ryu school which was led by a top master in the style and was located only blocks away.

After training with Nagaoka Sensei for several months I happened upon a Wado Ryu school on the other side of Yokohama and I joined briefly, but it was a bit out of the way so I remained at the Kobukan. The Wado school was taught by Kawaguchi Yoshio Sensei, a well-known master of the style. I was not dissatisfied with Nagaoka's school, but he was not there every night and I wished an alternate place to receive instruction on those evenings. That problem would be solved later when Ohnishi Sensei opened up a club in Yamato, which was near the base.

Q: What did the Kobukan dojo itself look like?

There was no insulation anywhere on the wood structure. The windows were about six feet off the ground so there was no danger of breaking through them. Near the bottom of the walls were a number of sliding vents designed to allow flow-through air in the hot months. They were kept closed in the winter but let a strong draft through. In the winter it was very cold and in the summer quite hot. The floor was basic tatami mat laid directly on the ground. It was canvas on top made of woven straw. Periodically Nagaoka Sensei would move some mats around as they got worn. As mats were picked up and moved, various forms of wildlife scurried back out of site. In every mat there were usually a few straws that stuck up, waiting to impale a foot, and many sections of the mats had areas that were worn through.

There was a frame structure in one corner that held a sandbag for kicking and punching, and a makiwara on the side for punching practice. A broken mirror about 2' x 3' was on the wall at one end, along with a small Shinto shrine.

Q: Could you discuss the content of Shin Kage Ryu a little more?

Shin Kage Ryu was a mixture of karate and jujutsu techniques. For my Shodan (1st Dan) test, I had to learn five empty-hand kata unlike any I have seen in other karate styles. I also had to learn a kata with the sword, which was a variation of one of the empty-hand kata. We also practiced a grappling kata similar to that practiced by Judo players. Kicks, punches, strikes and blocks were identical to those I have seen in Shotokan, but stances were a bit higher and shorter. This was to allow greater shifting movement in preparation for throwing techniques.

From time to time, Nagaoka Sensei taught us various throws to be used in conjunction with our kicking and punching techniques. In all, it was a very well-rounded system. I would estimate that the style was actually about 75% karate techniques. On occasion I still

Front of the Kobukan in the Chinatown section of Yokohama in 1963.

Robin Rielly (left) and Satoshi Kikuchi (right) practice the kata GoJu at the Kobukan Karate School, Yokohama in spring of 1963.

practice the original kata, but now my long training in Shotokan takes over and I note that my stances are much longer and lower than they were when I was practicing Shin Kage Ryu.

Q: What was class like with Nagaoka Sensei? Did he focus heavily on kata, basics, sparring, partner drills, etc.?

Generally we began with warm-ups and basic techniques, not unlike the karate I practice today. There was a great emphasis on two-man drills. As opposed to Shotokan, where we practice a decisive single blow as a counter, there were many drills where the offensive side used a number of attacks and involved a series of blocks and counter attacks. Sparring in Shotokan basically stops if someone goes down. In Shin Kage Ryu, the combatants might wind up on the floor at which point they would be expected to grapple, using choking or joint locking to finish the opponent. Class ended with kata practice.

After class ended, Sensei would stay on the floor and work with us individually. On two or three of the nights, our training was followed by a J.K.A. Shotokan group that allowed us to cross train with them if we wished. It was taught by a Sandan (3rd degree black belt) named Suzuki. Keep in mind that at that time J.K.A. only had five dan ranks, so a Sandan was pretty high. Suzuki Sensei helped me understand hip movement, and another member, Tachikawa, spent a good deal of time helping me with my roundhouse kick. He was a Shodan and a member of the Tokyo University team. Tachikawa commuted to school from Yokohama and thus was able to get in some extra training at our school. I found out many years later that one of the Shotokan black belts there, Arai, was a student of Okazaki Sensei. So while I was practicing Shin Kage Ryu, I also had some exposure to Shotokan.

I think it is necessary at this point to discuss the belt rank system. The only belts I ever saw in Japan, both in Shin Kage Ryu and Shotokan, were white, brown, and black. Students began training with a white belt. There were no smaller ranks within the white belt group. When ready, one tested for brown belt, making first, second, or third kyu. Once brown belt had been obtained, there was no further testing within that belt category. One simply remained a brown belt until he took the Shodan test. Then ranks tiered in terms of black belt grades. I never saw green, purple, or any other colored belt until I returned to the States.

Q: In general, how did the native Japanese residents treat you being an American and a military member? Was there still a lot of tension hung over from World War II?

I would have to consider it mixed. It was clear that many did not want us there. In the dojo there were two brothers who went out of their way to make us feel welcome. Yoshio and Satoshi Kikuchi became good friends of mine, and I spent a lot of time with them after practice on the weekends. Satoshi and I maintained a long relationship over the years, and it was always my wish to return to Japan to visit him and his family. Unfortunately he passed away in his late 50s from stomach cancer.

Toward the end of my tour in Japan, a local yakuza (Japanese organized crime member) joined the dojo. He was supposed to be a black belt from another style. Nagaoka Sensei asked me to spar with him and told me to take it easy. I did and my opponent rewarded me with a strike to the jaw full force. So I side kicked him and sent him flying into the wall. Nagaoka Sensei stopped the match at that point. The next day he wanted us to spar again and the man refused (I guess he had had enough).

Satoshi Kikuchi (front) and Robin Rielly (rear) practicing the side thrust kick at the Kobukan in 1963.

Q: As a World War II researcher, how do you think the war affected the people, government, and general health of the country during the era you were there?

That is difficult to assess. At the time I was in Japan, I was not really interested in things academic; that came later in my life. The Japanese seemed to be hard working and in good health. I saw nothing really negative about their condition. Keep in mind that I lived on a military base and my forays into Japanese society were limited. The only real contact I had was with people training in the dojo and my girlfriend and her family. Other servicemen frequented bars and came into contact with the lower elements in Japanese society. I had little experience there as I have never been a drinker and bar girls held little interest for me.

After I had been in Japan for about a year, I read an ad in the English version of the Japan Times. It said that some Japanese college students wished to meet with an American for the purpose of English language practice. It sounded like an interesting idea; at last I would meet with some people my own age who were educated. I made the contact and arranged a meeting. The train ride to the town in which they resided took about a half hour. It was near the seashore south and west of Yokosuka, on Sagami Bay. I got off the train at the town station looking for the students and found two girls approach me who were about the same age as me. They were sisters. Itakura Yoko was a junior at Meiji University majoring in law and her sister Satchiko was an elementary school teacher. They introduced themselves and took me to their home where I met their parents. Their father was a famous scientist and was head of the Chemistry Department at Tokyo University.

From that point on, many Sunday afternoons were spent with the family and they took me to various places that foreigners never got to see. All the while we spoke English so that they could practice. I indicated that I would also like to learn some Japanese, and so Yoko began to give me some Japanese language instruction. In time I began to develop other interests in her, and within a few months she took me to the junior prom at Meiji University in Tokyo. Her sister knew that we were dating, but both sisters kept if from the parents.

Yoko normally rode the train from her home town to Tokyo for daily classes. The train passed through Yokohama, so on her way home she would get off there and we would go to a local coffee shop to spend some time together. After she got back on board the train, I would continue on to the dojo for training. It was a sad parting for both of us when my tour and extension ended and I had to return to the States. We continued writing, but soon it became obvious to me that we really had no future and so the relationship ended.

Q: Did Japanese karate students treat you differently as a Westerner who spoke little of their language?

Several months after we joined, Don McNatt was transferred south to Iwakuni. He continued to train there under a Shotokan instructor named Akiyama and eventually became the first American to achieve Nidan rank in the Japan Karate Association. After he left the Marine Corps, he went home to Florida and began teaching Shotokan there. He joined with Okazaki Sensei and was heading the organization there until J.K.A. politics disrupted things when they sent Ueki Sensei to take over Florida. I have been in touch with Don over the years, and he is still active in the martial arts.

Once Don left, I was the only American in the club. By that time I was friendly with the Kikuchi brothers and the other Japanese accepted me, particularly after I made it to brown belt. After class, Nagaoka Sensei and the Kikuchi brothers frequently took time to explain movements to me.

Sitting in seiza was very difficult for me as I was initially very stiff. Yoshio and Satoshi decided to fix this, so each evening after practice they would sit in seiza with me and talk, to help me overcome my initial discomfort. It was that kind of treatment that made us friends — they were willing to spend time with a stranger to help him. They were all willing to assist me with learning their language, and I made every effort to do so. As a result, my impressions of the Japanese people have always been very positive and, as I look back, I must admit that I was treated very well by them. In addition, they all knew about Marines and had a great respect for us. Nagaoka Sensei had been a Colonel in the Army during WWII, so the Marines' military heritage was well-known to him.

The various high ranking Japanese instructors had a mixed attitude toward Americans. Some would allow foreigners to train, and others made it clear we were not allowed. A local Wado Ryu dojo wanted no Americans, but a fellow Marine, Paul Fenimore, continued going back until they finally let him in. The understanding was that they would allow him to train, but it was his responsibility to tell other Americans that they were not allowed. Paul was quite good and left Japan with his black belt. He subsequently returned to his home in Chicago and taught karate there for some time. Another local dojo, taught by Kawanabe Sensei, welcomed Americans, and several soldiers on the base trained there.

In many areas of Japan, mainly away from the bases, it was not uncommon to see signs on the doors of Japanese restaurants and other businesses stating that Americans were not welcome there. The war was not that far in the past. If I walked down the street with my Japanese girlfriend, the other Japanese assumed that she was a prostitute, as no self-respecting Japanese woman would be seen with an American.

Q: In 1963 you began splitting your training time between Nagaoka Sensei and Ohnishi Eizo Sensei. What can you tell us about Ohnishi Sensei's style, background, and teaching methods?

On some occasions I worked later hours and could not make it to Yokohama for class on time. On the way to Yamato one day I saw a sign on a post indicating that there was to be a new karate school opening in the town recreation center. This was only a few hundred yards outside the main base gate. There was a Japanese man about my age looking at it as well and he translated parts of it. We became acquainted and decided to train there when it opened the following week. About 30 people showed up on opening night, and I was the only American. Everything was in Japanese, so I followed as best I could. Onishi's style was one of the Shorin styles, but I am not sure exactly which. There are some Americans in New Jersey who trace their lineage to Onishi and call their style Koeikan, but I never heard that name in his classes. It is possible that he identified the system and organization to the students at some point, but my Japanese was not good enough to pick up on it.

I just got in line and followed as best I could. When he saw that I already had some training, he had me spar with his assistant instructor. I didn't embarrass myself, but the assistant instructor was pretty far out of my league and easily evaded my attacks. Onishi presented me with a lapel pin to his organization and a copy of a small book he had written. His training methods were fairly standard — basics, sparring drills, and kata. His kicking technique, however, was quite different. In all of the karate I had learned up to that point, the hips were thrust forward to add power to the kick. Onishi's method was to incline the upper body forward and tense the abdominal muscles to add power to the kick. This shortened the range of the kick but probably added a different type of power.

Many of the sparring drills had jumping movements, so it was a bit different than what I had learned previously. I only spent a few months with him, so I did not learn any of the basic kata as he did not cover any when I was there. However, I managed to pick up on his Kusanku kata, as he demonstrated it several times for the class. Kusanku was also shown step by step in the book he gave me, so I practiced that version until I switched to the Shotokan kata Kanku Dai. I have seen several varieties of the form over the year, but his was a bit different. He was small and very quick, so his kata included many jumps and dodges.

I believe that Onishi was affiliated with Toyama Kanken Sensei, as Toyama is pictured in his book. Additionally, the title page of his book indicates that he was a member of the Zen Nihon Karatedo Renmei (All Japan Karate Do Federation). Toyama Kanken is generally associated with Shudokan Karate. Onishi's teaching method was basically to demonstrate a drill or technique and then walk around as everyone practiced it, correcting where necessary.

Q: What differences did you experience in the Ohnishi program as compared to the Nagaoka program?

The main difference was that there was no throwing or grappling taught with Ohnishi Sensei, at least not on the level that Nagaoka Sensei was teaching at that time. The front kicking took some adjusting as I had to kick one way with Ohnishi and another way with Nagaoka. Instead of working on mats, Ohnishi Sensei worked on a wood floor in the town's recreation center. The floor was well-used, full of splinters and very dirty, but that was the venue in which we had to operate.

One night while I was training, my foot was snagged on a large nail head that protruded from the floor and it began bleeding. I showed it to Onishi Sensei and he sent his assistant to the local drugstore for some Mercurochrome, which we proceeded to dump on the wound. Having done that, the cut was wrapped in a dirty rag and I finished training that way. The bottoms of my feet were black from the dirty floor, so once back at base I headed directly to the infirmary where the corpsman on duty cleaned and dressed the wound properly. He also gave me a tetanus booster shot. Fortunately I did not get an infection.

Q: Was it difficult maintaining a full military work schedule as well as training seven days a week? Did you ever have an inclination to quit given the difficulty of training?

Life in the Marine Corps is generally difficult and you make time as best you can.

Fortunately, there were a number of us training at various dojo(s) in the area so if we couldn't get off base we trained together in the gym. After I had been in Japan for several months I landed a new job working in the training office and doing other administrative chores, so my job had regular hours. Also, many of us would get back to the base at 10-11 at night and run the perimeter of the airfield to give us additional conditioning.

As I noted earlier, I am not a drinker, so the nightlife in town had little appeal. There was not much else to do but go to the gym and workout. The base had a photography club, model airplane club, a diving club, etc. I joined the diving club for a while, but couldn't get used to diving with partners. Spearfishing was always a solitary endeavor. I decided I would rather take my chances with the elements alone than risk getting shot by another spear fisherman's gun in murky water.

Q: Are there any particularly difficult or rewarding memories you have from that time in Japan?

There are none that stand out, with the exception of my Japanese girlfriend, which was very positive. One thing I do remember is the weather. Japan has a rainy season and it seems as though it will never stop. The Japan Guide lists it as running from June 8 to July 20. During that time there is a good amount of rain, and on some days it seems that it will never end. Many of the places we had to patrol were covered with a foot or two of water, but we still had to slog through it on our rounds. The rubber ponchos we wore kept us from the rain, but the rubber just made us sweat so you never seemed to get dry. During that period, everything always seemed damp.

The two months after the new year, January and February, were particularly difficult for us. Walking the flight line on guard duty or guarding the radar installations at the ends of the runways was extremely cold. The wind howled out of the mountains and swept across the Kanto Plains to the sea. We wore our regular dungarees, a cold suit over that, and a field jacket with a hood on top. Long winter underwear was the norm as well as gloves. We carried .45 caliber M-1911 automatic pistols and a sawed off 12 gauge riot gun slung on our backs. It was so cold we could barely move, and our patrols consisted of shuffling along as best we could. At one o'clock in the morning, one hour into a four hour watch, you would give anything to be anywhere else. That is probably the only time I regretted being in the Corps. Many of the Marines I worked with had gone through boot camp at Parris Island with me, so we had a lot of friends around most of the time. More is better when you have to share misery.

Q: In 1963, you returned to the U.S.A. and began your relationship with Okazaki Sensei. Can you describe how that meeting came about and what your early impressions of Okazaki Sensei were?

When you return from an overseas tour, the Corps allows you 30 days leave. So in late August of 1963, I found myself back home in New Jersey. I was due to report to Camp Lejeune, North Carolina, after that. While I was in Japan, an issue of *Strength and Health Magazine* came out that had a story about Okazaki Sensei and how he had just come to Philadelphia. Fortunately the address was listed. After a few days at home, I packed my gi in a gym bag and headed for Philadelphia, a two hour drive.

I managed to find the dojo after a bit of city driving confusion. I parked around the corner and walked up the street to the dojo location. A couple of members were out front, and when they saw me coming, they looked at me strangely and moved away. Perhaps the Marine Corps haircut confused them. I walked through the front door at 222 S. 45th St. and entered the dojo that would be my focus for the next 51 years.

The office was in back, as indicated by a sign. I bowed to the pictures, took off my shoes, and crossed the empty training floor to the office area. It was midday, so Okazaki Sensei was out to lunch. One of his workers questioned me about whether I had trained before, and I told him I was just back from Japan where I had been training. He informed me that I "had not been trained." I wasn't sure who this guy was, but before any confrontation could take place, Okazaki Sensei came in. In my best (and probably very poor) Japanese, I introduced myself and showed him my rank from the Kobukan in Yokohama (I was ranked as a Shodan by Nagaoka Sensei). Okazaki Sensei explained to me that my style and school was unknown to him, but it didn't matter. I was welcome to train as a guest while on leave.

So I joined the Philadelphia Karate Club and trained a number of times over the next few weeks, prior to heading for Camp Lejeune. Okazaki Sensei explained that I could wear my black belt as a guest, but if I became a member I would have to put on a white belt and train for a minimum of six months until I could be tested. I told him it didn't matter to me as long as he would teach me. The first time training with him was revealing — he was just as good as I expected, and better. From that point on, I considered him to be my teacher.

Wearing a white belt while visiting a different dojo was a well-established Japanese tradition and showed humility. I had seen it many times in Japan when visiting "white belts" showed up at the Kobukan. The first time it happened, I thought that the guy was really good for a white belt. In time I came to understand that the new white belt might be a Nidan with many years of training. So I did not feel that it was a problem for me to wear a white belt. I was there to learn, not flaunt any prior knowledge.

Okazaki Sensei's teaching style was very technical and he emphasized the basics. Although Nishiyama Sensei in California was teaching a number of kata, Okazaki kept us on the five Heians, Tekki Shodan, Hangetsu and Bassai Dai. I was allowed to perform Gankaku in tournaments and practice it since I knew it prior to beginning training with him. One of my students at Camp Lejeune had trained with Mikami Sensei in Kansas City and knew a number of Shotokan kata, which he helped me learn as I taught him Shin Kage Ryu. A tremendous mix of karate styles existed on Marine bases, and that allowed us to expand our knowledge. Virtually all of it was Okinawan or Japanese as there were very few Marines stationed in Korea. Army and Air Force members were in Korea, and many of them brought back Korean styles of karate. From other Marines I learned some kata from Shorin Ryu and also learned to use the sai. We were all very open to what others knew and eagerly latched on to any knowledge we could get. For us, there were no styles, only karate, and we all wanted to increase our proficiency.

My time with Okazaki Sensei was limited by my long drive and the full class, so I did not get to spend much individual time with him in that first year. I soon returned to Camp Lejeune, NC, to finish out the last year of my enlistment.

At Lejeune I settled in to a desk job at the Base Motor Transport Company. This was a job with regular hours, and my rank of Corporal E-4 gave me a bit more responsibility and a bit more freedom. Camp Lejeune is next to the town of Jacksonville, which held little interest as it was filled with bars and pawn shops. I went to the gyms in search of a karate club.

There were several clubs on base at the time. Staff Sergeant Sam Pearson was the highest rank on the base, having been awarded a Yondan (4th degree black belt) in Shorin Ryu by Shimabuku Eizo Sensei during the last of his several tours in Japan and Okinawa. He had a nice club going and he trained alongside his students. Although I liked SSgt. Pearson, the style was just too different from the Shotokan I had decided to practice. So after a month or two with him, I quit.

I then went to the Area 10 Gym and contacted the manager about potentially starting my own group. At that point, the Kobukan Karate Club was formed and I taught a combination of Shin Kage Ryu and Shotokan as best I could. The 1963 Marine Corps Championships were held at Lejeune a month or so later and I participated, winning first place in sparring, third in kata, and the Grand Champion trophy. This was totally new as it was my first tournament (we never practiced sport karate at Nagaoka Sensei's dojo).

Members of the Kobukan Karate Club practice the knife hand block outside the Area 10 Gym at Camp Lejeune, NC, in February 1964.

At the end of 1963, SSgt. Sam Pearson was instrumental in forming the first Marine Corps Karate Team at Camp Lejeune. In early 1964, the base put about 15 of us on a bus and sent us to Toronto, Canada, to represent the Corps in the North American Karate Championships being run by Tsuruoka Mas Sensei. Tsuruoka Sensei was a traditional, respected Chito Ryu practitioner.

Black belt members of the Marine Corps Karate Team pose with other black belts and officials at the 1964 North American Karate Championships hosted by Tsuruoka Mas Sensei in Toronto, Canada. Back row standing 2nd from left is Corporal Peter Musachio, 4th from left is Corporal Robin Rielly, Front row kneeling 2nd from left is Sergeant Roland Albarado and 3rd from left is Staff Sergeant Sam Pearson. Tsuruoka Sensei is kneeling front and center wearing glasses.

We spent a week in Toronto visiting dojo(s), meeting with the American Ambassador, and participating in the tournament. We all won a few matches and Ssgt. Pearson placed in sparring, so we left the city with a sense of accomplishment. Later that year we had the 1964 Marine Corps Championships at the base and I won a few matches and then lost a close match to Gunnery Sergeant Don Bohan, an Isshin Ryu black belt who had trained on Okinawa. GySgt. Bohan went on to win the tournament.

My club on the base was doing well, and the Marine Corps Team was asked to participate in a publicity tour. It was to be about a six month tour and my time was running out, so I declined rather than extend my enlistment. I was granted an early out to attend college and left the Corps a few days short of my three years so as not to miss the opening of classes.

Q: Coming from a background in Shin Kage Ryu, was it a jarring experience becoming part of a big organization like the Japan Karate Association? Could you describe how it seemed to operate in those early days?

In Japan, I never paid much attention to organizations. Training day-by-day was my only concern. I know that Onishi Sensei was part of an organization, but I do not know about Nagaoka Sensei. However, I did know that J.K.A. rank was highly respected in Japan and so I was pleased that I could practice in that organization and achieve rank in it. There were a number of new American karate organizations looking for men like me with Japanese experience, and several offered me advanced rank if I were to join their group. My response was that I was not worth a higher rank. I preferred to be a J.K.A. Shodan (1st degree black belt) as opposed to a watered down Godan (5th degree black belt) in one of these groups.

Since I was one of the early black belts in Okazaki Sensei's group, I know that we all experienced the same thing — we were Shodans and figured we might never get any higher. Then, around 1966 or so, Maynard Miner made Nidan and we figured we might have a chance. In any case, we did not ask for testing — it was something you did not do. In 1967, Enoeda Sensei told me that I had to test for Nidan at the spring test; however, before the test, he was sent to England and courtesy dictated that I didn't bring the matter up again on my own. Two years later, in 1969, Okazaki Sensei realized I hadn't tested for a while, so I took the Nidan test and passed.

Q: Was there a strong focus on tournament play throughout the '60s and '70s in the J.K.A.? What were those early tournaments like?

When I first got out of the Marine Corps, it was fall of 1964. Since I was not able to get to Okazaki Sensei's dojo as much as I would have liked, I attended open tournaments in New York City for the next year. They were fairly wild, with some good competitors and some not so good. There were a few contestants who had obviously trained in Japan, and we stuck out like sore thumbs. After I saw one fighter in particular, I introduced myself to him and found that he had been in the Air Force in Japan about the same time I had. He trained in Shudokan, a style connected to Toyama Kanken. We became close friends, and he introduced me to his other friends who trained with him. Together we formed a small organization that existed for about a year.

1963 Marine Corps Championships at Camp Lejeune, NC. It was not uncommon for the winner in lower ranked belt classes to fight the winner in the brown belt class. The winner of that match then fought the winner in the black belt class for the Grand Championship. Here Corporal Glenn Premru (brown belt) squares off against Corporal Robin Rielly (black belt) (right) in the final match. The referee is Sergeant Roland Albarado. Rielly won the match and the Grand Champion's trophy taking first in sparring and third in kata.

Philadelphia was a long trip for all of us, so we depended on each other for training. In short order we realized that our knowledge was limited and we would have to find an instructor. No one in the New York metropolitan area impressed us, so by the end of 1964 we connected all five of our clubs to Okazaki Sensei formally. He and the J.K.A. would be our instructor and our home from that point on.

Understand that competition karate was quite new to the J.K.A. at this time. It had only begun in the late 1950s, so in 1964 J.K.A. tournament karate was in its infancy. As a result, tournament fighting was much different than it is today.

I asked Okazaki Sensei if I could compete, but he told me to just send my students. This was upsetting to me as I really liked the competition. Finally, in 1966, I competed in the East Coast Championships and did well. I continued to compete for the next couple of years until 1969. During that time I won first placed in kata twice and second and third a couple of times. Sparring was never very successful for me; I tended to be a bit wild. I usually won several matches and got to the semi-finals. Frequently at that point I would get disqualified for excessive contact.

In 1967, I was on the East Coast team and fought in the nationals run by Nishiyama Sensei in Los Angeles. After winning my first match, I drew Ken Funakoshi from Hawaii. I lost to him, and he went on to take second after losing to Frank Smith. On the East Coast there was always great rivalry between the Philadelphia club and the New York club run by Mori Masataka Sensei. My greatest challenges always came from Joe Gayol and Bob Shapoff, both of whom were excellent karate men. Nationally, there was a great rivalry between the East and West Coast, but the Hawaiians had been taught by Mori, Asai, and Kanazawa Senseis and were always strong. Ken Funakoshi and George Sasano were always right at the top, but no one seemed to be able to beat Frank Smith from Nishiyama's dojo.

J.K.A. tournaments were always hotly contested, and those fighting in them were very strong. Techniques were definitely killing blows, mostly front kicks and counter punches. We all knew how to back kick, but to turn your back on a Shotokan player was akin to committing suicide. We were not trained to go back, but to charge straight in as soon as we perceived an opening. I recall team training with Kisaka Sensei standing behind us as we sparred. If you backed up or didn't press an attack, you got slammed across the back with the kendo shinai as he screamed, "Attack!" Our philosophy was that we'd rather get hit coming in, rather than stand there and get beaten with the shinai.

In 1969, I prepared for the nationals tournament which was held in Philadelphia. On

Saturday evening, I took my Nidan test in front of Miyata Sensei and Okazaki Sensei. I passed (as mentioned earlier), but broke my right big toe in the process. When I got up in the morning, it was so swollen that I could barely walk and could not compete. It would have been my last tournament. That fall, as I prepared for the next East Coast event, I received a call from Okazaki Sensei telling me that from that point on I would not compete — I had to be a judge. And so ended my competition career.

In the late 1960s and early 1970s, the J.K.A. clubs were one organization (All American Karate Federation) and were serious competition for the Japanese. Frank Smith beat Ueki Mas Sensei in a famous match in Los Angeles, and we could compete with anyone in the world. Unfortunately, the A.A.K.F. came apart in the early 1970s and our strength was divided.

Q: Has there ever been a heavy focus on application in kata (bunkai) during your Shotokan training? If so, how important is it to the curriculum?

We did applications as we practiced the various kata so that we could understand the importance of certain body positions and perform the kata movements correctly. It was a given that each movement could have a variety of applications. So while it was important in the curriculum, it never formed the single focus for a class.

Q: Do Shotokan basics evolve throughout a practitioner's career or do they always involve deep stancing and large movements?

Shotokan uses large movements and deep stances for training as it helps to build muscle strength and reinforce correct movement. In actual fighting, stances are shorter. As a result of large movement and deep stance training, it is easier to build power for short movements. As one advances in their training, this becomes evident. It is not usually evident to those who do not practice Shotokan as they tend to focus their interest on basic training and kata. If one watches a Shotokan match, he will notice that the long, deep stance is usually used at the moment you deliver a technique against the opponent. At other times, you keep a shorter stance to improve mobility. Every fighter is different, and the basic training gives them the ability to vary movement.

Q: Did you ever integrate hojo undo (basic body conditioning) into your training?

Although we had a sand bucket in the gym to strengthen our hands for spear hand thrusts, we did not have a makiwara. We simply chopped down oak saplings about head height, taped a paperback novel over them, and then an old rag or towel. They worked very well, and we had a number scattered through the area. We frequently made runs through the tank tracks near the base, stopping at various makiwara we built, doing drills in the open spaces in the woods.

Q: When did you decide you wanted to become an author on the topics of Shotokan Karatedo and World War II? Was writing something you always enjoyed?

After I left the Marine Corps in late August 1964, I attended Rider College to finish my BA degree. I spent three years there supporting myself by teaching karate at three locations. After my first year back the G.I. Bill came through, and between that and my

Corporal Robin Rielly practices against a makiwara at Camp Lejeune, NC.

three karate clubs I did very well. An additional source of income came from my wife. She had continued in school when I left to go into the service and was an elementary school teacher. In all, we were financially stable. I graduated from Rider in 1967 with a Bachelor of Arts degree in political science. By that time I had a great interest in Japanese history and culture. I enrolled in a Master's Degree program in Japanese Area Studies at Seton Hall University, graduating in 1969. One of the requirements for the degree was the completion of a thesis. My original plan was to do something on Japanese politics or culture, but the department chairman, Dr. John B. Tsu, persuaded me to write about karate since it was something I knew about and little had been done in research on the topic. So my master's thesis was entitled, "A Study of the Development of Karate in the United States."

While at Seton Hall, I formed a karate club there and also had another in the nearby town of Millburn. One of my students in the Millburn branch of the Kobukan was a printer by trade, and we photographed and produced study sheets on the first three Heian Kata for sale to my students. That was my first foray into writing about karate. It occurred to me that my thesis might be marketable, but I had little knowledge of how to get published, so I asked my student if he knew. After consulting with his family, they decided that they would publish my book and distribute it. The initial printing was 1,000 copies and it was entitled *The History of American Karate*, and it was published in 1970. It sold the initial printing, but marketing was difficult for the printing company, so that was the end of that project. However, it was well-received by the university and was written up in the *New York Daily News* along with a photo of my wife and me holding the book.

My WWII research and writing came from my attempt to learn more about my father's WWII experiences in the Navy. Like many veterans who have been in serious combat, he spoke little about it, except to mention some friends that he had served with. In 1989, the National Association of U.S.S. LCS(L) 1-130 was formed. Within a few years he had heard of it and went to his first convention. In 1993, I attended one with him for a couple of days in Washington, DC. There I met some of his shipmates and saw a model of the LCS(L) gunboat type on which he served. It was my original plan to build a model of his ship for him, however, plans were hard to find so I decided to write the history of the ship. I learned that his ship had been on the infamous radar picket line off Okinawa in the summer of 1945, where the picket ships bore the brunt of the kamikaze attacks. His ship, LCS(L) 61, had been under attack a number of times and had shot down five kamikazes. One of them, a Betty twin-engine bomber, missed his 160' long gunboat by only about ten feet.

Q: Could you tell us a little about the other J.K.A. seniors you spent time with and what they added to your overall training?

Between 1967 and 1968, Enoeda Keinosuke Sensei was here on the East Coast as Okazaki Shihan's assistant. He visited my clubs regularly, and I traveled to wherever he was teaching each Saturday to further my knowledge. Many who trained with him in England for a much longer time would probably tell you he was inspirational. I always looked forward to his classes, and even though they were hard he did not abuse his students.

Q: You've described in a previous interview how Kisaka Katsuya Sensei taught, going so far as to deliver frequent high impact punches and kicks on students. In hindsight, do you believe this "spirit testing" kind of aggression was healthy for students, and do you think it has a place in modern martial arts?

Spirit training yes, but abusing students is a definite no. A competent instructor knows just how far he can push students so that they learn to perservere, even if they think they can't. It is the instructor's responsibility to foster student growth and to prevent injury wherever possible.

Q: Did you ever get to see and spend more time with your original two instructors from Japan, Nagaoka and Ohnishi?

Once I left Japan, I kept in touch with Nagaoka Sensei for a couple of years. My friends in Japan told me he closed the Kobukan in Yokohama and moved to Tokyo. At that point I lost contact with him. One of my American friends went to work in Tokyo in the 1990s and I asked him to look for Nagaoka Sensei, but he couldn't locate him. At the time I trained with him, in 1962-63, he was 48 years old and I was 20-21. Since I am now 72 years old, he would have to be around 100, so I am sure that he has passed on. I hope the book I wrote on Shin Kage Ryu for him will preserve his memory for awhile. I only trained with Onishi Sensei for a few months, so I have never had any contact with him, with the exception of getting some knowledge of him from Ed Kaloudis years ago. Mr. Kaloudis trained with him and represented his style on the East Coast for many years.

Q: How have you seen yourself grow both as a practitioner and teacher as you've become a senior in the art of Shotokan?

I think that I have matured in my approach to teaching. In my younger days as an instructor, I pushed my students just as I had been pushed. They achieved proficiency and had great fighting spirit. The things we did in the '60s and '70s would simply generate lawsuits today, so instructors really have to be careful.[91]

As far as my personal practice is concerned, now that I am 72, it is obvious to me that my body cannot perform as it did when I was 25 or 30. So I have to adapt techniques and practice them in such a manner that is practical for me.

---

[91] Image courtesy of the I.S.K.F.

Q: How would you like to see Shotokan grow as future generations take the responsibility of carrying on the art?

I would like to see it grow, but not at the expense of watering down karate or changing the traditions. As each country adopted karate, they changed it to suit their culture. I would like to see karate keep its traditional aspects as I feel there is much to be gained in learning that way.

Chapter 15 –
Shuri Ryu

Of all the styles included in this book, Shuri Ryu is the sole art created by a Westerner. Style creation is a subtle matter, born of either organizational necessity or significant technique alteration. Robert Trias, founder of Shuri Ryu, traveled extensively but found himself stationed back in the United States with no karate precedent to rely upon. So, in 1946, Trias Sensei began teaching out of his small home dojo located in Phoenix, Arizona. Two years later, he established the United States Karate Association, and began the long road to prominence.

Trias Sensei's personal training came during his time in the military. His primary instructor was Hsing Tong Gee, whom he met in the early 1940s. Hsing Sifu was said to teach both Hsing-I (Xing Yi Quan) and Shuri Tode Ryu (Shuri Te), and was purported to be a nephew of Motobu Choki, the great Okinawan fighter.[92] Trias Sensei combined this foundational training with his prior experience in boxing, later expanding his knowledge with Chinese Kempo, Judo, and Goju Ryu. The result was Shuri Ryu, born as a result of Trias Sensei's travel while in the military and tireless efforts to research and innovate in the martial arts.

As one of the earliest and most recognizable masters in America, Trias Sensei attracted a wide variety of students from all over the country. Many of the early Western practitioners were multi-style men, similar to Trias Sensei himself. Under Trias's guidance, they all grew

---

[92] Corcoran, John, Emil Farkas, and Stuart Sobel. *The Original Martial Arts Encyclopedia: Tradition, History, Pioneers.* Publisher Location: Pro-Action Pub., 1993. 230. Print.

together and the U.S.K.A. organization became one of those most well-known in the country, its events drawing hundreds if not thousands of participants and spectators.

Victor Moore

Victor Moore is a unique martial arts personality and competitive champion. Moore Sensei is an eclectic stylist yet traditionalist at the same time. His earliest martial experience came in the form of Judo, however he branched out into Chinese Kempo in the mid 1950s. He continued to expand his knowledge, studying Chito Ryu, Goju Ryu, Shotokan, and Shuri Ryu, while also pursuing Judo and winning competitions.

Moore Sensei was a staple on the tournament circuit during a time of great prestige and exposure for tournament-style karate. He fought and defeated some of the biggest name competitors of the day, including Joe Lewis, Mike Stone, and Glenn Keeney. He also distinguished himself as an instructor and became one of the trusted keepers of Shuri Ryu, appointed to the prestigious Trias International Society. He accomplished all this while facing serious racial prejudice from other martial artists and society at large.

Q: Moore Sensei, could you describe when and where you were born?

I was born in 1943 and am originally from the Cincinatti, Ohio, area. My neighborhood was pretty rough, what you might consider a ghetto. There was some activity in the way of gangs, people fighting, that sort of stuff.

Q: Did you ever find yourself getting mixed up in gang activities?

No, I never did. I had strict parents and they kept us in line. We had to learn how to take care of ourselves, too. My father was loving, but ran a tight household and insisted I join a number of organizations in the area (Cub Scouts, Boy Scouts, explorers, etc.). I got started in the Boy Scouts around seven years of age, and joined sports clubs early, too, so I had good structure.

Q: What was your earliest introduction to the martial arts?

In the mid-1950s there was an older boy in my neighborhood who would show some of us younger kids basic jujutsu techniques. That interested me since I knew trouble might find us on any given day. Shortly after, a local Y.M.C.A. opened a Judo program in addition to weightlifting and boxing programs. This started at the Melrose Y.M.C.A. and then the 9th Street Y.M.C.A.

The Melrose Judo program was operated by a gentleman named Buzzy Smith. The boxing coach was Joe Joiner. I worked out there and became a sparring partner for "Tiger" Joe Harris at the age of 14, and often fought with the adults.

Q: Could you describe the teaching style of the early Judo programs?

They were pretty militaristic in nature. The instructors had gained their skills during wartime. The military style followed them into the dojo and we trained with strict discipline and behavior.

Q: Considering the rigors of militaristic training, what kept you engaged in martial arts?

There was just a general excitement to it. I was always involved in physical fitness. I found that my active lifestyle and interest in fitness allowed me to excel in the martial arts arena.

During that time I began competing in boxing, managing to win all 12 of my amateur matches. My love of competition certainly aided in my martial pursuits, all of which helped keep me from getting beat up and picked on, that's for sure.

Q: When did you branch out into karate itself?

My introduction to karate came in 1956. I had seen some demonstrations from Oyama Masutatsu Sensei on TV, and since I was already doing Judo and jujutsu I felt like I wanted to learn what karate was all about. Unfortunately, karate schools were few and far between.

One day I found out about a gentleman named Ronald Williams who worked out in the woods near where I lived. I went up the hill and told him that I was hoping to learn some of the techniques he was doing. He just said, "You're too young, boy. Go away." I kept bugging him every day, and finally he let me visit. Shortly after, I became his little punching bag. Ronald's brother heard about the training and decided he wanted to try as well. Mr. Williams's goal was to make us reconsider and go away, but we just stuck with it.

Victor Moore during his early days of kempo and karate training.[93]

So while studying with Mr. Williams I noticed that a Judo program had opened up on

---

[93] Images courtesy of Chad Wissler.

Vine Street in Cincinnati. I was interested in continuing my Judo, but the Vine Street school was located in a section of town that black folks didn't go. I decided to venture up anyway. I got there and asked if I could come in. It took a little while but they finally relented, although it was clear they were uncomfortable with me entering a white establishment. I became their uke in the Judo program, figuring they would be more at ease if I let them throw me around a little bit. Eventually the instructor, Ray Hughes, got used to the idea of me being there.

After becoming a regular student at the Judo school, I noticed there was also a small karate class operated by a gentleman named Harvey Eubanks. There were no black people in that program at the time, so it was an unusual request when I asked to join. They decided to accept me, but I had to start all over in terms of style and rank — my experience with Mr. Williams did not cross over. In fact, by the time they had accepted me I had already been a student of Mr. Williams for a number of years and had achieved black belt status with him. That didn't matter of course. I was a white belt again in the new program.

They were very exacting, and we had to do everything specific to the way the style demanded it. It felt like they were trying to get me to quit, but by then I had gotten somewhat used to that sensation. I made sure to work hard, clean the dojo, and do all the things a good student would do so they wouldn't have a reason to expel me. Eventually Eubanks Sensei took a liking to me.

Q: You mention a strict adherence to style at the Vine Street dojo. What style did they teach?

The first instructor, Harvey Eubanks, was a Goju Ryu practitioner. Later the program was taken over by William Dometrich who had direct experience studying with Chitose Tsuyoshi of Chito Ryu. Mr. Eubanks had studied Goju Ryu on Okinawa while in the military, although I don't recall his specific instructors.

Dometrich Sensei, who had studied in Japan with Chitose Sensei, was a tough teacher and karate man. He would have us do fingertip pushups, knuckle pushups, and the like. He taught in a regimented style, which was typical for military men and Japanese teachers. It was thanks to him that I actually got to meet and train with Chitose Sensei himself, which was a great honor.

Coincidentally, it was only after studying with Mr. Eubanks and Mr. Dometrich that I realized my first instructor, Ronald Williams, had been teaching a style more heavily influenced by Chinese elements (we had just called it "kempo"). Thanks to his military experience, Mr. Williams was able to travel around the Far East, so he also had experience in Japanese influenced karate, which he was able to integrate into his teachings.

Around 1961, I met an exchange student at the Vine Street school named Chung Leang who studied Chi Un Fa. He was a big influence on me, especially in terms of combative effectiveness. He stressed being light and mobile and would test us in unique ways. I remember one time he was focusing on us removing as much tension from our bodies as possible. He would come up to us, one at a time, and blow at us. He would then analyze how much that blow made us waiver, determining how light we were. He explained that an inward drawing of breath should be sensitive enough to actually pull your body forward. This meditation and concentration allowed us to control minute distances, giving us enhanced quickness and deceptiveness.

Chung Leang Sifu had tough training methods, including hitting us with bamboo. He had a method where he suspended a string in front of us and made us kick over it. If we didn't get our knee up high enough we would interfere with the string, and he would punish us with pushups. During kumite he would tie two opponents together about a foot apart so that they could not retreat from each other, relying instead on angling and technique. He would also hold a stick at about waist level and make us kick before the stick hit the ground. Then he would lower the stick to knee level and make us kick again. The stick got lower and lower and it felt like a quickdraw contest. Through him I learned that timing is just as important as speed, if not more so.

Q: After your time at Vine Street, where did your martial arts journey take you next?

Eventually the karate program on Vine Street closed, but luckily a school opened up not long after on Redding Road. This was operated by a gentleman named James Wax. I went up first to join the Judo program but found out that Mr. Wax was operating a Shorin Ryu Karate outfit as well. This turned out to be a time of growth for me in both arts.

As a teacher, Wax Sensei followed the formula of being tough and trying to make you quit. Robert Yarnall was a good student of his, whom I had met during tournaments and the like. I found the stances and hip movement to be fairly similar to my previous experiences, so I didn't have too much trouble adapting. Of course, the kata had their own flavor and I had to make sure to do it their way without influence from my previous styles.

One time we were jogging around the training floor and there was a little *tick, tick, tick* sound as we went. Wax Sensei stopped the class and asked, "What's that ticking sound?" We didn't know, so we just went back to running. Once we started there it was again, *tick, tick.* He stopped us and said, "Something must be on somebody's foot." I looked down and right in the ball of my foot was a roofing tack.

Thanks to all of my training, I had developed very thick calluses and the roofing nail just happened to end up in there. I didn't feel it, which was lucky because it would have hurt like heck. That moment made me think about all the tough training like kicking makiwara, running around in the forest with Williams Sensei and kicking trees, as well as holding class out on the hot blacktop where your feet were almost blistering. It was pretty brutal, but I was thankful that day for it.

One of the other great things about the Redding Road program is that one of the top Judo men in the world taught there. He was a Detroit and Chicago man but found his way down to Cincinnati. His name was John Osako.

Q: What was it about Osako Sensei that made him so special?

Besides just being an outstanding instructor, he knew how to counter, work sweeps, and adapt to people from other

John Osako, a renowned Judo champion in America.

styles. He could beat folks from Aikido, Judo, jujutsu . . . it didn't matter. One time I almost threw him. I had him up and over and was getting ready to slam him but somehow he rolled off, reversed it, and I hit the mat. I would often say that whenever I was training with Osako Sensei all I got to see was the ceiling because I was flat on my back so often.

I learned a lot of excellent techniques from him, and he improved my Judo greatly. I'm glad I had an opportunity to work with him. Osako Sensei ran a strict class, and, much like some of my prior experiences, I got the feeling that he was daring us all to quit. We had to work hard to keep up.

Q: Did Redding Road become a permanent home for you in terms of training?

Unfortunately that school ended up closing as well, and I wasn't sure what to do next. I was in the process of trying to go to college. I had a desire to be an engineer, helping to design and build buildings. I was accepted into Central State College in Wilberforce, Ohio. I wasn't that great of a student, but I was really drawn to engineering so I decided to try anyway.

At college I met a wrestling champion from Pennsylvania named Johnny Henderson. He and I hit it off pretty good. He wanted to learn something about karate and I was interested in learning more wrestling. So just about every day we got out onto the mat, showing and sharing. We were two peas in a pod. We got some funny looks and were laughed at for training so much, but we didn't care.

Eventually it got to the point where my training was taking over social activities and studies. Whenever I got back to my dorm room my roommate had to scold me and tell me to focus on my class work. Thanks to him I was able to stay in college and even found time to join the Pershing Rifle Team for the Army Reserve Officer's Training Corps (R.O.T.C.). The drill team started with 50 or so interested members but got whittled down to about 15. I'm sure without the discipline of martial arts I wouldn't have been one of the remaining members.

Q: Did you continue your karate training while in college?

Yes, I did. While there I met a Japanese professor by the name of Barry Yasuto. He was versed in Shotokan, and as Shotokan schools tended to be in those days, he was very regimented and tough. While working with him, I had to start over as a white belt despite some of my previous experience. That was fine with me . . . I just wanted to learn.

Eventually, over the years, I was able to achieve my black belt in Shotokan thanks to Yasuto Sensei's consistent teaching. I felt like I earned it since I did things his way, starting over from scratch, and coming up through the ranks. After achieving black belt I was hoping to get a membership card to join the Japanese Karate Association, but I was told

Americans couldn't join the J.K.A. I never found out the true motivation for keeping me out, whether it was race, ethnicity, or something else.

One thing I was sure of at that time is that blacks were not being accepted into engineering jobs. I was applying all around, even in my home town, and could not break into the field. I couldn't even secure an apprenticeship, despite being properly educated. That's when I decided to drop out of college and put my efforts somewhere more useful.

I told my mom, "Why keep spending all this money if I can't even get a second glance in this field?" She replied, "Well what are you going to do for money? You need a job!" I said, "I think I'm going to teach karate." She replied, "How are you going to make a living doing that juju stuff?"

Truthfully, I didn't have a good answer for her at the time. There weren't many long-term success stories of people teaching karate for a living. Worse yet, there wasn't an abundance of karate schools in the country to help develop a large amount of interest from the public. The general American interest was still in Judo at that point.

Around 1962, I made the leap to start teaching. I was still living with my folks, so I was able to save up a little bit of money and rent out a storefront. Luckily for me the school picked up some momentum which allowed me to travel and compete. From there I was able to grow a bit of a name for myself and the school.

Q: Was it difficult attracting students with the lack of general public knowledge of karate and the potential for racial prejudice against a black teacher?

I found it wasn't as hard attracting them as it was keeping them. I had come from a long line of very tough instructors, so naturally I was as hard as they were. A lot of students experienced the pushups, low stances, and repetitions, and realized it wasn't something they wanted to put themselves through.

A funny thing started to happen at tournaments in those days. We instructors would get together and compare numbers of students. If you had too many students, everyone assumed you were soft. It became an odd badge of honor to be able to say you only had a few students, because that meant you were tough.

Q: Having a diverse background in Goju Ryu, Shorin Ryu, Shotokan, and Chinese kempo, what did you actually teach when you opened your school?

Throughout my training in Cincinnati and college I maintained my relationship with Ron Williams up in the hills. He was skeptical of me teaching other folks and sharing what I had learned. Despite his reservations, I taught some of the soft system he shared with me but also some of the hard systems of Shotokan and Goju Ryu.

Some days we would study the way the body worked (things like anatomy, pressure points, etc). Then we might work circular and soft methods. Other days we would do hard techniques and object breaking. I think my success and the success of my students can be attributed to this mix of softness with speed and agility and hard power with toughness.

Q: After you opened your school, you started getting seriously involved in tournament competition, wherein you became one of the great champions of your generation. Did you find success right away or was there a steep learning curve with lots of barriers in the way?

That reminds me of a funny question my son asked me one day. He said, "Dad, I heard you telling the story about how you placed in every tournament between 1965-1975 and won all of these championships . . . but what about *before* 1965?"

I told him, "Shhh, nevermind that! Hahaha."

But no — I think it's important to note that some of the earliest tournaments we gathered at were in Canada, namely Ontario. They actually started there before becoming popular here in the U.S.A. They had published little magazines about the events and sent them down to instructors here in the States, saying that everyone was welcome from all styles. This started in the late 50s, and I made my first trip up around 1960-1961.

I had competed quite a bit in that early era with mixed results. I frequently got to the quarter and semifinals in tournaments, but was struggling to secure first or second place. One time I was on the way back from Canada with my wife and she started in on me saying, "You let them boys beat you? You let them get the best of you again?" My wife, Nancy Allen Moore, had started her own karate training in 1962 and was able to critique the matches. She started her competitive career in 1965 in kata and joined in with kumite in 1966.

Victor Moore shown in strong physical condition during his tournament years.

We got into this big argument, and I pulled the car over so that we could argue better. She was getting on me saying that I had to make more contact, and so on and so on. She was a great student of karate so she knew what she was talking about. I got so steamed that day that I vowed never to lose another match. I trained so hard when I got back home that when the next tournament came around I was dominating my opponents at will. From then on, until my retirement in 1975, I placed in every tournament I entered. Not only that, but I was consistently winning in kata, weapons, and breaking as well.

Q: In regards to your success in kumite (fighting), you were one of the smaller fighters on the circuit. How did you manage to keep up with the men that were bigger, longer, and stronger?

It was mostly about knowing how to move. Thanks to my mixture of Chinese, Japanese, and Okinawan training, I could get down in very low stances where they couldn't get me and then spring in quickly with force. I made sure never to back up on a straight line, but to sidestep in order to gain an angle advantage. Good, fundamental karate technique is really what did it.

In 1963, Robert Trias Sensei was testing me for my Nidan. As part of the test he wanted to find out just how good I was at fighting. To test my limits he had me fight John Keehan, later known as "Count Dante" and founder of the Black Dragon Fighting Society. Keehan was a top level fighter and experienced martial artist. I didn't beat him, but neither did he beat me. Being able to take Keehan to a draw was good enough proof for Trias Sensei, and he granted me the promotion. John Keehan turned out to be a strong advocate for allowing minorities into the U.S.K.A. and tournaments.

Q: One of your milestones was in 1965 when you won the United States Karate Association National Championships, making you the first African American to accomplish such a feat. What did it mean to you to win that?

It actually means a little more to me now than it did back then. At the time I was deep in the circuit and fighting everybody. At the U.S.K.A. events, I came to know Master Trias, and he would go so far as to request which techniques he wanted to see me fight with. I had some of the animal forms (tiger, leopard, snake, crane), and he would want to see those type of movements.

In 1965, big Mike Foster, 6'7" or so and about 270 pounds, used to travel with Dr. Chitose and some others as a bodyguard (or so I heard). He would get down in a low, wide kibadachi and crawl in toward you, getting closer and closer. He would use little scoots to make subtle advances. From there he could reach out, grab you, snatch you up, throw a reverse punch, and either knock you down or throw you around. He was that strong and big that he could make it work on a regular basis. He would also transition into a side stance and throw a sidekick and knock people clear out of the ring.

I was set to face Foster at the U.S.K.A. event and I thought to myself, if I have to fight this guy I better go into a light cat stance, slightly crouched for speed, and make my blocks from there. It had worked in the past where I blocked from this position and then sprung in with a reverse punch or what have you. I began my fight with Foster using this tactic, but he kicked me so hard that it hit my block, sending me back out of the ring and into the bleachers. I said, "Wow! Oh shoot, this isn't gonna work."

So, when I got back into the ring, I stopped waiting for him to come to me. Instead, I went into him, around him, jumped up onto his leg, grabbed his gi, swung up onto his back, etc. Master Trias said I looked like a monkey swinging on a branch (not a racial comment, just based on the way I had to climb all around Mike). I had to use all kinds of techniques, but in the end I won. Afterward Trias Sensei said, "That is one of the best matches I have ever seen!"

Q: Did you feel any pushback after that victory from individuals who didn't like seeing an African American winning national events?

Well, there were certainly folks who didn't even like seeing me compete in the first place. There were times when I had to be escorted into events. On some occasions Master Trias or the Black Dragon Fighting Society had to step in and insist that I be permitted access.

The resistance came from event staff, but also from hotels and venues associated with the tournaments that simply didn't want blacks in their establishments. I remember one time being held outside a hotel and Master Trias said, "Well if you don't let him in there won't be any tournament because he is the defending champion."

Q: Could you talk a little bit more about how your relationship with Trias Sensei grew and what he contributed to your overall learning?

I was fortunate in that Trias Sensei took me under his wing. Master Trias knew a lot about the formal ways of Asian training and shared a lot of that with me. He stressed things like proper bowing and etiquette just as much as technique. If you recall, I mentioned earlier that I got to train with Chitose Tsuyoshi when he was brought over by William Dometrich. As Chitose Sensei was greeting all the students, he noticed the formal way I did my bowing. This really caught his eye, and we spent more time together after that. Chitose Sensei showed me a number of techniques that I ended up using in tournaments and were key to some of my victories. To think, it all started with proper bowing as shown to me by Trias Sensei!

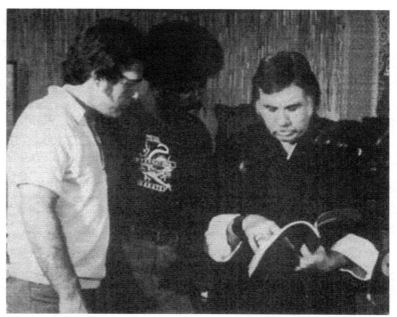

Victor Moore with Robert Trias (right) and Jim McLain (left).

Q: Were there any other tournaments or events in the 1960s that stand out in your memory?

Quite a few, as I was very active during those times. In 1966 I attended the U.S.K.A. World Championships held in Richmond, Virginia, hosted by Daniel Pai. In that tournament I was able to defeat the All Hawaiian Champion. My wife was able to win the brown belt division against male competitors.

I remember in 1967, at the Jhoon Rhee International, they had brought the All Korean Champion over from Korea and had a delegation of about 16 people. This champion was putting on a demonstration of splits and kicks, putting his foot up over his head and touching the wall behind him. I had some people come up to me and say, "Oh, Vic Moore, do you see who you're going to have to fight? You got your hands full now!" I said in response, "Yea that looks good, but the walls aren't hitting back." Word got out that I had said that, and there was some buzz around the gymnasium about "Vic Moore calling out the champion."

When it finally came time for the fight, I don't believe he was prepared for my Judo background. I was able to grab him, spin him around, and control him. Also, I don't think he expected me to be able to jump as well as him, since I was a karate guy and not a taekwondo guy. This worked to my advantage, and one time when he jumped to do a flying side kick I jumped up too and kicked him out of the air. I'll never forget that because the Koreans got very mad at me. The tournament directors actually had to call in highway patrol toward the end of the event because they were worried there would be an incident.

Unfortunately, despite the fact that I had won my match during this round-robin style tournament, Jhoon Rhee did not let me compete in the final round. Joe Lewis ended up winning that tournament, but it was sad because I wasn't given the opportunity to compete in the appropriate matches.

Even with incidences like the one at Jhoon Rhee's tournament, I have to say the quality of the competitors was very high at most of the bigger events in those days. There were times when you had half a dozen champion level competitors lining up against one another. You couldn't just worry about winning, you had to worry about placing at all! It was a pleasure competing against quality individuals, and we would seek each other out.

A few other notable tournaments for me include the U.S.K.A. 1ˢᵗ World Pro Karate Championships at the World's Fair in 1968 where I beat Joe Lewis. I also defeated Mike Stone in 1969 at the 1ˢᵗ U.S.A. Pro Team Karate Championships in Long Beach, California. I remember that Mike Stone would come in hard and catch guys with a sweep and ridgehand. He would hit them right between the eyes and send them flying to the mat. When our match came up, he hooked me and was coming in hard, but thanks to my Judo background I knew how to counter it. I was able to throw him down on his head and shoulder. He dislocated his shoulder at that time and was disqualified because he couldn't continue. Also, in 1970, I was able to defeat Bill "Superfoot" Wallace at the U.S.K.A. Pro-Am World Championship.

Victor Moore Sensei during a classic bout against Bill "Superfoot" Wallace.

As a sidenote, I often get asked about the time Bruce Lee and I did a demonstration together in 1967. This has become somewhat infamous because the clip of Bruce Lee punching at me is used in a lot of his highlight reels. Bruce was trying to build his reputation in Hollywood, and one of the things he anchored his reputation on was speed.

During the 1967 demo he asked for an assistant to help show how he could punch faster than anyone could block. In truth, a lot of the champions of the day didn't pay too much mind to him because he had never proved himself in real matches. However, Robert Trias told me to hop up and be Bruce's partner. I did what I was told. Without going into excess detail, I will say that Bruce was fast . . . but not so fast that I couldn't block him. To learn more about that encounter, go online and search for "Vic Moore: The Man That Fought 'Em All." It is a small biographical explanation of this particularly interesting encounter.

Vic Moore and Bruce lee during the speed test.

Q: Could you discuss your transition into full-contact-style fighting?

The transition started around 1970 when we put on the first kickboxing tournament in California (Lee Faulkner, Joe Lewis, Greg Baines, Jim Harrison, myself, and a few others). These proved to be some rough competitions. Joe Lewis had hit Greg Baines so hard and so many times that Greg ended up having open brain surgery.

Joe Lewis and I had actually introduced kickboxing on American TV on the Merv Griffin Show. We weren't going full speed at each other, but we weren't going slow either. We decided that we wanted to put on a good show and let the American people see how karate competition was being translated into full contact. Even though it was called kickboxing early on, it still operated with good karate technique.

During the demo we were tagging each other solidly, laughing and smiling and having a good time. Even though we were enjoying ourselves, it was so vicious looking that the producer of the TV show stopped the match. He thought it was far too violent to continue. This was an early sign — full contact would have to be adapted and softened for popular public consumption in the coming years.

Victor Moore during his victory over Joe Lewis in 1968. Moore Sensei and Lewis Sensei would go on to demonstrate full contact kickboxing on the Merv Griffin Show.

Q: In the late '60s and early '70s, Robert Trias set about establishing the Trias International Society, an early Hall of Fame model used to honor impactful martial artists. You were one of the first 10 inductees. What did that mean to you to receive that honor?

With Ed Parker, Allen Steen, Jhoon Rhee, and others putting on tournaments, there became a challenge for who could put on the biggest and best events. Master Trias had to work hard to keep the best fighters and most well-organized events. I was succeeding in tournaments but was also preserving the Shuri Ryu curriculum in terms of the techniques, kata, and waza. I was producing good quality students who were also winning in competition. I helped teach a number of Master Trias's early students, including his daughter Roberta. As a result, I was honored to be the first African American inducted into the group.

The Trias International Society was indeed like a Hall of Fame, except you didn't have to pay $300 to get inducted and treated to a fancy dinner.

Q: As you got older, did you see any negative health effects from the intensity of your training?

No, and I attribute that to getting good advice from my teachers. I haven't had to change my techniques, but I have gotten more wisdom on how to use them. One of the things that makes me wonder about modern karate — everybody is a Soke (founder) of some new style, 10th Dan in five or six different styles. It's impossible for them to have perfected anything, let alone invent something new. I've been asked if I ever wanted to create a new style based on my unique background, and I always say no because I haven't mastered any one of my core styles.

The question remains for new Soke: what is it that you have developed that hasn't already been developed? Is it possible you think you've created something new because you didn't learn enough about your core arts? Mixing and mashing techniques from different styles is fine for cross training, but it does not warrant a new style complete with self-promotion to high ranks.

Q: What made you decide to ultimately retire from competition?

I didn't like the direction karate was going. I was first involved in competition with kata, breaking, point sparring, and so on. Later I got involved with full-contact kickboxing-style matches. However, I noticed padding was becoming more and more prevalent. That was fine at first as it allowed us to throw full intensity techniques while protecting the other person in case there was a slip in control. However, the pads became an excuse to lose technique entirely and just swing wildly with full contact.

The pads also led to the popularity of techniques that, without the pads, could be dangerous to oneself. For example, we rarely kicked with the instep of the foot in our karate training. The instep is full of nerves and weaker bone structure than the ball and the heel. For roundhouse kicks we would always use the ball of the foot. The padding on top of the foot was there to protect the naturally weaker structure. Unfortunately, kicking with the ball is more difficult and can lead to jamming the toe if the technique isn't good. Kicking with the instep was easier and padded, so it became popular.

Tournament judges back in the early days would judge the quality of a punch just as much as the impact of the punch. They would check if the person was striking with the front two knuckles and with proper bone alignment. When pads came along, we were no longer able to tell the bone alignment. In addition, the striking surface mattered less so you started seeing a great deal more boxing style technique since it made sense with the thick gloves on. This moved us further away from real karate during competition.

I also noticed there was more and more jumping up and down while people were fighting. This is something you might see during a street fight when boys are trying to dance around each other while throwing jabs. You might also see it in sport fights like kickboxing. You do not (and should not) see it in karate, yet it was becoming popular in karate matches.

As time went on, these things became the norm and people didn't know what they didn't know. They were moving away from karate and not even realizing it, especially as teachers began propagating popular tournament methods in their own schools. You can only imagine how quickly things broke down in just a few short generations.

I'm open to new ideas and methods — that's why I got involved with kickboxing. But when kickboxing required the use of big gloves and operated by its own rules, I never confused it for karate. Tournaments started adding and changing all these elements, but still called it karate. I could not endorse that and decided to retire.

In 1975, I created the World Karate Association in an effort to establish a traditional set of standards that would be upheld by all the instructors who joined. My goal was, and continues to be, to set an attainable minimum set of standards for good fundamental karate punches, kicks, blocks, stances, and techniques. Then, from there, increase the standard as individuals go up in rank. It's my hope that in this way we can elevate people to at least a fundamental understanding of what karate should be about. Later I renamed my organization the Traditional World Karate Association just for clarity and separation from a similarly named kickboxing group.

Q: Have you noticed any other concerning trends in the karate world?

Yes, and I think it starts by looking at the exterior. The colors and decorations of gi (uniforms) have spiraled out of control. People seem to be losing the connection of a plain white gi (or plain black gi for an instructor). The gi was made in such a way so as to tolerate grabs, holds, and attacks. A good gi kept both practitioners safe without things ripping off or hands getting stuck on extra decorations. In addition, the gi symbolized the purity of mindset that was supposed to go with training.

The exterior noise is reflected in the behavior of practitioners as their attitudes and egos worsen. It points back to a lack of discipline and focus on the right things during training. As kids became more involved in the arts, karate started reflecting the culture of little league games with awards all over the place and parents screaming and yelling. Karate is not a little league game — it is a life and death art. The black belt used to be something that commanded respect, with the understanding that the wearer was an individual of deadly skill and intent. If you see eight year olds with black belts, it can no longer command that same kind of respect.

One final note in regards to external trappings — there seems to be an ever increasing assortment of belt colors as time goes on. However, the red belt should always be reserved for 9th and 10th Dan Grandmasters in all arts. In some Korean styles we see the red belt used as a brown belt. When studying history, you can see the rocky relationship between Korea and Japan. When Japan occupied Korea, a lot of the freedoms, rights, and arts of Korea were repressed. As a result, when Korea was freed from Japanese control, one of their reactions was to re-institute the learning of martial arts. They preserved their own cultural styles and sometimes mixed in the karate brought over by the Japanese. However, as an intended slight, the Koreans made the red belt just below the black belt in their rankings. Readers should understand why there is some confusion in the modern martial arts world regarding how the red belt is used, and it is my opinion that it should remain reserved for Grandmasters.

Q: For individuals looking to preserve the old ways of karate, what kind of advice could you give them in terms of the focus and intent needed to keep the spirit of karate alive?

Carrying on despite adversity and grouping together are two of the most important keys to remember. There is strength in numbers, but the numbers need to be aimed at the right goal. Right now the numbers are in favor of pageantry, lack of discipline, and non-karate technique. When a number of low quality black belts look around at each other and are all at the same level, they come to agree that they are all at an acceptable level. This is how a lowering of standards becomes the norm.

Good karate folks need to band together in practice and in tournaments. They need to adhere to good karate stances, techniques that target vital areas, and strikes that utilize proper bone alignment and are executed with power but also control.

The key is not to give up, let things slide, or go with the flow. We see now that money is best made through events that reward both children and adults for fancy outfits, sloppy kata, and wild fights. As such, it is easy to chase that money . . . but chasing money does not create a bright future for karate.

GRANDMASTER VICTOR MOORE
VIC MOORE INTERNATIONAL KARATE SCHOOLS
NKJC

Chapter 16 –

Conclusion

The history of karate is deep and complex, but its legacy as a global art is still very new. Sometimes it can be difficult to see history happening around us, yet we are living in a critical time for karate's dissemination. How we treat it, respect it, and develop it will have lasting implications. It was the Western Generation who helped bring karate to the world, and it is the rest of us who will take the gift and cultivate it.

Each reader will likely have drawn his or her own conclusions while reading this book, maybe even developing new theories about the past, present, and future of karate. If so, then this work has accomplished its primary objective. However, while in the process of crafting interviews and researching history, I noticed some recurring themes and came to a few realizations that I would like to share. Understand that these conclusions are subjective, so weigh them against your own research accordingly.

The Use and Abuse of Storytelling

Stories have a way of growing in scope over time. Tales of "glory days" are common, but in the martial arts they can become part of our shared mythology.

Revered men like Matsumura Sokon, Funakoshi Gichin, and Kyan Chotoku are rightfully thought of as great heroes of karate, but they were men, too. They had vices and personality quirks which sometimes got them into trouble. This is true of every karate generation. When listening to tales from the interview guests in this book, it is easy to observe the courtesy and tact they exhibit when discussing matters of their seniors. Yet, we can't ignore the fact that there were plenty of acts of ego, jealousy, anger, and violence . . . even during karate's golden era.

Why bring this up? Because just as respect and courtesy are important in the preservation of karate, so is observing the art's potential perversion. Built into the nature of karate training is a tendency to obey the sensei and not ask questions. Some teachers in both the East and West have found ways to leverage that trust and authority, building their own power and influence. While some sensei exhibit great wisdom and care with their authority, many others use it as a tool for mental, physical, and emotional control. Storytelling and exaggeration are subtle tools that can be used to alter credentials and events in order to suit the needs of the storyteller.

Every martial artist must find a balance between respect and critical thinking. As time goes on, more senior sensei will pass away and fewer resources will exist to dispute individuals looking to make bold (sometimes fictitious) claims. Karate's history will never be clear cut; there are even different perspectives of the stories told in *this* book. But research, technology, and open communication amongst stylists will be the key to getting as close to the truth as possible while preventing rampant abuse by those looking to enhance their own agenda.

Training was Sporadic, and so was Rank

We live in an amazing era of communication and information. We walk around with devices in our pockets that, until just a few years ago, were the stuff of science fiction. We can access a global network of videos, articles, conversations, and images on every topic of the martial arts. We can travel across the globe in record time physically, or do so digitally in mere moments.

When the Western Generation was coming of age, information in the United States regarding karate consisted of a few scattered books and a handful of apocryphal stories. Early teachers often took guesses at history and technique, and sometimes just made things up because they couldn't be disproved.

To get any sort of training, individuals in the United States had to first locate a program in their city or state, then get as much training as they could while hoping the program didn't move, shut down, or otherwise became unavailable (which happened often). Individuals in the military were subject to the whims of their service, even if that meant sending them far away from their teacher after a few short months.

The effort to achieve consistent and long-term training required a massive commitment, often forcing the practitioner to study diligently on his / her own for months or even years. Sometimes small details were lost or changed as the practitioner grew without direct oversight.

The Okinawan / Japanese sensei and their American students did their best to manage rank in those early, uncertain times. Some instructors chose a very classical approach, only giving rank after years of study, regardless of travel difficulty. Other teachers gave rank based on ability and aptitude, ignoring time-in-grade. Still others gave rank in hopes that the student would train on their own and one day grow into the grade.

The whole thing was messy, complicated, and resulted in confusion and even abuse (both on the part of Western students and Eastern teachers). It's easy to scoff at the lack of organization or raise an eyebrow at early rank practices, but the truth is, we're still feeling the long-term effects of those early days, and we may never come to a consensus as a global karate community regarding what rank means and how it should be given.

Heavy Military Influence on Karate was a Double-Edged Sword

The bulk of karate's introduction to the West was conducted through military channels. The earliest pioneers, like Robert Trias, were military men. Many members of the Western Generation came from the armed forces as well. As a result, the U.S. military structure has left an irreversible impression on how we perceive karate and how it has grown since its earliest days on American soil.

The 1940s-70s was an interesting era of growth for the U.S. Military. World War II, the Cold War, the Korean War, and the Vietnam War each provided innovation, revision, and reorganization of military life. Internally, the military was attempting to handle racial strife and bring its broad collective of soldiers into cohesive order. The end result was (and still is) an incredibly potent and confident fighting force.

One of the great, lucky circumstances of karate's dissemination is that the United States sent some of its most capable physical warriors to Okinawa and Japan. Karate instructors were often tough and demanding, the work ethic of their students infamous. A more delicate portion of Western society might have been scared off, but the American soldiers arriving needed the physical skills of karate to help them survive, so they engaged in training with a fierce dedication.

The existence of influential American military bodies in Japan and Okinawa helped soldiers navigate the seemingly mysterious cultures of the East. The Army, Marines, Navy, and Air Force all eventually realized the value of integrating karate into soldiers' lives, capitalizing on improved physical fitness, increased fighting effectiveness, and prevention of "idle hands." The efforts of those early organizations allowed soldiers to quickly and reliably gain access to some of the best teachers alive.

Unfortunately, many early soldiers who learned karate were irrepressibly focused on fighting. While looking for techniques, sparring challenges, and hard contact drills, many failed to realize the value of the kata, philosophy, and culture that were as critical to understanding karate as actual physical combat. Some soldiers eschewed the culture outright, opting to stay purely "Western" despite what was going on around them. The end result was propagation in the West of a lot of karate-looking technique that lacked the heart and soul of karate itself.

American soldiers sometimes accepted karate technique, but focused on fitting it into their military lifestyle. When teaching back in the United States, many instructors recreated the reality of boot camp as opposed to the reality of karate. The end result was the propagation of a hybrid karate / military experience. Many civilians who could have benefited from nuanced guidance, infused with culture and philosophy, were drilled out of karate altogether.

In order to survive the ordeals of their time, many military members had to adopt (or were born with), a heightened alpha mentality. In modern psychology, alpha males / females are considered those individuals who are natural leaders and who generally possess extroverted qualities. By necessity, the military developed a hierarchical operational structure, utilizing commanders and subordinates to varying degrees throughout its ranks. This inevitably fostered alpha mentality, and many of the individuals who excelled at karate also achieved success in their military careers, becoming respected leaders.

When it came time to bring karate back to the United States, alpha individuals naturally started up their own schools and organizations. However, as karate grew, more and more interaction was required between various alpha factions. Students also began to grow under alpha teachers, mirroring the traits of their teachers. This all coalesced in a tumultuous fashion where martial arts politics and ego friction became more common than cooperation. Of course, military culture was far from the only cause of friction in the U.S., but it certainly was a factor.

One intriguing side effect of both alpha culture and Western culture in general was a distaste for the subtleties of Japanese and Okinawan etiquette. Americans readily adopted the surface matters of courtesy and respect, like bowing and using titles. However, they often eschewed the quieter skills of courtesy, preferring instead to "shoot straight" or not "mince words." This duality sometimes transferred into actions, wherein a sensei might bow respectfully into a dojo or tournament and then proceed to exhibit traits of cockiness, ego, and bravado.

Many of the old teachers in Okinawa and Japan expressed concern that Westerners could never truly learn karate. They were referring to the mindset as much as the technique. We have to honestly analyze ourselves in order to keep the best of what the Western military brought us, while having the courage to fix what doesn't reflect the old ways.

Crossing Paths is as Important as Ever

One of the hottest debates of our generation is in regards to cross training. Some staunch traditionalists believe that the purity of their art demands seclusion; influence from other arts only serving to water down the careful construction of their style. Modern freestyle practitioners believe that picking and choosing from different systems will lead to a collection of the best techniques from every style. As in most martial arts matters, the solution here lies in the balance.

The long-standing tradition of preserving karate is part of what makes it special. It's exciting to think that the same fighting principles taught today could have been used by warriors hundreds of years ago. The strict adherence to stylistic detail, when done right, helps guide students through the maze and haze of fighting, delivering a coherent methodology to them in a repeatable way. Traditionalism is wonderful, until it starts to exhibit signs of exclusionism.

It's not a well-known fact that the Okinawans loved to learn different fighting arts while they were developing karate and kobudo. Karate's influences range from China, to Japan, to Malaysia, and more. In the end, it became something unique to Okinawa, but its influences were numerous. Cross training is not a new concept, and neither is learning about fighting at different ranges. When the Okinawans found a weakness in their abilities, they discovered ways to improve and develop while still preserving what their instructors gave them.

Before the Western Generation arrived in Japan and Okinawa, small groups of sensei were getting together for research and training purposes. As Westerners landed, those groups continued to develop, disband, and grow anew. Many Western students were exposed to multiple different instructors on the island, and it was not uncommon for one sensei to send a student to another sensei in order to learn about that particular teacher's specialty.

As time has gone on, stylistic prejudice has proven both profitable and popular. Staunch lines have been drawn between arts, and there is an ever-increasing splintering of styles with new systems being created under the guise of political or technical necessity. Sadly, the splintering is reducing our ability to learn from one another and is swaying the balance of training away from productive sharing.

Karate is an art that can provide a lifetime of deep study. It is also a framework that can tolerate an influx of new ideas. A classical karate practitioner can learn the core of his / her art and use other influences to provide a fresh perspective on the core style. It is important to understand that this growth of perspective and understanding does not indicate the need for a new style. It just means the practitioner is exploring the art as it was intended. It is still the job of the practitioners to preserve the framework and pass it on as it was given to them, so that others can explore it, share it, and grow in their own way.

Preserving a Proud Legacy . . . and Improving Upon It

The role of history is to help us appreciate the efforts and beliefs of those who have gone before us. With proper study we might be able to "stand on the shoulders of giants," as Isaac Newton once famously wrote. As each modern generation comes to prominence, it is their duty to understand the goals and motivations of those that came before them.

The Western Generation experienced rare days, acting as heralds for the West and becoming the first wave to undergo extended, in-depth training in karate. It was their strength that helped karate spread so quickly and voraciously across the United States.

Our role in more modern generations is to observe, appreciate, honor, and improve upon what the Western Generation has delivered to us. We must do more to learn about the culture from which karate came and strive to live up to its highest ideals. We must be loyal to our instructors and styles, but observe them honestly and do our best to correct a style or organization's course, should it drift.

Every generation has the ability to find new abuses for karate. The allure of external trappings, money, accolades, ego, control, and power will always be present for as long as karate is practiced. The more one trains, the more the soft touch of ego and power can infect the mind. That is why we must routinely and diligently recall the lessons shared by our seniors. We must strive to exhibit their greatest traits while burning away flaws and distractions in the cauldron of our training.

We now operate as an imperfect global karate community who carries with it the small jewels of karate's true heart. We must continue to learn and share as much as we can, so as to create a path that all prior generations can look upon and be proud of. We are the beginnings of a legacy whose story has yet to be written.

Glossary

Aikido   Japanese martial art developed by Ueshiba Morihei OSensei. Known for its blending and throwing techniques.

bogu kumite   Live, unscripted fighting using hand, body, and head padding that resembles traditional kendo garb.

budo   Term for "the way of martial arts".

bunkai   Martial analysis of movements in kata.

bushi   Warrior. In Okinawa, often reserved for gentlemen of accomplishment in the fine arts as well as fighting arts. Bears a a connotation of prestige and etiquette.

dan   A ranking in karate above that of black belt. There are generally 10 dan ranks.

dojo   A place for training in the "way" of martial arts.

G.I.   Generic term for American military member.

gamaku   The waist and small of the back.

gasshuku   A special or enlongated training event.

gi   a karate uniform.

hakutsuru   White Crane.

hanshi   Highest title attainable in karate. Generally reserved for 8th-10th dan practitioners, depending on the style.

hinkaku   Special dignity.

hojo undo   Supplementary exercises and equipment used to build the body and technique.

Judo   Throwing art developed by Kano Jigoro.

kai   A club or association.

karatedo   The "way" of the empty hand.

karateka   One who practices karate.

kendo   Japanese sport of sword fighting.

kiai   Expression of spirit and intent. Often verbalized as a shout.

kihon   Basic or fundamental movements.

kobudo   The "way" of Okinawan weaponry.

kumite   Unscripted fighting, often with pads.

kung fu   Generic term for Chinese martial arts.

kyu   Karate rankings under black belt.

kyusho   Method of vital point striking.

makiwara   Padded hitting board used to develop striking technique.

menkyo kaiden Certificate of stylistic transmission.

Naha Te Term used for karate styles associated with the area of Naha, Okinawa.

obi Belt.

OSensei Term reserved for the founder of a martial arts style.

oyo bunkai Higher level of analysis and kata application, allowing for creativity and flexibility.

renmei Organization or association.

renshi Title reserved for karate practitioners in the 5th dan to 7th dan range, depending on style.

sensei Instructor, guide, or teacher.

Shuri Te Term used for karate styles associated ith the area of Shuri, Okinawa.

sumo Japanese sport of unbalancing your opponent and forcing them out of the ring.

taijiquan Tai chi chuan. Chinese art known for its harmonious and flowing movements.

tatami Padded or woven floor mat.

te Hand.

ti chi ki Term used in regards to a higher level of karate understanding beyond that of bunkai.

Tomari Te Term used for karate styles associated with the area of Tomari, Okinawa.

tuite Joint manipulation or hand grappling.

U.D.T. Underwater Dive Team associated with the U.S. Navy.

U.S.M.C. United States Marine Corps.

Index

About the Author

Matthew Apsokardu is a professional writer and martial artist. He began his study of Okinawa Kenpo Karate Kobudo in 1995, eventually becoming a direct student of C. Bruce Heilman. He expanded his martial education into the world of Japanese budo, first studying Muso Jikiden Eishin Ryu followed by Muso Shinden Ryu. Matthew continued to extend his learning by attending seminars and gasshuku with gentlemen of various karate styles, which eventually led to the "Tales from the Western Generation" project. Matthew also took his training outside of the dojo by volunteering with the Douglas County Sheriff's Community Safety Patrol.

Matthew graduated from Penn State University in 2006 with a degree in Professional Writing. He created the website Ikigai Way, a compendium of original martial arts articles and interviews. He expanded those articles into full ebooks and magazine publications. Matthew also founded Apsos Media (http://apsosmedia.com) and Apsos Publishing (http://apsospublishing.com), designed to help small businesses and private authors bring their brands to life.

See more about "Tales from the Western Generation" and the interview guests at **http://westernkarate.com**. Reach out to the author at westernkaratebook@gmail.com.

View a wider variety of martial arts articles by the author at **http://ikigaiway.com**.

41879965R00292